S0-AIE-099

JUST JAMES

*The Brother of Jesus
in History and Tradition*

Studies on Personalities of the New Testament
D. Moody Smith, Series Editor

JUST JAMES

The Brother of Jesus
in History and Tradition

John Painter

UNIVERSITY OF SOUTH CAROLINA PRESS

For Gillian
worth waiting for

© 1997 University of South Carolina Press

Published in Columbia, South Carolina, by the
University of South Carolina Press

Manufactured in the United States of America

01   00   99   98   5   4   3   2

Library of Congress Cataloging-in-Publication Data

Painter, John.
    Just James : the brother of Jesus in history and tradition / John
Painter.
        p.   cm.—(Studies on personalities of the New Testament)
    Includes bibliographical references and index.
    ISBN 1–57003–174–6
    1. James, Brother of the Lord, Saint.   I. Title.   II. Series
BS2454.J3P25   1997
225.9′2—dc21
[b]   97–21237

CONTENTS

PREFACE

Just James is the consequence of an invitation by Moody Smith (toward the end of 1988) to contribute to this series of Studies on Personalities of the New Testament. I accepted without hesitation. Because my research and teaching have been directed to the history and literature of early Christianity, rather than narrowly to the New Testament, I was aware that there was more to this James than generally meets the eye. In my days as an undergraduate student, reading Streeter's *The Four Gospels* and *The Primitive Church* convinced me of the diversity of earliest Christianity. This view is reflected in my earlier studies of Johannine Christianity and Mark as well as in my teaching of Paul and the Synoptic Gospels. I am glad to find opportunity to acknowledge the debt my generation of students owes to Streeter, not least in the recognition that the literary diversity of the New Testament is rooted in the historical, and probably geographical, diversity of earliest Christianity. Study of James has deepened and enriched this sense of diversity and significantly changed my understanding of the history of early Christianity, leading to conclusions about which I had no inkling when this study began. In this process James the brother of Jesus emerges as one of the outstanding figures in early Christianity.

If this has been obscured in the New Testament, it is because these documents do not derive from pro-Jamesian circles. A tradition of reading the New Testament has developed that is more negative in relation to James than the documents demand. Once certain presuppositions are laid aside, James emerges as the leading figure of the Jerusalem church. This perception of James is strengthened by paying attention to traditions about James outside the New Testament. *Just James* rereads the evidence about James free of some of the dominating interpretative paradigms. In the study of James there is no safety or security for the unwary, because the sources take sides and should be read in the light of this fact. While there are those who defend the historical accuracy of Acts, the bias of this work is commonly recognized and preference is given to Paul's letters where the two overlap. Even this can be too simple because, although Paul wrote of what he knew at first hand, he was not a disinterested observer. In many instances we need to allow that other participants in the events described, such as James and Peter, saw things in ways quite different from Paul's account of the events. Only careful, critical reconstruction can recover awareness of this with some degree of probability.

That the role and influence of James continued after his death is partly a consequence of the way his death was portrayed, though it can also be argued that his death was so portrayed because of his outstanding influence. But once the story of his death was told, it became evidence for the dominating influence of James that continued after his death. *Just James* attempts to recover awareness of the significance of the life and work of James. It also seeks to trace the unexpected ways his influence spread following his death. This theme is picked up in the introductory "Just James: The Death of a Legend." What follows is a detailed and critical treatment of all the significant evidence about James that was preserved by the early church both in its "Catholic" form and in its other forms. We begin in part one with the New Testament, treating first the Gospels, then Acts, and then the Letters of Paul. Part two examines the tradition about James preserved by Eusebius, the Nag Hammadi Library, and later Christian material. Finally, part three brings sharp focus to Jewish Christianity, featuring the role of the righteous sufferer and the Epistle of James. At every point the approach adopted is to examine the evidence in its literary and historical context. This is crucial because evidence about James is not straightforward, and the nature of the evidence must be weighed carefully.

Work on James was delayed by the writing of *The Quest for the Messiah* (1991) and interrupted by the need to provide a revised edition at the end of 1993. Nevertheless my manuscript on James was complete by late 1994. For a variety of reasons the process of publication has been drawn out, and since the completion of my work, two studies on James have appeared in English. First, Richard Bauckham contributed "James and the Jerusalem Church" to *The Book of Acts in Its Palestinian Setting* (1995), volume four, edited by Bauckham, of a series on Acts. Bauckham operates within the recognized boundaries of contemporary scholarship, and many of his detailed positions are covered in my discussion. What drives his contribution, and the volume in which it appears, is an attempt to demonstrate the historical accuracy of the Acts account. Perhaps the least satisfactory part is his attempt to reconcile Acts with Paul's letter to the Galatians. Tensions that most scholars regard as irreconcilable are declared to be no problem by Bauckham. His identifications of Gal 2:1–10 with the famine relief visit of Acts 11:30 and of the problem at Antioch in Acts 15:1–2a with Paul's confrontation with Peter (Gal 2:11–14) are unlikely to convince many scholars today. Nevertheless, in the light of the early Christian evidence, Bauckham recognizes the leadership of James but, on his reading of Acts, allows for its emergence only from Acts 12:17. His conflation of the evidence suggests that the acceptance of a law-free mission to the nations was accomplished without serious complication. The evidence independent of Acts suggests that this is an oversimplified view. Consequently, *Just James* differs greatly from his understanding of the role of James and the history of early Christianity and provides a much more detailed treatment than Bauckham was able to provide in the space at his disposal.

The second work, by Robert Eisenman, *James the Brother of Jesus,* was published in 1997 and arrived on my desk on the 20th of May. By then my own manuscript was in page proofs. There I discussed his earlier studies of James (see pp. 230–34). His latest work, however, is a massive increase in detail, though without significant change of any important view, and has been dealt with in an excursus (pp. 277–88). In *Just James* the point of view manifest in the evidence about James is taken into account as is the question of the evidence's independence from or dependence on other traditions. In this way distinctions can be made about probable historical credibility over against views that express ideological or theological positions in which earlier history is constructed in the image of later realities. A conscious, critical use of the sources is crucial if the perils of historical reconstruction are to be negotiated successfully.

I am grateful to Margaret "Peggy" Hill for her care and professionalism in picking up *Just James* just when I thought it had become becalmed in the editorial doldrums. Working with Peggy and her staff has been a pleasure and has improved the book as well. An author could have no more enthusiastic and critical publishing editor, and for this I am most grateful. It remains only for me to thank Moody Smith for inviting me to write this volume and for the collegial friendship over the past, almost twenty years. Meetings of SNTS in various parts of the world have been enriched by our exegetical exercises.

The study of James remains neglected. I hope that *Just James* will encourage a recovery of the recognition of how significant James was in the history of earliest Christianity and provide some explanation of how and why that significance has been obscured in most of the surviving traditions, most of which have been filtered by emerging "Catholic Christianity."

ABBREVIATIONS

1 QH	*Hymn Scroll* from Qumran
1 Qp Hab	*Habakkuk Pesher* from Qumran
1 QS	*Community Rule* from Qumran
Adv. Marc.	Tertullian, *Against Marcion*
AH	Irenaeus, *Against Heresies*
ANCL	Ante-Nicene Christian Library
ANF	Ante-Nicene Fathers
ANRW	*Aufstieg und Niedergang der römischen Welt*
Ant.	Josephus, *Jewish Antiquities*
ATR	*Anglican Theological Review*
BJRL	*Bulletin John Rylands Library*
CBQ	*Catholic Bibilical Quarterly*
CD	*Damascus Document* from Qumran and the Cairo Geniza
CmSBF	Collectio minor Studium Biblicum Franciscanum
De Carne Christi	Tertullian, *On the Flesh of Christ*
De monog.	Tertullian, *On Monogamy*
De vir. ill.	Jerome, *Lives of Illustrious Men*
ECL	Early Christian Library
EPRO	Etudes préliminaires aux religions orientales dans l'empire romain
EQ	*Evangelical Quarterly*
FRLANT	Forschungen zur Religion und Literatur des Alten und Neuen Testaments
FZB	Forschung zur Bibel
HE	Eusebius, *History of the Church*

HNT	Handbuch zum Neuen Testament
HTKNT	Herders theologischer Kommentar zum Neuen Testament
ICC	International Critical Commentary
JBL	*Journal of Biblical Literature*
JR	*Journal of Religion*
JSNT	*Journal for the Study of the New Testament*
JSNTSS	Journal for the Study of the New Testament Supplement Series
JSOT	*Journal for the Study of the Old Testament*
JSS	*Journal of Semitic Studies*
JTS	*Journal of Theological Studies*
LCC	Library of Christian Classics
LCL	Loeb Classical Library
MMT	Halakhic Letter(s) from Qumran, *4Q MMT*
NHS	Nag Hammadi Studies
NICNT	New International Commentary on the New Testament
NIGNTC	New International Greek New Testament Commentary
NovT	*Novum Testamentum*
NPNF	Nicene and Post-Nicene Fathers
NRSV	New Revised Standard Version
NTS	*New Testament Studies*
NTSMS	New Testament Studies Monograph Series
Pan.	Epiphanius, *Panarion*
P Oxy.	Papyri Oxyrhynchus
Ref.	Hippolytus, *Refutation of All Heresies*
RestQ	*Restoration Quarterly*
RGG	Die Religion in Geschichte und Gegenwart
RHR	*Revue de l'Historie des Religions*
RNEB	Revised New English Bible
RSV	Revised Standard Version
SBL	Society of Biblical Literature
SBS	Stuttgarter Bibelstudien
SBT	Studies in Biblical Theology
SNTSMS	Studiorum Novi Testamenti Monograph Series

SPAW	Sitzungberichte der preussischen Akademie der Wissenschaften
ThLZ	*Theologische Literaturzeitung*
ThR	*Theologische Rundschau*
TU	Texte und Untersuchungen zur Geschichte der altchristlichen Literatur
TZTh	*Tübinger Zeitschrift für Theologie*
UBS	United Bible Society
WUNT	Wissenschaftliche Untersuchungen zum Neuen Testament
ZKG	*Zeitschrift für Kirchengeschichte*
ZNW	*Zeitschrift für die neutestamentliche Wissenschaft*

JUST JAMES

The Brother of Jesus
in History and Tradition

JUST JAMES

The Death of a Legend

The James who is the subject of this study is not prominent in any contemporary church tradition. Roman Catholicism looks to Peter as the apostolic founder of its tradition, and the churches of the Reformation look back to Paul. Even when James is spoken of, the son of Zebedee and brother of John normally comes first to mind. He has become known as the greater James, while our James is sometimes known as "the less" and thought to be the son of Alpheus.[1] With this identification goes the assumption that the so-called brother of the Lord was, in fact, a cousin, distancing him from Jesus. From this perspective he is *just* James.

One of the aims of this book is to show that the grounds for dismissively regarding James the brother of Jesus as "less" are misguided and that it is necessary to recognize him as a towering figure in the earliest church. Here we exploit a potential double meaning in the epithet *"Just James,"* drawing attention to the tradition of righteousness associated with James, so much so that he came to be identified by the title *James the Just*. It is not simply that he was regarded as a just man. The title was given to him as the one who, in the minds of those who so named him, epitomized righteousness and justice. But if this was the case, why has his role been almost obliterated from the consciousness of continuing church traditions?

Reference to "the death of a legend" is similarly multivalent. In the first instance this statement recognizes that part of the legendary greatness of James finds focus in the various early traditional accounts of his death. These might equally be called "legends" of his death, although the unquestionable historical kernel makes clear that James himself had become legendary, especially in relation to his righteousness. The righteousness of James led to various elaborations

---

[1] See R. Bauckham, *Jude and the Relatives of Jesus in the Early Church* (Edinburgh: T & T Clark, 1990), 20–21.

1

about the consequences of his death, while at the same time the death of James contributed to the appreciation of his righteousness in legendary terms. The focus on the death of James in the tradition justifies the caption "The Death of a Legend."

The developing tradition found expression in the legend of the perpetual virginity of Mary, the mother of Jesus, which was made possible by teaching found in such infancy Gospels as the *Protevangelium of James*. There, in narrative form, it was taught that Joseph was a widower with children (including James) when he became betrothed to Mary. Mary was a virgin when she conceived Jesus, and she remained a virgin through the process of birth and throughout her life. With the influence of Jerome, whose views were adopted and spread by Augustine, this legend was suppressed in the West and another legend put in its place. According to Jerome, those referred to as brothers and sisters were actually Jesus' cousins. Jerome sought to preserve the virginity of both Joseph and Mary. The death of one legend saw the birth of another.

Modern study, beginning with the work of J. B. Lightfoot, has shown that the theory advocated by Jerome entails insuperable problems. Modern Western scholarship has tended to regard this approach to the "brothers" of Jesus as indefensible legend. Lightfoot, however, began a process of reexamining the viability of the older tradition in the *Protevangelium of James*. From the point of view of the present study, Lightfoot announced the death of one legend only to replace it with another. Although Lightfoot's position has been supported by other, more modern studies,[2] most modern research on the subject seeks to show that both legends are dead.

The name James is derived from the Semitic *Jacob*,[3] a name that recalls the third of the great patriarchs of the Jewish people. It was a common Jewish name in the first century. In the New Testament the name is used over sixty times of as many as eight persons:

1) the patriarch Jacob; 2) the father of Joseph, the supposed father of Jesus; 3) the son of Zebedee and the brother of John, one of the twelve; 4) the son of Alpheus, one of the twelve; 5) James the "less," son of Mary and Clopas and brother of Joses (Joseph); 6) the father (brother?) of Judas, one of the twelve, who may be identified with Thaddaeus (Lebbaeus); 7) James the brother of Jude and author of the Epistle of James; 8) James, the brother of the Lord and leader of the Jerusalem church. It is possible to reduce this number by arguing that some of these uses are to be identified with the same person. *Jacob* ('Ιακώβ) is used twenty-four times of the patriarch Jacob and twice of the father of Joseph the supposed father of Jesus (Matt 1:15, 16).[4] Other references in the

---

[2] See, e.g., Bauckham, *Jude*.
[3] 'Ιακώβ, which is hellenized as 'Ιάκωβος.
[4] In Luke (3:23) the father of Joseph is named Eli.

New Testament use the hellenized form ('Ιάκωβος) which is consistently translated as *James*. About half the uses are to be identified with James the brother of John and son of Zebedee, while almost a third probably refer to the James known as the brother of Jesus. The remaining references relate to figures often difficult to identify, though some refer to the other apostle named James.

The differentiated use of the two forms of the name in the New Testament, where figures in "Christian" history are given the hellenized form while those from Jewish history prior to Jesus, especially the patriarch Jacob, retain the Semitic form, may have led the English translators of the Bible to retain *Jacob* as an Old Testament name, while using *James* as the name for the Christian apostles. The two names in English are derived from Latin, in which *Jacobus* and *Jacomus* are variants of the same name. The same variants exist in some European languages: for example, in Italian *Jacapo* and *Giacomo,* in Spanish *Iago* and *Jaime.* But in English *Jacob* and *James* have tended to be regarded as two different names. The one name (Jacob), apart from times when there has been an attraction to the use of Old Testament names, has tended to be used by Jews, while the other (James) has been used by Christians. Reference to the supporters of the Stuart Jameses as *Jacobites* and to their period as *Jacobean* shows awareness of the etymological relation of the two names.

In the Christian tradition the name James is sometimes used without clarification. This contributes to the confusion and difficulty of identifying our subject within the documents of the New Testament. Such confusion is rare in the other early Christian literature. One reason for this is that the martyrdom of James, brother of John and son of Zebedee, is narrated in Acts 12:1–2. He was executed by King Herod (Agrippa I), who was king of "Palestine"[5] from 42–44 CE. This time frame leaves little room for notable activity by this James, and early legendary development is restricted to elaborating the tradition concerning his death. Eusebius (*HE* 2.9.2–3) records a report from Clement of Alexandria (ca. 200 CE) saying that James forgave his accuser, and the apocryphal Apostolic History of Abdias describes the miracles and controversies leading up to his execution. This James was, according to the Synoptics, a notable figure among Jesus' disciples, being (according to the Synoptics) one of the first four called by Jesus and one who remained part of a significant nucleus reduced at times to the three, Peter, James, and John.

In early church tradition, however, James the brother of Jesus held central stage for some time. He was the fountainhead of traditions used to further the interests and causes of a variety of groups, including Jewish Christian, the Great Church (Catholic), and Gnostic. By the end of the patristic period, this fountain had run dry.

---

[5] While this name is an anachronism, it conveniently signifies collectively what were separate political regions in the first century.

In the traditions recorded by Eusebius (Hegesippus, Clement of Alexandria, Origen), James was the first bishop of the Jerusalem church. His election to this position is located at the beginning of the life of the Jerusalem church. He was thus the first bishop of the leading (mother) church of the growing Christian movement. The account in Acts portrays the key role of the Jerusalem church, and even the letters of Paul confirm its importance because they show that Paul contested and struggled against that leadership. But according to popular understanding, in Acts Peter is at first portrayed as the prominent leader among the twelve, giving way to James only when he is forced to leave Jerusalem (Acts 12:17). The account of the Jerusalem assembly (Acts 15) portrays James "presiding," and this position of leadership is consistent with the remainder of the narrative of Acts.

The tendentious nature of Acts is widely recognized, and this is crucial for the study of James. But that this is also true of the letters of Paul is not always remembered because awareness that his letters provide firsthand knowledge of people and events often seduces scholars to forget that primary sources also need critical evaluation. These comments apply particularly to the discussion of the relation between Paul and James.

In spite of the suppression of the importance of the family of Jesus in the New Testament texts there is ample evidence of its presence. Matthew and Luke reduce the cohesion of the family by affirming that Jesus was conceived by Mary while she was a virgin, so that other children born to the family did not share a biological father with Jesus. Although the point of the infancy stories in Matthew and Luke was to affirm the significance of Jesus, they had the effect of minimizing the importance of the family, apart from Mary. In following centuries the continuing virginity of Mary became important as a way of affirming the uniqueness of Jesus and of developing a focus on Mary herself as an idealization of the feminine and of virginity.

As we noted above, the *Protevangelium of James* preserved the virginity of Mary perpetually. Jerome went further and maintained the virginity of Joseph also by arguing that those called brothers (and sisters) were actually cousins. These views become known by the names of leading exponents in the fourth century. The first was advocated by Epiphanius and remained the dominant view of the Eastern Church, while Jerome's view became dominant in the West. Until recently Jerome's was the Roman Catholic view, though Catholic biblical scholars do not uniformly hold this view today. A mural in the crypt of the Benedictine Dormition Abbey in Jerusalem depicts a scene which portrays the Epiphanian view. Portrayed in a scene of the flight into Egypt, the youthful James is seen leading the donkey upon which sits Mary with the infant Jesus.

The writings of the New Testament represent different interest groups. None of those groups represents the interests of James. In the early church traditions representing both Peter and Paul obscured the importance of James and the family of Jesus. In spite of this, in traditions from the second century on, there re-emerges awareness of James as the leading figure in the Jerusalem church. According to Hippolytus (*Ref.* 5.2) James was venerated by the Naassenes as the figure by whom the secret teachings were transmitted to the sect via Mariamne. Thus there is evidence of an early (Jewish) Gnostic appeal to the traditions of James. Hegesippus provides evidence of the reclamation of James by the Great Church. But that reclamation is unintelligible unless there was an awareness of the tradition that established the importance of James in the life of the church. James was too important to surrender to the Gnostics.

Tradition names James the first leader of the Jerusalem church. The list of the bishops of Jerusalem, the first fourteen Jewish (Hebrew) and the next fourteen Gentile, cites James as the first of the Hebrew bishops.[6] Various traditions affirm his appointment, directly by the risen Jesus,[7] by Peter, James, and John,[8] or by the apostles as a group.[9] These variations make best sense if the earliest tradition affirmed that the risen Jesus directly appointed him. In the variant traditions James is brought back under the control of the Great Church by attributing his appointment to the apostles. James is also made the recipient of special revelations from the risen Lord.[10] Because this tradition exposed James to the whims of the Gnostics, James is sometimes linked with Peter.[11] Underlying the choice of James as the first leader and his position as the repository of the secret tradition is his acknowledged position as the "brother" of Jesus. Even Eusebius, who qualifies his understanding of that tradition, acknowledges that James was known as the brother of Jesus and attributes tradition to this effect to Hegesippus.

Tradition of the martyrdom of James is known to us in Josephus (*Ant.* 20.197–203) and Christian traditions gathered by Eusebius from a variety of sources of which Clement of Alexandria and Hegesippus are named. James, in addition to being called the Lord's brother, is referred to as "the Just" or "the Righteous." Use of this epithet manifests the status of James in the role of the righteous sufferer. He is at once perceived in this role in the company of Jesus and of other Jewish righteous martyrs. Once in this company, the epithet

---

[6] See the tradition reported by Eusebius, *HE* 4.5.1–4. Epiphanius, *Ref. (Pan.)* 66.19.7–66.20.1, mentions thirty-seven bishops.

[7] See *Kerygmata Petrou, Ascents of James,* and the *Gospel of Thomas* logion 12. Perhaps implied by Clement of Alexandria as reported by Eusebius *HE* 2.1.4, where James is named first, followed by John and Peter, in the group of three to whom the risen Lord gave higher knowledge after the resurrection.

[8] Clement of Alexandria according to Eusebius in *HE* 2.1.3.

[9] *HE* 2.23.1.

[10] Clement of Alexandria in *HE* 2.1.4; the *Apocryphon of James*; the *First* and the *Second Apocalypse of James*.

[11] Clement of Alexandria in *HE* 2.1.4; the *Apocryphon of James*.

"Righteous" takes on a sense of piety and asceticism for which James became famous, so that Mary-ever-virgin is joined by the virgin James.

Eusebius acknowledges no Petrine leadership of the Jerusalem church. He does refer to Peter as the leader of all the apostles in the context of asserting that Peter brought the treasures of the gospel from the east to Rome in the reign of Claudius (*HE* 2.14.6). The authority of Peter is identified with Rome in a time too early (the reign of Claudius) and in a tradition too late (Eusebius) to be historically credible. But there is no suggestion that Peter was the leader of the Jerusalem church. Eusebius quotes Clement of Alexandria (*HE* 2.1.3) as saying that, after the ascension, Peter, James, and John chose James as the first bishop of Jerusalem.[12] In his own interpretation Eusebius equates the time of James's appointment with the martyrdom of Stephen (*HE* 2.1.2). While this shows that Eusebius has no detailed information, it is clear that he knows no tradition of Petrine leadership of the Jerusalem church. Like the tradition he quotes, he was concerned to show that the authority and leadership of James were rooted in the authority of the apostles. The Petrine tradition of leadership was associated with Rome (not Jerusalem). For Eusebius there was nothing superior about the authority of either Jerusalem or Rome. What was important was the tradition of apostolic churches, which were a bulwark against the aberrations of heresy.

One of the aims of this book is to show the central role of James in the life of the earliest church. If it is true that he had this role, we also need to show what obscured the significance of his role in the ongoing mainstream traditions. James is central in certain traditions, but at some point these traditions ceased to be influential. What attracted the shapers of these traditions to James, and why did these traditions not continue to be influential? Attempting to provide some answers to these questions we gain a clearer perception of the life and struggles of the early church. We are forced to penetrate beneath the answers that were provided by the post-Constantinian Church, which read its kind of orthodoxy back into the earlier period. Perception of the significant role of James is only possible if we break through this construct.

Modern studies of James have concentrated on a relatively limited number of questions. Naturally, the old question of the relationship of James to Jesus and Mary continues to be important and with this the question of which references to James, in the New Testament, are to this James. Was he the author of the letter that we know by that name? While the early church assumed that he was, this conclusion is widely questioned today. Since the time of F. C. Baur, who developed the hypothesis of a conflict between Jewish Christianity and Gentile Christianity, leading to a synthesis in Catholic Christianity, the question of the relationship of James to Paul has been crucial.

---

[12] See also logion 12 of the *Gospel of Thomas*.

Baur's position, developed from 1831, is seminal for our discussion.[13] He argued that the four apparent parties at Corinth were in fact two; that the party of Paul and Apollos stood over against the party of Cephas, i.e., Peter, and Christ.[14] The latter represented Jewish particularism against the universalism of a spiritual gospel.[15] He identified the Jewish Christian opposition to Paul with "false apostles" who are not to be identified with the original apostles (Peter and James). At that time he traced a line of continuity between the false apostles as the common opponents of Paul in Galatians, Philippians, 1 and 2 Corinthians and the opposition to Paul in the second century evidenced in Justin, the Pseudo-Clementines, and Irenaeus. While tracing this line of continuity was an important contribution, it is now widely recognized that Baur was too hasty in assuming that the second-century evidence to which he appealed referred to a single common front. The major development in his view was a consequence of historical critical attention to the Pastoral Epistles (1835) and Acts in work culminating in his *Paul* (first published in 1845). Baur began to show that the account in Acts ought not to be treated as accurate history, concluding that Peter and James were the leaders of the anti-Pauline movement. Consequently, our discussion of the question has been expanded to take in the relationship of James and Paul to Peter.

In his introductory essay to the study *Antioch and Rome* (1983), by Raymond E. Brown and J. P. Meier, Brown outlines a model of four types of Jewish Christianity, based on an analysis of different attitudes to the law. Brown acknowledges that the use of such a typology is heuristic and does not mean that historical reality was as clear and simple as the model might seem to imply. In historical reality people and groups often overlap the types. The value of the types is that they make clear a series of distinct options that were open on the question of the observance of the law. The typology assumes that each of the Jewish groups spawned Gentile converts who adopted their views of the law. The first group insisted on full observance of the law, including circumcision. The second did not demand circumcision. The third did not demand circumcision or that one follow the food and purity laws but insisted on keeping the ten commandments and continued to observe the Jewish festivals. The fourth saw no relevance at all in any of the Jewish rituals. Brown thinks that James and Peter belonged to the second group, but that, while James inclined to the position of the first group, Peter was closer to the position of the third. Paul fits into the third, and a more extreme position is represented by the Hellenists.

---

[13] "Die Christuspartei in der korinthischen Gemeinde, der Gegensatz des petrinischen und paulinischen Christentums in der alten Kirsche, der Apostel Petrus in Rom," *TZTh* (1831): 61–206.

[14] "Christuspartei," pp. 77, 83–84, 114.

[15] "Christuspartei," p. 107.

The position of Wilhelm Pratscher is similar in some respects to that of Brown and Meier.[16] Pratscher, however, takes the differences between James and Peter further and sees some rivalry between Peter's people and those who supported James, arguing that 1 Cor 15:7 is a "Rivalitätsformel" (contrast 1 Cor 15:5). Instead of seeing Peter wavering somewhere between James and Paul, Pratscher argues that there is no trace of evidence concerning the anti-Paulinism of James, who should be seen rather as one who mediated between Paul and the Jewish Christians who opposed Paul.[17] Thus Pratscher sees James playing a reconciling role. While these may appear to be small differences, they lead to a very different understanding of early Christianity and, of course, to the role of James within it.

Historically, much depends on the way the accord negotiated at the Jerusalem assembly is reconstructed. It is frequently recognized that the account in Acts cannot be read as straightforward history. Paul's firsthand account is not without its own *Tendenz*, or bias.[18] The terminology used by Paul in Galatians is likely to favor his interpretation of the events, and the reader needs to be sensitive to alternative understandings that were open to other participants in the dialogue. This would include (minimally) different understandings of the language of the agreement and perhaps even completely alternative accounts of the accord.

---

[16] See Pratscher's *Der Herrenbruder Jacobus und die Jacobustradition* (Göttingen: Vandenhoeck & Ruprecht, 1987).

[17] This is the position of H. J. Schoeps, *Theologie und Geschichte des Judenchristentums* (Tübingen: J. C. B. Mohr [Paul Siebeck], 1949), 261, and R. B. Ward ("James of Jerusalem in the First Two Centuries," *ANRW* II, 26.1, p. 784), who builds on the work of J. Munck (*Paul and the Salvation of Mankind* [London: SCM, 1959], 107).

[18] Since I wrote the first draft of this study M. D. Goulder's *A Tale of Two Missions* (London: SCM, 1994) has appeared. Goulder notes the tendentious nature of Luke but appeals to the letters of Paul for evidence of what actually happened because, after all, "Paul was there at the time." See *A Tale of Two Missions*, pp. x–xi.

Part I

The Gospels, Acts, and the Letters of Paul

CHAPTER 1

THE GOSPELS
James and the Family of Jesus

THE FAMILY IN THE GOSPELS

While the earliest and most direct sources for our knowledge of James are the letters of Paul, these letters presuppose a knowledge of the fundamental relation of James to Jesus. This relationship is more visible in the Gospels than in the letters of Paul. We have no assurance that the evangelists knew James directly, as Paul did. The critical reader will be suspicious of tendencies that present the family of Jesus in a manner that becomes dominant in the emerging Catholic Church—that is, tendencies to standardize one position as orthodox. The Gospels were shaped by ideological positions in the reporting of history.[1] Ideological struggles were already under way in the time of James, and participants, such as Paul, are not free from ideological bias.

Talk of ideological bias needs some qualification. All accounts reflect a point of view. Some bear little relationship to the events they purport to report. Others are justifiable in terms of the events that they report and are verifiable through independent accounts. Firsthand accounts are also subject to point of view and can be unjustifiably biased. There is no doubting the ideological bias in the letters of Paul, though whether this bias is justifiable in terms of the events reported is another question. One of the tasks undertaken in the present study is to chart the struggle in which James and Paul were involved. In dealing with the Gospels the critical reader should be alert to recognize tendencies from the Pauline struggle and other ideological struggles of the later Church. Points of view that are free of these influences need to be taken seriously as transmissions from an earlier time, perhaps even from the time of Jesus.

The first major question concerns how we are to understand the family of

---

[1] M. D. Goulder, *A Tale of Two Missions* (London: SCM, 1994), xii, argues that the Gospels are to be understood in relation to the two missions, the one based on the demand for circumcision and the other law-free (free from the demand to be circumcised and all that entails).

Jesus. Mary is portrayed as his mother, and Joseph is called his father. The infancy stories of Matthew and Luke assert that Jesus was conceived while Mary was betrothed to Joseph but before they were married, that the child was conceived without the participation of a human father but by the intervention of God. Other texts of the New Testament provide no evidence of knowledge of this teaching. Absence of this evidence from the Gospels of Mark and John as well as from the letters of Paul is a basis for questioning how early this tradition is, although this absence of evidence need not imply the falsity of tradition in Matthew and Luke.

Paul, Mark, and John give the reader no reason to think that those called brothers and sisters of Jesus were anything but full brothers and sisters.[2] There is no suggestion anywhere in the New Testament that there were children born to Joseph by an earlier marriage. The narrative of the virginal conception in Matthew and Luke provides a basis for christological development and for this reason alone must be questioned. Given that evidence of this story is absent from Paul, Mark, and John, and other parts of the New Testament, the most obvious conclusion to be drawn is that Jesus and those called his brothers and sisters were children of Joseph and Mary. While it might be argued that the virginal conception of Jesus was a secret and the New Testament generally reflects the state of public knowledge, there is no reason to suggest that, had there been children of Joseph by a first marriage, this would not have been public knowledge.

The Role of the Family

The study of James in the New Testament has been hindered by assumptions which, in spite of being based on little evidence, have largely gone unquestioned. The precise relation of James to Jesus has been a long-term preoccupation because of the commitments of ecclesial traditions, deflecting attention from other important assumptions crucial for understanding the significance of James in the early church. Those assumptions emerged in my detailed survey of the secondary literature on James. Only when this had been done did I discover, in the article on James in the *Encyclopaedia Britannica,* a succinct summary of the three points that emerged in my study.[3] They are:

---

[2] While "brother" could be used loosely to describe other kinship relationships, the fact that only this term is used of the so-called brothers of Jesus makes any other relationship unlikely. The theory that the "brothers" were cousins thus runs against the fact that they are never called cousins (ἀνεψιόι). On the use of ἀδελφός see J. Blinzler, *Die Brüder und Schwestern Jesus,* SBS 21 (Stuttgart: Katholisches Bibelwerk, 1967), 39–48, and L. Oberlinner, *Historische Überlieferung und christologische Aussage: Zur Frage der "Bruder Jesus" in der Synops,* FZB 19 (Stuttgart: Katholisches Bibelwerk, 1975), 16–49.

[3] 15th edition (Chicago: Encyclopaedia Britannica, 1978), vol. 5, p. 507.

1) James and the brothers and sisters of Jesus were not believers during the ministry of Jesus (John 7:3–5; Mark 3:21, 31–35);
2) James became a believer through a resurrection appearance of Jesus to him (1 Cor 15:7);
3) a transition from the leadership of Peter to that of James was made necessary by the forced flight of Peter (Acts 12:17).[4]

None of these positions is clear on a face-value reading of the texts, and there is good reason to question such a reading because it minimizes the importance of James and the family of Jesus. Apart from the Epistle of James, none of the New Testament texts is written from the point of view of James. The problem for the study of James is complicated further because no contemporary ecclesiastical tradition looks back to James and the family of Jesus as its fountain head. When one fails to assume the three points outlined above, the flimsy evidence of the New Testament is open to a very different reading.

James: Follower or Opponent?

The evidence of the Gospels does not single out James, and what we can say of him needs to be discussed in relation to the presentation of the family. Conclusions drawn about the mother of Jesus have not been as negative concerning her relationship to Jesus as those drawn concerning James because she attracted an ongoing tradition of support. While it is generally argued that the Synoptic Gospels present the family (without any exceptions) in a negative relation to Jesus, it is John (7:5) that is thought to single out the brothers as unbelievers. Even if this text is read in this way, it needs to be asked whether the Johannine position on the brothers is historical. The position on James generally builds on the assumption that it is. Separating tradition from redaction makes it possible to speak of the historical James as distinct from his image in the Gospels. Tradition is not necessarily straightforwardly historical, and the evangelist's redaction may not be unhistorical, but the distinction is important in establishing a sound historical methodology.

Early tradition about James not found in the New Testament also has a bearing on the way the New Testament evidence is read and assessed. In particular, account needs to be taken of the pervasive tradition of James as the first bishop of Jerusalem. This tradition makes clear that James was chosen because of his relationship to Jesus and because of his piety.[5] His legendary piety appears

---

[4] Goulder, p. ix, argues that the Jerusalem mission was at first run by Peter and the sons of Zebedee and later by Jesus' brother James and other members of his family.

[5] Eusebius, *HE* 2.1.2.

to be rooted in history because Josephus's account of the martyrdom of James confirms the honor in which he was held by those Josephus considered most concerned with maintaining the law in his day. James's reputation for piety was reinforced by his martyrdom, and the accounts of his life as well as his death are shaped by the tradition of the righteous sufferer. Indeed, this genre of literature is almost certainly responsible for the attribution of the epithet "the righteous" to James.[6]

Studies attempting to reconstruct something of the time of Jesus normally begin with the Synoptics. In this instance the explicit statement that "his brothers did not believe in him" justifies starting with John (7:5). Recognition of tendencies of interpretation in the early church helps us discern the bearing that the tradition in John has on our understanding of James and the family of Jesus. The tendency to idealize the mother of Jesus in John should alert the reader to the possibility that the portrayal of the family has been subjected to certain pressures which have skewed the picture.

JOHN: THE FAMILY AS FOLLOWERS

References to the family of Jesus in John are few but significant (2:1–11, 12; 7:3–5; 19:25–27). The references in 2:1–11 and 7:3–5 are frequently assigned to the signs source (a collection of miracle stories that John might have used). Regardless of whether a signs source theory is accepted, it is probable that the references to the mother and brothers of Jesus are traditional, although there is evidence that the evangelist has significantly reworked the traditional elements in the interest of his own purposes. John may have been completed in the light of the knowledge of one (Mark) or more of the Synoptics. The position taken here is that the evidence suggests that the substantial shaping of John was achieved independently of the Synoptics.[7]

The treatment of tradition concerning the family of Jesus in John has been subordinated to the overriding ideology of the Beloved Disciple, which has also influenced the treatment of the disciples, especially Peter. The Beloved Disciple

---

[6] On the use of Δίκαιος in relation to James, see the accounts of the martyrdom of James in Eusebius, *HE* 2.23, which include those written by Josephus, Hegesippus, Clement of Alexandria, and Origen. See also the *First Apocalypse of James,* the *Second Apocalypse of James,* and the *Ascents of James* in the Pseudo-Clementines. On the model of the righteous sufferer see the texts concerning the Qumran Teacher of Righteousness. Righteousness applied to this teacher also has a bearing on the perception of him as a suffering righteous martyr.

[7] The independence of the Johannine tradition from the Synoptics is argued by P. Gardner-Smith, *Saint John and the Synoptic Gospels* (Cambridge: Cambridge University Press, 1938); C. H. Dodd, *Historical Tradition and the Fourth Gospel* (Cambridge: Cambridge University Press, 1963). For a more nuanced position see D. M. Smith, *John among the Gospels: The Relationship in Twentieth-Century Research* (Minneapolis: Fortress, 1992), and my *The Quest for the Messiah: The History, Literature and Theology of the Johannine Community* (Nashville: Abingdon, 1993), 99–105.

is portrayed as the legitimate leader of the Johannine community. In the Johannine context Petrine authority constituted the most serious challenge and, because of this, Peter appears alongside the Beloved Disciple, always in an inferior position.

The mother of Jesus appears alongside the Beloved Disciple as another ideal disciple. The rest of the family does not fare so well. The treatment of the brothers of Jesus must be read against the tendency to exalt the Beloved Disciple. The evangelist's treatment of the family is more or less straightforward and not without importance. Discerning what is derived from tradition is much more difficult.

John 2:12: The Faithful Family

The reference to the brothers of Jesus in John 2:12 follows the gathering of the first disciples (1:19–51) and the provision of wine at the wedding in Jesus' first sign at Cana of Galilee (2:1–11). In this sign the mother of Jesus was instrumental in leading Jesus to act in a way that revealed his glory so that his disciples believed in him. Then we are told that Jesus

> went down to Capernaum with his mother, brothers and disciples and remained there not many days.

We are led to assume that the retinue of Jesus' followers is made up of family and disciples. Jesus went to Capernaum, and family and disciples went *with him*. The family group is made up by his mother and his brothers. James is not mentioned by name in John, but we may safely assume that the most prominent of the brothers of Jesus is included in the collective reference to "his brothers."

We should be cautious about assuming that Joseph was dead simply because he is not mentioned. The sisters of Jesus are not mentioned either, and we have no reason to think that they were dead. Rather, the mother of Jesus and the brothers are specifically mentioned because of the prominent role that they play in the early church.

John 2:12 has no Synoptic parallel and is a summary statement. It can be seen as an editorial bridging composition by the evangelist. The disciples are included, connecting their presence in 2:1–11 with what is to follow, 2:17, 22. The mother of Jesus has a crucial role to play in the first Cana sign (2:1–11) but has no continuing role in what follows. The mention of the brothers in 2:12 is completely gratuitous. They are mentioned at neither the Cana wedding nor the subsequent events in the Temple. Had the evangelist freely composed 2:12, those mentioned in the linking verse might be expected to be present in the preceding and succeeding incidents. What 2:12 does is to create the impression that the brothers were an essential part of the following of Jesus. John may have used a traditional summary to this effect. This is the view the reader must draw from 2:12.

John 7:3–5: The Brothers as Unbelievers?

John 7 confirms the impression that the brothers of Jesus were present in his retinue. They were with him in Galilee. Even if their advice to him—

> "Go down from here and go to Judaea that your disciples may see your signs which you do; for no one does anything in secret and himself seeks to be in public"

—does not meet with immediate approval, it confirms their presence with Jesus. The narrator's comment "For his brothers did not believe in him," more than any other evidence, has led to the widespread view that James and the brothers did not believe in Jesus during his ministry.

Given that this incident is peculiar to John, we may doubt the validity of it as historical evidence about James, especially as the narrator here gives expression to the Johannine redaction even if the incident is based on tradition. There are also good reasons for doubting that the evangelist intended to portray the brothers straightforwardly as unbelievers. Because John does not portray the brothers in any prominent role, reference to their presence with Jesus is all the more important. But how are we to take the statement that "his brothers did not believe in him"? From the Johannine perspective, belief prior to the resurrection/glorification of Jesus is thought to be suspect, so that right at the end of his farewell discourses Jesus challenges the affirmation of belief by the disciples, "Do you now believe?" (16:31). He goes on to tell them that "the hour comes when you will all be scattered" (16:32), an event which falsifies their claim to believe. If Jesus puts the belief of the disciples in question at this point, we should hesitate before concluding that the narrator's comment in 7:5 indicates that the brothers were total unbelievers. By Johannine standards of "authentic" or ideal belief neither the disciples nor the brothers qualified until after the resurrection of Jesus and the coming of the Paraclete.

Literary parallels with other Johannine narratives suggest that reading 7:5 as if the brothers were not followers of Jesus is mistaken. In John 2:1–11 the sign was initiated by the mother of Jesus whose report to Jesus constitutes an implied request. But Jesus rebuffs his mother:

> "Woman, what is there between us? My hour has not yet come."

The rebuff or objection is an essential aspect of the quest story.[8] In spite of this rebuff his mother persisted and Jesus acted to supply the need, with the

---

[8] See my *The Quest for the Messiah,* p. 177.

consequence that the disciples believed. In a similar way the request/suggestion by his brothers that Jesus should go to Judaea is met by a rebuff by Jesus:

"My time is not yet present, but your time is always ready."

Mention in each case that the time/hour has not yet come confirms that the pattern of the narratives was intended to make the connection between the two stories, especially as the family of Jesus is involved in each. Jesus told them to go up to the feast, asserting that he was not going because "my time is not fulfilled" (7:8). However, when the brothers had gone up, Jesus also went, but secretly, not openly (7:10). In each of the narratives Jesus apparently rejects the request only to comply with it *in his own time*. In the second sign at Cana Jesus also rebuffs the request of the "nobleman"—"Unless you see signs and wonders you will not believe" (4:48)—but in response to the persistent request heals the man's son with the consequence that his whole house believed. Thus we have a Johannine pattern in which the petitioner is rebuffed, but Jesus accedes to the request and the petitioner appears in a positive light.

The reason for Jesus' reluctance to go up to Jerusalem (Judaea) is stated in 7:1. The Jews there are seeking to kill him. There is no suggestion that the brothers hope to have Jesus entrapped in Jerusalem. Their suggestion is that Jesus should act in the most public context, where his actions will have greatest effect. Later (in John 11), when Jesus has been called to Bethany and announces that he is about to go, the disciples object:

"Rabbi, the Jews now seek to stone you and do you again go there?" (11:8)

When Jesus persists with that intent, Thomas (Didymos, "the twin") says:

"Let us also go that we may die with him." (11:16)

This remark shows as little perception of what Jesus had in mind as do the comments of his brothers.

The evangelist is also intent to portray the hiddenness of Jesus, the hiddenness of the Messiah, the hiddenness of the revelation. Consequently, everyone in Jerusalem is seeking Jesus and cannot find him. Even if 2:1–11 and 7:1–9 are from tradition, perhaps a signs source, there is evidence of the evangelist's interpretative work. Had the presence of the brothers with Jesus during his ministry not been traditional, and very likely historical, they would have played no part in the Gospel narrative. Even in the evangelist's interpretation of their role, they are portrayed as "fallible followers" rather than as outright unbelievers. In this their portrayal does not differ greatly from that of the disciples, except that the role of the family is marginal while the disciples regularly appear with Jesus.

The overall effect of John 2:1–11, 12 is to lead the reader to the conclusion that the mother and brothers of Jesus were among his intimate supporters. This impression is not altogether undone by John 7:3–5, in which the narrator informs the readers that they did not believe in him at this stage. Yet, the impression that his brothers were followers is confirmed by their presence with Jesus. Consequently, we should not build up a theory of opposition to Jesus by his natural family. It is significant that, in John 4:44, there is no reference to the kinsfolk of Jesus (contrast Mark 6:4) when the evangelist describes the contexts in which Jesus was accorded no honor. Rather, in John the family of Jesus, especially his mother, is portrayed positively even if in a somewhat paradoxical fashion. I refer here to the way the Jesus of John refers to his mother as "Woman" (2:4; 19:26). While such a form of address is not in itself derogatory, it is abrupt to the point of being dismissive when addressed by a son to his mother.

John 19:25–27: The Ideal Disciples and the Absence of James

As the followers present with Jesus at his crucifixion, John 19:25–27 mentions the mother of Jesus, his mother's sister, Mary the [wife] of Clopas, and Mary Magdalene, together with the Beloved Disciple. The absence of Jesus' brothers is notable, and the women mentioned provide pieces in a puzzle for those seeking to harmonize the Gospels.

In Mark 15:40 three women are named as Mary Magdalene; Mary the mother of James "the less" and Joses; and Salome. In an attempt to harmonize the Markan account with John 19:25, Mary the mother of James and Joses (Mark 15:40) is sometimes identified with the sister of the mother of Jesus. Her two sons bear the same names as two of the "brothers of Jesus," and here they are identified as cousins rather than brothers. Because Mark mentions only three women it is sometimes assumed that (in John) "Mary the [wife] of Clopas" does not refer to an additional person but names the sister of the mother of Jesus. The case is built up by other references to the women in the crucifixion, burial, resurrection narratives.[9] The motivation for this harmonization, essential to Jerome's hypothesis, is to identify those known as brothers of Jesus as cousins.

---

[9] See the account of the crucifixion in Matt 27:56 (Mary Magdalene; Mary the mother of James and Joseph; the mother of the sons of Zebedee), which differs from Mark 15:40 by omitting the epithet "the less" and, in the place of Salome, mentions the mother of the sons of Zebedee who could be identified with Salome.

At the burial Mark (15:47) mentions Mary Magdalene and Mary the [mother?—assuming identity with the second Mary of 15:40] of Joses, who in Matthew (27:61) are named Mary Magdalene and the other Mary.

At the empty tomb Mark (16:1) mentions Mary Magdalene and Mary the [mother?—again

The attempt to harmonize Mark 15:40 with John 19:25 fails because there is no place in Mark 15:40 for the mother of Jesus (or the Beloved Disciple), mentioned by John. If John has introduced them into his account this is probably true of the sister also. Further, John 19:25 distinguishes four, not three, women. The first two are not named but identified by their relationship to Jesus and each other. The second group of two is made up of two women named Mary. The first of these is normally understood to be Mary the wife of Clopas, but, given the form of the first half of 19:25, which mentions the *mother* of Jesus and the sister of his *mother,* it may be that Mary was the *mother* of Clopas. There is no persuasive reason to harmonize Mark's reference to Mary the mother of James and Joses with John's to the sister of the mother of Jesus. Other features of the Johannine account suggest that ideological considerations are at work in this part of the passion narrative.

As he did in 2:4, Jesus addresses his mother as "Woman" in 19:26: "Woman, behold your son." The words spoken to the Beloved Disciple make clear that he is the son in view, "Behold your mother" (19:27). Because the brothers of Jesus are not mentioned and the mother of Jesus is committed into the care of the Beloved Disciple, it can be argued that the brothers are not believers. Such a conclusion is precarious. The narrative is peculiarly Johannine and serves Johannine purposes. The role of the Beloved Disciple is elevated so that his position as the ideal disciple is heightened as is that of the mother of Jesus. It is unlikely that this narrative is based on independent historical tradition. In other scenes the ideal role of the Beloved Disciple is elevated at the expense of Peter.[10] Here the Beloved Disciple and the mother of Jesus are portrayed as ideal disciples and are committed each to the other's keeping.

The absence of Peter and the other disciples should not be taken to mean that they were in no sense believers or followers at the time. Having suffered a failure of nerve, they have fallen short of the response of the ideal disciples. The absence of the brothers from this scene can be understood in the same way. Michael Goulder is right in asserting that "In John Jesus takes away from them [the brothers of Jesus] their privilege of looking after his mother, and gives it to the disciple whom he loved. John's feelings were not ambivalent."[11] Histori-

---

with reference to 15:40] of James and Salome; or, again on the precedent of Mark 15:40 where the meaning is clear, it is probable that Salome is a third woman present. Having mentioned both sons in 15:40, Mark mentions only one in 15:47 and the other in 16:1 in the reverse order of the first mention. Matthew (28:1) takes the reference as being to the same two Marys who were at the burial, naming the second again as "the other Mary." This confirms that Matthew understands Mark's reference first to the mother of Joses and then to the mother of James on the basis of Mark 15:40, where Mary is named the mother of both sons. Matthew omits Mark's reference to Salome. John (20:1) mentions only Mary Magdalene.

[10] See especially John 13:23–30; 18:15–17; 20:2–8; 21:7–24.

[11] Goulder, p. 15.

cally this scene provides no evidence to support the view that the brothers were not followers of Jesus. Their absence from this scene is no more incriminating than the absence of Peter and the rest of the twelve. Because of the evangelist's ideological concern to undergird the authority of the Beloved Disciple, the Gospel has portrayed him in some tension with the twelve, and always to the advantage of the Beloved Disciple. We should expect no less in the portrayal of the family of Jesus. Given the evidence of the leading role of the family in the early church, we should expect the evangelist to suppress that role to the advantage of the Beloved Disciple in a way similar to that in which he has deemphasized the role of Peter. Nothing in this Gospel gives us any reason to think that the brothers were anything but part of the following of Jesus during his ministry.

THE SYNOPTICS: THE MARKAN FRAMEWORK AND ITS INTERPRETATION BY MATTHEW AND LUKE

Our treatment of the family of Jesus in the Synoptics assumes the priority of Mark,[12] and some account is given of the differences from Mark found in Matthew and Luke, including those parts of Mark that are omitted by Matthew and Luke and the additions that they made to the Markan framework. Matthew and Luke provide accounts of the infancy of Jesus, a perspective totally lacking from Mark. Generally speaking, we have given priority to the Markan material although the possibility that modifications might be based on a knowledge of tradition independent of Mark cannot be ruled out.

MARK: A CRITIQUE OF DISCIPLES AND FAMILY

Several passages in Mark have contributed to the negative view of the family of Jesus that is commonly thought to be historical. Attention needs to be given to evidence of underlying tradition as distinct from the meaning of these passages within the Markan framework. Mark has a negative view of the family and of the twelve. It is also comparatively easy to see how Matthew and Luke have modified Mark. Discerning what can be said on the basis of the underlying tradition in Mark is much more difficult.

It has become standard approach in the commentaries to see Mark 3:20–35 as a sandwich structure in which the incident introduced in 3:21 concerning the family of Jesus is completed in 3:31–35. According to this reading, the

---

[12] The hypothesis of the priority of Mark and its use by Matthew and Luke, together with the hypothetical sayings source generally known by the symbol Q, is accepted as the most useful working hypothesis. See M. D. Hooker, *The Gospel according to Saint Mark* (Peabody, Mass.: Hendrickson, 1991), 15. Further research is likely to confirm the general theory while showing that the reality was more complex, rather than simpler, than the popular form of the hypothesis suggests. For example, there is a growing tendency to return to the view that the Synoptics were dependent on a common source to which Mark provides closest resemblance.

action of the "filling" (3:22–30) throws light on the action of the family, setting it in an extremely negative context. The family, supposing Jesus to be "beside himself," is portrayed in terms little better than the scribes from Jerusalem who accuse him of being possessed by the prince of demons. This reading is not likely to clarify the historical role of the family during the ministry of Jesus because 3:20–21 is probably a Markan bridging summary, and without it the story of 3:31–35 ceases to be negative. Nor is it altogether satisfactory as a bridging passage because there is minimal continuity between 3:13–19 and 3.20–35 on this reading. It simply serves to move Jesus from one situation to another. According to our reading, Jesus chose the twelve to be with him (3:14), then moved with the twelve into the next scene (3:20–21). Thus 3:20–21 refers to the disciples, not to the family.

Mark 3:20–21: Disciples or Family?

The incident follows immediately after the choosing and naming of the twelve (3:13–19), which is the opening of an *inclusio* completed by the sending out (mission) of the twelve (6:7–13).[13] The account of choosing and naming says that Jesus appointed twelve "so that they may be with him [μετ' αὐτοῦ] and so that he may send them to announce the news." Mark goes on in the connecting editorial (3:20–21) to describe the activity of the disciples with Jesus.

> And he comes [or they come] into a house; and again the crowd comes together, so that they were not able even to eat bread. And when his associates [οἱ παρ' αὐτοῦ] heard they went out to take[14] him; for they were saying, "He is beside himself."[15]

The account of the sending out of the twelve does not appear until 6:7–13. In between the choosing and the sending of the twelve they are with Jesus. Mark introduces the incident concerning the charge that Jesus is demon-possessed (3:22–30), which is connected by 3:20–21 to the choosing and naming of the twelve (3:13–19) and is followed by incidents concerning the family of Jesus, their arrival seeking him (3:31–35), and the rejection of Jesus at his hometown, Nazareth (6:1–6, especially 6:3–4). In this way the status of both the

[13] An *inclusio* is the framing device whereby all of the narrative between 3:19 and 6:7 is seen in terms of the first of the two purposes of the appointment. The twelve disciples were chosen to be with Jesus. Only in 6:7–13 is the second purpose of sending them out as apostles realized. Hence 3:20–6:6 is framed or sandwiched.

[14] Means to restrain, arrest.

[15] D. Wenham, "The Meaning of Mark 3.21," *NTS* 21 (1974–75): 295–300, supports this interpretation.

twelve and the family, in relation to the mission of Jesus, is put in question. The evidence and arguments now need to be examined in detail.

Scholars generally argue that 3:20–21 refers to the family of Jesus, and there are two broadly different approaches to this position. Both argue that the Greek phrase οἱ παρ' αὐτοῦ is a reference to the family of Jesus. But this expression could also mean "his associates" or "adherents." In so-called classical Greek it means "envoys" (Thucydides 7.10) or "ambassadors" or is used with the dative to refer to those of someone's household and rarely with the genitive to denote friends or dependents. In the LXX it means "adherents," "followers" (1 Macc 9:44; 11:73; 12:27; 13:52; 15:15; 16:16; 2 Macc 11:20), "parents" or "relatives" (Prov 31:21; Sus 33; cf. *Ant.* 1.10.5), meanings which are also to be found in the papyri. Yet commentators invariably opt for "his family." Recently Raymond E. Brown wrote, "Only Mark (3.21) associates this seeking at Capernaum with the fact that 'his own' (= family at Nazareth) think that he is beside himself and set out to seize him."[16] Brown gives no indication of any possible alternative reading. This is characteristic. Both the NRSV and the RNEB translate the phrase as "his family." In an attempt to justify this understanding C. E. B. Cranfield asserts: "Here in Mk 3.21 it must mean 'his family'; not 'his disciples'—described as οἱ περὶ αὐτὸν in 4.10. . . ."[17] But we can hardly think that οἱ περὶ αὐτὸν and οἱ παρ' αὐτοῦ have become, for Mark, technical descriptions, one for the disciples and the other for the family of Jesus. The linguistic evidence is even more complex. For example, when Jesus goes to a desert place, Simon and those with him (οἱ μετ' αὐτοῦ) pursue him (1:36). Very likely we are to think of this as a group of the disciples. The same expression (μετ' αὐτοῦ) is used in the account of the choosing of the twelve, whom Mark says Jesus chose "to be with him" (3:14). Thus we have three different linguistic formulae. It is unlikely that they indicate specific groups, so that οἱ παρ' αὐτοῦ clearly *identified* "his family," who have not yet appeared in the narrative of Mark. More evidence must be used to establish to whom the expression refers.

Both also argue that 3:20–21 forms a sandwich structure or *inclusio* with 3:31–35, thus identifying οἱ παρ' αὐτοῦ as the family. The family goes out in 3:21 and arrives in 3:31. Robert A. Guelich argues that the conclusive evidence in favor of understanding οἱ παρ' αὐτοῦ in terms of "his family" is "the evangelist's 'sandwich' structure of 3:20–21 and 3:31–35 around 3:22–30. Mark 3:31 makes clear that Jesus' 'family' is the subject of 3:21."[18] See also Robert Horton Gundry: "The charges against Jesus and his responses to them are sandwiched between the starting out of his family to seize him because they think

---

[16] *The Death of the Messiah* (Garden City, N.Y.: Doubleday, 1994), 1025 n.99.

[17] *The Gospel according to St Mark* (Cambridge: Cambridge University Press, 1972), 133.

[18] *Mark 1–8:26,* Word Biblical Commentary 34A (Dallas: Word Books, 1989), 172.

he has gone berserk (vv20b–21) and their arrival and his response (vv31–35)."[19] Cranfield makes the same point in other words: "The natural assumption is that οἱ παρ' αὐτοῦ here denotes the same people as are mentioned in v.31, and so includes the mother of Jesus."[20]

The notion of the sandwich structure implies that 3:20–21 introduces 3:31–35; that without 3:20–21, 3:31–35 is introduced abruptly and without adequate preparation while 3:20–21, without 3:31–35, is a narrative going nowhere. This interpretation ignores the problem of the abrupt and enigmatic introduction of the family in 3:21. Understood in terms of this sandwich structure, "the family" first appears in Mark in a bad light, although the hostility attributed to the brothers is rarely aimed at Mary also. The family is portrayed as unsympathetic to Jesus, asserting that "he is beside himself,"[21] out of control and in need of forcible restraint. The notion that the abrupt introduction of the family in 3:31 is overcome by 3:20–21 is strange. It is asking too much of the reader to recognize the vague expression in 3:21 as a reference to the family members who are not specifically mentioned until 3:31. If the disciples are in view in 3:20–21, the narrative continues their presence with Jesus from 3:13–19. This reading seems more obvious.

Finally, both positions assert that Mark portrays the family as "outsiders" (3:31–32; 4:11). This reading depends on the Markan framework where the significance of "outsiders" becomes clear in 4:11. Thus, in an independent tradition about the arrival of the family of Jesus, the mention of the fact that the family is outside the house carries no strongly negative message like the one that Mark might intend the *rereader* of his Gospel to discern. John Dominic Crossan rightly argues that Mark shows hostility toward Jerusalem and the relatives of Jesus.[22] That hostility is moderated progressively by Matthew and Luke.

The first of the two positions that reads 3:21 in terms of the family of Jesus is represented by Cranfield. He takes the reference to a house that Jesus enters in 3:20 to indicate the "family home" because when Jesus enters the house "some of them at any rate are actually in the house already."[23] The argument that this excludes identification with the disciples is unconvincing. It depends on one particular interpretation of "he went into a house" (ἔρχεται εἰς οἶκον), taking it to mean "he went home," which is followed by the RSV and other English translations. It is also assumed that those who came out to take/restrain Jesus (ἐξῆλθον κρατῆσαι αὐτόν), "some of them at any rate," according to Cranfield, were already "at home" when he arrived. But the text is not as

---

[19] *Mark: A Commentary on His Apology for the Cross* (Grand Rapids: Eerdmans, 1993), 170.

[20] Cranfield, p. 133.

[21] Gundry, *Mark: A Commentary on His Apology of the Cross*, p. 171.

[22] "Mark and the Relatives of Jesus," *NovT* 15 (1973): 81–113.

[23] Cranfield, p. 133.

specific as this. Nothing indicates that they were already in the house when Jesus arrived.[24] One variant reading, using the plural "they went into a house," which might well be original, has Jesus enter the house with a group.[25] In context, those entering with Jesus can only be understood as his disciples. They may have gone into the house with Jesus and come out *after* him. Even if the singular is accepted, the reader might have been expected to know that the disciples went with him.[26] In 3:20 it is said that Jesus went into a house, and we must assume (it is not specifically mentioned) that he came out. The group that sought to restrain Jesus came out, it must be assumed, after Jesus had come out. The disciples went in with Jesus before coming out to restrain him. On the plural reading, 3:20–21 is more effectively a linking narrative connecting 3:13–19 to 3:22–30, and οἱ παρ' αὐτοῦ is a reference to the twelve.

Also against the view that the family followed Jesus out of the house in 3:21 is the announcement of their arrival only in 3:31. But if 3:21 refers to them, are they not already present? To suggest that in 3:21 they go out to restrain Jesus but actually only arrive in 3:31 is hardly convincing. No great distance is involved, so little in fact that Jesus' own exit need not be mentioned. Further, 3:31–35 appears to be a new scene, with Jesus inside and the family outside. It is true that Mark does not say that they were outside "a house," though the narrator's statement that they were outside (3:31), which is taken up and repeated by the crowd, gives the impression that Jesus was inside and the family was outside the house.

A second approach that takes 3:21 as a reference to the family copes better with the itinerary of Jesus and the movement of the family. It is argued that Jesus had abandoned the family home in Nazareth and had set up his own establishment in Capernaum. The basis for this position is the reference to Jesus being "in a house" (ἐν οἴκῳ) in Capernaum in Mark 2:1. Here the RSV and other English versions translate "he was at home." On this basis it can also be suggested that Jesus was the host at a meal in his home in Mark 2:15.[27] In this

---

[24] The assumption that some members of the family were already in the house, made explicit by Cranfield, provides strong motivation for the choice of the singular "he went into the house" rather than the plural, "they."

[25] The singular (ἔρχεται) is supported by ℵ* BW (εἰσέρχεται is read by syr^s and cop^{sa,bo} Victor-Antioc), the plural (ἔρχονται) by ℵ^c ACKLΔΘΠ f^1 f^{13} (D εἰσέρχονται). This is far from clear-cut evidence in favor of the singular. The singular reading might be explained in terms of the desire to protect the disciples from the stigma of the action described. But Mark is not sensitive about portraying the disciples in a less than complimentary light.

[26] If the plural reading is thought to be a scribal "correction," it indicates that 3:20–21 was read by these early scribes on the understanding that the disciples were with Jesus. If such is the case, their interpretation correctly caught the Markan meaning.

[27] Thus E. S. Malbon, *Narrative Space and Mythic Meaning in Mark* (San Francisco: Harper & Row, 1986), 117–18, and S. C. Barton, *Discipleship and Family Ties in Mark and Matthew*, SNTSMS 80 (Cambridge: Cambridge University Press, 1994), 68.

context 3:20 is taken to mean "he went home," not to the family home in Nazareth but to his own establishment in Capernaum from whence he, with his disciples, conducted his mission. The family was not in this house but in Nazareth, and it was in Nazareth that news of Jesus' frenetic behavior reached them, provoking them to set out to restrain Jesus in Capernaum. They arrived only at 3:31 in the narrative.

Against this view, Cranfield is right to think that the expression οἱ παρ' αὐτοῦ implies that, whoever they are, they are in the company of Jesus, not a family that has been rejected and left in another village some miles away. No other house is mentioned, and it is asking a lot of the reader to know that those who went out to restrain Jesus went out, not only from another house but from another town that has not been mentioned.

Further, in none of the references that are taken to indicate "the home" of Jesus does Mark make the details clear. In each case (2:1, 15; 3:20) Mark literally refers to "a house." In Mark 2:1 there is no reason to think that the house is anything but a house visited by Jesus, one where it came to be known that he was present. Once 2:1 is taken to be the home of Jesus, however, the temptation is to read other indefinite references to "a house" in the same way. While it is possible to read 2:15 as a reference to Jesus' home, most commentators take 2:15 to be a reference to the house of Levi. Mark has just narrated the call of the tax collector, Levi, and Luke (5:29) certainly understood the text of Mark to mean that the meal was in "his house," that is, the house of Levi. This is a reasonable reading of Mark. The assembly of tax collectors is easily understood as one of friends and associates of Levi. Mark does not provide any indication of the location of this house. He mentions Jesus' movements beside the sea (2:13) without suggesting that he was still in Capernaum. In 3:7 Jesus again withdraws somewhere beside the sea before going to a mountain to call, appoint, and commission the twelve (3:13–19). Without any further indication of location Mark mentions Jesus' entry into a house (3:20). The RSV translates this as "he went home," prejudicing the reading of 3:21 by which οἱ παρ' αὐτοῦ are taken to be "his family"! The meaning is compromised in favor of "his family" once the indefinite "house" is translated "home." Where "home" is intended it is clearly indicated, as in 5:19 in which Jesus tells the healed demoniac to go home: "Go to *your* house" (Ὕπαγε εἰς τὸν οἶκόν σου). The reference in 3:20 is indefinite, and there is no reason to think that the house was Jesus' own establishment or that he was still in Capernaum. There is as little reason to think of this house as the home of Jesus as there is to think that Jesus resided in the house that he enters (εἰσῆλθεν εἰς οἶκον) to escape from the crowd in 7:17, and no one would suggest that the house he enters (εἰσελθὼν εἰς οἰκίαν) in the region of Tyre was his home (7:24). Here we have examples of Jesus making use of houses in the course of his mission. There is no reason to think that any of them should be identified as his own home.

The view that Jesus operated his mission from his home runs contrary to the tradition in Q (see Matt 8:20 = Luke 9:58: "The foxes have holes and the birds of the air have nests but the Son of Man has nowhere to lay his head") as well as to Mark (see the mission charge of Mark 6:6b–12, especially 6:10). These traditions indicate that Jesus conducted an itinerant mission without any settled base. The notion of Jesus' home base has been imported into texts that mention only a house in which Jesus is present. Jesus not only had no home base; he also called on his disciples to leave families and homes to follow him. In this the Markan narrative, corroborated by Q, is probably consistent with the historical Jesus.

If it is argued that Jesus remained in the house throughout the events of 3:20–35, with the family coming from Nazareth, then the scribes from Jerusalem must also have been gathered around Jesus and would have been included among those designated by him as his eschatological family. Against this view it seems that Mark has strung together independent traditions in a way that does not make explicit the movements of all parties. Jesus left the house to encounter the scribes and had reentered to talk with the crowd of disciples by the time the family arrived for the first time in 3:31. Thus 3:21 refers to the twelve, revealing that Mark has an ambivalent attitude toward them. Chosen in 3:13–19, they are shown to be fallible followers of Jesus in 3:20–21.[28]

The text of 3:20–21 compels the reader to fill gaps in the narrative. The identity of those who went out to restrain Jesus is not made explicit. While the flow of the narrative from 3:13–19 implies the presence of the twelve with Jesus, this conclusion must be drawn by the reader. Mark provides a reason for the disciples' action by saying that because of the press of the crowd "they were unable even to eat bread" (3:20), *implying* that Jesus and his disciples were unable to eat, which lends weight to the plural reading. There is then the description of two negative verbal responses to Jesus, first by a group not clearly identified (3:21) and then by the scribes from Jerusalem (3:22–30). The severity of the criticism of the first group is apparent only when the parallel with the second is recognized because Jesus' critique explicitly deals only with the second.

It is not actually said who was saying of Jesus, "He is beside himself." It may be those who went out to restrain Jesus. The flow of the narrative, however, implies that this was the conclusion drawn by the crowd. The twelve went out to restrain Jesus because of what they heard. The narrative supplies the reader with the report that they heard the crowd saying, "He is beside himself."

---

[28] See R. C. Tannehill, "The Disciples in Mark: The Function of a Narrative Role," *Journal of Religion* 57 (1977): 386–407, and E. S. Malbon, "Fallible Followers: Women and Men in the Gospel of Mark," *Semeia* 28 (1983): 29–48.

The crowd's view of Jesus ("He is beside himself") agrees in principle with the evaluation of the scribes from Jerusalem who said of Jesus, "He has Beelzebul" (Mark 3:22). This is signaled by the agreement in the introductory quotation formulae: "they were saying" in each instance. The use of the imperfect tense implies repeated assertion, not casual remarks, and the parallelism draws attention to the common assertion made in popular and more technical terms. Jesus condemned their views as blasphemy of the Holy Spirit, and such blasphemy was said to be beyond forgiveness because it named goodness as evil and called God the devil (3:27–30). What is not immediately apparent is that the views of the crowd fall under the same condemnation because their evaluation of Jesus is the same, only stated in more popular terms. There is little to choose between madness and possession. This phenomenon is understood at three levels in Mark. In the incident described in Mark 3:20–30 the crowd, with its popular view, diagnoses the "madness" of Jesus (3.21); the scribes, adopting a theological perspective, accuse him of "demon possession," understood as a manifestation of evil opposed to God and his purposes (3:22); the narrator identifies this in priestly terms as possession by an unclean spirit (3:30), rendering the possessed unclean.

The question of what is from tradition and what is Markan redaction is important although, even if 3:20–21 is from tradition, the enigmatic nature of the reference does not permit any clear and straightforward identifications; gaps must be filled by the reader before 3:20–21 can be understood precisely. Contextually 3:20–21 serves to introduce the charge of demon possession in 3:22–30.

While Mark 3:22–30 and 3:31–35 contain traditional material, Mark 3:20–21 is Markan redaction. According to Lorenz Oberlinner, there is linguistic and contextual evidence suggesting that 3:21 is Markan redaction.[29] In Mark the verb translated "to take" has a hostile sense, meaning to restrain or arrest.[30] The incident described in 3:20–21 is missing from Matthew and Luke, which could mean that they regarded it to be Markan redaction. The redactional nature of this linking narrative means that no historical weight can be placed on it. Hence, even if it refers to the family, and we have argued it does not, the most that could be drawn from it is that Mark had a negative view of the family. In our view it is Mark's ambivalent attitude toward the twelve that emerges from 3:13–19 in relation to 3:20–21. Further, on our reading it is the crowd who was saying that Jesus was beside himself (not the twelve), and thus the crowd is associated with the negative attitude of the scribes from Jerusalem. By

---

[29] Oberlinner, pp. 167–75. Markan redaction is often introduced by participles (ἀκούσαντες). Further, ἐξέρχεσθαι and κρατεῖν are characteristic Markan terms.

[30] For the use of κρατῆσαι see Mark 3:21; 12:12; 14:1, 44, 46, 49, 51. It is similar to the hostile use of πιάσαι in John 7:30, 32, 44.

attempting to restrain Jesus the twelve take a step in the direction of this negative response. Thus the limitations of the twelve are accentuated at this point.

Such a critique of the disciples is characteristic of Mark. They are not
charged with the guilt of the unforgivable sin directly (as are the scribes) or
indirectly (like the crowds). They are, however, depicted as fallible followers of
Jesus, and this is already signaled in description of the choosing and naming of
the twelve (3:13–19), which concludes by naming "Judas Iscariot, who also
betrayed him." If the one who betrayed Jesus is among the twelve, it is no
surprise that the twelve as a group should have been guilty of an attempt to
restrain Jesus.

Our reading of Mark 3:20–21 acknowledges the obscurity of the Greek
text. There are gaps that the reader must fill as this material is read. It is not said
who the "they" are who were not able to eat bread and only the context reveals
to whom the expression οἱ παρ' αὐτοῦ refers. Mark does not specify what
they heard nor who was saying, "He is beside himself." Gundry holds that it
was not the crowd who said this because in 3:31–35 the crowd is revealed as
the true family.[31] The crowd of 3:20–21 is not identified straightforwardly with
those gathered around Jesus in 3:31–35, which recounts a separate incident
even if Mark has linked it thematically with the earlier sequence. From 3:22 to
3:30 Jesus' dispute is with the scribes from Jerusalem, and there is no reference
to the crowd of 3:20–21. Verses 31–35 imply a new situation. Certainly the
crowd gathered around Jesus is not the hostile scribes. This crowd is made up
of unspecified followers of Jesus, and it seems to be implied that they are now
inside the house, for they report to Jesus, "Behold, your mother and your
brothers are outside seeking you."

On our reading of Mark four successive groups fall under critique: first the
disciples, then the crowd (3:20–21); then the scribes from Jerusalem (3:22–30);
and finally the natural family (3:31–35). The critique of the family is obviously
quite central to the present study.

Mark 3:31–35: The Eschatological Family

For those seeking to reconstruct the history of James and the family,
3:31–35 should be read, in the first instance, as a free-standing tradition. It is
also of interest to see what Mark makes of it in the context of his Gospel,
although the views expressed there may be a departure from a fair account of
the historical role of the family during the ministry of Jesus.

Certainly Mark is handling old tradition, as signaled by the biographical
apophthegm.[32] In terms of the analysis of the chreia this should be seen as an

---

[31] *Mark: A Commentary on His Apology of the Cross,* p. 171.

[32] R. K. Bultmann, *History of the Synoptic Tradition* (Oxford: Oxford University Press, 1968), 29.

inquiry story.[33] In it the mother and brothers of Jesus come seeking Jesus (3:32). This provides him with the opportunity to make his pronouncement concerning the eschatological family. Unlike a quest story, the narrative here does not trace the fate of the family. The arrival of the family is used to introduce the inquiry about the true family. Mark is content to allow the family to disappear from the scene, and, for all we know, they might still be waiting outside. Unlike a quest story, in which the quester is important and the outcome of the quest is indicated, in an inquiry story the inquirer is important only to provide the opportunity for a pronouncement.

The story sets an ideal scene in the life of Jesus, showing his relationship to his followers. That the story is traditional is no guarantee of the historical accuracy of the events described. Markan redaction of the traditional story is in evidence.[34] Jesus' mother and brothers are specifically mentioned and perhaps his sisters also. In all probability "and your sisters" is a scribal addition.[35] Reference to the sisters in 3:32 has been introduced because of the mention of sisters by Jesus in 3:35.

In Mark the incident follows immediately after Jesus' controversy with the scribes concerning the source of his power. Without any indication of a change of scene the reader is told:

> And his mother comes and his brothers and standing *outside* they sent to him calling him. And a crowd was sitting around him and they say to him, "Behold your mother and your brothers [and your sisters] are outside seeking you." And having answered he says to them, "Who is my mother and [my] brothers?" And looking around at those sitting around him he says, "Behold my mother and my brothers. [For] whoever does the will of God, this one is my brother and sister and mother."

The mother and brothers of Jesus came *seeking* him. This suggests nothing sinister. The fact that they await *outside* implies a respectful approach. Their arrival and the report of it to Jesus imply an inquiry. His answer first makes explicit the nature of the inquiry, "Who is my mother and [my] brothers?" (3:33). Jesus' answer to this inquiry is given first by his action, in looking at those gathered around him; and then in his words, "Behold my mother and my brothers. [For] whoever does the will of God, this one is my brother and

---

[33] See the analysis by R. C. Tannehill in *Pronouncement Stories,* ed. Tannehill, *Semeia* 20 (1981): 10, 114–16.

[34] R. Pesch, *Das Markusevangelium,* vol. 1, HTKNT (Freiburg: Herder, 1977), 221; Oberlinner, *Überlieferung,* pp. 179–83.

[35] The editors of the third edition of the UBS Greek New Testament give the reading only a "C" rating on a scale of A to D, when A notes the highest degree of probability for a reading where there are variants.

sister and mother" (3:34–35). In this way Mark has Jesus delimit the "eschatological family," which is distinguished from the natural family waiting outside
and from the twelve, who are not mentioned at this point. This family is identified with the anonymous crowd gathered around Jesus (3:32).

It may be that this double stress on the family being "outside," expressed
first by the narrator and then reported to Jesus by the crowd, foreshadows the
reference to outsiders by Jesus in Mark 4:11. This negative sense is a consequence of Markan redaction. In the isolated narrative itself it means no more
than that the family waits outside, seeking (to speak to?[36]) Jesus. There is no
doubt that in Mark 3:31–35 Jesus distinguishes the eschatological family sitting
around him from his natural family outside. This view is softened in Matthew
and Luke.

The reader is not told why the mother and brothers of Jesus come seeking
him. We are not told that they have come to restrain Jesus. Rather, consistent
with an inquiry story, their coming allows Jesus to make his pronouncement.
According to Jesus, his natural family has been replaced by his eschatological
family, those who do the will of God. The point of this saying is not to indicate
that the family of Jesus is opposed to Jesus' mission. It is to assert the place
of the eschatological family. The (twelve) disciples are not identified with the
eschatological family any more than is the natural family. The challenge to do
the will of God lies equally before them.

The incident under discussion takes on a particularly negative tone only
when it is read in the framework of Mark. If the incident is based on old
tradition, as seems likely, what we learn is that the mother and brothers of Jesus
came seeking him. There is nothing negative in this. Even the reference to
them being outside, unable to enter because of the crowd in the house, is not
at all sinister. Only when this is read in the light of Mark 4:11 does it suggest
that they are to be seen as "outsiders." That Mark intends this is probable,
revealing that he is not positively inclined to the leadership role of the family
of Jesus in the early church. Mark was no more sympathetic to the leadership
of the twelve.[37] They are not identified with the eschatological family and are
even more stringently criticized in Mark 3:20–21.

Mark aims to elevate the eschatological family of Jesus. No conclusions
should be drawn about the opposition of the natural family or of James in
particular. Mark's treatment of the natural family and the twelve puts in question leadership aspirations arising from both groups. The twelve are fallible
followers, and the way in which Mark portrays them in a bad light is commonly
treated in the literature. The treatment of the natural family may well signal a
rejection of James and his successors. Might it be that Mark looks to Paul as the

---

[36] Thus Matt 12:47. According to Luke 8:20, the family members "wish to see" Jesus.

[37] Thus, rightly, J. D. Crossan, "Mark and the Relatives of Jesus," *NovT* 15 (1973): 81–113.

one who manifests the leadership arising from the eschatological family? There is a strong case for seeing Mark as a pro-Pauline Gospel because the Pauline gospel is understood more adequately in Mark than in any other Gospel. With its focus on the passion of Jesus and the rejection of Jewish food and purity laws (Mark 7:1–23), Mark alone asserts that Jesus declared all food to be clean. Consistent with Paul, Mark also gives expression to a more radical view of the sabbath than does Matthew.

Stephen C. Barton has shown that in depicting the subordination of family the Gospels are consistent with other Jewish (Philo, Josephus, and Qumran) and Hellenistic (Cynic and Stoic) traditions.[38] Some elements in the early Christian movement have distanced Jesus from his family in the interest of the universal spread of the mission beyond the range of kinship ties. Consequently, it is not surprising that Jesus asserted that participation in his mission involved loyalty that overrode family and friendship ties. His own relationship to his family was a test case. The true family of Jesus is found within the community of his followers, and here, according to this incident, not even the twelve have a special place. Obedience to the will of God is the sole criterion for membership in this family. This opens the way equally to all who respond positively to the call of Jesus, and we might suspect that, for Mark, Paul holds a special place among those who do the will of God. According to this reading, the story tells us more about the limits Jesus placed on family ties and the attitude of Mark to the family of Jesus (as outsiders) than it tells us about the attitude of the family to Jesus.

Set in the Markan framework the reference to the family being outside (3:31–32) takes on a more negative sense, especially in the light of 4:11. The family members now emerge not simply as outside the company of 3:32 but as "outsiders." Yet this Markan evaluation of the family is not really any more negative than the view of the twelve that emerges in Mark 4. The twelve were supposed to be "insiders," but by their failure to understand the parable of the soils they showed themselves to be "outsiders" (4:10, 13).

Mark 6:3–4: Jesus' Rejection in His Own Country

Mark 6:3–4 provides further evidence concerning the family of Jesus and the only specific reference to James in Mark. Between the previous reference to the mother and brothers of Jesus (3:31–35) and 6:3 is the account of Jesus teaching beside the sea (4:1–34); the sea-crossing with the calming of the storm (4:35–41); the healing of the Gerasene demoniac on the eastern side of the sea (5:1–20); the return to the western side of the sea, where an account of two healings is given (5:21–43). The reference to the family and to James is followed

---

[38] *Discipleship and Family Ties in Mark and Matthew*, pp. 23–56.

by a description of the mission of the twelve (6:6b–13). Thus the treatment of the family falls between the choosing and naming of the twelve (3:13–19) and the mission of the twelve (6:6b–13). This suggests a parallel evaluation of the family and the twelve. If the twelve, having been chosen and named, are called into question, they are nevertheless entrusted with mission by Jesus. The same may be true of the family.

Jesus, followed by his disciples, goes to his own country, presumed to be Nazareth (specifically named only in Luke 4:16), where, teaching in the synagogue on the sabbath, he evokes amazement because of his wisdom and his mighty works (6:1–6a). A basis of the amazement is the fact that Jesus, who did these things, is a person well known to them. They ask in amazement:

> "Is this not the carpenter, the son of Mary and the brother of James and Joses and Jude and Simon? And are not his sisters here with us?" And they were scandalized by him.

In Mark no paternity is ascribed to Jesus; instead he is described as "the carpenter."[39] Without any reservation he is described as the son of Mary and the brother of James, Joses, Jude, and Simon. In addition sisters are mentioned but not named. We may well ask why Mark has omitted reference to Joseph and why the sisters of Jesus are mentioned but not named. It may be for no other reason than that Mary and the brothers became notable figures in the early church.

The absence of Joseph from all narratives in Mark is remarkable and unexplained. It is often taken to mean that Joseph died early in the life of Jesus which, if the case, would be consistent with Joseph's being older than Mary, if she were his second wife, as proposed by the Epiphanean view. But there is no evidence to support this view. Perhaps Joseph remained aloof from the Jesus movement and, as a consequence, achieved no prominence in the early Christian tradition. However this is to be understood, it should be noted that, according to the narrative, it was not the family of Jesus who were scandalized by Jesus but the people of Jesus' own country. These same people referred to the mother, brothers, and sisters of Jesus as being among them. While Mark records the rejection of Jesus in his home country without excluding the family from this response, he does not involve them in this action either. The proverb—"A prophet is not without honor except in his own country, amongst his own relatives, and in his own household" (6:4)—was used to reinforce that rejection. Mention of the family in the proverb should not be taken to mean that the

---

[39] Compare the modifications made in Matt 13:54–56.

family was opposed to Jesus. Mark's own antipathy to the family meant that he had no concern to exclude them from any possible blame.

The proverb appears in comparable incidents in Matt 13:57 and Luke 4:24. Matthew omits any reference to "his own relatives" and Luke omits both the relatives and "his own house." It appears in a somewhat different context in John 4:44. John assumes that Jerusalem is Jesus' home country and makes no reference to the negative role of kinsfolk and household. In Mark the narrator informs us that Jesus was not able to perform any mighty works, although he healed a few sick people. And he marveled at his hometown people's unbelief (6:6), unbelief because they were scandalized by him (6:3) because he was known to them as one of a familiar family. The proverb confirms that they were scandalized simply because they knew the family, although something about the particular family may have accentuated the scandal.

The Markan form of the proverb includes Jesus' family among those who give him no honor, but there is no specific reference to the mother, brothers, and sisters of Jesus in the proverb, and they are not named as unbelievers. Reference to the family is made by those who belonged to his own country as a way of identifying Jesus in relation to them. It would be risky to assert, on the basis of the proverb, that the family of Jesus did not believe in him, especially as Mark has a tendency to play down the roles of the family. The inclination to take the proverb as indicating in detail the groups who rejected Jesus is strengthened for those who take 3:21 as a reference to the family, especially if it is accepted that it is they who say of Jesus, "He is beside himself." Both of these conclusions are incorrect in our view. Further, Mary the mother of Jesus is commonly excluded from this evaluation of the family. If the proverb is not applicable in her case, then there is no good reason to think that it applies to James either.

The proverb is probably traditional and, because it is known in other contexts, it may have been Mark who located it in the context of the rejection at Nazareth. It should carry no weight in an argument about whether the family of Jesus rejected him during his ministry. Mark has filled out the basis for the rejection by reference to the known family of Jesus the carpenter, the son of Mary, naming his brothers and mentioning his sisters. James is named first, perhaps in order of age, because Mark had no wish to accentuate the leadership of James in the early Church. From this perspective, Jesus' "home crowd" finds him to be a member of an ordinary family, making the assessment of him as anything but ordinary a difficulty for them. Yet, from Mark's point of view, the evidence of Jesus' own teaching and activity is extraordinary. The paradox of the extraordinary Jesus is set against the ordinary family, and this leads to amazement, scandal, and rejection.

Mark 15:40 and Parallels: The Women at the Cross

Reference to women watching the crucifixion from afar names Mary Magdalene and mentions two other women (15:40).[40] Mary Magdalene is the only constant figure in the group of women mentioned in the passion story of each of the Gospels. In Mark a second Mary is identified as the mother of James, who is called the small or young, and Joses ('Ιωσῆτος), while the third woman is identified as Salome. A variant allows for reading Mary Magdalene, Mary (the wife) of James and the mother of Jesus, and Salome. There are other variants, but none of these makes this group of women relevant to a discussion of the family of Jesus. Matthew's treatment of this pericope is similar to Mark's, except that Matthew uses the Semitic form of the name Joseph ('Ιωσήφ), and, instead of Salome, the mother of the sons of Zebedee is mentioned. Luke (23:49) mentions the women but does not name them.

There have been attempts to identify the James and Joses in Mark 15:40 with the brothers of Jesus of the same names. The argument is that the Mary named as their mother was the sister of Mary the mother of Jesus. This arrangement involves accepting that those called brothers (and sisters) were actually cousins. Vincent Taylor rightly notes that the two groups should not be identified.[41] The identification presupposes a particular reading of John's account of the presence of the women at the cross in John 19:25–27. According to this reading, the sister of the mother of Jesus is named Mary the wife of Clopas. This reading of John is improbable. This Mary is probably a third woman, not the sister of the mother of Jesus. She is identified as the wife of Clopas but could be the mother of Clopas.

The mother of Jesus is not mentioned in the Markan passion story. The final reference to the family occurs in the account of the rejection in Jesus' hometown (6:3–4). Thus Mark leaves the reader with a negative view of the family.

MATTHEW: NATIVITY AND REJECTION

Matthew and Luke add nativity stories to the framework of the Markan narrative. Because the two nativity accounts are difficult to reconcile with each other while serving clear christological purposes, little confidence can be placed in the historicity of the traditions embodied there. Matthew and Luke do not reproduce Mark 3:20–21, but both make some modifications to Mark 3:31–35 and 6:3–4.

---

[40] The word order, placing "mother" before "and Salome," makes clear here that the second Mary was the mother only of James and Joses and that Salome was a third woman present at the crucifixion.

[41] V. Taylor, *The Gospel according to St Mark* (London: Macmillan, 1966), 598.

Matt 1:18–25: The Nativity

Mark provides no evidence of any knowledge of the birth traditions about Jesus; Matthew leaves readers in no doubt (1.18–25).

> Now the birth of Jesus Christ was thus. When his mother Mary was betrothed to Joseph, but before they came together, she was found to be pregnant by the holy spirit.

All of this is conveyed by the narrator who tells of the response of Joseph to the miraculous conception and the confirmation of the miracle through an angel of the Lord in a dream to Joseph. The narrator then concludes, concerning Joseph:

> And he did not know her until she bore a son; and he called his name Jesus. (1:25)

The natural way to read this implies that Joseph did come to "know" Mary after she bore her son, just as "before they came together" (1:18) implies that they did not "come together" until later. In this context "to know" carries the meaning, common in biblical texts, "to have sexual intercourse" (see, for example, Gen 4:1). In 383 CE Helvidius of Rome used both of these texts from Matthew, together with Luke 2:7, which refers to Jesus as Mary's "firstborn son," implying that there were others born later, a view which he found to be confirmed by references to the brothers and sisters of Jesus in other parts of the New Testament. Opponents of this position that Mary bore other children after Jesus stress that the point of the statement is to assert that Mary remained a virgin until she bore a son and that there is no intention to say anything about the situation after that event. They are right about the point in view but it would not have been made in this way by a writer who wished to maintain that Mary remained a virgin even after the birth of Jesus. Given that Matthew later introduces the reference to the mother of Jesus with his brothers and sisters (13:53–58), the reader naturally assumes that they were children born to Mary and Joseph subsequent to the birth of Jesus.

Matt 12:46–50: The Eschatological Family

Matthew's treatment fundamentally follows Mark 3:31–35. There are, however, certain important differences. Matthew omits the critique of the disciples (Mark 3:20–21) but maintains the sequence of the second and third incidents (the Beelzebul charge and the discussion of the true family), although Matthew 12:24 names the critics of Jesus the Pharisees (they were the scribes in Mark 3:22). Matthew and Luke appear to have drawn on Q in addition to

Mark for the second incident, but Matthew's critique of the family is based on Mark. Differences from Mark do not converge with similar differences in Luke and appear to be a consequence of Matthean redaction.

Matthew omits reference to the family's standing *outside* the house and says that they were seeking *to speak* to Jesus (12:46). Instead of having the crowd inform Jesus that his family is here, Matthew has one of the crowd perform this function. The report in Matthew takes account of the Matthean modifications to the introduction. Jesus is informed that his mother and brothers are standing outside "seeking to speak to you." The textual evidence concerning 12:47 is ambiguous, and this verse may be a scribal addition. Matthew's practice in general is to compress the Markan narrative, and he may have done this by having the narrator inform the reader that the mother and brothers of Jesus are seeking to speak to Jesus. The addition of 12:47 makes Matthew conform more closely to Mark, a characteristic scribal tendency. Against this conclusion is the fact that, without 12:47, Jesus would be made to respond to the arrival of his family, of which the reader has been informed, but Jesus has not.

Matthew has Jesus extend his hand to his disciples (point to them) and announce that they are his eschatological family. Here Matthew affirms that this family comprises the disciples rather than some unspecified group, which is important for Mark in his critique of the twelve. Matthew changes Mark's "will of God" to "the will of my father who is in heaven," which can be regarded as a characteristic Mattheanism. There are other minor stylistic changes. The incident reveals Mark's critique of the disciples and Matthew's affirmation of them. Neither Matthew nor Mark implies that the natural family is included in the eschatological family. By identifying those around Jesus (Mark) and the disciples (Matthew), another, alternative family is indicated, even if the words about "those who do the will . . ." do not exclude the family.

Matt 13:53–58: The Proverb of Rejection

While the account of the "rejection" in Jesus' home country generally follows Mark 6:1–6a, there are differences, some of which can be put down to Matthean sensitivity; others provide Johannine echoes, and some do not seem to have any particular point of reference. The teaching in the synagogue is not specifically set on the sabbath (as in Mark). Matthew probably took it for granted that Jesus would teach there on the sabbath. The form of the objection voiced by the synagogue congregation also provides some variations.

> "Where did this man get this wisdom and these mighty works? Is this not the carpenter's son? Is not his mother called Mary and his brothers James and Joseph and Simon and Judas? And are not all his sisters with us? From whence are all these things [given] to this man?"

Matthew does not describe Jesus as the carpenter, but shows no sensitivity to recording the attribution of paternity to the carpenter (Joseph) because the Gospel has already made quite clear that Joseph is not the biological father of Jesus.[42] Taylor notes that it is contrary to Jewish custom and insulting to describe a man as a son of his mother.[43] This fact might explain Matthew's change at this point, if he were sensitive to Jewish values where Mark was not, though Matthew then mentions "his mother called Mary."

The context in Luke is the same as in Matthew and Mark. The setting in John is the bread of life discourse, in which the speakers are "the Jews" in Galilee. They not only name Jesus the son of Joseph but assert rhetorically, "Is this not Jesus the son of Joseph, whose father we know and whose mother we know?" The agreement between John and Luke in naming Joseph the father of Jesus need not imply dependence of the one on the other because the name of Joseph as the father of Jesus was widely attested in tradition. They follow the tendency in Matthew to identify Jesus by paternity. While Matthew and Mark report the crowd asking "Are not his sisters with us?," in John the question asked by the Jews implies that they know his father and mother.

There are also some differences between Matthew and Mark in the forms of the names of the brothers.[44] Matthew and Luke read the proverb as if it gave detailed reference to those who rejected Jesus, leading Matthew to omit reference to the relatives and Luke to omit reference to relatives and household. Their omission of these references simply clarifies Mark's use of the proverb. There is no indication in Mark that the family is present on this occasion or that Mark intended to show that they rejected Jesus as a prophet. But Mark's use of the proverb could be read as if that were intended. Matthew and Luke edited the proverb to exclude that meaning.

LUKE: THE IDEALIZATION OF THE FAMILY

While the Lukan nativity scene is independent of Matthew, it tends to have the same implications for an understanding of the family of Jesus. According to Luke's understanding, John the Baptist also belonged to the wider family of Jesus. But our attention is turned to the understanding of Mary and the consequences of her role for the significance of those known as the brothers of Jesus. Even though Luke implies a relationship qualified by the teaching of the vir-

---

[42] In Luke (4:22) and John (6:42) neither Jesus nor Joseph is called the carpenter. Paternity is asserted, but Jesus is simply called the son of Joseph. Matthew's infancy story is told from the perspective of Joseph, magnifying his righteousness.

[43] See Taylor, p. 300.

[44] Here, as in Matt 27:56, Matthew has the Semitic Ἰωσὴφ where Mark has the Hellenistic Ἰωσῆτος (Mark 15:40; 6:3). Matt 13:55 reverses the order of brothers three and four as found in Mark 6:3. By doing this he makes the names conform to the order of the disciples as they appear in Mark 3:18–19, with which Matt 10:3–4 agrees.

ginal conception of Jesus, so that those called his brothers and sisters did not have a common father, he modifies the Markan narrative so that the family of Jesus is portrayed more positively than in Mark.

Luke 1:26–56: The Role of Mary in Luke's Nativity Story

As in Matthew, in Luke at the time Mary conceived, she was betrothed but not married to Joseph. The child was conceived through the intervention of God. In Matthew the revelation of this circumstance and of the name of Jesus and his saving role is made to Joseph. In Luke the angel Gabriel makes the revelations, including the name of Jesus and his messianic role, to Mary. In Matthew (1:19) Joseph is portrayed as a righteous man; in Luke Gabriel announces to Mary that she has found grace with God and the Lord is with her (Luke 1:28, 30). Mary is immediately portrayed as a faithful follower by her assent to the role revealed to her.

"Behold the servant of the Lord; let it be to me according to your word." (Luke 1:38)

Luke 4:16–30: The Rejection at Nazareth

Luke has reversed the Markan order, followed by Matthew, of the apparent rejection by Jesus of his mother and brothers (Mark 3:31–35 and Luke 8:19–21) and the rejection of Jesus by the people of his own town, Nazareth (Mark 6:1–6a and Luke 4:16–20). In each incident Luke has reduced or removed any negative understanding of the role of the family as portrayed by Mark.

In Luke the rejection at Nazareth (4:16–30; compare Mark 6:1–6a and Matt 13.53–58) is placed at the beginning of Jesus' ministry. What Mark and Matthew identify as Jesus' "home country" is specifically named Nazareth by Luke and interpreted as the place "where he was brought up" (4:16). Luke does not use the expression "home country" at this point. The term is introduced in the distinctively Lukan proverb (Luke 4:23). These changes are explanations of the tradition for readers who would not identify the Markan reference to Nazareth or know that it signified the place where Jesus was brought up.

Like Mark, but not Matthew, Luke locates Jesus' presence in the synagogue on the sabbath. The setting enables Luke to provide an example of Jesus' synagogue sermons, much in the same way as he uses the exemplary speeches of Peter, Stephen, and Paul in Acts. Jesus' sermon is based on the reading from Isaiah 61:1–2 (and 58:6?). He announces the fulfillment of the prophecy there enunciated and those who hear him bear witness to the gracious words proceeding from his mouth. This response is more positive than the response depicted in Mark and Matthew, perhaps necessarily because of the nature of the "sermon" Luke has introduced. Those who hear and respond in this way also say incredulously, "Is this not the son of Joseph?" (Luke 4:22). The use of the imperfect ("they were saying") implies saying repeatedly, not offhand or casual remarks. There is no mention here of the carpenter (as in Mark), or the carpenter's son (as in Matthew), or Jesus' mother Mary and his brothers and his sisters, as in Mark and Matthew. Thus James the brother of Jesus is not mentioned by name in Luke. Luke, like Matthew, does not think of Jesus as the biological son of Joseph.

Luke has introduced an additional proverb spoken by Jesus, perhaps suggested by the use of "home country" in the Markan tradition (Mark 6:1, 4).

> "Doubtless you will quote this proverb to me, 'Physician, heal yourself. What we have heard you did in Capernaum, do here also in your own country.' " (Luke 4:23)

The proverb assumes the miraculous activity of Jesus in Capernaum, but, according to the Lukan order, the ministry at Nazareth is the subject of the first detailed account of Jesus' activities. Only the summary statement of Luke 4:14–15—that Jesus, filled with the power of the Spirit, became known throughout Galilee—precedes it, and, while it can be argued that Jesus was active in Capernaum, there is no account of Jesus' ministry there prior to Luke 4:16–30. In Mark, however, the rejection in Jesus' home country is preceded by the healing of Jairus's daughter and of the woman with the issue of blood. These miracles occurred after Jesus' return from the eastern side of the sea of Galilee to the western side. No town is named, but it might be assumed that Jairus was ruler of the synagogue in Capernaum, a town beside the sea of Galilee. The Lukan proverb might presuppose the Markan order of events. Luke has Jesus suggest that his reception at Nazareth is a consequence of his failure to produce there such miracles as he had worked in Capernaum. In Mark (6:5) Jesus' failure to work many miracles at Nazareth is a consequence of the Nazarenes' unbelief.

Luke provides a different perspective altogether. The initial reception of the synagogue sermon is described in positive terms (4:21). The interjection "Is this not the son of Joseph?" is not scornful but an incredulous wondering in the face of the evidence of Jesus' words. Jesus' response is to quote the proverb "Physician, heal yourself" that Luke found in Mark and to provide two precedents from scripture.

The second proverb, of the prophet's rejection in his hometown (4:24), is introduced with a second quotation formula, although Jesus continues to be the speaker ("But he said . . ."), suggesting that Luke has brought together independent proverbs. This quotation is introduced by the solemn formula, "Truly I say to you, 'No prophet is accepted in his hometown,' " which Matthew and Luke found in Mark. The proverb is abbreviated and given in an idiom different from the Markan form which, apart from an abbreviation, was followed by

Matthew. The Lukan form is explicable in terms of Lukan editing. The term "acceptable" is introduced from Isaiah 61:1–2 so that there is a play on the idea that what is acceptable to God is not acceptable to the people of Nazareth. By omitting any reference to kinsfolk or those of Jesus' own house Luke has followed a tendency in Matthew. The proverb in Luke deals only with the rejection (non-acceptance) of Jesus by the townspeople of Nazareth. Any critical reference to the family of Jesus has been removed. Luke only makes explicit what Mark has intended, though Mark has no concern to safeguard the family from any suspicion of criticism.

Following the proverb the words of the Lukan Jesus turn to two precedents from scripture. In these the point is made that, although there were many widows and lepers in Israel at the time of Elijah and Elisha, each helped only one, and in each case the one helped (widow and leper) was not an Israelite (Luke 4:25–27). Those in the synagogue are filled with anger. They cast Jesus out of their town and seek to kill him by throwing him down a cliff. He escapes from them, passing through the midst of them, and goes his way (Luke 4:28–30). Luke, who initially describes a positive response by the synagogue congregation, finally signals the most violent and decisive rejection of Jesus by the people of Nazareth. The Lukan narrative has a Johannine ring about it. From John 5:16, 18 onward the evangelist records repeated attempts to arrest or kill Jesus, and in 9:22 the decision is announced to cast out of the synagogue any who confess Jesus to be the Christ.[45] In Luke the basis of the violent rejection is the argument that God has chosen to favor those who are not Israelites, as demonstrated by the cases of the widow of Zarephath and Naaman the leper from Syria. This basis of violent reaction has more in common with the treatment of Paul by the Jews as portrayed in Acts than it does with John. In Acts the reaction is a consequence of Paul's freely preaching the gospel to Gentiles. Already Luke is preparing his justification for the mission to the nations and the violent response of unbelieving Jews to this mission. Given that this response appears to be Lukan redaction and that it fits the situation of the early church, no weight should be placed on it in relation to reconstructing the ministry of the historical Jesus in Nazareth.

Luke mentions no miracles at all in Nazareth and gives no reason for the lack of miracles. The scriptural precedents tend to suggest that such was the plan and purpose of God. Given the initial favorable response to Jesus recorded by Luke, it would not have been convincing for him to suggest that the townspeople's unbelief is the cause of the failure. Rather, Luke portrays the unbelief as the consequence of the failure of Jesus to perform signs in Nazareth. This is consistent with his understanding of Jesus' failure to perform signs there as part

---

[45] See John 9:34; 12:42; 16:2 and chapters 5 and 8 of my *The Quest for the Messiah: The History, Literature and Theology of the Johannine Community* (Nashville: Abingdon, 1993).

of the divine plan. Luke already has in mind the view that the rejection of Jesus by Israel (Nazareth) provides the opportunity for the Gentile mission. The rejection at Nazareth is shown to be part of the divine plan for bringing the mission to the Gentiles.

Luke 8:19–21: The True Family of Jesus

The idealization of Mary has an effect on Luke's use of traditions in which Mary is portrayed negatively by Mark, such as Luke 8:19–21 (cf. Mark 3:31–35; Matt 12:46–50). Most likely the abbreviation and reversal of order are a consequence of Lukan redaction.

The arrival of the mother and brothers of Jesus is described by the narrator and reported to Jesus. According to Mark, it was reported to Jesus that his mother and brothers "are outside seeking you." Matthew qualifies this, "seeking to speak to you," and Luke omits reference to the family being "outside" and has them "wishing to see you." Jesus announces that his mother and brothers are those who hear and do the word of God. The variation in wording from Mark can be understood in terms of preferred Lukan idiom.

Luke's account in much abbreviated form removes any contrast between the natural family and the "true" family. Luke omits Jesus' question concerning who are mother and brothers that leads to the contrast with the natural family. Nor does Jesus identify the eschatological family with those sitting around him (Mark) or with the disciples (Matthew). Certainly Luke makes clear that the eschatological family, those who hear and do the word of God, is not restricted to the natural family, though the natural family are not excluded either.

Our study so far has argued that the evidence used to document the unbelief of the family, the brothers in particular, will not bear the weight of the case that has been built on it. Although Luke does not include the mother of Jesus among the faithful witnesses at the passion, his treatment of the family allows a positive evaluation of their role as followers of Jesus.

CHAPTER 2

ACTS

James as Convert or Foundation Leader?

In Acts the family of Jesus appears among his followers, and James is portrayed as the leader of the Jerusalem church. There is nothing to suggest that this view represents a radical change within the Jesus movement. There is no evidence of a "conversion" of James from unbeliever to follower, nor is it clear that Peter was first the leader of the Jerusalem church, giving way to James only after a decade or so of leadership.

ACTS 1:14: THE ROLE OF JESUS' FAMILY IN THE EARLIEST CHURCH

The conclusion to Luke's presentation of the family is found in Acts 1:14. Following this, only James is mentioned, and without identifying him as the brother of Jesus. After the ascension of Jesus, Luke portrays the return of the disciples from the Mount of Olives to an upper room in Jerusalem where they are depicted (in 1:14) gathered for prayer with women, including Mary the mother of Jesus, and his brothers. Luke portrays the mother and brothers of Jesus as "believers" and faithful followers of Jesus, and there is no indication of their recent radical "conversion" subsequent to his death, through, for example, some resurrection appearance. They are mentioned as a group. The brothers are not named. The omission of the names from Luke 4:16–30, which is dependent on Mark 6:1–6a, in which the brothers are named, means that the reader is not prepared for the appearance of James in Acts 12:17. That Luke assumes that James is well known is implied by the way he introduces him simply as James, with no further clarification.

ACTS 12:17: THE LEADERSHIP OF JAMES

Although the James mentioned in Acts 12:17 is not called the brother of Jesus, he cannot be the brother of John and son of Zebedee whose execution by Herod is described in Acts 12:2. Mention of the execution makes clear the identity of the James in Acts 12:17 by removing the other notable James from the scene. Peter, who was imprisoned at the time of that James's execution, has been miraculously released and has come to the house of the mother of John who is called Mark.[1] Peter's message is:

"Announce these things to James and the brothers." (12:17)

That this refers to James the brother of Jesus, not James the son of Alpheus, is confirmed by Paul. He identifies James the brother of the Lord as one of the apostles and the first of the three pillars of the Jerusalem church (Gal 1:18–19; 2:9). Later tradition also names this James as the first bishop of the Jerusalem church. This information cannot be gleaned from Luke-Acts. The reader may well ask whether Luke intends to obscure this or expects his readers to be aware of the connection.

The singling out of this James by name is an indication of his prominence in the Jerusalem church. The "brothers" mentioned here are widely assumed to be the disciples and believers generally. But if James is the brother of Jesus, "the brothers" might be the other brothers of Jesus who also at this time had leading roles in the Church,[2] though their roles were secondary to that of James, who was the preeminent leader. Against this reading is the fact that reference is simply to "the brothers" and not to the more specific "his brothers" or "brothers of Jesus" or "of the Lord." The specific terms are used only of actual relatives, whereas all believers can be spoken of as brothers. The possibility that the brothers of Jesus are here in view, in spite of the less-than-specific "the brothers," is kept open by the close association with James. Peter, it will be recalled, instructed, "Report these things to James and the brothers."

It has been suggested that the narrative of Acts portrays the leadership of the Jerusalem church at first by the apostles, headed by Peter. Even in the early persecutions, when the Hellenists were scattered out of Jerusalem, the apostles remained (Acts 8:1). However, when the Antioch church sent famine relief to Jerusalem by the hands of Barnabas and Saul, there is no mention of the apostles. The relief was sent to "the elders" (Acts 11:30), indicating a transition in leadership from the apostles to the elders. Thus when the Jerusalem church sent Barnabas to Antioch, there is no mention of the apostles. It is assumed that he was sent by the elders and that by then James had replaced Peter. Acts 12:1–24 can be read as a kind of flashback to explain how James came to leadership. Herod

---

[1] The introduction of Mark is reminiscent of that of Joseph, called Barnabas *by the apostles* (Acts 4:36–37). Mark is mentioned because of the role he is to play with Barnabas and Saul, just as Barnabas has been singled out from among those who sell land because of the role he is to play with Paul. The introduction of John, called Mark, also signals that another John is in view for the first time, not John the Baptist (e.g., Acts 1:5) or John the brother of James (Acts 1:13, etc.).

[2] See Eusebius, *HE* 3.19.1—20.7; 3.32.1–6. Cf. Acts 21:17.

Agrippa had James the brother of John executed and Peter was thrown into prison.

The transition of authority from Peter to James is often taken to be implied by Acts 12:17. If James were already the leader, nothing would be more natural than for Peter to report back to him. This reading is at least as plausible as the one that takes Peter's message to be a passing on of the authority of leadership. If this is what Luke meant to convey, why does Peter not resume leadership on his return to Jerusalem? In Acts 15 James is portrayed as the leader of the Jerusalem church even though Peter was then present again. It seems that the prominence of Peter in Acts has been interpreted in terms of his leadership. But that prominence is described more in terms of his activity in relation to those outside the believing community than in terms of leadership of the community. Peter, like Paul, is portrayed as a "missionary" rather than as the leader of a settled community.

Acts explicitly names no single leader of the Jerusalem church. The conclusion that Peter was the leader at first is the consequence of the influence of an interpretative tradition that has no support in relation to Jerusalem. Nothing in Acts supports this view. Peter's prominence is in terms of his missionary activity in relation to the community at large rather than as leader of the church community. Indeed, the notion that Peter was the leader runs contrary to tradition concerning the Jerusalem church. That tradition names James as the first leader ("bishop"). The nomenclature is anachronistic, but the leadership of James is supported by the way in which James is portrayed in Acts 15 and 21 as well as in Paul's letter to the Galatians. Even in Acts and Galatians the sole leadership of James is not explicit. More than likely James was one of a group of leaders among whom he stood out, from the beginning, as the leading figure and dominant influence. Upon this basis the tradition of James as the first bishop of Jerusalem was developed.

The Hebrews and the Hellenists

The *Tendenz,* or bias, of Luke in Acts does not express the point of view of James or Paul. Yet Acts provides evidence of the rivalry between these two and the groups they represent. Acts 6 refers to the rivalry between the Hebrews, represented by the apostles, and the Hellenists, represented by Stephen and Philip and others with Greek names chosen to represent the Greek-speaking Jewish believers in Jerusalem.[3] The leadership of the Hellenists increased persecution, culminating in the martyrdom of Stephen and the scattering of the Hellenists. Acts 8:1 refers to the scattering of all except the apostles, the leading Hebrews. The Hellenists were scattered "over the country districts of Judaea

---

[3] See C. C. Hill, *Hellenists and Hebrews: Reappraising Division within the Earliest Church* (Minneapolis: Fortress, 1992).

and Samaria." The mission of Philip (a Hellenist) to Caesarea in Acts 8 is followed (allowing for the break in narrative to describe the conversion of Saul) by the mission of Peter to the same place in Acts 10. While it was not Luke's intention to show a continuing rivalry between the two groups, Acts provides evidence of rival missions in action. The appointment of the seven Hellenists to oversee the distribution of aid in Acts 6 is a consequence of the rivalry and conflict between the two groups. Acts goes on to show that the scattering of the Hellenists resulted in the spread of their mission and the proclamation of the gospel to Gentiles without demanding that they accept circumcision or keep the Mosaic law (Acts 8:1; 11:19–24). In a very understated way Acts reveals an important basis of conflict between the two missions.

At this point Acts (11:22) indicates that news of developments at Antioch reached the Jerusalem church and that Barnabas was dispatched to Antioch. Luke makes no mention of the apostles or elders or indeed of any other leadership group. The decision to send Barnabas was made, according to Luke, by the church, which might have involved a group or a leader acting for the church.

Barnabas, first introduced (Acts 4:36–37) as a Levite from Cyprus named Joseph, was (re)named Barnabas by the apostles. The name, supposedly meaning "son of encouragement" (4:36) means, in fact, "son of Nebo." On a surface reading of Acts Barnabas epitomizes encouragement, first to Saul and then to John Mark. Luke's skillful introduction of Barnabas subtly reinforces his role as a representative of the Jerusalem church, a situation that remains a sinister undertone in his relationship with Saul/Paul. At his introduction, Barnabas is portrayed as one of those who sold property and laid the proceeds at the apostles' feet. Thus Luke establishes Barnabas as a longtime member of the Jerusalem church, in good standing with the apostles. That he, along with Peter and other Jewish believers, under pressure from James, withdrew from table fellowship with Gentile believers in Antioch confirms Barnabas's alignment with the Jerusalem church and those known as "Hebrews" (Gal 2:11–14).

Mention that he is from Cyprus prepares the way for his initial mission with Saul (and John Mark) in Acts 13:4–13. The mission to Cyprus should be seen in the light of the mission of the Hellenists who, when they were scattered because of the persecution that arose after the martyrdom of Stephen, traveled to Phoenicia, Cyprus, and Antioch. Just as Peter had followed Philip to Caesarea, so Barnabas followed the Hellenists to Antioch and then to Cyprus.

Acts does not indicate what role the Jerusalem church (James?) expected Barnabas to play. It reports that on arrival he rejoiced at what he saw of the grace of God, and he exhorted the believers to remain faithful and steadfast (11:23). The narrative suggests that as a result of his coming a large number of converts joined the believers (11:24), but, as this information more or less repeats the description of the growth which had brought Antioch to the attention of the Jerusalem church (11:21), we may doubt that it is intended to indicate that the coming of Barnabas was the cause of another spectacular growth.

That the Jerusalem church intended Barnabas to have a role of oversight is suggested by the decision of Barnabas to seek out Saul in Tarsus to assist in the work once he had discovered the scope of it (11:25–26). They stayed in Antioch for a year, meeting with the church and teaching a large number of people. The terminology of Acts 11:26 suggests a single church at Antioch. If a single, mixed (Jew and Gentile) church developed there, this helps to explain why the withdrawal of Jewish believers from table fellowship with Gentile believers, as described by Paul in Gal 2:11–14, was so disruptive. The emergence of a large and rapidly growing mixed church at Antioch soon came to the notice of the citizens of Antioch, who named the new group "Christians," meaning the household of Christ.

The role of Barnabas in bringing Saul to Antioch is mentioned only in Acts. Acts 9:26–30 prepares the way by asserting that Saul was introduced to "the apostles" by Barnabas. What gave Barnabas the confidence to meet Saul remains unexplained. Following the introduction, Saul is said to have reported to the apostles and then to have preached boldly in Jerusalem, disputing with the Hellenists who were seeking to kill him.[4] Because of the danger "the brethren" brought Saul to Caesarea and sent him to Tarsus. Paul's letter to the Galatians (1:18–21) does not mention the role of Barnabas or any attempt by the Hellenists to kill Paul. In both of these matters the narrative of Acts has been shaped to provide a basis for the role of Barnabas in the calling of Saul to Antioch, giving the impression of basic agreement between him and the apostles in the Jerusalem church. There is also a distancing of Saul from the Hellenists, whose work he joined at Antioch, according to Acts, as a representative of the Jerusalem church through the invitation of Barnabas.

Gal 1:21 indicates that after his initial visit to Jerusalem Paul went into the regions of Syria and Cilicia. There is no indication of how he came to Antioch from whence he went up to Jerusalem with Barnabas (2:1). It is possible that Paul in Galatians has obscured the initial leadership of Barnabas in bringing him to Antioch. Alternatively, by having Barnabas bring Saul to Antioch Acts has achieved a view of the unity of the mission of the church, showing that the mission of Paul arose from initiative originating with the Jerusalem church. There is quite a strong case for thinking that when Barnabas came to Antioch he found Paul there already, recognized as one of the local leaders. The question of the relationship of Paul to the church at Antioch is crucial. It is unclear to

---

[4] Were the "Hellenists" followers of Jesus or part of the wider Jewish group known as Hellenists of which the believers were a small part? If they were followers of Jesus, they might have sought to kill Saul because he had persecuted them. Acts provides no answers to these questions, and there is reason to doubt the historicity of the account.

what degree the church at Antioch derived its character and mission from the initiative of Paul or, alternatively, to what degree Paul derived his own missionary strategy and understanding of the church from Antioch.

It is of great interest that Saul of Tarsus, a diaspora Jew, appears to have been a zealous adherent of strict law observance until his conversion (Gal 1:13–16).[5] He describes himself as

> a Hebrew of the Hebrews, with reference to the law, a Pharisee, with reference to zeal, persecuting the Church, with reference to righteousness which comes by the law, blameless. (Phil 3:2–11 especially 5–8; cf. 2 Cor 11:18–29)

In both the passage from Galatians and the one from Philippians Paul refers to his persecution of the church (see also 1 Cor 15:9) in relation to his zeal for the law. The reference to his zeal for the traditions "of my fathers" in Galatians may be the equivalent of the reference to himself as a Pharisee in Philippians, where he also describes himself as "a Hebrew of the Hebrews." This probably signifies a Hebrew-speaking son of Hebrew-speaking parents (perhaps actually speakers of Aramaic). For a Jew of the diaspora to be a Hebrew involved a self-conscious commitment to the traditions of the fathers and strict law observance, including the practice of circumcision.

Paul's identification of himself as a Pharisee and Hebrew, in the days before his "conversion," associates him with the Hebrews of Acts 6. The same group is probably to be identified with those in Acts 15:5 called Pharisees, who are probably from the same group as those from Judaea who came to Antioch in Acts 15:1 demanding strict observance of the Mosaic law by all who wished to be "saved."

The tension between the Hebrews and the Hellenists in the early church was a manifestation of a similar tension in Judaism. Prior to his conversion, Paul had been a zealous and active member of the Hebrews, insisting on the need for circumcision and law observance. This led him into conflict with the Hellenists, especially with those who were followers of the Way, a designation used of the followers of Jesus before they became known as Christians. Acts may well be right in associating Saul with the execution of Stephen and in naming Saul as a legal witness of the stoning (Acts 8:1). Paul himself acknowledges his role in persecuting the church (Gal 1:13; Phil 3:6; 1 Cor 15:9).

What is surprising is that, after his conversion, Paul did not join the faction of the Hebrews in the church but became a leading representative of the faction

---

[5] While Paul's letters confirm his role as persecutor, they nowhere indicate he was formerly known as Saul, a name used of him only in Acts (7:58; 8:1, 3; 9:1, 8, 11, 24; 11:25, 30; 12:25; 13:1, 2, 7, 9).

of the Hellenists (Acts 11:25–26).[6] This situation raises a question as to whether the respective gospels preached by the two missions differed in any way. Gal 1:6–12 make clear, in spite of Paul's protestations, that there were rival gospels, though only one "true" gospel. In 1 Cor 15:1–11 it is asserted that there was no difference as far as the gospel history was concerned, even though the Hellenists included (as far as we know) none of Jesus' disciples, and we might question whether their gospel made use of the sayings of Jesus or of any narration of his deeds. Too much has been made of the absence of such material from the letters of Paul which are, after all, letters and not Gospels.[7] The differences did not arise from the "data" but emerged in the interpretation and application of the gospel history.

The account in Acts has obscured the conflict between the Hebrews and the Hellenists and leaves no trace of tensions between Paul and Barnabas or Peter and James. Such tensions are apparent in Gal 2:11–14, as are the greater tensions between Paul and Peter and Paul and James. When, on the second missionary journey, Paul and Barnabas part company, the reason, according to Acts, is that Barnabas wished to take his cousin John Mark with them, but Paul did not (Acts 15:36–41). A more likely reason for the parting is the disagreement between Peter and Paul over common meals shared by Jewish and Gentile believers, a conflict which also involved Barnabas (Gal 2:11–14). The fundamental differences between Paul and Barnabas are sufficient to make us question whether Barnabas would have asked Paul to join him in the mission at Antioch. It seems more likely that when Barnabas came to Antioch he found Paul already there and that Paul's own approach to mission grew out of the Hellenist law-free mission at Antioch.

ACTS 15: JAMES AND THE COUNCIL OF JERUSALEM

According to Acts, the council was a consequence of some people from Judaea (a delegation from James?) asserting to the believers in Antioch that

"Unless you are circumcised according to the custom of Moses you are not able to be saved." (Acts 15:1)

---

[6] For evidence of Paul's change in favor of the Hellenists, see Phil 3:7–11; Gal 2:15–17.

[7] The position stated here is opposed by such scholars as F. Neirynck in "The Sayings of Jesus in 1 Corinthians," paper given at Colloquium Biblicum Louvaniense XLIII, August 8–10, 1994. In support of his "minimalist" position Neirynck appeals to N. Walter, "Paulus und die urchristliche Jesustradition," NTS 31 (1985): 498–522, and A. J. M. Wedderburn's Paul and Jesus: Collected Essays, JSNTSS 37 (Sheffield: JSOT, 1989), 51–80. Advocating a more substantial awareness of and dependence on the Jesus tradition are M. B. Thompson, Clothed with Christ: The Example and Teaching of Jesus in Romans 12.1–15.13, JSNTSS (Sheffield: JSOT, 1991); V. P. Furnish, Jesus according to Paul (Cambridge: Cambridge University Press, 1993).

It is possible to see the group that delivered this message as a delegation from James without revising the role of James in Acts if the order of events in Gal 2:1–10 and 2:11–14 is reversed. The confrontation in Antioch then precedes the meeting in Jerusalem. The only reason for making this reversal is to harmonize Galatians with Acts. But Peter/Cephas is not mentioned among those present in Antioch at the beginning of Acts 15, so that the two accounts are not easily harmonized, and there is no good reason for making the attempt. The group coming from Judaea to Antioch is not identified in Acts. When Paul and Barnabas and certain others went to the apostles and elders in Jerusalem (15:2)[8] they encountered a group described as "certain of the believers from the sect of the Pharisees" (15:5). Acts does not say so, but it seems that these people belonged to the same group as those that arrived in Antioch expressing the demand of circumcision of those who would be saved. That demand is now further elaborated.

> "It is necessary to circumcise them and to charge them to keep the law of Moses." (15:5)

Two matters have been clarified. The demand of circumcision in 15:1 implies, as we might have guessed, the keeping of the law of Moses (15:5). Those making the demand are believers belonging to the sect of the Pharisees. In Acts there is no indication that James himself was associated with this group. But the tradition that named James "the Just" or "the Righteous" implies that James was faithful to the law, and the (Pharisaic?) response to his execution/murder suggests that even unbelieving Pharisees might have been sympathetic to James.

According to Acts, the church at Antioch was established by Hellenists who were scattered from Jerusalem at the time of the martyrdom of Stephen. The Judaean believers of Pharisaic persuasion should be identified as "Hebrews." Hellenists and Hebrews adopted different approaches to mission, and at Antioch representatives of the Hebrew mission expressed the demands of their mission to the church at Antioch. Those demands were reiterated when the delegation from the church at Antioch came to Jerusalem.

According to Acts 15, James supported Paul and Barnabas in their law-free mission to the Gentiles (15:6–21), and it was James's judgment that prevailed in the policy toward the Pauline mission to the Gentiles. James B. Adamson goes so far as to suggest that James's speech and the substance of the "decree" were James's formulation communicated to Gentile Christians in a letter.[9]

---

[8] Interestingly, when Paul's arrival in Jerusalem is described in Acts 21:18–26 only the elders are mentioned along with James. Are we to assume that the apostles were no longer present?

[9] J. B. Adamson, *James: The Man and His Message* (Grand Rapids: Eerdmans, 1989), 22–23. This position is now supported in more general terms by R. Bauckham, "James and the Jerusalem Church," in *The Book of Acts in Its Palestinian Setting*, ed. Bauckham, vol. 4 of *The Book of Acts in Its First Century Setting* (Grand Rapids: Eerdmans, 1995), 462–67.

James's decision was that circumcision was not to be required of Gentile believers, but that those not circumcised were to abstain from the pollution of idols, immorality, things strangled, and from blood (15:20, 29 and see 21:25). Even in Acts, which appears to give a picture of accord between the Jerusalem church and Paul and Barnabas, the demands of the Jerusalem church (James) are not conveyed by Paul and Barnabas but by Judas Barsabbas and Silas, leading men of good standing with the Jerusalem church. The episode of the council closes with the church at Antioch rejoicing in the message brought by the two envoys from Jerusalem, who then leave while Paul and Barnabas remain in Antioch, teaching and preaching (15:30–35).

The evidence suggests that there was no unanimity between Paul and the Jerusalem church on the question of his mission to the nations. Even according to Acts, three different views can be discerned within the Jerusalem church. First, there were those who insisted that Gentile converts keep all the demands of the Jewish law. This position can be understood as a rejection of any Gentile mission as such because Gentiles were required to convert to Judaism. Second, Peter affirmed the validity of the Gentile mission. In his apologia there are no indications of any specific conditions arising from distinctive elements of the Jewish law. Third, James, who, with Peter, appears to support Paul and Barnabas, adopts a mediating position by calling on Gentile converts to observe certain practices that were especially sensitive for Jews. These requirements were set out in a letter addressed to the Gentile converts of the Pauline mission (with Barnabas).

It will be recalled that, according to Acts 15:36–41, Paul and Barnabas parted company after their return from the Jerusalem assembly because of a disagreement about whether to take John Mark on the second mission. Mark had turned back on the previous mission. Consequently Paul and Barnabas parted, and Barnabas took Mark (his cousin)[10] with him, while Paul chose to take Silas (15:40). Plausible as this disagreement might seem as the basis for this breakdown of partnership, a more convincing reason emerges in the reading of Gal 2:11–14[11]: Paul and Barnabas separated over differing understandings of the role of circumcision and the demands of the law. The withdrawal from table fellowship by Peter and Barnabas was not a temporary situation, and the falling out of Paul and Barnabas confirms this.

Even though the falling out is cloaked in Acts,[12] when the account of Acts is read in the light of Galatians it throws further light on the differences between Paul and Barnabas. In the missionary journey described in Acts 13:1–12, Barna-

---

[10] At least this is the view given in Col 4:10 and may or may not be presupposed by Luke.

[11] See J. P. Meier in R. E. Brown and J. P. Meier, *Antioch and Rome* (New York: Paulist Press, 1983), 39.

[12] Ibid., pp. 4, 39.

bas and Saul took John Mark with them as an assistant and traveled through Cyprus. Apparently Barnabas was the leader of the mission. It was on his initiative that Saul was invited to join the leadership of the church in Antioch (11:19–26). When the names of the prophets and teachers at Antioch are listed (Acts 13:1), Barnabas is mentioned first, while Saul is last. John Mark is not mentioned. When "the Holy Spirit" issues a command to the mission (Acts 13:2), Barnabas is again named first. Finally, at the end of the mission in Cyprus, at Paphos it is said that the governor, Sergius Paulus, sent for "Barnabas and Saul" (Acts 13:7). All of these details support the impression that Barnabas was the leader of the mission when it set out and when it arrived at Paphos. The reader knows that Barnabas was a native of Cyprus (Acts 4:36–37), making it a natural choice for the mission with him as leader.

During the meeting with Sergius Paulus two details prepare the reader for change. First, it is Saul (not Barnabas) who is filled with the Holy Spirit and becomes the chief spokesman for the mission, leading to the conversion of the governor (Acts 13:9–12). Second, the narrator informs the reader for the first and only time that Saul is "also known as Paul" (Acts 13:9). From Paphos the mission leaves Cyprus and journeys to Perga in Pamphylia (Asia Minor). Two changes call for attention. The company is now described as "Paul and his companions." Paul is obviously named as the leader, and the other members of the mission are designated simply as his companions. The change of name from his Hebrew name Saul to his Roman name Paul signals the decision of Paul to direct his mission as the apostle to the nations. Without warning, Luke has introduced the mission to the nations, and it is appropriate that Paul should now appear as leader. No indication is given of any dispute between Paul and other members of the party at this time. From Perga, we are told, John Mark departs this company and returns to Jerusalem (Acts 13:13).

Following the accord at Jerusalem, Paul suggests to Barnabas that they revisit the converts from their earlier mission. Barnabas wishes to take Mark, but Paul objects because Mark had deserted on arrival in Pamphylia. Objection to Mark probably went deeper than that occasioned by simple desertion. Mark returned to Jerusalem. He was a Jerusalem believer, and the Jerusalem church used to meet in his mother's house. Paul perceived Mark to be ideologically opposed to his mission to the nations. The issue was particularly sensitive after the "incident at Antioch" (Gal 2:11–14). The controversial issue of eating with Gentiles led to a bitter conflict not only between Peter and Paul but also between Paul and Barnabas. In Acts 15:36–41 the disagreement between Paul and Barnabas over taking Mark with them barely hides the ideological conflict over the ground rules of the mission. Barnabas, by choosing Mark, is reaffirming the ground rules of the Jerusalem church and its mission. As an emissary of the Jerusalem church to Antioch (Acts 11:22), he is working out the Jerusalem view in new contexts. In the company of Paul it had taken him some time to get his position clear. When he and Paul parted company, he and Mark returned to Cyprus, where he had led the mission, and Jerusalem rules had more or less applied. But Paul took Silas through Syria and Cilicia to revisit the churches founded under his leadership and on the basis of his mission to the nations.

The differences between Paul and the Jerusalem pillars are also cloaked by the suggestion that a compromise was accepted by both sides, a compromise expressed in the requirements set forth in the so-called Jerusalem decree. The letter embodying these demands is not entrusted to Paul (and Barnabas), but Paul's tacit approval is implied by the naming of one of the two messengers as Silas, who was to be Paul's new partner. Paul's choice of Silas is an enigma, given that he was one of the two selected to deliver the message from the Jerusalem church to the church at Antioch. We must conclude that naming Silas as one of the bearers of the letter is a Lukan strategy to endorse the compromise position. There are two ways of resolving this puzzle.

First, if the account of the decree is historical, it may be that Luke has chosen to name Silas in order to suggest that the Pauline mission accepted the decree (see Acts 16:4). Even if the account is not historical, Luke's intent in naming Silas as one of the messengers has the same effect.

Second, the Jerusalem decree may be the creation of Luke, who wished to present a moderate (compromise) position, one between the demand of full observance of the law and the rejection of observance, as the one that finally prevailed. Paul shows no awareness of the content of the decree in his letters. His own views are contrary to those expressed in the decree. That the decree of the council was a Lukan creation is also suggested by the way in which the decree requirements are introduced in Acts 21:25. In this context the elders, after hearing Paul's report on his mission, call on him to observe how many thousands of Jews who are zealous for the law have come to believe (Acts 21:20). The requirements of the decree are presented then without any reference to their earlier promulgation. They are seen as a compromise between the position of the Jews zealous for the law and the Pauline reputation for a law-free mission (Acts 20:21). The triumph of the compromise position appears to be a Lukan construction and perhaps represents the reality of his time and place. By naming James the "author" of the decree Luke makes him the exemplary moderate in a situation of conflict between two extremes. Paul has also been drawn into this moderation by being shown as a party to the accord. Luke strikes this balance by distancing James from those who demanded circumcision and law-keeping of all who would be saved and by distancing Paul from the rejection of all the demands of the law by those who preached a faith-only gospel of salvation.

Focus on the Jerusalem decree obscures the radical decision giving recognition to the Pauline mission, free from the demand of circumcision in the Jerusalem accord. Complexities emerged as new situations unfolded. Were the rules of this mission legitimate for Jewish as well as Gentile believers? What were the rules to be for Jews like Paul and Barnabas who were engaged in the mission to the nations? It is likely that conflicting expectations were hidden under apparent verbal agreement, and it is difficult to fit the terms of the decree into all of this because nothing in the discussion prepares the way for the requirements issued at the end of the assembly.

It is likely that Luke understood the terms of the decree to be relevant for Gentile believers without reference to the sharing of table fellowship with Jewish believers. By Luke's time of writing, toward the end of the first century, this had ceased to be an urgent question. The four demands of the Jerusalem decree, arising from Lev 17–18, were known and observed as late as the third century.[13] But the situation in Antioch (Gal 2:11–14) raised a host of problems not covered by the decree. There was, first, the situation of circumcised and uncircumcised eating together, quite apart from the question of food purity laws. These problems would not have been overcome even if Gentile believers had observed the requirements of the decree. Indeed there is no indication that the decree was formulated to deal with the problems hindering the relationship between Jewish and Gentile believers. Rather, as Acts itself suggests, through the interpretative role of James, the decree is an expression of a reading of the Mosaic law (Lev 17–18) as relevant to the situation of Gentiles living in the midst of Jews, the situation of resident aliens.

At some point the dominantly Gentile church came to accept that there was a minimal continuing relevance of Jewish law, beyond the moral demands, that remained relevant for the church. Given the early Christian, Jewish, and Gentile acceptance of the Jewish scriptures as Christian scriptures, some attempt had to be made to come to terms with the demands of the Jewish law. In a way it is surprising that so little of what we recognize as ritual law was retained.

In his use of tendency criticism in his later work F. C. Baur captured *something* of Luke's position. From this perspective the account in Acts appears to be a compromise of the Jewish particularism (attributed to Pharisaic Christians by Luke but, according to Baur, actually represented by Peter and James) and the universalism of Paul. The compromise was achieved by separating Peter and James from the conservative reaction of the Pharisaic believers so that they no longer demanded circumcision and by portraying Paul as a faithful Jewish believer who observed Jewish festival and rites when he was in Jerusalem. Baur recognized that, in the light of Paul's own letters and other literary evidence, this position is something of a distortion.[14] Reality was more complex than Baur supposed.

---

[13] See Bauckham, "James and the Jerusalem Church," pp. 464–66.

[14] *Paul, the Apostle of Jesus Christ: His Life and Work, His Epistles and His Doctrine* (1876; London, 1978), 5–6 and p. 5 n.1.

ACTS 21:17–26: JAMES AS LEADER OF THE JERUSALEM CHURCH

At the conclusion of the so-called third and final missionary journey Paul returned to Jerusalem via Miletus and Caesarea, where he was warned that imprisonment and death awaited him. From Romans we know that preoccupation with the necessity of bringing to a conclusion the collection for the poor saints in Jerusalem drove Paul to continue in spite of forebodings (Rom 15:25–33; cf. 1 Cor 16:3; 2 Cor 8–9). The question of whether the collection would be accepted was prominent because acceptance was a symbol of the acceptance of the Pauline mission by the Jerusalem church. The outcome of this episode is absent from the account in Acts, which does not make explicit either acceptance or rejection of the collection. Only in Acts 24:17, in his defense before the Governor Felix, does the Lukan Paul mention that he had come to Jerusalem, "to bring to my nation alms and offerings." James D. G. Dunn argues that there is no certainty that the Jerusalem church received the collection, while M. I. Webber suggests that the collection was rejected.[15]

The description of the events related to Paul's return to Jerusalem occurs in one of the so-called "we passages" of Acts. When Paul and his party arrived in Jerusalem they were warmly received by the brethren (21:17). More than likely "the brothers" indicates fellow Christians, although the close association with James (21:17–18; cf. 12:17) opens up the possibility that the other brothers of Jesus are in view. Only on the day after his arrival did Paul and his party go to see James, and we are told that all of the elders were present (21:18). The narrative in Acts 21 assumes the leadership of James. There is no mention of Peter or of other apostles in conjunction with the elders, as there was in Acts 15. As far as Paul's party is concerned, his leadership is clear in the narrative. Paul greeted James and the elders and reported what God had done among the Gentiles/nations through his ministry (21:19).[16] The elders' response was to rejoice and praise God. At the same time, however, they drew attention to "how many thousands of Jews had believed and all of them zealous for the law" (21:20). This piece of information is used as a basis for a call on Paul to manifest his true Jewish credentials. The pretext is that all have been told that Paul teaches all Jews everywhere who live among nations to forsake circumcision, the law of Moses, and Jewish customs (21:21).[17] This "rumor," which Acts assumes to be false, is to be proved false by the purifying rites that the elders recommend to Paul. The evidence from Paul's letters suggests that the

---

[15] J. G. D. Dunn, *Unity and Diversity in the New Testament* (London: SCM, 1977), 257; M. I. Webber, "ΙΑΚΟΒΟΣ Ο ΔΙΚΑΙΟΣ: Origins, Literary Expression and Development of Traditions about the Brother of the Lord in Early Christianity," Ph.D. dissertation, Fuller Theological Seminary, 1985, pp. 117–19.

[16] The expression ἐν τοῖς ἔθνεσιν is ambiguous and the ambiguity has important consequences.

[17] "Living among nations" means as part of the diaspora, although some situations in Palestine would also be covered by this description.

rumor was justified. At the same time, for the sake of accord in Jerusalem, Paul might well have been willing to follow the recommended course of action (1 Cor 9:20). Apparent agreement covers up what was a serious point of conflict.

Luke's account in Acts 21:19 portrays Paul as the successful missionary to the Gentiles,[18] reporting back to the Jerusalem church which is described as undertaking a successful mission to the Jews, a mission based on the acceptance of the demands of the Jewish law (Acts 21:20). The assumption implied by the Acts account is that two independent missions existed, the one wholly restricted to Gentiles and the other wholly restricted to Jews. In the middle of this is Paul, a Jew and at the same time the leading figure in the mission to the Gentiles. According to Acts, the Jerusalem church maintained a mission to the Jews based on circumcision and the keeping of the Mosaic law, including Sabbath, food, and purity laws. Paul's circumcision-free mission in the diaspora was restricted to Gentiles, and confirmation of this was intended by the account of Paul's compliance with the request of the Jerusalem leadership that Paul take part in the rites of purification.

Paul was urged to pay the expenses of four men who had taken a (Nazirite?) vow and to join them in their purification, demonstrating that he lived as a good Jew. On this practice see 1 Macc 3:49; Josephus, *Ant.* 19.294; Num 6:2; and M. Megillah 1.10–11. Paul agreed to this. At the same time the requirements of the Jerusalem accord for Gentiles are *restated,* but in a way that suggests that Paul is hearing them for the first time (21:22–25).[19] At the end of the period of purification Paul went to the Temple, into which it was wrongly assumed that he had taken a Gentile. It could be that Paul's accusers were believing Jews zealous for the law and belonging to the Jerusalem church, but Luke identifies them as Jews from the province of Asia where Paul's relationship with Gentiles was known. Their assumption proceeds from their impression of Paul, which the action prescribed by the elders (described in 21:22–25) has done nothing to change. The visit to the Temple led to the arrest and deportation of Paul to Rome. From one point of view this was disastrous. Acts portrays it as the means whereby Paul achieves his plan to extend the mission westward.

Acts has reduced the tension between Paul and the Jerusalem church by implying that the Pauline mission was directed wholly to Gentiles. Yet this is inconsistent with the Pauline strategy Luke describes, whereby Paul first preached in the Jewish synagogues before turning to the Gentiles. Luke also describes a situation in which the Jerusalem church recognized the mission to the Gentiles free from the demands of the law except for the requirements expressed in the Jerusalem "decree." Paul did not submit the mission to the

[18] Acts understands ἔθνεσιν as Gentiles, but Paul understood his mission to be to the nations, including the Jews.

[19] Thus M. Hengel, *Acts and the History of Early Christianity* (London: SCM, 1979), 117.

nations to the demands of the so-called Jerusalem decree, which Luke on more than one occasion introduces (15:19–20, 28–29; 21:25). Nor is it likely that the reduced demands of the law expressed in the decree as formulated in Acts would have satisfied those described as zealous for the law, whose leader was James. Here Acts is not plausible, presenting an oversimplified account of the situation. Such a compromise would not have been acceptable to those described as "zealous for the law" any more that it would have been for Paul.

In all of this it is clear that James was the leading figure in the Jerusalem church. In spite of this fact, Luke mentions him on only three occasions (Acts 12:17; 15:13; 21:18). This is puzzling. Martin Hengel has described the treatment of James in the New Testament as one-sided and tendentious.[20] Luke may have known of the martyrdom of James in the year 62 CE but chose not to mention the event because of the prestige attached to James as a martyr. It could be that the title "the Just" or "the Righteous" was attached to James in the context of his martyrdom. If so, this fact was also ignored by Luke.[21] It is as if Luke has pushed James into the background, but, because of his prominence, has been unable to obscure totally his leading role. He sought to minimize the role of James because he was aware that James represented a hard-line position on the place of circumcision and the keeping of the law, a position that Luke himself did not wish to maintain. In contrast Paul had adopted a law-free policy in relation to his mission, and, while Luke might have been more in sympathy with this, he harbored reservations and modified Paul's mission to the nations into a mission to the Gentiles which did not take in Jews. Because he has done this inconsistently it is possible to recover evidence of Paul's mission to the nations and the historical position of James.

ACTS 21:27–36; 23:12–22: JAMES AND THE ARREST OF PAUL

The course of action recommended by James and the Jerusalem elders led to Paul's arrest, and there is no evidence that James or members of the Jerusalem church came to the aid of Paul after his arrest. There is no suggestion of any concern for Paul. In the narration of the plot to kill Paul (Acts 23:12–22), it is not the intervention of the Jerusalem church that saves Paul but the action of the son of his sister (Acts 23:16).

---

[20] "Jacobus der Herrenbruder—der erste 'Papst'?," in *Glaube und Eschatologie: Festschrift für W. G. Kümmel zum 80. Geburtstag,* ed. E. Grässer and O. Merk (Tübingen: J. C. B. Mohr [Paul Siebeck], 1985), 72.

[21] Though there was ample opportunity for the martyrdom to have made some impact on all but the letters of Paul, none of the New Testament writers mentions the death of James or names him "the Just." The deaths of neither Peter nor Paul give cause for comment in the NT because they were executed by the Romans. Acts records the execution of Stephen (Acts 7:54–8:1a) and of James the brother of John and son of Zebedee (Acts 12:2) by "the Jews." Another explanation must be sought for the silence concerning the death of James "the Just," who was executed at the instigation of the High Priest Ananus.

Knowing the harmonistic tendencies of Acts enables us to question whether James and the elders, in suggesting that Paul participate in an act of purification in the Temple (Acts 21:20–21), might not have hoped for Paul's arrest. It could be argued that the Jews who created the turmoil that led to his arrest were members of the Jerusalem church zealous for the law. The same suggestion might be made concerning those who bound themselves by an oath to kill Paul (Acts 23:12). But such assertions go much further than is justifiable on the basis of the criticism of Acts. In both instances the opponents of Paul are described simply as Jews (Acts 21:27; 23:12). The narrative of Acts suggests that James and the Jerusalem elders foresaw that Paul's presence in the Temple in Jerusalem was likely to precipitate a riot and nevertheless urged this course of action on him. When Paul was arrested, James and the elders made no representations on his behalf. Paul's hope of a successful completion of his work in bringing the gifts of the largely Gentile churches to Jerusalem was sadly disappointed, and his relationship with James and the elders was less than cordial.

CHAPTER 3

THE LETTERS OF PAUL

Paul and James

A careful examination of the letters of Paul confirms that the role of James the brother of Jesus has been obscured in the Gospels and Acts. Because Acts has influenced all subsequent sources, any independent early evidence is invaluable. The earliest evidence comes from Galatians, which could be the earliest writing in the New Testament, and from another letter, written not much later.

GALATIANS: THE TWO MISSIONS IN ANTIOCH AND JERUSALEM

Most commentators date Galatians in the late 50s, grouping it with Romans toward the end of Paul's missionary career. Thematically, it is close to Romans. Each letter deals with the role of the law. But there are important differences in their treatment of this common theme. The assumption that Paul's early theology is found in the eschatology of 1 Thessalonians, rather than in Galatians or Romans, fails to recognize that apocalyptic elements are fundamental to Paul's theology.[1] From Galatians we learn that Paul encountered the problem of the law at least from the time of the Jerusalem accord. He might have written a letter dealing with related issues at any time after the events narrated in Gal 2:1–10, 11–14. These events were hardly early in his Christian formation, taking place seventeen years after his "conversion." All of the surviving letters come from the relatively short period of the ten years following these events.

Significant differences between the accounts in Gal 2:1–10 and Acts 15 put in question whether Galatians refers to the Jerusalem assembly described in Acts 15. Gerd Lüdemann attempts to reconcile these by suggesting that Gal 2:2 implies two meetings or at least a meeting within a meeting: the first with the

---

[1] See J. C. Beker, *Paul the Apostle* (Philadelphia: Fortress, 1980).

assembly and the second with the limited circle of "the pillars."[2] It may be that the account in Acts 15 has influenced his judgment concerning Galatians 2. Differences between the two accounts are far-reaching.[3] If, in the light of these differences, the second visit noted in Galatians is identified with the so-called famine-relief visit (11:27–30), we might need to conclude that the Jerusalem assembly had not yet taken place at the time of the writing of Galatians. In support of this scenario, it is noted that both visits (Gal 2:1 and Acts 11:27) are described as second visits by Paul after his conversion, and the visits are said to be based on some revelation.[4] But there are problems with this view also.[5] Luke's account is so driven by his tendency to remove tensions between Paul and the Jerusalem church that the actual historical sequence is no longer recoverable in Acts. Most scholars identify the visit described in Gal 2:1–10 with the Jerusalem assembly. If this view is accepted there is no need to date Galatians much later than that event.

Gal 1:17–19: Leadership in Jerusalem

Paul's letter to the Galatians makes clear that James was known to Paul by reputation and in person. Here Paul attempts to establish his independence of the authority of the Jerusalem church and its leaders, whom he describes as "apostles before me" (Gal 1:17). Thus when Paul calls himself an apostle he ascribes to himself status equal to that of the original Jerusalem apostles. He argues (Gal 1:18–19) that, after his conversion from the role of a persecutor of the followers of Jesus to a proponent of the new movement, he did not go up to Jerusalem for a period of three years.[6] When he did go up to Jerusalem he went with a limited and specific agenda (to see Peter) and stayed only fifteen

---

[2] *Opposition to Paul in Jewish Christianity* (Minneapolis: Fortress, 1989), 36.

[3] The reasons for the visits to Jerusalem differ in the two accounts: Paul and Barnabas meet with a restricted group in Galatians but with the church in Acts; the mission is accepted without conditions in Galatians but the demands of the decree are specified in Acts.

[4] In support of this view, see D. Wenham, "Acts and the Pauline Corpus II. Evidence of Parallels," in *The Book of Acts in Ancient Literary Setting*, ed. B. W. Winter and A. D. Clark, vol. 2 of *The Book of Acts in Its First Century Setting* (Grand Rapids: Eerdmans, 1993), 215–58, esp. 226–43.

[5] The account in Acts 11:27–30 does not indicate any discussion of the Gentile mission so fundamental to Galatians. To overcome this, D. R. Catchpole ("Paul, James and the Apostolic Decree," *NTS* 23 [1977]: 428–44) ingeniously suggests that the accounts of Acts 11 and 15 are the results of Luke's use of duplicate accounts of the same visit. This view is the consequence of a determined attempt to reconcile Paul with Acts. In practical terms it might lead to the same position as would ignoring the visit in Acts 11, unless it is argued that chronologically Acts 11 is the correct point in the narrative for the visit.

[6] On the appropriateness of the use of the term "conversion" in relation to Paul, see A. F. Segal, *Paul the Convert: The Apostolate and Apostasy of Saul the Pharisee* (New Haven: Yale University Press, 1990), 1–183.

days. This visit took place sometime before 36 CE.[7] The visit, with the expressed purpose of seeing Peter, is commonly taken to indicate that at this time Peter was the leader of the Jerusalem church (Gal 1:18).

Coincidentally, Paul acknowledges that during the visit he also saw James and implies that James is an apostle: "But I saw none of the other apostles except James the brother of the Lord" (1:19).[8] Walter Schmithals argues that Paul did not wish to call James an apostle but has achieved a studied ambiguity, "leaving room for the possibility that one could, if need be, count James among the apostles—something he [Paul] himself was not accustomed to doing."[9] This is an extraordinary reading of Gal 1:19. One reason for this seems to be the assumption that the status of true apostleship was limited to the twelve. Was Paul's claim to apostleship a claim to be one of the twelve? This is most unlikely. Rather Paul claimed apostleship of equal status with the twelve. The evidence of 1 Cor 15:5–7 implies that he recognized that James shared the status of "all of the apostles." Thus the apostolic band included Peter and the twelve, James and all the apostles, and last of all Paul himself (15:5–8).

Paul might have chosen to see Peter because Peter was perceived to be more sympathetic to Paul's cause. James, as the leader, was too important to be missed,[10] and Peter may have effected an introduction for Paul. But Acts 9:27 says that Barnabas introduced Saul to the apostles! If, in Paul's terms, James was the only other apostle seen by him in addition to Peter, it is clear that he is not using the term apostle in the restricted sense of the twelve. This is confirmed by his own claim to be an apostle, which he defends at length (1:1, 11–17). Paul did not claim to be one of the twelve, a group which he elsewhere recognized by that name (1 Cor 15:5). While there appear to be those who wished to restrict the status of apostle to the twelve (perhaps the author of Acts), Paul showed no inclination to accept this view. Of course he was aware that those who did this were prepared to recognize (as he himself also did) those who were apostles of churches (Rom 16:7; 2 Cor 8:23; Phil 2:25) and not on the same level as the apostles of Jesus. It may be in the sense of apostles of the church at Antioch that Acts 14:14 refers to Paul and Barnabas. That was certainly not the status that Paul claimed for himself or recognized in James. Gal 1:17 shows that Paul placed his apostleship on the same level as those who "were apostles before me." This includes James.[11]

---

[7] See G. Lüdemann, *Paul, Apostle to the Gentiles* (Philadelphia: Fortress, 1984), 262.

[8] Paul uses the expression "brother(s) of the Lord" elsewhere only in 1 Cor 9:5.

[9] *The Office of an Apostle* (Nashville: Abingdon, 1965), 65.

[10] See S. G. F. Brandon, *Jesus and the Zealots* (Manchester: Manchester University Press, 1967), 163.

[11] The basis of Paul's claim to apostleship is set out in Gal 1:1, 11, in which he claims to have seen the risen Lord and to have been commissioned by him. The same basis is apparently assumed for the apostleship of James.

Gal 2:1–10: The Pillars and the Leadership
of the Two Missions

"After fourteen years" (46–50 CE) Paul made another visit to Jerusalem, this time with Barnabas and Titus (Gal 2:1–10).[12] The purpose of the later visit was to place Paul's mission to the nations/Gentiles with its gospel on a firm basis (2:2) because it was being threatened by "false brethren" (2:4). The term translated "Gentiles" or "nations" is ambiguous and can be used by the same person with more than one meaning.[13] Contrary to common opinion ἔθνη is not used exclusively for Gentiles, with "people" reserved to describe the Jewish people.[14] In John 11:50 Caiaphas refers to Jews as both "people" and "na-

---

[12] It is uncertain whether the fourteen years commences from the time of Paul's conversion, that is, whether the count begins from the same point of time presupposed by Gal 1:18, in which the same temporal introduction (Ἔπειτα) is used, or whether the count recommences from the time of the first visit. If the former, the date of the second visit can hardly be later than 46 CE, and, if the latter, the date is hardly earlier than 48 CE. Most commentators opt for the later date.

[13] James Barr's attack on the reading of complex concepts into single words (in *The Semantics of the Bible* [1961] and *Biblical Words for Time* [1962]) has not prevented this practice in the interpretation of ἔθνη in the New Testament. To read ἔθνη as if it were a technical term for "Gentiles" overlooks the complexity of the evidence. A person can use the same word with varying shades of meaning. If ἔθνη can mean "Gentiles," it is only from the perspective of the Jew who views the other nations. The same person can include his own people among the nations. The inclusive sense is found in the expressions "every nation" (Acts 10:35; 17:26); "all the nations" (Mark 11:17 = Isa 56:7; Mark 13:10; Luke 12:30; 21:24; 24:47; Acts 2:5; 14:16; Rom 1:5; 4:17–18; 15:11, Rev 14.8, 15.4, 18:3), an expression which would not need "every" or "all" if ἔθνη meant "Gentiles." Inclusiveness is clear in the lists of Rev 5:9; 7:9; 11:9; 13:7; 14:6; 17:15. Only 17:15 uses the plurals throughout; the singulars using "every" instead of "all" have the same inclusive meaning. Here a very clear difference from the use of the term "Gentile" emerges. The New Testament does not use ἔθνος of an individual Gentile because the word signifies a single nation. Although Paul, on two occasions, contrasts "Jews" and "Gentiles" (Rom 3:29; 9:24), using ἔθνη exclusively of Gentiles, when speaking of the individual Jew, Paul must use "the Greek" as the corresponding term (Rom 1:16; 2:9, 10; 3:9; 10:12). Here Paul deals with the priority of "to the Jew first" in the economy of God's salvation. The linguistic contrasts show that Jews and Gentiles, or the Jews and the Greeks, are included in the salvation of God. The distinction between Jews and Greeks is also used in Acts 14:1; 16:1, 3, although reference to devout Greeks in the synagogue at Thessalonica (18:4) could be a reference to hellenized Jews. Compare the reference to the Hellenists (the Ἑλληνισταί are contrasted with the Ἑβραῖοι in Acts 6:1; 9:29; 11:20. Here Jews who have adopted Greek culture (language) are contrasted with Hebrew-/Aramaic-speaking Jews. Jewish members of the Pauline churches in the diaspora are included in "all the churches of the ἐθνῶν" (Rom 16:4), just as there were Jewish members of the church at Antioch, and Acts 2:5 implies that Jews of the diaspora came to Jerusalem from "every nation under heaven." When Paul asserts, "I am under obligation to Greeks and Barbarians" (Rom 1:14), he is using the nomenclature of the Greeks to affirm his universal obligation. Here "Greeks" signifies all who were shaped by the Greek paideia, including hellenized Jews. The rest were "Barbarians," including Aramaic-/Hebrew-speaking Jews.

[14] In the LXX ἔθνος and its plural are used to translate fifteen Hebrew expressions, the most frequently occuring of which are "goy(im)" and "am(iym)." In spite of this fact, following the

tion,"[15] and in Rom 4:17–18 Paul speaks of Abraham as the father of many nations, a description that includes Israel among the nations.

Paul's mission was directed to the nations (Rom 1:5), all of them, and his modus operandi was determined by this orientation. Luke might have understood Paul's "to the Jew first" to mean that he systematically began his mission in the synagogues (Acts 13:14; 14:1; 16:13; 17:1–2, 10; 18:4), asserting that this was his custom. While Paul's letters do not confirm this, it is clear that the churches founded by him were mixed, including both Jews and Gentiles. It is also clear that the presence of Jews did not determine the mode of Paul's mission. Rather they were expected to modify their behavior to the practice of the mission to the nations. This expectation was the cause of the problem in the mixed church at Antioch.

The false brethren of Gal 2:4 are not specifically identified but are said to have crept in under false pretenses. They should be associated with a faction of the circumcision party (Gal 2:7, 9). Apparently they tried to compel Titus, a Greek, to be circumcised (Gal 2:3). But where was it that they carried out this activity? The narrative order of Gal 2:4, which is placed in the context of the visit to Jerusalem, implies that their activity took place in Jerusalem. This order, however, might be explained as follows: Paul first describes his visit to Jerusalem. He then gives the reason he felt the need to lay his gospel before those of repute in Jerusalem. The false brethren crept in and were accepted in Antioch, only later to manifest their demands.[16] With Acts in mind it could be argued that the problem first appeared in Antioch, with the Judaeans of 15:1. This motivated the journey of Paul and Barnabas to Jerusalem, where the Pharisaic believers of 15:5 insinuated themselves into the private meeting. In spite of their intervention Paul gained recognition for his mission. While this reading is not a consequence of undue pressure to harmonize Galatians with Acts, Paul does not mention the "false brethren" in relation to his meeting with "the pillar apostles." Paul's account assumes that the problem emerged in Antioch but

---

article by G. Kittel on ἔθνος (*Theological Dictionary of the New Testament,* vol. 2, pp. 364–72), most scholars assume that ἔθνη must mean "Gentiles" in Paul and the New Testament generally. But this ignores the fundamental meaning of the term in Greek and in the LXX. In the Psalms ἔθνη and λαοί are used thirty-five times in synonymous parallelism (*Dictionary of the New Testament* vol. 2, pp. 365–66). Further, ἔθνος is repeatedly used to translate "goy" in the promise to Abraham that God would make of him "a great nation" (Gen 12:2; 46:3; Exod 32:10; Num 14:12; Deut 9:14). And Abraham is described as "the father of many nations," which surely includes Israel (Gen 17:4, 5, 16; cf. Rom 4:17–18), and it is said that two nations were in the womb of Rebekah, Israel/Jacob and the nation(s) that descended from Esau.

[15] See John 11:48–52 and cf. references to the Jewish nation in Luke 7:5; 23:2; John 18:35; Acts 10:22; 24:2, 10, 17; 26:4; 28:19. See also my "The Church and Israel in the Gospel of John," *NTS* 25 (1978): 525–43.

[16] Lüdemann (*Opposition,* p. 35) draws this conclusion.

specifically mentions the false brethren at a point which implies their presence in Jerusalem.

On the assumption that the challenge came in Antioch, the response came through a revelation that Paul and his party should go up to Jerusalem and lay the matter before those of repute (2:2, 6×2, 9), who are eventually named as James, (Cephas) Peter, and John, the pillars. Paul's elaboration in 2:6 shows that he set no store by their reputation.[17]

> And from those who were reputed to be something (what they were does not matter to me; God shows no partiality)—those, I say, who were of repute added nothing to me.

Those who regarded them as "pillars" probably had in mind the image of the church as a building, possibly an image of the Jerusalem church. More likely they thought of these three as the pillars of the church, wherever it might spread. The image expresses a territorial claim that constituted a problem for the Pauline mission.[18] The narrative implies that the James in question has already been identified as the brother of the Lord.

This second visit to Jerusalem for a private meeting with the reputed pillars concludes with the recognition of a policy of two missions; the success of Paul's mission to "the uncircumcision" is presented as comparable to Peter's success among "the circumcision" (2:7). Compare the indirect reference to the two missions and their modes of operation in Acts 21:19–20 and the discussion of that text above. Gal 2:6–10 is important enough to quote in full.

> From those reputed to be something (what they were does not matter to me; God shows no partiality[19]) for those people of repute added nothing to me; but on the contrary, seeing that I had been entrusted with the gospel of the uncircumcision as Peter [was] of the circumcision, for he who worked through Peter for an apostleship of the circumcision worked also through me to the Gentiles/nations and knowing the grace that was given me, James and Cephas and John, those reputed to be pillars, gave the right hand of fellowship to me and Barnabas, that we [should go] to the Gentiles/nations, and they to the circumcision; only that we should remember the poor, which very thing I was eager to do.

---

[17] See J. D. G. Dunn, "Echoes of the Intra-Jewish Polemics in Paul's Letter to the Galatians," *JBL* 112/113 (1993): 459–77.

[18] The Qumran texts (see esp. 4 QpIsa[d]) portray leaders and members of the community in terms of parts of the Temple. See B. Gärtner, *The Temple and the Community in Qumran Scrolls and the New Testament* (Cambridge: Cambridge University Press, 1965).

[19] The expression πρόσωπον ὁ θεὸς ἀνθρώπου οὐ λαμβάνει has the same meaning as οὐ προσωπολημψία. See James 2:1–4.

The stress on those of repute (2:2, 6ˣ², 9) reflects tension between Paul and the reputed "pillars" that is especially clear in 2:6. There Paul questions what the pillars actually were, setting aside their reputations as irrelevant to God. Whatever Paul thought of the pillars, he acknowledges their reputation in the Jerusalem church. James is mentioned as the first of three exalted, reputed "pillars."

The precise terminology used in 2:7–9 is important. Lüdemann thinks that there was a transition from Petrine leadership at the time of Paul's first visit to Jerusalem to the leadership of James at the time of Paul's second visit.[20] He notes that Barnabas, James, and John are not mentioned in 2:7–8. There the Greek name Peter is used, whereas the Semitic Cephas is used in 2:9, reflecting the Judaizing context of the second Jerusalem meeting where Barnabas, James, and John are also mentioned. The transition brought a tightening of the demands of the circumcision party concerning the relationship of Jewish believers to Gentiles. But if 2:7–8 reflects the first meeting between Paul and Peter only, Paul has obscured this by commencing 2:7 in a way that presupposes continuity of reference to those of repute in 2:6. It is they who have seen that "I [Paul] was entrusted with the gospel of the uncircumcision" (2.7). Thus, while James and John are not named in 2:7, the plural ἰδόντες assumes their presence with Peter. These verses all belong to the situation of the Jerusalem accord. Some other explanation must be sought for the use of the name Peter in 2:7–8 and Cephas in 2:9.

The interchange between the use of Cephas (Gal 1:18; 2:9, 11) and Peter (2:7) probably reflects the traditional use in the Jerusalem church (Cephas), on the one hand, and the characteristic name used by the Galatians (Peter), on the other.[21] In naming the pillars the Semitic form of the name, Cephas, appears in place of the Greek, Petros, in recognition that the status of the pillars was accorded by the Jerusalem church. The priority of James reflects the prominence of the brother of the Lord and his leadership in the Jerusalem church.

Lüdemann also argues that the absence of "apostleship" from the reference to Paul, in contrast to the reference to Peter, reflects the fact that Paul's apostleship was not recognized in Jerusalem.[22] His argument fails to take account of the chiastic parallelism of the statements in Gal 2:7–8.

(a1) but on the contrary they, seeing that I had been entrusted with the gospel of the uncircumcision

---

[20] *Paul,* pp. 69, 120 n.78.

[21] Given that the gospel tradition identifies Cephas as the Aramaic equivalent of Petros, there is no case for suggesting that two different people in the Jerusalem church are in view, as Eusebius does in *HE* 1.12. Eusebius's motivation was to clear Peter of the charge leveled by Paul in 2:11–14.

[22] *Opposition,* p. 37.

(a2) as Peter [had been entrusted with the gospel] of the circumcision

(b2) for the one who worked with Peter for an apostleship of the circumcision

(b1) worked also with me [for an apostleship] to the nations. . . .

The use of the "gospel of the uncircumcision" with an implied gospel "of the circumcision" in 2:7 finds a chiastic parallel in "apostleship of the circumcision" with an implied apostleship "to the nations" in 2:8. Reference to the gospel is explicit only in relation to Paul, just as reference to apostleship is explicit only in relation to Peter. In each case specific mention is made only concerning the first person named and implied in relation to the second. Nevertheless, Lüdemann rightly suspects that Paul's apostleship was contested in Jerusalem. But we learn this from Paul's polemical defense of his apostleship (1:1) and his gospel (1:6–9, 11–12). In the light of this contest 2:8 is a subtle claim to equal apostleship which avoids explicit use of the term. If Paul reports the exact terms agreed to by the parties, the chiastic formulation might have been designed to avoid a confrontation. But this is Paul's account of the meeting, and it reflects his perspective. The Jerusalem apostles would have allowed only a minimalist interpretation of Paul's apostleship, recognizing his mission to the Gentiles authorized by the Jerusalem church. Paul's use implied a maximal interpretation of his apostleship to the nations, claiming equality with the twelve.

An amicable agreement appears to be described between the "pillars" and Paul and Barnabas. In 2:7–9 Paul claims that the reputed pillars acknowledged his gospel and mission alongside the gospel and mission of Peter. Throughout this passage Peter's gospel, apostleship, and mission are said to be of and to "the circumcision." The parallel statements concerning Paul speak of his gospel of "the uncircumcision," but apostleship and mission to "the nations." The parallelism of the statements concerning the two missions could be taken to imply that ἔθνη here is to be understood in the sense excluding the Jews, that is, as the uncircumcised Gentiles. But if this is the case, why did Paul change the idiom, breaking the linguistic parallelism between circumcision and uncircumcision? Rather the change signals a crucial aspect of Paul's point of view. The expressions "gospel of the circumcision" and "of the uncircumcision" signify the demands made as preconditions of the two gospels. Paul's gospel repudiated the demand for circumcision. But in the accord he acknowledged the gospel of the Jerusalem pillars that demanded circumcision in exchange for their recognition of his gospel which did not demand circumcision.[23] Thus this first state-

---

[23] The description of the gospel of the uncircumcision, implying also a gospel of the circumcision (2:7), is somewhat perplexing in the light of Paul's insistence that there is no other gospel (1:6–9). What is envisaged in 2:7–9 is not the absolute demand for circumcision because a gospel of the uncircumcision is acknowledged. In spite of the agreement there is a sense in which the gospels of the two missions are irreconcilable. Paul wished to obscure this point to his own advantage.

ment concerning the gospel refers to the conditions required by the respective gospels. This statement makes no reference to audience. This comes in the last two statements, concerning apostleship and mission. Paul characterized Peter's apostleship and mission as of and to the circumcision. Thus the gospel demanding circumcision was restricted to the scope of the already circumcised, the Jews. In contrast Paul characterizes his own apostleship and mission not as to the uncircumcision but as to the nations.

There is a great deal of room here for misunderstanding between the two parties. The "accord," even as described by Paul, does not easily provide a single, unequivocal solution. It is not surprising that the various parties to the accord appear to have understood it differently, and it was not long before accord gave way to discord.

There are two missions, but how were they distinguished? In geographic terms—the one mission restricted to "Palestine" and the other aimed at the Roman world beyond Palestine? Or are we to think of an ethnic distinction: one mission restricted to Jews only and the other to Gentiles? Or is the difference ideological—the differing demands made by the two missions, the one mission demanding circumcision and all that this entails and the other mission free of those demands? If the last, then both missions might include both Jews and Gentiles. Paul's characteristic description of his mission was "to the nations," not simply to the uncircumcised, and this included the Jews as one of the nations. The conditions each demanded of converts distinguished the two missions. The one required circumcision and law observance, while the other did not. Naturally the latter was characterized by converts from many nations, including some Jews, while the former remained dominantly Jewish and required Gentiles to convert to Judaism.

The pillars assumed that Paul's mission would be restricted to Gentiles, whereas Paul understood it as a universal mission to "the nations," including Jews. At the same time, Paul would not tolerate the extension of the preaching of the gospel based on the demand of circumcision and law observance for the uncircumcision (the Gentiles). The conflict that soon emerged in Antioch (2:11–14) was inevitable.

From the point of view of the circumcision mission, those who did not keep the law were inferior to those that did. This position was prepared for by the inferior place of Gentile godfearers in Jewish synagogues, as was argued long ago by Sir William Ramsay.[24] Paul later responded with his own evaluative distinction between the strong and the weak (1 Cor 7:1–13). At the time of writing Galatians, the issue was the equality of the mission to the nations. When this was challenged Paul responded by questioning the consistency of those who belonged to the circumcision mission (2:11–14).

---

[24] *St Paul the Traveller, and Roman Citizen* (London: Hodder & Stoughton, 1895), 4.

The strategy of two distinct missions with independent ground rules might have been an attempt to find a diplomatic solution to a difficult problem. It allowed the Jerusalem pillars to acknowledge the legitimacy of a circumcision-free mission to the Gentiles without giving up their own position of demanding circumcision and law observance. Had it been possible for the two missions to remain separate and distinct, the one to the Jews and the other to the Gentiles, the solution might have worked. The result would have been two quite distinct missions, as James, and perhaps Peter, envisaged. But this was not a real possibility. Conflicting understandings of the accord made actual conflict inevitable. The complexity and impracticality of the solution became apparent when (Cephas) Peter came to Antioch (2:11). Perhaps the flaw in the accord was already foreshadowed when, as Paul notes, the pillars extended the right hand of fellowship to him and to Barnabas(2:9). Titus, who had accompanied Paul with Barnabas, is not included. He is not mentioned again after the note that, although he was a Greek, he was not compelled to be circumcised (2:3).

Gal 2:11–14: James and the Dispute at Antioch

Many commentators think that the incident described in 2:11–14, though narrated after the agreement between Paul, Barnabas, and the Jerusalem pillars, must have occurred prior to it.[25] It is argued that, whereas a sequence of events might be indicated (in 1:18 and 2:1) by the use of "then" or "next" ("Επειτα), no time sequence is indicated by the use of "When" ('Οτε). While no time sequence is necessarily indicated by that expression, the event could just as well be in sequence as out of sequence, and the order of narration would need to be put in question if that order is to be rejected. Only the conviction that Peter would not have gone back on the "accord" favors the reversal of the sequence. But it is not inconceivable that Peter might have been inconsistent. The inconsistency of Peter was precisely the point of Paul's criticism, although these events are described to Paul's own advantage. Consequently, it may be that Peter's action was not inconsistent from Peter's point of view.[26] Thus we should look for acceptable ways of reading 2:11–14 in its present narrative sequence because, although the text does not demand this, there is nothing in the text to indicate that we should do otherwise.[27]

Paul entered the discussion with the pillar apostles with a view to securing

---

[25] Thus both H. Zahn and J. Munck. See G. Howard (*Crisis in Galatia: A Study in Early Christian Theology*, SNTSMS 35 [Cambridge: Cambridge University Press, 1979], 22) and Lüdemann (*Paul*, pp. 75–77), who is followed by R. B. Ward ("James of Jerusalem in the First Two Centuries," *ANRW* II.26.1, 783–84).

[26] See H. D. Betz, *Galatians: A Commentary on Paul's Letter to the Churches in Galatia*, Hermeneia (Philadelphia: Fortress, 1979), 106.

[27] Ibid., p. 105 n.436.

the recognition of the gospel he preached (2:2) and of his mission to the nations. The specific form of the gospel preached by Paul and his approach to mission to the nations were closely related. The same was true for the gospel and mission of the circumcision carried on by the pillars. The problem of intersecting missions is already in view in the second visit to Jerusalem because Titus, a Greek, traveled with Paul (2:3). In terms of stressing the recognition accorded to his mission by the pillars, Paul notes that "Not even Titus who was with me, being a Greek, was compelled to be circumcised."[28] Paul expected the ground rules of the "home side" to apply when the two missions intersected. The account of Paul's relationship with the Jerusalem church in Acts 21 suggests that Paul complied with the Jewish law when he was in Jerusalem. While this could be Lukan apologetic, it could be a point of detail that Luke has accurately described (see 1 Cor 9:19–23). Thus, when Peter came to Antioch he at first complied with Paul's expectation of the outworking of the accord. He lived by the ground rules of the predominantly Gentile church at Antioch which was represented by Paul in his mission to the nations. The use of the name Cephas rather than of Peter signals that Cephas/Peter represents the Jerusalem community in Antioch,[29] which was dominantly a manifestation of Pauline Gentile Christianity. Peter and the other Jewish Christians at first ignored the Jewish purity laws and ate with Gentile Christians.[30]

According to Paul, the situation exploded when representatives from James appeared on the scene and Peter and the other Jewish Christians, including Barnabas, withdrew from table fellowship.[31] Paul says specifically of Peter, "he

---

[28] The wording might be significant. Paul does not deny that Titus was circumcised but affirms only that he was not *compelled* to be. Paul denies that he gave way, even for a moment (Gal 2:5). But if in Jerusalem the "reputed pillars" acknowledged the validity *and equality* of Paul's mission to the nations without demanding circumcision, or so it seemed to Paul, magnanimously now Paul might have conceded the circumcision of Titus, not of necessity but as an offering of good will and as an expression of his understanding of the accord, *that the rules of the home church apply.*

[29] See Betz, *Galatians,* p. 106.

[30] If Gentile Christians were viewed as a "third race," it is possible that Jewish Christians might not have considered them to be impure. But the notion of the "third race" (in, e.g., the Epistle of Diognetus) is a somewhat later development, and there is no evidence that the notion was used in relation to Jewish perceptions of Christians. Rather the classification is evidence of Christian self-awareness of their distinctive nature.

[31] There is a widespread tendency to distance James from the circumcision party that exerted pressure on Peter at Antioch. (See B. H. Streeter, *The Four Gospels: A Study of the Origins Treating of the Manuscript Tradition, Sources, Authorship and Dates* [London: Macmillan, 1924], 232; Streeter, *The Primitive Church: Studies with Special Reference to the Origins of the Christian Ministry* [London: Macmillan, 1929], 55; Meier in Brown and Meier, p. 42; H. J. Schoeps, *Theologie und Geschichte des Judenchristentums* [Tübingen: J. C. B. Mohr [Paul Siebeck], 1949], 261. This distancing serves the inclination to minimize any conflict between Paul and James, and it is thought that the conflict depicted in Gal 2:11–14 could not have involved James after the accord depicted in Acts 15 and Gal 2:1–10. But there was a conflict between Peter and Paul that even drew in Barnabas. Conflict with James should not be ruled out.

separated himself fearing those of the circumcision [party]," as did the other Jewish Christians (2:12–13). The circumcision party is to be identified with James and those who had come representing him to Antioch.[32] How to interpret the position of Peter is more difficult. He may have wavered from the Jerusalem position under the dominant influence of Paul until the messengers arrived from James. Raymond E. Brown[33] thinks that Acts 15:20 and Gal 2:12 suggest that the enforcement of the food laws associated with the name of James was not Peter's idea and that he acquiesced only under pressure.[34] Strangely, Meier[35] argues that, in this incident, Barnabas sided with Peter against Paul because Peter's influence was so strong. But, in this, Meier leaves out of account the authority of James which, once it was asserted by the delegation, caused Peter, Barnabas, and other Jewish Christians to defect also.

The situation in Antioch provided the first test of the accord for representatives from Jerusalem, and it was James who gave the definitive Jerusalem position, and Peter bowed to his leadership. James intervened through anonymous delegates (2:12) who are sometimes identified with the messengers of Acts 15:22–35. To do this it must be assumed that James sent them independently subsequent to the assembly. In that case they represented his views rather than the agreed and known position of the assembly. Their message did not concern minimal requirements for Gentiles but demanded fundamental separation of the two missions in the withdrawal of Jewish believers from table fellowship with Gentile believers.

It is rather dramatic to say that Peter withdrew, "fearing those of the circumcision party."[36] A precise translation is "fearing the circumcision," and it has been argued that unbelieving Jews in Antioch were the source of Peter's fears.[37] Peter feared the reaction of the Jews to the failure to keep the Jewish food and purity laws. But why should this fear emerge only after the appearance of the messengers from James? Fear of the circumcision *party* is implied by comparison with the use of the term in 2:1–10, in which James is portrayed as the party's leading representative. Given the status and standing of Peter, some great authority must have been behind the circumcision party and been the source of his fear. This can only be James. That Barnabas and the other Christian

---

[32] This is denied by Schoeps (p. 261) and W. Pratscher, *Der Herrenbruder Jacobus und die Jacobustradition* (Göttingen: Vandenhoeck & Ruprecht, 1987).

[33] Brown and Meier, p. 4.

[34] D. R. Catchpole ("Paul, James and the Apostolic Decree," *NTS* 23 [1977]: 428–44) argues that the decree was communicated for the first time by the messengers from James, who caused the problem in Antioch (Gal 2:12). But the problem was the reassertion of the demand for circumcision (2:14).

[35] Brown and Meier, p. 24.

[36] Paul's evaluation of Peter's response is charged with polemical passion.

[37] See R. B. Ward, "James of Jerusalem in the First Two Centuries," p. 784.

Jews also withdrew is significant, suggesting that Barnabas might not have been in full agreement with Paul's circumcision- and law-free mission to the nations. This interpretation is supported by our reading of Acts 15:36–41 above.

That Paul does not harken back to the accord in the debate with Peter indicates that he knew there was more than one way to read the accord.[38] There is no need to resort to the desperate measure of reversing the order of 2:1–10 and 2:11–14. After the making of the accord Paul accused Peter (and the others who had withdrawn) of hypocrisy because Peter had not lived consistently as a Jew himself and yet was attempting to compel Gentiles to live as Jews (2:11–14). Paula Fredrikson argues that the attempt to compel Gentiles to live as Jews was an innovation not only in the early Church but also in Judaism.[39] This is an overstatement, although Fredrikson makes a useful correction to the view that such a demand was the norm. The position of Peter outlined here goes beyond the maintenance of a circumcision mission to the Jews. A mission to Gentiles involving the demand of circumcision is indicated by the reference to compelling Gentiles to live as Jews in 2:14.[40] The issue that gave rise to this criticism was the demand that Gentile members of Paul's mission should be circumcised if they were to share in table fellowship with Jewish believers.[41]

The argument that follows (2:15–21) to the effect that no one, Jew or Gentile, is justified by the works of the law but only through faith in Jesus Christ is theologically more significant. Paul is dealing with an issue that was, for him, non-negotiable. The discussion leading to the accord did not work at this level. Rather there the discussion concerned the ground rules for two separate missions, to Jews and to the nations. What Paul now does, arising out of the conflict consequent on the intersection of the two missions, is to question the validity of the gospel of the circumcision, the gospel for which James was the figurehead but of which Peter (as well as Barnabas?) was also a representative.

The description indicates a conflict between Paul and the circumcision mission and rifts within the two missions. There is no evidence that James was involved in any mission to Gentiles. His activity was confined to the Jerusalem church. Even if it is thought that the Jerusalem community had an influence beyond its own boundaries, exclusive mission to Jews is one interpretation (James's) of the circumcision mission.

---

[38] See Betz, *Galatians,* p. 106.

[39] "Judaism, the Circumcision of Gentiles, and Apocalyptic Hope: Another Look at Galatians 1 and 2," *JTS* 42 (October 1991): 532–64.

[40] The use of ζῆς in the first half of the verse makes clear that what is in view is the attempt to compel Gentiles to live as Jews (τὰ ἔθνη ἀναγκάζεις ἰουδαϊκῶς).

[41] While there was now no absolute demand for circumcision, such as was expressed in Acts 15:1, 5, full table fellowship between the two missions was made to depend on the acceptance of the rules of the circumcision mission.

Peter undertook a mission to the Gentiles as part of the circumcision mission. His mission demanded the circumcision of converts, compelling them to live as Jews. If such a difference existed between James and Peter, other differences probably existed between them over the question of the relationship of the circumcision mission with the mission to the nations. Those differences emerged in Antioch.

Gal 2:11–14 narrates a conflict, not only between Paul and Peter but also with Barnabas. This conflict is one reason why Paul next teamed with Silas rather than with Barnabas. Galatians does not indicate this turn of events because it was written after the breach with Barnabas but before Paul teamed with Silas. The Silas named in Acts 15:22, 40; 16:19; 17:14; and 18:5 is probably named Silvanus by Paul in 2 Cor 1:19; 1 Thess 1:1 (cf. 1 Pet 5:12). Because Paul's letters confirm this teaming we must question whether Silas was entrusted with the "Jerusalem decree," if the account of the sending of this decree is historical.

After the conflict, whose views prevailed at Antioch? Did the views of Paul and/or Barnabas or the views of James and/or Peter prevail there? Did Paul's views win the day? It is often assumed that they did not. Streeter asserts: "If we are to associate the outlook of Antioch—the first capital of Gentile Christianity—with the name of any Apostle it will be with that of Peter."[42] Meier asserts, in common with Streeter: "But Peter, having won out over Paul at Antioch, may have remained the dominant figure there for some time. This may be the historical basis of the later, anachronistic tradition that Peter was the first bishop of Antioch. . . . Downey thinks that Matt 16.18 represents the tradition of Antioch concerning the foundation of the church there."[43] Why Meier appeals to Downey at this point is inexplicable, as Streeter had propounded this same view in 1924. Michael Goulder makes the point that the Petrines won the round at Antioch (Gal 2:11–14), but that in the long run (in the second century) the Pauline party won, as is shown by Christian non-observance of circumcision and Jewish purity laws; the Aramaic churches split away and became heretical sects.[44] R. P. Martin argues that the emissaries from James "were in a measure successful (Gal 2.13)" and that "Paul moved away from this base in Antioch, having suffered a defeat there."[45]

There is nothing in the letters of Paul or in Acts to suggest that the church at Antioch rejected Paul's understanding of the gospel and the mission. The suggestion that Acts portrays a break of relationship because Paul hardly visits

---

[42] *Primitive Church,* p. 45, and see p. 58.

[43] Brown and Meier, p. 24, and see also pp. viii, 39, 46.

[44] *A Tale of Two Missions* (London: SCM, 1994), 3, 108.

[45] *James,* Word Biblical Commentary 48 (Waco, Tex.: Word Books, 1988), xxxvi–xxxvii. See also J. D. G. Dunn, "The Incident at Antioch (Gal 2.11–18," *JSNT* 18 (1982): 3–57, and P. J. Hartin, *James and the Q Sayings of Jesus,* JSNTSS 47 (Sheffield: JSOT, 1991), 230.

Antioch after this point is not persuasive. Acts 15:30–35 narrates the return of Paul and Barnabas to Antioch, where they remain teaching and preaching the word of the Lord. Then the disagreement between Paul and Barnabas is described (15:36–41). This is as close as Acts comes to acknowledging the conflict that emerged in Antioch, not only between Paul and Peter but also between Paul and Barnabas (Gal 2:11–14). There is no hint of which side the church at Antioch might have taken in this disagreement.

The narrative of Acts portrays Paul's continuing relationship with Antioch. At the conclusion to the next phase of his mission, Paul returns to the church at Antioch and,

> After spending some time there he departed and went from place to place through the region of Galatia and Phrygia, strengthening all the disciples. (Acts 18:23)

To suggest that Paul did not stay long on the basis of the brevity of the reference is hardly convincing. Brevity is a consequence of the perspective of Acts, which is concerned to portray Paul's continuing mission. For this purpose Paul needs to move on. Acts 18:23 tells us that he stayed there "some time," which implies a significant stay.

That Paul did not visit Antioch at the conclusion of his "third" missionary journey is explicable in the light of his letters, especially Rom 15:25–33. Paul was preoccupied with the difficult situation awaiting him in Jerusalem, where he was to deliver "the collection" for the poor saints. Acts makes no mention of this in its account of Paul's meeting with James and the elders. Paul mentions the collection to Felix (Acts 24:17) to explain his presence in Jerusalem. Had Paul not been arrested we may reasonably suppose that, having fulfilled his obligations in Jerusalem, he would have made his way to Antioch. His failure to do so should not be construed as evidence of a rift between Paul and the church at Antioch.

The conclusion that Paul lost the contest arises from assumptions about the subsequent nature of Christianity at Antioch.[46] In particular Matthew, seen as a pro-Petrine document, is today widely thought to be the Gospel of the church at Antioch. Evidence for locating the writing of Matthew in Antioch is sparse, but there is reason to think that traditions now embodied in Matthew came to Antioch and that Matthew came to be influential there. A good case can also be made for arguing that Matthew, embodying the special source M, was fashioned in response to Paul's law-free mission and gives expression to a law-based

---

[46] Thus R. P. Martin (*James*, p. xxxvii) argues that "all the inferential evidence points to Antioch as the seat of the anti–Pauline missionaries."

mission. It can hardly be understood as a gradual dilution of Pauline Christianity in the years following the Jewish war. But this scenario does not presuppose that Paul lost the contest at Antioch.

The prominence of Matthew must be recognized alongside the continuing influence of Paul. Either at the time of the Jewish war, or immediately thereafter, refugees from the Jerusalem church arrived in Antioch, bringing with them their commitment to the ideology symbolized by James and the tradition expressing this ideology. This was more than fifteen years after Paul's dispute with Peter and Barnabas and the delegation from James.

Two Missions, Many Factions

There is some virtue in maintaining a simple vision of a conflict between two missions. To some extent the missions can be characterized in categories supplied by Acts. There the Jerusalem church is described in terms of two groups, the Hebrews and the Hellenists. They manifest a division originating in Judaism. The terms designate two broad Jewish orientations rather than factions, and there were serious divisions within these two. The orientations can be delineated in terms of language preference, Hebrew or Greek. Language reveals cultural preferences so that the Hebrews can be understood as conservatives, maintaining the old (Mosaic) traditions, while the Hellenists are to be seen as progressive, open to radical reinterpretation of the tradition in new situations. The Hebrews maintained the Mosaic law, including the practice of circumcision, while the Hellenists adopted an approach to mission that did not require circumcision, maintenance of the food and purity laws, or observance of the sabbath. It is probably an oversimplification to identify the Hellenists with the uncircumcision mission and the Hebrews with the circumcision mission but, given our present state of knowledge, this hypothesis makes a good deal of sense.

Clarity is no virtue if it obscures a more complex situation. Our approach attempts to do justice to clarity and complexity. The evidence of Galatians indicates two missions. But if the account in Acts is tendentious, so also is Paul's account in Galatians. A critical reading of Galatians provides evidence of a more complex situation that is supported by a critical reading of Acts. From reading Acts we suggest that there were as many as six factions within the two missions. Our analysis is clearer than it was for those who participated in the events because it has the benefit of hindsight. Yet there are many dark spots hidden from our knowledge.

Each of the two missions was made up of three factions. Some of the factions overlapped, while others were more or less opposed to one another.

The Circumcision Mission

The first three factions of the six were intent on maintaining Jewish identity and an ongoing mission to "the Jewish people."

FIRST FACTION.   It is evident in Acts 15:1, 5 and Gal 2:4, where Pharisaic believers insist that all believers (Jews and Gentiles) should be circumcised and keep the Mosaic law, that for this faction there was no salvation without full law observance. This faction was not party to the accord. We have no knowledge of its leading personalities, but James and Peter were not part of it. F. C. Baur ("Christuspartei") oversimplified the situation. He was not wrong, in his later work (*Paul*), in seeing James and Peter as part of the opposition to Paul, but they were not his most extreme opponents.

SECOND FACTION.   There were those who recognized the validity of the two missions but were themselves committed to the mission of and to the circumcision. For this group the uncircumcision mission was meant to be a mission exclusively to the Gentiles, and the mission to the Jews was focused on "Palestine," perhaps even primarily on Judaea. The missions were understood in both ethnic (cultural rather than genetic racial) and geographic terms. The leading exponent of this faction was James the brother of Jesus. While the other mission was acknowledged, this one assumed the total independence of the two missions but also the acceptance of the rules of the circumcision mission if the two intersected. Thus when members of this faction went outside Palestine they were required to be law observant. In this vein we are to understand the role of the messengers from James in Gal 2:12. Further, Jewish members of the uncircumcision mission were expected to keep the law. Hence not only Peter but also Barnabas and other Jews in Antioch came under pressure to comply with the demands of James. This faction allowed that the uncircumcision mission could operate on a law-free basis only in relation to Gentiles. If the "Jerusalem decree" is not a fiction, even the Gentiles were required to abstain from certain practices particularly offensive to Jews, although nothing in Acts suggests that observance of the Jerusalem decree provided a basis for full table fellowship between Jewish and Gentile believers. Rather these were the requirements laid on Gentiles living in Jewish territory.

Gentile converts were not actively sought, but proselytes were permitted to convert by submitting to the demands of the law. The primary objective of the mission was to maintain the messianic proclamation of Jesus to the Jews, and nothing that might compromise this objective was allowed to stand in the way. What Walter Schmithals says of the Jewish Christians of Palestine fits well the analysis of this faction. Schmithals notes that, from the early days, there was a "party," or faction, in the Jerusalem church that observed the law and another that did not. The Hellenists, those who did not observe the law, were persecuted by the Jews and fled from Jerusalem, while those who observed the law were unmolested. He continues: "Therefore, for the Jewish Christians in Palestine the question of their attitude to the Law was not only, perhaps not even principally, a theological problem, but a question of their existence as a Church in the Jewish land."[47]

Schmithals's insight should not obscure the importance of theological defense of the law for this faction. In the Gospels the M tradition now embodied in Matthew best represents the position of this faction. Because there was no active Gentile mission, there is little trace of this faction after the Jewish war.

THIRD FACTION.   Others acknowledged the validity of the two missions but understood the differences between them more in terms of the ground rules by which the two missions operated than in terms of the groups targeted. This third faction was committed to a mission based on circumcision and law-keeping. It was oriented primarily to all Jews, including the diaspora, and overflowed in a mission to Gentiles. An alternative mission to the Gentiles free from the demand of circumcision and the keeping of the Mosaic law was recognized. Peter was the most notable representative of this faction, and, in later times, the Gospel of Matthew gave expression to this group's views and supported the leadership of Peter. Evidence suggests that Peter traveled widely in his mission, which extended beyond Palestine to Corinth and Rome. Later evidence (e.g., from Nag Hammadi and the Pseudo-Clementines) portrays James in Jerusalem while Peter was occupied in a widespread mission. The incident at Antioch suggests that this faction supported the view that the rules of the home mission applied when the two missions intersected, although members of this faction were subject to pressure from the second faction, especially from James. Members of the third faction chose the "superior way" of circumcision and law-keeping for their own mission to both Jews and the nations. Matt 5:19 implies that circumcision and law keeping are not necessary to enter the kingdom of heaven, but those who did not meet these conditions and taught others to follow their example would be least in the kingdom. Very likely this was intended as a critique and evaluation of the Pauline mission to the nations and may have been common to the second and third factions.

These three factions broadly fit the description of the first of two types of Jewish believers distinguished by Justin (*Dialogues* 47):

1) Those who insisted that Gentile converts keep all aspects of the Mosaic law;
2) Those who kept the law themselves but did not insist that Gentile converts should do so.

---

[47] *Paul and James*, SBT 1/46 (London: SCM, 1965), 39.

The Uncircumcision Mission

Only the first of the factions described below reveals a concern to maintain Jewish identity, and it fits the second type of Jewish believer mentioned by Justin.

FOURTH FACTION. The fourth faction largely overlapped the third except that members were involved in mission to the Gentiles on a law-free basis. The third and fourth factions each recognized the validity of the other, the difference between them being that the one had chosen to maintain a dominant mission to the Jews while the other was confined to a mission to Gentiles. Their policy was that home rules applied when the missions intersected, but there was also the tendency to be influenced by James and the policy of the second faction on this issue, as illustrated in Gal 2:12. Jewish members of this fourth faction were law observant, Barnabas being the outstanding representative of this group, which might have been more ambivalent than the third on the question of the superiority of the circumcision mission and its gospel.

FIFTH FACTION. The fifth faction affirmed a mission to all the nations, including the Jews, a mission free from circumcision and the ritual elements of the Mosaic law. Paul was the leading exponent of this faction. While it acknowledged the expediency of a mission restricted to the Jews based on circumcision and the Mosaic law, the law-free mission to the nations was affirmed as the true expression of the gospel (Gal 2:15–21). Because the circumcision mission was viewed as an expediency, this faction adopted the view that home rules should apply and that there was a special case for adopting the rules of the circumcision mission in Jerusalem.[48]

Paul also affirmed the priority of the Jews: "to the Jew first" (Rom 1:16; 2:9, 10). The gospel was to the Jew first. That was a fact of history, and Paul's policy gave recognition to the Jerusalem church as the source of the whole Christian mission. He recognized the debt owed by the Gentile churches as a basis for his collection for the poor saints of Jerusalem (Rom 15:25–27). But Acts suggests another construction of that priority. According to the narrative, Paul programmatically offered the gospel first to the Jews, and only when it was rejected by them did he turn to the Gentiles (Acts 13:46). Yet this appears to be an oversimplification because, even in Acts, it is clear that the initial offer of the gospel in the synagogue was not restricted to Jews (Acts 13:44). Indeed it was reception by this broader audience that caused the Jews to reject the gospel (Acts 13:45). To the Jew first, as a principle, shows that Paul did not exclude the Jews from his mission to the nations. They were given some priority, recognizing their foundational role. But Paul was not ready to constrain the gospel

---

[48] See 1 Cor 9:19–23 and Acts 21:17–36, which tell how Paul, on the recommendation of James, submitted to Jewish practice on return to Jerusalem.

by restricting its scope to Jews or by subjecting those who responded to the demands of the Mosaic law. Nor was Paul willing, not even for a moment, to constrain the gospel to allow his own people opportunity to respond. Rather he argued that their present rejection of the gospel was the opportunity for the nations (Rom 11:11–12).

Given that Paul was himself a Jew and that, at the same time, he understood himself to be the apostle to the nations, the place of the Jews in the purposes of God was a thorny problem for him. It is not that his mission to the nations excluded the Jews. But his argument in Romans 9–11 suggests that he knew in his heart that his approach to mission jeopardized the success of the mission to the Jews. Had he not known, his opponents would certainly have made the point in no uncertain terms. But Paul was the prisoner of a vision, impelled by the conviction that the mission to the nations could not wait, nor could it be constrained by the demands of the Jewish law.

SIXTH FACTION. The sixth faction is not evident in Galatians, but in 1 Corinthians there is evidence of a faction that advocated an absolutely law free mission recognizing no constraints whatsoever, ritual or moral. No names can be put to this faction, but it was seriously opposed by Paul, although his name was sometimes associated with it (Rom 3:8). It is unlikely that this faction acknowledged the validity of the circumcision mission at all. Raymond E. Brown outlines a typology of four kinds of Christianity which overlaps the typology provided here.[49] In the fourth group, more radical in its rejection of Jewish festivals and worship than Paul, Brown identifies the Hellenists of Acts 6:1–6 and the Beloved Disciple of the Fourth Gospel. This group, as understood by Brown, lies somewhere between the fifth and sixth factions in our analysis. It seems overly simple to place the Hellenists all in one group or faction. Rather they appear to have been spread across what have been described as the fifth and sixth factions, groups marked by a spectrum of different positions. While the first three factions were intent on maintaining a Jewish identity, factions four to six, especially five and six, threatened to destroy the Jewish identity of the Christian movement. If James the brother of Jesus is the most notable representative of the first three groups, then Paul held that position for groups four through six. In the middle, Peter and Barnabas appear to hold mediating positions but from either side of the division of the two missions.

The typology of two missions recognized in six factions is obviously a simplification of what was a highly complex historical situation. It gathers nuanced shades of difference into six factions. This also inevitably hides overlapping agreements. Where possible we have sought to identify these. The typology is put forward as an advance on the view that assumes agreement of all parties or simple polarization of two opposed parties. Aided by the recogni-

---

[49] Brown and Meier, pp. 1–9.

tion of the tendentious nature of the sources, we are alerted by the evidence of Acts alone to the more complex situation, and the letters of Paul help us to see something of the different positions. Although we are dependent on sources dominated by the Pauline perspective, the role and influence of James emerges as a dominating factor.

1 Corinthians: Rivalry between James, Peter, and Paul

There are two important references relevant to James in 1 Corinthians. The first is in 9:5, while the second concerns the resurrection appearances described in 15:5–8.

1 Cor 9:5–6: The Role of Wives and Work in the Two Missions

In 1 Cor 9:5–6 Paul sets up a contrast between himself and Barnabas, on the one hand, and "the rest of the apostles and the brothers of the Lord and Cephas" (Peter), on the other. Given that Peter is named separately from the rest of the apostles, and Paul has no reason to deny Peter's apostleship, we should not conclude that the specific reference to the brothers of the Lord implies that they are not viewed as apostles. Rather it shows that, among the apostles, Peter and the brother of the Lord rated special mention. Reference to "the rest of the apostles" implies that Barnabas and Paul are also apostles.

Two things distinguish Barnabas and Paul from the others. The others traveled about with their wives and apparently did not need to work to support themselves but were supported in their mission (see also 1 Cor 9:14). This says nothing explicitly about whether Paul was married or not, though the idiom is strange if he was not. By implication he says that his wife did not travel with him and that it was necessary for him to work to support himself and his mission and that the same was true for Barnabas. Perhaps we should say of Paul that he chose to work so that the gospel could be offered free of charge.

Practice was divided on party lines. Those of the circumcision mission traveled with their wives, while those of the uncircumcision mission did not. This mention of travel opens up the possibility of activity of James in the diaspora. There is no evidence to confirm this possibility. At Corinth, where Paul's comment about the travel practices of the apostles, the Lord's brothers, and Peter was relevant, it is important to notice the evidence concerning party strife (1 Cor 1:10–12; 3:3–4:21). There is no mention of James or a James party here, but the Peter party is prominent. Perhaps that is why, of the brothers of the Lord and the apostles mentioned in 1 Cor 9:5, only Peter is named (as Cephas). This tends to confirm the view suggested by the evidence of Galatians, that when Paul encountered opposition from the circumcision mission in the diaspora, it was associated with Peter, although there might be influence of James in the background.

1 Cor 15:5–8: Rival Appearance Traditions

That the James mentioned in 1 Cor 15:7 is the brother of the Lord is readily recognized by commentators. This fact was already accepted by Eusebius (*HE* 1.12), who glosses his reference to 1 Cor 15:7: "He was seen by James— one of the reputed brothers of the Lord." Given that the appearance of the risen Jesus to Peter and the twelve is mentioned (and that these are mentioned in that order in 15:5), the only James notable enough to be mentioned in this company simply by name is James the brother of the Lord who was the pre-eminent figure in the Jerusalem church in Paul's time. The sequence of appearances is important, and there is little doubt that Paul meant this to be understood as a temporal sequence: first to Peter, then to the twelve, then to five hundred brethren at once, then to James, then to all the apostles, and last of all to Paul (15:5–8).[50] Many questions remain concerning the list of witnesses to the resurrected Jesus. Is the list traditional, apart from the reference to Paul? Is the tradition all of a piece or are there layers of tradition?

1 Cor 15:3b–7 is bounded by Paul's formula introduction in 3a and his account of Jesus' appearance to himself, which is given in the first person and is obviously not traditional. That 15:3b–7 is traditional is supported by:

1) similar formulations found in non-Pauline works (Mark 8:31; 9.31; 10:32–34; Acts 10:42; 2 Tim 2:8; 1 Pet 2:21–25; 3:18–22);
2) the concentration of non-Pauline language and stylistic features in the section;
3) the fact that the section is self-contained.

There are, however, difficult questions to be answered concerning how the tradition in 15.3b–7 came to be in its present form.

1 Cor 15:3b–4 is formally distinct from what follows. In this passage the death (according to the scriptures), burial, and resurrection (according to the scriptures) of Jesus are proclaimed without any mention of witnesses. There is a formal distinction between the proclamation of the gospel data (15.3b–4) and the list of witnesses (15:5–7). But there was hardly need to provide evidence of the death and burial of Jesus. Rather, what was needed was evidence that his death was according to the scriptures. While this was also affirmed of the resurrection, credible evidence of the resurrection was more important. The judgment that 15:3b–4 is the earliest part of the tradition is based on the assumption that there was no empty tomb and that there were no resurrection appearances.

---

[50] The apparent temporal sequence has been questioned, but the sequence of first to Peter and last of all to Paul makes unlikely the attempt to read the εἶτα ... ἔπειτα ... ἔπειτα ... εἶτα ... ἔσχατον δὲ πάντων without reference to temporal sequence.

Contrary to this view, Paul and the Gospels base the resurrection faith on the appearances of the risen Jesus.

Hans Conzelmann argues that the linguistic evidence supports the view that the tradition includes the appearance to Peter (consistent with Luke 24:34) and then to the twelve (see Acts 1:22) in verse 5.[51] Others consider that the earliest tradition includes 15:6a (15:6b is Pauline commentary). Against this, Conzelmann argues that 15:6 is a new grammatical construction.

1 Cor 15.7 commences in the same way as 15:6 (ἔπειτα ὤφθη). If the evidence suggests that 15:3b–7 (apart from 6b) is pre-Pauline, then it would seem that either 15:6a and 7 belong to the same stratum of the tradition or that 15:7 was modeled on 15:6a. Indeed the appearance to James and all the apostles is part of a sequence beginning with 15:5.

and he appeared [ὤφθη] to Cephas, then [εἶτα] to the twelve; (15.5)

next [ἔπειτα] he appeared [ὤφθη] to over five hundred brethren at once; (15:6a)

next [ἔπειτα] he appeared [ὤφθη] to James, then [εἶτα] to all the apostles. (15:7)

In each verse (15:5, 6, 7) there is a single use of "he appeared." Like 15:6, 15:7 connects the sequence by the use of "next," which is absent from 15:5 because it comes first in the sequence. But 15:7, like 15:5, describes two appearances, although the verb "he appeared" is used only once in each case.

According to Adolf von Harnack, the tradition assumes that Jesus first appeared to Peter in Galilee before appearing to James in Jerusalem and that the appearance to James was subsequent to the appearance to the five hundred brethren at Pentecost.[52] Harnack argues that 15:5 and 15:7 reflect a shift from the leadership of Peter and the twelve in Jerusalem to the leadership of James. Pratscher, building on the work of Harnack, argues that 15:7 is based on 15:5 and is a *Rivalitätsformel* reflecting the rivalry between the followers of James and the followers of Peter.[53] Lüdemann develops a similar position but refers to "legitimization formulae."[54] A complementary position is expressed by Streeter concerning Matt 16:18, "You are Peter . . ."; Streeter argues that this formula

---

[51] *1 Corinthians: A Commentary on the First Epistle to the Corinthians,* Hermeneia (Philadelphia: Fortress, 1975), 251. Each of the assertions in 15:3b–5 begins with a ὅτι–clause.

[52] "Die Verklärungsgeschichte Jesus, der Bericht des Paulus [1 Kor 15.3ff.] und die beiden Christusvisionen des Petrus," *SPAW. PH* (1922): 62–80, esp. 62–68.

[53] Pratscher, pp. 35–46.

[54] *Opposition,* pp. 46–52, esp. 51–52.

was not opposed to the authority of Pauline leadership but to the leadership of James and the extreme Judaizers.[55]

In these formulae (1 Cor 15:5, 7) the followers of Peter and James each asserted that the risen Lord had first appeared to their leader. If the original leadership of Peter is accepted the *Rivalitätsformel* reflects a change of leadership in the Jerusalem church. Lüdemann fixes the time of this shift between Paul's first and second visits to Jerusalem, and appeal has been made to Gal 1:18–19; 2:9; and Acts 12:17 to support this view. Alternatively, we have argued that there was continuing tension between James and Peter (Gal 2:11–14).

Paul's use of composite tradition does not suggest rivalry between Peter and James. Rivalry is evident, but it is the distinctive appearance to Paul that is controversial. In Paul's use of the tradition, Peter and James stand together against him. The appearances of the risen "Christ" to them were part of the regular order, while Paul was forced to argue for the validity of the irregular appearance to himself. This circumstance is reflected in the formula introduction ("last of all") and the extended explanation (15:8–10). In 1 Corinthians 15 Paul neither sees in the tradition in verse 7 a basis for setting the authority of James before Peter nor does he treat that tradition as a rival to the Petrine tradition. The view that it is, is the consequence of scholarly reconstruction. Lüdemann correctly argues, however, that the polemical use made of the tradition by Paul does not preclude another context and use of the tradition at its source.[56] Here it is possible to see the imposition of Petrine leadership as the later move. This view is supported by the recognition that Matthew develops the view of Petrine leadership on the basis of Mark, from which the tradition used by Matthew is absent.

The formal identity of the confessions in 15:5 and 7 shows that they express conflict. Because the role of the twelve soon vanished from Jerusalem, they are not mentioned by Paul in Galatians; it is argued that reference to the appearance to them belongs to early tradition in which the authority of Peter was paramount. Understood as an alternative tradition, 15:7 asserts that the foundational appearance was to James. This is supported by the quotation from the gospel to the Hebrews translated by Jerome (*De vir. ill. 2*): "But the Lord, after he had given his grave clothes to the servant of the priest, appeared to James." In the place of the twelve 1 Cor 15:7 mentions "all of the apostles" who (contrary to the view of Harnack) are to be understood as more inclusive than the twelve, though still a restricted group which does not include Paul, only because his exceptional commissioning had not yet been narrated. When Paul does narrate the event, he claims the title of apostle, noting the exceptional circumstances (15:8–10).

---

[55] *The Four Gospels*, p. 258.
[56] *Opposition*, pp. 52–53.

The formulation of neither 15:5 nor of 15:7 specifically says "first to Cephas," "first to James." Had this been the case in the tradition, Paul would need to have assimilated the two confessions into a comprehensive list including both Peter and James because there cannot be two firsts in the same series. The argument assumes that in each case a first appearance is claimed, on the one hand to Cephas and on the other to James, and that the claims were made by rival groups asserting priority for their own leader. While an underlying tension between James and Peter is evident, Paul saw the two as part of the common circumcision mission.

CHAPTER 4

JAMES, PETER, MATTHEW, AND PAUL

Diversity and Conflict in the Two Missions

For F. C. Baur, Peter was the leading figure in the circumcision party, the outstanding opponent of Paul. Peter confronted Paul in Antioch, and his party caused trouble at Corinth. He failed to recognize the dominating influence of James behind Peter in his conflict with Paul.

PETER AND JAMES AS OPPONENTS OF PAUL

James differed from the hard-line Pharisaic Christians of Acts 15:1, 5 in recognizing a law-free mission to Gentiles but was resolute in demanding that the mission to the circumcision observe the law completely. At Antioch Peter wavered at first or perhaps was inclined to follow Paul's understanding of the two missions strategy. But he was part of the circumcision mission, the mission that demanded circumcision of those who became a part of it. Baur rightly recognized the relevance of 1 Corinthians for this debate. The problems caused by the presence of Peter in Corinth support the view that he, along with James, continued to assert the authority of the law.

The Peter party at Corinth should be seen as the Judaizing party and the major opponent to Paul. There is no evidence to suggest that the party misrepresented Peter or that he was a reluctant leader of it. Consequently, we must align Peter and James more closely than is often done. Without 1 Corinthians it might have been possible to argue that Peter reluctantly adopted the Judaizing position only under pressure from James. But there is no evidence of any influence of James at Corinth. No James party is mentioned, confirming that Peter was the main missionary of the pillar apostles of the circumcision party outside Judaea. Peter differed from James in extending the mission beyond "Palestine" and in actively seeking to extend the mission to Gentiles, even if this aspect of the mission was secondary to the mission to Jews.

PETER AND JAMES AND THE LEADERSHIP QUESTION

Although Cephas and James stand close together as representatives of the circumcision party, evidence of a leadership struggle surrounds these two figures. Historically it is likely that James was the first leader of the Jerusalem church. In Acts Luke tried to reconcile conflicts and to reconcile the later tradition of Petrine leadership in the church at large with the tradition of the original leadership of James in Jerusalem. This strategy was possible because of the prominence of the public role of Peter from the beginning. The evidence of the authority of James over Peter, even exercised at a distance, is demonstrated in Gal 2:11–14, and there is no reason to think that the situation was different at the beginning of the Jerusalem church.

There were traditions that rejected the leadership of both Peter and the twelve and of James and the family of Jesus. Mark is critical of the twelve and of Peter. After the confession of Peter at Caesarea Philippi (Mark 8:27–30) Mark describes the way Jesus spoke to Peter, calling him Satan.

> "Get behind me Satan, because you do not mind the things of God but the things of men." (Mark 8:33)

In this way Mark puts the leadership of the twelve in question. But this does not mean that he establishes the leadership of the natural family of Jesus and of James. Rather Mark shows that the natural family is displaced by the eschatological family (Mark 3:31–35). Just what shape this leadership would have taken is unclear, though Mark may have looked to Pauline leadership. Luke abbreviated this section of Mark (Luke 8:19–21), omitting reference to Jesus' looking around at the crowd that was listening to him (Mark 3:34), a reference which implies that they are the true family; Luke also omits the question

> "Who is my mother and brothers?" (Mark 3:33; Matt 12:48)

The question implies that the natural family is not the true family; without the question, the statement of Luke 8:21 can include them:

> "My mother and my brothers are those who hear the word of God and do it."

Thus Luke allows that the family of Jesus, as much as the twelve or any other hearers, can be true family if they obey the word that they hear.

It is commonly recognized that Matthew does not follow Mark in his critical presentation of the role of the twelve and of Peter in particular. Matthew does not include the reference to the disciples and their attempt to restrain Jesus (Mark 3:20–21). While Matthew reports Jesus' reference to Peter as Satan (Matt

16:23), which Luke omits, only Matthew has the immediate response of Jesus to Peter's confession of him as the Christ in the following terms.

> "Blessed are you Simon son of John, because flesh and blood has not revealed this to you but my Father who is in heaven. And I say to you that you are Peter, and upon this rock I will build my Church, and the gates of Hades will not stand against it. I will give you the keys of the kingdom of heaven, and whatever you bind on earth will be bound in heaven, and whatever you loose on earth will be loosed in heaven." (Matt 16:17–20)

These words, addressed directly to Peter, support a tradition of Petrine leadership, even if the scope of that authority is explicitly broadened in another passage peculiar to Matthew. In Matt 18:18, the last part of this saying to Peter, which deals with the authority of binding and loosing, is addressed to all of the disciples who are identified as the audience in Matt 18.1 (cf. John 20:23). Nevertheless, Matthew upholds the tradition of the leadership of Peter in the church as the leading representative of "the twelve."

Michael Goulder argues that the Gospels need to be understood in relation to their loyalty to one or other of the two missions.[1] He argues that Luke and John are Pauline Gospels, while Mark and Matthew form bridges to the Jerusalem mission. This is something of an oversimplification because the two missions were themselves divided into factions, and the Gospels are expressions of these. Mark does not fit the Jerusalem mission, and John must be located independently of Paul. Though embodying traditions shaped by the factions before the Jewish war, the Gospels attained their final form in the period following the war.

MATTHEW AND THE GENTILE MISSION

Matthew is widely thought to be a Jewish Gospel adapted to the situation of the Gentile mission following the Jewish war and as a result of the emergence of Formative Judaism, which excluded from the Jewish community those who believed Jesus to be the Messiah.[2] A minority of scholars think of Matthew as a Gentile Gospel.[3] Either way, Matthew, in its final form, is understood as directed to the Gentile mission. Against this view I have long taught that Mat-

---

[1] *A Tale of Two Missions,* pp. x, 41, 42, 44, 74, 93, 94.

[2] Thus W. D. Davies and D. C. Allison, *Matthew: A Critical and Exegetical Commentary on the Gospel according to Saint Matthew,* 2 vols. (Edinburgh: T & T Clark, 1988, 1991).

[3] Thus G. Strecker, *Der Weg der Gerichtigkeit: Untersuchung zur Theologie des Matthäus* (Göttingen: Vandenhoeck & Ruprecht, 1971), 34–35, and K. W. Clark, "The Gentile Bias in Matthew," *JBL* 66 (1947): 165–72.

thew is a Jewish Gospel from the circumcision mission proclaiming Jesus as Messiah and taking in a mission to the nations on these terms.

Evidence concerning the circumcision mission reflects a situation around 50 CE. If Matthew was written around 85 CE, can we suppose that a mission based on circumcision and the demands of the law was maintained until this time? That such a mission was sustained, especially in Jerusalem, until the Jewish war scarcely needs to be argued. After the destruction of Jerusalem we might doubt the survival of that mission. But members of the Jerusalem church were dispersed, and we should think of worsening relations between Jews who believed Jesus to be the Messiah and other Jews, rather than of an immediate breakdown of relations. The pressures of Formative Judaism are likely to have strengthened the resolve of the circumcision mission to maintain fidelity to the Mosaic law rather than making that mission irrelevant.

B. H. Streeter and the Conflict between the Two Missions

It is generally thought that the *Sitz im Leben* of Matthew was Antioch.[4] An early exponent of this view was B. H. Streeter, whose views are complex and worth restating.[5] In dating Matthew around 85 CE in Antioch Streeter is part of the contemporary consensus. But his understanding of the composition of Matthew is nuanced and provides a basis for understanding conflicting tendencies. Streeter was ahead of his time in asserting the diversity of earliest Christianity, stressing the importance of the different great cities that were centers of Christian community. Streeter's *The Four Gospels* was first published in 1924, some years before Walter Bauer's celebrated *Orthodoxy and Heresy in Earliest Christianity*. In addition to the sources of Matthew, Streeter identified the special Lukan source (L) from Caesarea around 60 CE and the special source of the Lukan infancy narrative, as well as the Johannine tradition from Ephesus.[6] He located the major Gospel sources in different cities, and this enabled him to account for differences in the sources by means of the differences in the character of Christianity in those cities. Streeter also related the Gospel sources and the Gospels themselves to the factionalism of early Christianity.

Tradition associated with Antioch includes the important "You are Peter . . ." of Matt 16:18. The Greek translation of Q, which Streeter dates around 50 CE, was probably the original Gospel of Antioch.[7] It is unclear where the Q tradition originated, although it was probably by Matthew and written in Aramaic.[8] The M tradition was produced in Jerusalem, expressing the au-

---

[4] See Brown and Meier, pp. ix, 15, 22–29.

[5] *The Four Gospels,* pp. 16, 500–527; *The Primitive Church,* pp. 58–65.

[6] See *The Primitive Church,* pp. ix, 44, 50–65. The whole book addresses the question of the role of the great centers of early Christian community.

[7] *The Four Gospels,* p. 513.

[8] Ibid., p. 232.

thority of James the Just, the brother of Jesus. James was the leader of the "Palestinian" Christians who zealously observed the law and worshipped in the Temple.[9] At the onset of the Jewish war the Jerusalem Christians fled, some to Pella while others went to Antioch, to which the refugees from the first persecution had fled and where they had founded a church (Acts 11:19–20) that maintained links with Jerusalem (Acts 11:28). It was natural, therefore, for a second wave of refugees to flee to Antioch.

When the Jerusalem refugees came to Antioch they brought with them their collection of the sayings of Jesus (M). This interpretation of the Jesus tradition was a reaction against what was perceived as Petro-Pauline liberalism in relation to Gentile mission and observance of the law. It came with the authority of James, enhanced by his recent martyrdom in 62 CE. Antioch, like Corinth, was divided by parties. The James tradition (M) strengthened the party of strict law observers. Previously the pro-Gentile mission party and the Jamesian circumcision, law-keeping party had been held together somewhat artificially and precariously by the Q tradition, which was more or less neutral on the question of Gentile mission and law-keeping. Peter was seen as a middle term between James and Paul in the Antiochene tradition, which embodied the slogan of the via media party ascribing the power of binding and loosing to Peter (Matt 16:18–19).[10] The slogan was not aimed against the leadership of Paul but against the leadership of James and the extreme Judaizers.[11] The coming of the Jerusalem refugees with M upset this delicate balance with an attack on what the Jerusalem refugees perceived to be Petro-Pauline liberalism.

About the same time the Gospel of Mark arrived from Rome and was hailed by the more liberal pro-Gentile party as the Gospel of Antioch's own apostle (Peter).[12] Thus, in Antioch, M and Mark were read side by side, helping to create conditions conducive to conciliation. The process was aided by: 1) a continuing tradition of Christian mission; 2) awareness that James, Peter, and Paul had not repudiated each other and all had been martyred recently; 3) the destruction of the Temple in 70 CE, which meant that half of the requirements of the law could no longer be fulfilled and suggested that Paul may have been right in asserting that Christ supersedes the law; 4) the fact that the Jews who stood for the old law had become the bitter enemies of Christians.

If these points suggest a situation favoring the law-free party, then it needs to be remembered that the Judaistic words of Jesus in M could not be and were not set aside. They were explored and reinterpreted in Matthew's Gospel which made use of a new exegesis in order to reconcile both parties. Here the restric-

---

[9] Ibid., pp. 511–12.
[10] Ibid., pp. 514–15.
[11] Ibid., p. 258.
[12] Ibid., p. 513.

tion of mission to the lost sheep of the house of Israel (M in Matt 10:6) was made to apply only to the time of Jesus' ministry, while the universal mission was commanded after the resurrection of Jesus (Matt 28:19–20). J. P. Meier, among others, now adopts this position. That universal mission is also foreshadowed in Matt 8:11. The five discourses of Matthew do, however, parallel the five books of the law and give expression to the teaching tradition of M with its demands. This tension makes good sense when it is seen to be an expression of the practice of Jesus, supported by James in relation to the practice of the later church, which was based on the position of Peter.

Streeter situates Matthew as a response to Jewish persecution subsequent to the Jewish war and at a time of imminent apocalyptic end expectation.[13] In relation to his sources Matthew increases the stress on imminence (Matt 10:23; 24:29; 26:64) and reference to the end of the age, with its trauma and "weeping and gnashing of teeth" (six times in Matthew and once in Luke and nowhere in the rest of the New Testament). The anti-Christ remains personal in Matthew and may well be associated with expectation of Nero *redivivus*. Three pretenders are known to have made their claims, in 69, 80, and 89 CE.

MATTHEW AND ANTIOCH

Today there are few who dissent from the view that the *Sitz im Leben* of Matthew was Antioch.[14] Yet there is little concrete evidence to support this view. While rejecting the view that Paul lost the struggle with Peter at Antioch, it is argued here that the position of the Jerusalem church (Peter) became dominant there after the Jewish war, perhaps as a consequence of the dispersal of (some members of) the Jerusalem church to Antioch and in the face of the growing influence of Formative Judaism. Thus only after the Jewish war were the more radical demands of the position of James successfully exerted at Antioch, and then they were moderated in their effect by the influence of Peter. Even this development was understood in the context of the Pauline legacy of continuing active universal mission.

Those who find the *Sitz im Leben* of Matthew in Antioch make use of evidence of the relationship of Matthew to the *Didache*.[15] But the evidence for situating the *Didache* in Antioch is as problematical as that in support of Matthew. When we do encounter tradition that is unquestionably from Antioch (the letters of Ignatius), it is explicitly Pauline in character, even if the form of

---

[13] Ibid., pp. 518, 523.

[14] A. F. Segal ("Matthew's Jewish Voice," *Social History of the Matthean Community,* ed. D. L. Balch [Minneapolis: Fortress, 1991], 26–29) argues for a Galilean origin of Matthew, as does J. A. Overman, *Matthew's Gospel and Formative Judaism: The Social World of the Matthean Community* (Minneapolis: Fortress, 1990).

[15] Streeter, *The Four Gospels,* pp. 507–11, and Brown and Meier, pp. 73, 81–84.

Paulinism is that of the early second century rather than of the time of Paul. Ignatius (*Eph* 12.2) looked to Paul as his prototype, and his letters show that he knew and used the letters of Paul. Ignatius also knew and used Matthew.[16] But by the time of Ignatius, Matthew was widely used.

Dating the letters of Ignatius is a problem. On the one hand Eusebius, in *Chronicles*, suggests a date of 107–108 CE but provides no evidence for this date apart from locating the events in the reign of Trajan (98–117 CE). On the other hand his list of the bishops of Antioch makes a date as late as 135 CE possible. Consequently a date between 105 and 135 CE is appropriate.[17] Within that range of dates there was ample time for Ignatius to become familiar with Matthew. Thus evidence to support the composition of Matthew in Antioch is not as clear or convincing as evidence of its use. Problems also emerge in the attempt to show that the form of Christianity at Antioch provides an intelligible *Sitz im Leben* for that Gospel. "The broad social and religious context reflected in Ignatius is not all that sets Ignatius apart from the Gospel of Matthew. The theological climate in which Ignatius worked also had undergone a sea of change."[18]

Clearly there is no straight line of development from Matthew to Ignatius either in terms of the situation reflected in Matthew and in Antioch at the time of Ignatius or in terms of the theology of Matthew and of Ignatius. The continuing influence of Paul on Ignatius sets him apart from Matthew, so that it must be said that the tradition of reading Matthew as mediated to Ignatius has lost its Judaizing edge. By then the influence of the M tradition had been thoroughly assimilated to the Petrine position and even that had been swallowed up and read in the light of the universal mission of the Great Church. Indeed a case can be made for understanding Ignatius's attack on Judaizers as aimed at Christians, "uncircumcised Gentiles who have developed an interest in things Jewish."[19] That Matthew was not read from an anti-Pauline perspective also suggests that the conflict with Paul lay in the distant past when the Gospel was first read in Antioch.

Matthew is an expression of the Petrine tradition, reinforcing Petrine leadership against the tradition that sought to reinforce the leadership of the family of Jesus and against the Pauline understanding of Christianity. This assessment differs from Streeter's view of a Petro-Pauline alliance at Antioch by distancing Peter from Paul, giving full weight to the conflict between Peter and Paul expressed in Gal 2:11–14 and in 1 Corinthians.

---

[16] See Streeter, *The Four Gospels,* pp. 504–7, and W. R. Schoedel, "Ignatius and the Reception of Matthew in Antioch," *Social History of the Matthean Community,* pp. 154, 175.

[17] Schoedel, p. 130.

[18] Ibid., p. 151.

[19] Ibid., pp. 144–45.

Petrine tradition is evident in the way Matthew handles the traditions concerning the authority of Peter and the twelve. Here it is necessary to question the Petrine tradition in relation to Mark. Mark is to be seen as a Pauline Gospel.[20] It is Matthew, in its final form, that is the Petrine Gospel. Matthew sets the authority of Peter and the twelve over the authority of the family of Jesus. In this Peter is seen in opposition to the authority of James and his successors. But Matthew's understanding of the gospel is an expression of the mission of the circumcision and a reconciliation of the positions of both Peter and James. Consistent with James and Peter, Matthew maintains a law-based mission, but, following Petrine practice, the finished Gospel directs that mission to the nations. Nevertheless Matthew preserves more adequately than any other source the way James interpreted the teaching of Jesus. For this reason a discussion of the law in Matthew is critical for our understanding of James.

THE LAW IN MATTHEW

Matt 5:17–20

Matt 5:17–20 programmatically sets out Matthew's understanding of the law in opposition to Formative Judaism and Pauline Christianity.

> "Do not suppose that I have come to destroy the law and the prophets; I have not come to destroy but to fulfill. Truly I say to you, until heaven and earth pass away, one *iota* or one *keraia* shall certainly not pass away from the law, until all things are fulfilled.[21] Whoever breaks one of the least of these commandments and teaches the same to others, he will be called least in the kingdom of heaven; but whoever does and teaches [these commandments], this person will be called great in the kingdom of heaven.[22] For I say to you, unless your righteousness exceeds that of the scribes and Pharisees, you will certainly not enter the kingdom of heaven." (Matt 5:17–20)

J. P. Meier and others think that the qualification "until all these things are fulfilled" means that in Matthew's interpretation of the teaching of Jesus some aspects of the Jewish law were no longer in force, having been already fulfilled, at least subsequent to the resurrection of Jesus if not as a consequence of the ministry of Jesus. The conflict between the command of Matt 10:6, which

[20] See my *Reading Mark: Worlds in Conflict* (London: Routledge, 1997), 4–6.

[21] Compare Luke 16:17 and see Matt 24:35 = Mark 13:31 = Luke 21:33 for a comparable saying about the words of Jesus.

[22] Streeter (*The Four Gospels,* pp. 256–57) sees the criticism aimed at Paul, while the praise has James the Just in view. H. D. Betz (*Essays on the Sermon on the Mount* [Philadelphia: Fortress, 1985], 20) agrees that Paul is the target of Matt 5:17–20.

restricts the mission to the lost sheep of the house of Israel, and the command to embark on a universal mission in 28:19–20 is also explained on the basis that the resurrection has intervened, bringing about that change. But those who adopt this view have not taken account of the fact that Matthew provides no instance of a biblical law that has passed away. In Matthew there is nothing to suggest that any aspect of the law has already been fulfilled and is no longer in force. Rather Matthew's interpretation provides an understanding of the intensified demands of the law.

Here Matthew is fighting on two fronts. He is confronting the continuing challenge of Pauline Christianity as perceived in his time. Paul and his contemporary (with Matthew) successors are portrayed as those who do not keep the commandments and teach others to break them as well (Matt 5:19 and cf. Acts 21:21). Streeter is right in seeing this criticism aimed against Paul, while the praise has James the Just in view. This strand of tradition, which is peculiar to Matthew (M), stems from James and Jerusalem but became embodied in what was to become ultimately a Petrine Gospel.

While Paul was a target of the M tradition, the primary target of the criticism in Matthew is the group described as the scribes and Pharisees who, in Matthew's time, are represented by Formative Judaism. In response to the criticism of Formative Judaism, Matthew makes clear that loyalty to the law is fundamental for the followers of Jesus, and Formative Judaism falls under the critique of Matthew's understanding of the law. Robert H. Gundry argues that Matthew's "antithetical manner puts distance between Matthew's community and anything recognizably Judaistic."[23] This argument overlooks the fact that, in spite of the antithetical form, the antitheses are not against the law. They do not advocate breaking or dispensing with the law but are intensifications of it. The righteousness of disciples must exceed the righteousness of the scribes and Pharisees. This means a more stringent interpretation of the demands of the law, a view expressed in material that is largely peculiar to Matthew (M).

The more stringent interpretation of the law is given in the six antitheses of Matt 5:21–48. Some of the antitheses and the adversative form of all are peculiar to Matthew (M). The adversative form, "You have heard that it was said to those of old. . . . But I say to you . . . ," suggests that the position of Jesus is new and is opposed to the old position that is to be found in the law.[24] This is, to some extent, misleading. Certainly this form gives expression to a polemical position, but the old is opposed only in one sense. The law, *as interpre-*

---

[23] "A Responsive Evaluation of the Social History of the Matthean Community in Roman Syria," *Social History of the Matthean Community,* p. 65.

[24] (1) Matt 5:21 and Exod 20:13; 21:12; Deut 5:17; Lev 2:17; (2) Matt 5:27 and Exod 20:14; Deut 5:18; (3) Matt 5:31 and Deut 24:1; (4) Matt 5:33 and Lev 19:12; Num 30:2; Deut 23:21; (5) Matt 5:38 and Exod 21:24; Lev 24.20; Deut 19:21; (6) Matt 5:43 and Lev 19:18.

ted by Formative Judaism, was opposed by the law as interpreted by the Matthean Jesus. Matthew does not propose breaking the law as interpreted by "those of old," who represent the position of Formative Judaism. Rather, Matthew proposes a more radical and demanding interpretation of the law, and this proposal is foreshadowed in the demand:

> "Unless your righteousness exceeds the righteousness of the scribes and Pharisees you will not enter the kingdom of heaven." (Matt 5:20)

The antitheses set out the demand for greater righteousness. There is nothing here to suggest any relaxation of the demands of the law.

Matthew and Q: Matt 11:12–13

Matt 11:12 (= Luke 16:16) is in tension with the distinctively Matthean Matt 5:17–20. This might be explained by Streeter in terms of Matthew's failure to reconcile conflicting tendencies in the generally neutral Q with the Judaistic M.

> "From the days of John the Baptist until now the kingdom of heaven suffers violence and violent people attack it. For all the prophets and the law prophesied until John."

First, we note the form of this Q saying in Luke 16:16:

> "The law and the prophets were until John; from then on the kingdom of God is preached and every one violently enters into it."

Matthew and Luke have treated this saying quite differently. Matthew has placed it in the context of his account of Jesus' witness to the role and significance of John the Baptist (Matt 11:7–19). Matthew's composition brings together John the Baptist and Jesus, shaping the Q saying to set John the Baptist on the side of fulfillment with Jesus, not with the law and the prophets. This alignment is made clear by the identification of John the Baptist with the eschatological coming of Elijah at this point (Matt 11:14, which is without parallel in Luke). Matthew also presents the message of the Baptist in exactly the same terms as the message of Jesus. Both are messengers of the kingdom who preach:

> "Repent; for the kingdom of heaven is at hand." (Matt 3.2; 4.17)

For Matthew this means that John the Baptist has been moved in the direction of the new order. He is not the last representative of the old but a representative of the new order. But Matthew's view can only be maintained by moving his understanding of Jesus in the direction of the old order at the same time. This shift is clear in the way Matthew treats Jesus' interpretation of the law. It is also to be found in the continuity between John and Jesus as messengers of cataclysmic judgment. The continuity is also evident in the account of the sending out of the twelve which includes the instruction of what they are to preach. This is identical to the message of Jesus and John, apart from the absence of the call to repent. They are to preach, "The kingdom of heaven is at hand" (Matt 10:7).

Matt 10:1–16

In Matthew's account of the sending out of the twelve Jesus commands the disciples:

> "Do not go into a way of the Gentiles, and do not enter a city of the Samaritans; but go rather to the lost sheep of the house of Israel." (Matt 10:5–6)

They are commanded to announce the arrival of the kingdom of heaven (Matt 10:7), to heal the sick, raise the dead, cleanse the lepers, and cast out demons (10:8) and to restrict the scope of their mission to Israel (10:5–6). That this charge expresses the understanding of the circumcision mission is confirmed by the fact that this command is peculiar to Matthew (M), where it indicates a restriction of the Jerusalem mission of the James faction. In Matthew this came to be understood as a limitation confined to the time of the mission of Jesus. Matthew understood that the mission was extended to the nations after the resurrection of Jesus but was based on the necessity of circumcision and the keeping of the law, which was the position of the Petrine faction.

Matthew and Mark

Matt 15:1–20 is based on Mark 7:1–23. Differences caused by Matthew's editing are illuminating. Although Matthew, like Mark, notes that the washing of hands before eating is a tradition of the elders, he omits Mark's reference to the fact that this practice was observed by the Pharisees and all the Jews (Mark 7:3). Because Matthew rejected this tradition without repudiating his Jewishness, it was in his interest to reduce the weight of Jewish support for it. Likewise, although Matthew shares with Mark the argument put forward by Jesus that food that goes into the belly and passes out of the body cannot defile a person but rather what proceeds out of the heart defiles a person, the conclusions that are explicitly drawn by Matthew and Mark are quite different. In both Gospels the argument is put forward to counter the accusation arising from the failure of the disciples to observe the tradition of the elders. The explicit conclusion drawn by (the narrator) Mark is that Jesus had declared all food to be clean (Mark 7:19), thus rejecting the Jewish food laws. This conclusion is absent from Matthew, and, given that Matthew has made use of Mark, we must assume that Matthew has rejected this conclusion. The explicit conclusion drawn by Matthew that "to eat with unwashed hands does not defile a person" (Matt 15:20) is explicitly absent from Mark, though it is implied. Matthew's rejection of Mark's conclusion implies the continuing force of the food laws for Matthew and his community, confirming that we have a form of mission based on circumcision and the observance of the law as understood in Matthew's presentation of Jesus' interpretation of the law. What Matthew rejected was the tradition of the elders, the extended interpretation of the law of Formative Judaism.

Matt 28:19–20

That the mission implied in Matthew, though based on circumcision and observance of the law, also had Gentiles in view is made clear by the narrative of the resurrection appearance and commission of Jesus to the eleven disciples to "go and make disciples of all the nations." If the Jews are included in the description "all the nations," it is clear that the mission cannot be confined to Israel, as was the case in Matt 10:5–6. The earlier restriction of the mission must now be understood as applying only to the time of Jesus' ministry. The form of the later commission signals the scope of the mission of the Matthean community and should be carefully examined. There is no command here to proclaim the gospel to all people. Rather the command is:

1) Make disciples of all nations. Focus on the new universalism of the mission has obscured what the mission was to accomplish. It is not the proclamation of the gospel but the communication of a life style to which the nations are to conform.
2) Baptize them. Baptism was important for the Matthean community but there is nothing to suggest that it took the place of circumcision. Rather the demand for the greater righteousness suggests that the requirement of baptism was an additional, not an alternative requirement.
3) Teach them to observe all the commandments of Jesus. This signals a law-based mission where the commands of Jesus are to be found in his interpretation of the law in its intensified form as found in Matthew.

What we find in Matthew is a mission based on the observance of the law. There is no reason to doubt that this included circumcision. In the new order of the greater righteousness Matthew developed a pattern of the intensification, not of the relaxation, of the law. Overall, this position was held by both Peter and James, although the active mission to the nations reflects the ultimate dominance of Peter's approach. Matthew provides an approach which incorporates tradition from James in such a way as to support Petrine leadership and legitimate a law-based mission to the nations. It is unlikely that Matthew would have survived in what became a dominantly Gentile church unless an alternative reading was possible. That this happened is supported by Ignatius, who refers to Gentile Judaizers who seem to have been Christians.[25] They read Matthew in a way relevant to what had become a Gentile church and for which the teaching of Jesus had become a new law. In this new setting many of the "ritual" elements of the Jewish law were disregarded, perhaps because Matthew was now read in circles that were not free from the influence of Paul. It was not noticed that Matthew did not share Paul's critique of the law, and no alternative rationale was sought for the abandonment of circumcision, Jewish food requirements, and other aspects of the law.

MODELS OF LEADERSHIP AND MISSION

If Matthew embodies the ideal of Petrine leadership, Luke-Acts combines the leadership of the twelve with a recognition of the leadership of the family of Jesus. Mark is critical of the leadership of the family of Jesus and of the twelve, looking rather to the eschatological family. John idealizes the role of the Beloved Disciple, linking him intimately with Jesus and the mother of Jesus although chapter 21 reconciles the leadership of the Beloved Disciple with that of Peter. Consequently we need to be aware of the role that competing leadership ideologies played in the portrayal of these leading figures.

Our task of reconstructing the role of James in the earliest church has been complicated by the widespread view that the family of Jesus, particularly the brothers, were unbelievers during Jesus' ministry. This picture is a result of an uncritical reading of the Gospels, which throw as much doubt on the belief of the disciples as on the family of Jesus. Coincidentally the Gospels bear witness to the presence of the family of Jesus among his "followers" (Mark 3:30–35; John 2:1–12; 7:1–9). Recognizing the ideological tendencies in the sources leads to a reconstruction in which the most likely scenario is that James was the first leader of the Jerusalem church, even when the twelve, including Peter, were present. What happened to the twelve is one of the mysteries of early church history.

James, as leader of the Jerusalem church, is identified with the circumcision party, that part of Jewish Christianity which demanded circumcision and the keeping of the Mosaic law, a position that became identified with the Jerusalem church. Within it were various factions agreed on the observance of circumci

---

[25] Schoedel, pp. 144–45.

sion and the Mosaic law though they were divided over the recognition of an alternative mission.

Acts has confused this picture in an attempt to present James as a moderate Jewish believer in harmony with Paul. The evidence justifies the description of his position as Judaizing.[26] While Peter was accused of Judaizing in relation to Gentiles, the pressure on Peter to maintain these standards came from James (Gal 2:11–12). Insistence that believers live as Jews is the essence of what Judaizing means (Gal 2:14). While James was not actively involved in a Judaizing mission to the nations, he exerted a Judaizing pressure upon those who were, such as Peter and Barnabas at Antioch.

Matthew's Gospel bears witness to the growth of a tradition that sought to establish the leadership of Peter as head of the twelve and the spearhead of a mission to the nations based on keeping the law as interpreted by Jesus. There is no reason to think that circumcision was not demanded. One reason for the shift of leadership from James to Peter was the need to legitimate the mission to the nations, the mission beyond Palestine. There is no reason to think that in Peter's lifetime, or in the intention of Matthew, anything but a law-based mission was intended. Matt 28:19–20 leaves no doubt that, according to Matthew, the mission to the nations was commanded by the risen Jesus. What is often missed are the careful conditions that are specified in relation to that mission: "teaching them to observe all that I have commanded you. . . ." In due course Matthew was read, and Peter was understood to validate the universal mission to the nations based on an understanding of the law *modified by the gospel*. The modification was not now understood in terms of the intensification of the demands as set out in Matthew. Rather a more moderate revision of the law was accepted, and this revision was reinforced by the domesticated understanding of Paul given in the Acts of the Apostles and the Pastoral Epistles.

The earliest documents of the New Testament portray James as the brother of Jesus without qualification. In Gal 1:19 Paul refers to James as the brother of the Lord, and it is clear from his description that it was James's relationship to Jesus that gave James his notable position in the early Church. Mark also portrays James as the brother of Jesus, one of a number of brothers and sisters. Nothing that is said in these documents gives the reader any reason to understand the relationship in anything but the straightforward sense.

Matthew and Luke provide accounts of the virginal conception of Jesus. Joseph is not thought to be the father of Jesus in these Gospels. The most natural reading of the relationship of the brothers and sisters of Jesus in these Gospels is that they are children of Joseph and Mary born subsequent to the birth of Jesus. From the point of view of these Gospels then, these children are half-brothers and half-sisters of Jesus.

---

[26] See the use of Ἰουδαΐζειν in Gal 2:14.

John, probably the last of the canonical Gospels, shows no awareness of the virginal conception of Jesus. While James is not mentioned by name, we may assume that he is understood to be one of the brothers mentioned as a group on two occasions (2:12; 7:2–13). The most natural reading of John is that those described as brothers are such in the normal sense. In the prologue John asserts that Jesus is the divine logos made flesh, but nothing suggests that this precludes the birth of Jesus under normal circumstances. It could be argued that "made flesh" implies a natural birth, with Joseph and Mary as father and mother. John's portrayal of the logos made flesh functions christologically like the Matthean and Lukan teaching of the virginal conception. John's distinctive christology does not necessarily involve any peculiar circumstances attending the birth of Jesus, and there is no reason to understand those described as brothers as anything but full brothers.

While there is nothing in Paul's letters or in Mark or John to show that they rejected the teaching of the virginal conception, the impression they give is that they do not know the teaching. Consequently, it seems safe to accept that Paul, Mark, and John understood the distinctive character of Jesus in a way that did not involve his virginal conception and accepted the brothers and sisters of Jesus straightforwardly. Thus the significant role of the family of Jesus, in particular the role of James, in the early Church is fully understandable.

The leadership of James in the Jerusalem church from the beginning gives weight to the view that the family of Jesus were followers of Jesus during his ministry. There is no doubt that Mark was critical of the role of the family. Mark was critical also of the twelve. In place of both of these groups the Jesus of Mark looks to the eschatological family. If Jesus intended a universal movement any privileged position given to his natural family would have constituted a problem. But Mark's critique of the natural family and of the twelve does not simply develop out of the teaching and practice of Jesus. It reflects his attitude to the leadership struggles going on in the church of his day. Opening the eschatological family to all followers of Jesus was crucial for a movement seeking to develop beyond "tribal" boundaries, making room for the leadership of Paul.

The role of James in the earliest Jerusalem church has been obscured because none of the authors of New Testament documents, except for the writer of the epistle of James, takes anything like a Jamesian point of view, and even the letter of James must be regarded as pro-Jamesian in a rather indirect fashion.[27] While Acts may not be anti-James any more than it is anti-Paul, it fits James into the author's ideological perspective, which differs somewhat from that of James. From our analysis James has emerged as the outstanding leader of

---

[27] While M emanates from James it has been shaped to conform to the point of view of a Petrine Gospel by Matthew.

the Jerusalem church, although various factions within the early church may well have challenged his leading role. In this context the conflict between Paul and James, which was perceived by the Tübingen school, needs to be reinterpreted. James appears on the side of those who were concerned to continue mission to the Jews. Paul emerges as the outstanding exponent of the mission to the nations, a universal mission that does not discriminate between Jews and Gentiles. The leadership of James presupposes the existence of the Jerusalem church. Yet it is clear from Gal 2:12 that the influence of James went beyond Jerusalem.

The differing roles of James and Paul pose the question of which of these two stands closer to the mind and practice of Jesus. The evidence of the Gospels suggests that James, in limiting his active role in mission to the Jews, was consistent with the practice of Jesus for whom, according to the Gospels (which reflect the reality of the mission to the nations), mission beyond the people of Israel was exceptional. The use of "Israel" presupposes the application of this term to the Babylonian exiles and their descendants. Israelite is the equivalent of "Jew" but was more likely to be used in the province of Judah than in the diaspora.[28]

James, centered in Jerusalem with a focus on the mission to the Jews, had every right to think that his approach to mission was true to the mission of Jesus and that the mission of Paul was without adequate precedent in the practice of Jesus. Such evidence as there is in favor of Paul's position is complex and can be employed only with difficulty. Much of it arises from exceptional encounters and incidents which can be suspected of having been shaped by the early Christian community. Nevertheless the most likely reading of this evidence suggests that Jesus was not strictly observant of Jewish purity laws, and it can be argued that the law-free mission to the nations is an extension of the logic arising from this aspect of the exceptional practice of Jesus.

A good example of the exceptional practice of Jesus is found in the story of the Greek Syro-Phoenician woman (Mark 7:24–30 = Matthew 15:21–28 where she is called a Canaanite woman). According to the Markan version, the blessings of the ministry of Jesus overflow to the nations, but Israel has priority. This is evident in the report of the words of Jesus, "First permit the children to be satisfied."[29] It is not likely that the story has come from the Gentile church because the Gentiles are represented by "dogs" (Mark 7:27). In spite of this derogatory reference, Jesus affirms that in due course the Gentiles will be fed. Further, the woman's persistent faith evokes from Jesus the response for which she hoped. Her daughter is healed immediately and without waiting for the

---

[28] See my "The Church and Israel in the Gospel of John," 103–12.

[29] Is this an expression of the Pauline principle of "To the Jew first . . ." (Rom 1:16; 2:9, 10; cf. Acts 13:46)?

children first to be fed. In Mark what is exceptional in the incident is its timing. The woman's faith, expressed in her assertion that even the dogs receive the crumbs (Mark 7:28–29), brings about the exorcism of her daughter before Jesus' mission to Israel had been completed.

Matthew's perspective is different. Matthew adds to the Markan story the saying of Jesus, "I was not sent except to the lost sheep of the house of Israel." Whereas Mark qualifies Jesus' mission in terms of the order, first Israel and then the nations, Matthew asserts that Jesus' mission was exclusively directed toward Israel. This view is consistent with the way James perceived his responsibility for mission. He maintained a mission to Israel in a way that preserved Jewish identity. Matthew acknowledged that the persistent faith of the woman was rewarded by the granting of her request and has Jesus pronounce, "Woman, great is your faith, let it be to you as you will" (Matt 15:28). Matthew recognizes the overflow of the blessings of the messianic ministry of Jesus beyond Israel to the Canaanite woman but marks this as exceptional in the reported words of Jesus, "O woman, great is your faith." Thus this exceptional activity outside the boundaries of Israel is a consequence of the woman's exceptional faith. As exceptional it provides no precedent. Nevertheless, it is in such an incident that the possibility of mission to the nations has its basis. The blessings of Abraham were to overflow to the nations (Gen 12:1–3). In the long run Matthew recognized the mission to the nations based on observance of the law as Jesus had expounded it (28:19–20). Peter and others extended the law-based mission to the nations in the regions beyond, thus reflecting a position somewhat different from James.

The Pauline position was an extension of the exceptional action of Jesus, which did not wait until Israel first enjoyed the blessings and was satisfied before extending the blessings to the nations. Paul concluded that Israel's rejection of the blessings provided the nations with their opportunity. This was not meant to exclude Israel from the blessings. Rather the inclusion of the nations was intended to lead to the inclusion of Israel as well (Rom 9–11).

But what of Israel's law? Was it to be set aside in the mission to the nations? It is clear, even in Matthew, that the blessings intended for Israel overflowed to the Canaanite woman on the basis of her faith alone.[30] Purity rules were ignored in Jesus' relationship with her, especially in the imagery of the sharing of a meal together, even if the meal consists only of crumbs that fall from the table and are eaten by the dogs. Although in the story the image was created by the woman, Jesus so approved of the woman's metaphor that he granted her wish (Mark 7:29).

---

[30] This Markan motif was not fully assimilated by Matthew. Though he stressed that Jesus' mission was to Israel alone and emphasized the exceptional nature of Jesus' action in this case, the basis for his action remains the woman's faith alone and is without reference to the requirements of the law.

Mark portrays the freedom of Jesus in moving among people considered to be unclean: notorious sinners, lepers, the demon-possessed. Jesus was not scrupulous in his observance of the sabbath. It is not that he went out of his way to break purity and sabbath observance, but these rules did not have high priority in his mission.

The incident in Mark 7:14–23 (= Matthew 15:10–20) is illuminating on this point. A discussion between Jesus and his disciples arose on the basis of Jesus' saying made to the crowd (Mark 7.15) in response to a controversy on the necessity of hand-washing. Jesus then explains to the disciples that nothing entering into a person defiles a person. In both Mark and Matthew this assertion was made in an incident in which the disciples were criticized by the scribes and Pharisees for eating with unwashed hands. This was a breach of Pharisaic tradition rather than of the written law. Matthew takes the saying of Jesus to mean only that "to eat with unwashed hands does not defile a person" (Matt 15:20), but Mark asserts that Jesus thus "declared all foods to be clean" (Mark 7:19). The conclusion given by the narrator in Mark is absent from Matthew, who has limited the application of the saying of Jesus to the specific matter under discussion—whether hand-washing before eating was a religious necessity.

The Markan conclusion is probably Markan redaction. It is not to be rejected as a distortion of the position of the historical Jesus for that reason because it is an obvious implication of the saying of Jesus which Matthew has used also. Mark has made explicit what was implicit in the teaching and practice of Jesus. Matthew, committed still to a law-based mission, could not follow Mark in this any more than could James.

The "converted" Paul moved from radical opposition to what he had perceived to be a lawless movement, to become a leading exponent of the law-free mission to the nations. His belief in the resurrection of Jesus was at the heart of this change. His opposition to the Jesus movement had been based on his view of Jesus as a lawbreaker, but his opinion had changed when he had come to see Jesus standing not against but on the side of God, a view that revolutionized his evaluation of the law, at least those elements which culturally separated Jews from the nations. His new sense of mission was grounded in his understanding of the gracious action of God revealed in Jesus.

Acts attempts to bring together radically different perceptions of the mission of Jesus which persisted among his followers. It does this from the perspective of the actuality of the successful mission to the nations. An exclusive mission to the Jews is not held out as a realistic possibility. From this perspective Acts does not adequately reveal the serious attempt of a significant proportion of the Jerusalem church to maintain a law-based mission. The author of Acts has obscured the significant conflicts which occurred in the interest of presenting a more-or-less unified movement and one that could be thought of as continuous with the church of all the nations that had emerged by the last decade of the first century. The situation before the death of James and the Jewish war was quite different from this, and Acts has had to adopt strategies to bridge significant gaps.

One strategy is found in Acts 10 which narrates an incident involving Peter and a Roman centurion, Cornelius, who was a "godfearer" (Acts 10:1–2).[31] In this episode Peter is taught, through a vision, that nothing that God has created is unclean. This resonates with the conclusion the Markan narrator draws (Mark 7:19), declaring all foods to be clean. If the Markan narrator is suspected of introducing this assertion anachronistically, we must suspect that Luke has done the same with Peter in Acts 10. There the vision, together with the evidence that Cornelius and his household have received the Holy Spirit without even being baptized, is used by Peter to justify his baptism of them and acceptance of them into the Christian movement (Acts 11:1–18). While Acts glosses over the conditions of entry for these Gentiles, the vision which provides part of the justification of the inclusion of the nations (Acts 11:18) also declares all food to be clean. Acts asserts not only that Peter accepted this but that, upon his report, the Jerusalem church also accepted it. In the light of subsequent events recorded in Acts and by Paul, the specific rejection of food purity laws at this point is historically unlikely. Cornelius, being a "godfearer," probably did not raise food- and purity-law problems but differed from Jews only in being uncircumcised.

Acts 15 suggests that Paul's mission to the nations had to be forcefully defended in Jerusalem, and even then the Jerusalem assembly laid certain obligations on Gentile converts in the so-called Jerusalem decree (Acts 15:19–20). In the light of Paul's letter to the Galatians the "decree" seems to be a Lukan accommodation or compromise which holds together the position of the later church of all nations with an approximation of the earlier position of the Jerusalem church. Luke's solution (the decree) was simple but the situation was complex, and Acts fails to do justice to the situation in Jerusalem and more or less loses Paul in the process. The outbreak of conflict between Paul and the leadership of the Jerusalem church in Antioch (Gal 2:11–14) exposes the problems which the account in Acts sought to "paper over."

Acts is an attempt to hold together the position of the church of all nations toward the end of the first century with the position of the mother church of Jerusalem between 30 and 60 CE. It is an attempt to bring together the regular practice of Jesus, which was the basis of the position of James and the Jerusalem church, with the position of Paul, which was rooted in the exceptional practice

---

[31] On "godfearers" see J. M. Reynolds and R. Tannenbaum, *Jews and Godfearers in Aphrodisias: Greek Inscriptions with Commentary, Proceedings of the Cambridge Philological Association* suppl. 12 (Cambridge: Cambridge University Press, 1987).

of Jesus,[32] who at times broke through the boundaries of Jewish law, enabling the benefits of his mission to reach the outcasts of Israel and even beyond to the nations. Luke acknowledged the differing approaches to mission, especially between Jerusalem and Antioch and sought to hold the two together. The actual problem was more serious because even Jerusalem and Antioch were not unified, being subject to further divisions in reaction to policy on mission.

In this context James was a significant and farsighted leader whose strategy was to preserve the mission to his own people. History proved his worst fears concerning the Pauline mission to be correct. The mission to the nations indeed ensured the ultimate failure of the circumcision mission.

---

[32] Jesus' proclamation of the kingdom of God might also have provided some basis for the Pauline mission. It was relevant to the poor and oppressed, the sick and the suffering; it entailed the overthrow of the forces of evil and the renewal of life in the fulfillment of God's purpose for human destiny.

Part II

Images of James
in the Early Church

CHAPTER 5

TRADITION IN EUSEBIUS

James the Just, Brother of the Lord, First Bishop and Martyr

Eusebius lived between ca. 260 and 339 CE and was bishop of Caesarea from ca. 313 to 339.[1] In Caesarea, before becoming bishop, he studied with Pamphilus, an admirer of the great Origen, who came to Caesarea from Alexandria. Thus Caesarea became a great center of Christian learning. Pamphilus himself was a noted Christian teacher, and his outstanding library became a rich resource for Eusebius the scholar, historian, and apologist. Although that library, like so many ancient libraries of the Mediterranean world, did not survive the vicissitudes of history, important selections from that treasury were incorporated into Eusebius's history of the church. Eusebius was not himself an original thinker or an elegant writer. He is notable because in his writing of history, more than any one before him, he identified his sources and quoted them verbatim. At the time that Eusebius wrote there was no expectation of exact quotation and identification of sources. A source was a resource. Authors, including historians, made their sources their own, using them as they wished and without reference. Eusebius changed this.

When dealing with his *Church History* it is necessary to distinguish the traditions used by Eusebius from his own compositions. Generally speaking, when we can check quotations against surviving works Eusebius proves to be a reliable scholar. But there are times when he summarizes rather than quotes, and,

---

[1] For the text of Eusebius's *History of the Church*, see *The Ecclesiastical History*, 2 vols., trans. K. Lake, J. E. L. Oulton, and H. J. Lawlor, LCL (Cambridge, Mass.: Harvard University Press, 1926, 1932); *The Ecclesiastical History*, 2 vols., trans., with introduction and notes, by H. J. Lawlor and J. E. L. Oulton (London: Macmillan, 1927, 1928); *Eusebius: The History of the Church*, trans., with notes, by G. A. Williamson. In this chapter, to assist readers in locating passages I include page references to Williamson's, generally available translation. Reference to the 1965 edition is given first, followed by reference to the 1989 edition in square brackets. Translations from Eusebius are my own, keeping as close as possible to one or another of the standard translations.

if we did not possess the source, the difference between these two practices would not always be clear. Even when we are dealing with a quotation, there are questions of the principles of selection and omission as well as of the original context and his purpose of use which may not do justice to the original settings. There is evidence that when Eusebius quoted his sources he sometimes left out sections without any indication that he was doing so.[2]

The first draft of the *History* was written before 300 CE, but the final work describes Constantine's victory over and execution of Licinius (324 CE) and cannot have been completed earlier than that date. The *History* makes no mention of the Arian problem or the Council of Nicaea in 325 CE, which sought to solve Arius's challenge to the belief in the fully divine status of the son of God. This could mean that Eusebius's history was completed before that date. This would be an insecure conclusion to draw because the Arian controversy marks a new phase in the history of the church, a controversy which remained unresolved even at the death of Eusebius. His role in the Arian controversy was ambiguous and enigmatic in that, although he was not an Arian, he was a supporter of Arius. The controversy does not serve the purpose of showing the victory of the one true universal church, which was one of Eusebius's objectives. It cannot safely be argued that his *History* was written after 325. It cannot have been completed before 324.

The *History* was based on Eusebius's earlier *Chronicles* (*Chronicorum*) which presupposed but was superior to the *Chronicles* of Julius Africarnus. Insufficient attention has been given to this work, which is clearly of interest to our study. Because a major investigation needs to be undertaken, here only a few points of interest will be noted. R. P. Martin, in *James* (1988), suggests that in *Chronicles* 2 Eusebius has two new pieces of information about James. Eusebius calls him "brother of God" (ἀδελφόθεος), a startling indication of his exalted status. He also is the earliest *extant* source to name James as *first* bishop of Jerusalem.[3] In making the latter point it is likely that Eusebius made use of a list of the bishops of Jerusalem which he might have taken over from Hegesippus. On our reading of *HE* 4.22.4 Hegesippus names Simeon as the second bishop of Jerusalem, implying that James was the first.

The *History* was compiled and written over more than a quarter of a century. It reflects changing perspectives and purposes between 300 and 324. In the early phases the problem of persecution was dominant, raising the question of the survival of the church. From the time of Constantine's victory at the

---

[2] See the evidence set out by H. J. Lawlor in *Eusebiana* (Oxford: Clarendon, 1912), 20, 96–97.

[3] In a fragment attributed to Hippolytus, "On the Seventy Apostles," the author lists first "James the brother of God [ἀδελφόθεος], bishop of Jerusalem." In the English translation this appears as "Lord's brother." Putting James first as bishop of Jerusalem implies that he was the first bishop. Eusebius makes no use of this quotation.

Milvian bridge and his edict of toleration (313), the new themes of the victory of the church and the godly emperor emerge. Thus, it is evident that Eusebius's *History* is motivated by apologetic tendencies. His aim was to show an innocent and virtuous church suffering persecution, and the providence of God at work in the godly emperor, leading to the triumph of the church. Another important theme relates to the description of the church and heresy in the past. Eusebius adopted the view that the major churches were apostolic foundations, united in the true faith against novel heresies. In the Arian controversy this was to prove to be an oversimplification. Nevertheless these perspectives have a bearing on the way Eusebius used his sources and should help to guide our reading of his account of them.

Although Eusebius was familiar with the book of Acts and made extensive use of it in describing the early history, he had his own agenda. His aim was to use Acts as a resource in the construction of his own independent work. This meant giving his interpretation of the account in Acts, using it selectively within his own framework. Thus Eusebius asserts that "James, who was called the brother of the Lord," was the first bishop of Jerusalem and was so appointed at the time of the martyrdom of Stephen (*HE* 2.1.2), although the quotation from Clement that follows fixes the appointment simply "after the ascension" (*HE* 2.1.3). Neither the timing nor the account of the event is derived from Acts. Eusebius provides no evidence of any implied early leadership of Peter, even though many scholars today think this is implied in the Acts account. Eusebius asserts the leadership of James more or less from the beginning.

HE 1.12.4–5: Paul on James, according to Eusebius

Eusebius first mentions James (1.12.4–5) in discussing the disciples of Jesus.[4] He writes to show that not only were these more in number than the twelve, but also they outnumbered even the seventy.[5] Here he makes use of the testimony of Paul who

> says that after his resurrection he [the savior] was seen first by Cephas, then by the twelve, and after them by more than five hundred brethren at once, of whom some, he says, have fallen asleep, but most remain alive at the time of writing. Next, he says, he was seen by James—who was one of the alleged brothers of the savior[6]—then,—as if in addition to these there had been, on the pattern of the twelve, a large number of apostles such as Paul himself, he adds—Later he was seen by all the apostles.

---

[4] Williamson, p. 65 [30].

[5] Eusebius names some of these as Barnabas, Sosthenes, and Cephas, whom he distinguishes from the apostle Peter. The conclusion that Cephas is not Peter is certainly incorrect but may have been drawn to save the face of Peter from the criticism of Paul in Gal 2:11–14.

[6] εἷς δὲ καὶ οὗτος τῶν φερομένων τοῦ σωτῆρος ἀδελφῶν ἦν.

This "quotation" is more or less fair, although in reporting 1 Cor 15:5–7 it adopts a *summary* idiom into which are inserted significant additions. We have no reason to think that Eusebius was making use of a different form of the text, although he might have derived the quotation of Paul from another source such as the writings of Origen.[7] Even if this was the case the additions are probably redactional comments by Eusebius. Some parts of the summary use the same words as Paul did but the inserted comments are not explicitly distinguished from the quotation and would be difficult to detect without an independent knowledge of Paul's letters. In the above translation the main insertions have been enclosed between dashes.[8] In one comment James is identified as "one of the alleged[9] brothers of the savior." This clarification of the text makes explicit which James is here in view, should the reader be in doubt. Eusebius supplies information given by Paul in Gal 1:19 but with his own characteristic qualification and in his own idiom. James is the "alleged" brother, and instead of brother of "the Lord" Eusebius has called him brother "of the savior." The use of "alleged" casts doubt on the actual relationship of James to Jesus. Eusebius generally makes this qualification when providing his own summary information but sometimes allows his sources to assert the actual relationship without qualification. Because we have detected Eusebius qualifying Paul where we know of no qualification, we are alerted to the possibility that he might have modified other sources in this way.

From this insertion onward the modifications by Eusebius are prominent in the paraphrase. Having explained who James was, it is then necessary to explain the reference to all the apostles, who they were, and why they are mentioned at this point. Reference to "on the pattern of the twelve" implies that the pairing of Cephas and the twelve is matched by James and all the apostles. Awareness of that parallelism provides some support for the view, going back to Harnack, that we have evidence of rivalry between groups supporting Cephas and James. While Harnack thought that "all the apostles" in verse 7 meant "the twelve" in verse 5, this is not the way the text was read by Eusebius. Eusebius does not mention any rivalry between the followers of Cephas and those of James. It is an important theme of Eusebius that the apostles, including Cephas, unanimously elected James as the first bishop of Jerusalem (2.1.2–5). But the formal parallelism, recognized by Eusebius, is suggestive of such a rivalry. In his attempt to identify "all of the apostles" he mentions Paul as an example.

---

[7] Eusebius probably derived a supposed quotation of Josephus from Origen, who also attributes it to Josephus. See *HE* 2.23.20 and the discussion of Origen on pp. 200–206 below.

[8] On the method of Eusebius in conflating separate statements from his sources see Lawlor, *Eusebiana*, p. 20.

[9] φέρω is used elsewhere by Eusebius in the sense of the alleged human relationships of Jesus. For comparable qualifications to 1.12.5, see 2.1.2 (in 2.23.1 there is no qualification).

Eusebius classes Paul's apostleship and resurrection experience on the same level with those of "all the other apostles." In 1 Cor 15:8–11 Paul stresses the exceptional nature of Jesus' resurrection appearance to him: "Last of all, as one born out of due time, he appeared to me." The burning issue of Pauline authority had been extinguished by the time of Eusebius, for whom all of the apostles had become a common bastion against heresy.

HE 1.13.1–22; 2.1.6–7: THE ABGAR INCIDENT—AN INTERLUDE?

Between the first reference to James (1.12.4–5) and the second (2.1.2–5) Eusebius has placed the story of Abgar V Ukkama ("the Black"), king (*toparch*) of Edessa (1.13.1–22) from 4 BCE to 7 CE and again from 13 to 50 CE. In his account of the disciples of Jesus, Eusebius noted that the names of (twelve) apostles are in the Gospels but that there was no known list of the names of the seventy, although he names, among others, Matthias and Thaddaeus, asserting that there were others in addition to these. The mention of Thaddaeus suggests the story about King Abgar of Edessa, although the story also has a connection to James. Eusebius claims to have found the story in the archives at Edessa and to have translated from Syriac the two letters that he includes.

The story, based on the letters, tells how Abgar, when he was dying, heard of the works of Jesus and sent a letter to him, begging relief from his illness. Jesus sent a reply by letter, promising to send one of his disciples to cure him and bring salvation. After the ascension of Jesus, Thomas, one of the twelve, sent Thaddaeus to Edessa, thus fulfilling the promise of Jesus. Given that Eusebius probably wrote this section of *HE* around 303 CE, the letters must be dated earlier, although we have no independent confirmation of their earlier existence. The letters also appear at the beginning of the *Doctrine of Addai*[10] from about 400 CE[11]; here Jesus speaks the letter to Abgar's messenger, Hanan, who puts it into writing. The Syriac wording is in agreement with the Greek of Eusebius. But there are two other new features in the *Doctrine of Addai*: 1) Jesus promised to protect Edessa (8.19–20) and 2) Hanan painted a portrait of Jesus and took it back to Abgar.

G. R. Horsley records an inscription concerning Edessa which might have been discovered in Ankyra. Horsley mentions the editor of the inscription, B. van Elderin, who has identified the name Ἰακώβ in the third line with James the Just. According to the inscription apparently James offered the city (Edessa) to God.[12] Just when James was supposed to have done this is unclear. The

---

[10] Addai is the Syriac equivalent of Thaddaeus.

[11] See G. Howard, *The Teaching of Addai*, SBL Texts and Translations 16 (Chico, Calif.: Scholars Press, 1981), 6–8, and W. Bauer, "The Abgar Legend," in *New Testament Apocrypha*, vol. 1, ed. W. Schneemelcher, trans. R. McL Wilson (Philadelphia: Westminster, 1963), 437–44. See also the Syrian *Acts of Thaddaeus,* which are probably from the third century.

[12] G. R. Horsley, ed., *New Documents Illustrating Early Christianity*, vol. 2 (North Ryde, Australia: Macquarie University, 1982), document 115, pp. 203–6.

inscription links James to Edessa, and he is party to the protection of the city promised by Jesus. Further, in the Nag Hammadi *First Apocalypse of James* 36.15–38.10 a chain of revelation is established from the risen Lord to James to Addai to the younger son of Addai. In this way James and the *First Apocalypse* are associated with Edessa.

Following the second reference to James in *HE* (2.1.2–5), in which Eusebius tells of the choice of James and the revelation of the higher knowledge to him, Eusebius returns to the fulfillment of Jesus' promise to King Abgar, which is now described in more detail. The conversion of the population of Edessa is said to have been largely a consequence of the cure of Abgar by Thaddaeus/Addai. These events, it is said, took place "at this time." Thus prior to 2.1.6 Eusebius describes the choice of James after the ascension, the giving of higher knowledge after the resurrection, and Saul's (Paul's) journey to Jerusalem to see Peter and his seeing James also. The reference to "at this time" is probably intended to indicate that the conversion of Edessa took place at the time of the latest event Eusebius mentions here, that is, the journey of Paul to Jerusalem. But the method of dating is too vague to be clear. Certainly the conversion is thought to have taken place fairly soon after the ascension of Jesus and in the time of the leadership of the Jerusalem church by James. The intertwining of James with this story implies a connection between James and Edessa.

HE 2.1.2–5: The Use of Unspecified and Specific Sources

Eusebius describes the work of the apostles from the choice of Matthias to the deaths of Peter and Paul (2.1.2–5[13]). He is summarizing unspecified sources as well as quoting from a specific source (Clement of Alexandria). Having dealt with the martyrdom of Stephen, he turns attention to James.

> Then there was James, who was called the Lord's brother;[14] for he too was named Joseph's son,[15] and Joseph Christ's father, though in fact the Virgin was his betrothed, and before they came together. . . . This James, whom the people of old called the Just[16] because of his outstanding virtue, was the first, as the records tells us, to be elected[17] to the episcopal throne (θρόνον) of the Jerusalem church. Clement, in *Outlines* (*Hypotyposes*), book six, puts it thus:

---

[13] Williamson, p. 72 [35–36].

[14] τὸν τοῦ κυρίου λεγόμενον ἀδελφόν.

[15] ὠνόμαστο . . . παῖς.

[16] ὃν καὶ δίκαιον ἐπίκλην οἱ πάλαι.

[17] ἐγχειρισθῆναι. See the use of ἐγκεχείριστο in 2.23.1 and contrast the use of ἑλέσθαι in 2.1.3 and κεκληρωμένου in 3.5.2.

"After the ascension of the savior, Peter, James, and John did not claim pre-eminence because the savior had specially honored them, but chose (ἐλέσθαι) James the Just as Bishop of Jerusalem."

In book seven of the same work the writer makes this further statement about him:

"James the Just, John, and Peter were entrusted by the Lord after his resurrection with the higher knowledge. They imparted it to the other apostles, and the other apostles to the Seventy, one of whom was Barnabas. There were two Jameses, one the Just, who was thrown down from the parapet and beaten to death with a fuller's club, the other the James who was beheaded."

James the Just is also mentioned by Paul when he writes:

"Of the other apostles I saw no one except James the brother of the Lord."

The quotation of Clement is set in the context of a summary statement about James, the sources of which, in addition to Clement, are not indicated. Eusebius not only names Clement; he also specifies the work and the two places, book 6 and book 7, from which the quotations have been derived. He does not, in this instance, simply run two quotations together, and we might expect that the accuracy of quotation is greater than in his earlier citing of Paul. Of this we cannot be sure because the *Hypotyposes* of Clement has not survived.

He 2.1.2: The Summary Statement

Here Eusebius indicates the basis of his qualification of James as one who is "called the Lord's brother." Both James and Jesus were known as the sons of Joseph, and James was known as the brother of Jesus, although Jesus was conceived by the Virgin. This Eusebius might have learned from Matthew and Luke. He is here dependent on the language of Matt 1.18 ("before they came together") and implies that Jesus and James were half-brothers, having the same mother, but not the same father, as was commonly supposed. The manner in which he has qualified this suggests he was dependent on Origen's treatment of "the brethren of the Lord" in his *Commentary on Matthew*.[18]

Eusebius tends to qualify statements about James being the brother of Jesus or Joseph being Jesus' father by using such expressions as "said to be," "named," "alleged." When he is quoting a source he generally reproduces without qualification "James the brother of the Lord" (2.1.5), but he has no compunction about adding his qualification concerning the "alleged brother of Jesus" (1.12.5), reading one source in the light of his own reading of others.

---

[18] See X.17 which provides commentary on Matthew 13:54–56.

In keeping with tradition, translation of the title given to James is rendered "the Just." It might often be more adequately translated as "the Righteous" in order to bring out the association of faithfulness to the law, which is the point of the reference to James's virtue. The title "the Righteous" also links James to a tradition of righteous sufferers. Eusebius's reference to James "the Just" is here dependent on Clement, although Clement does not justify this practice by reference to the virtue of James. In another, later quotation from Hegesippus (*HE* 2.23.4–7), it is said that James has been called the Just by all men from the Lord's time to "ours." This suggests that in his summaries Eusebius tends to draw on other relevant sources and not only on the ones under specific consideration.

Eusebius indicates that "the records tell us" that James "was the first to be *elected* to the episcopal throne of the Jerusalem church."[19] In the summary (2.1.2) the electing agents are not identified. According to the quotation from Clement (2.1.3), Peter, James, and John "chose" James the Just as bishop of Jerusalem. Although the episcopacy of James is clear, there is some confusion about the process of his election/appointment. Eusebius might not have perceived inconsistencies in these accounts, but modern critics cannot avoid them, especially when conflicting statements appear side by side as they do in 2.1.2–3.

The records of the list of the bishops of Jerusalem are now found in 4.5.1–5.[20] In 3.5.2[21] Eusebius again mentions James's appointment to the throne in terms that suggest that he is drawing on the language of the present passage (2.1.2)[22] The first quotation from Clement names James as bishop of Jerusalem in a context which implies that he was the first to hold that office but which does not name him as the first. There is also a quotation from Hegesippus that names Simeon, the successor of James, as the second bishop, thus implying that James was first (*HE* 4.22.4). While reference to James as the first bishop of Jerusalem comes in the summaries, it is misleading to suggest that Eusebius was the first to record this.[23] Even the terminology naming him as the first bishop is probably derived from the list of bishops that antedates Eusebius.

Eusebius introduces this account concerning James immediately after dealing with the martyrdom of Stephen. He continues "Then there was James . . . ," suggesting that his election to the throne of Jerusalem followed Stephen's death.

[19] Compare the summary statement in 2.23.1 concerning James, identified as the brother of the Lord, to whom the episcopal "throne" of Jerusalem was *allotted* by the apostles.

[20] Williamson, pp. 156–57 [107].

[21] Ibid., p. 111 [68].

[22] Thus G. Lüdemann, *Opposition to Paul in Jewish Christianity* (Philadelphia: Fortress, 1984), 161–62.

[23] This is the position of R. P. Martin, *James,* Word Biblical Commentary 48 (Waco, Tex.: Word Books), lviii, and Lüdemann, p. 162. Eusebius is the earliest extant source, but he indicates earlier sources.

The quotation from Clement that follows suggests an earlier date for the selection of James by situating it "after the ascension." While the martyrdom of Stephen occurred after the ascension, Stephen's demise was a little too much later to be what is at issue in the quotation from Clement. Eusebius was apparently unaware of this inconsistency in his narrative, but his narrative implies no leader prior to James.

This is the first of the frequent references to the "throne" of the bishop of Jerusalem, a term Eusebius uses of the seat of no other bishop.[24] There is no reference to the throne in the quotation from Clement or in the list of bishops. The throne is a redactional addition, perhaps based on Eusebius's knowledge of the throne in his own day (7.19.1).

Martin Hengel has drawn attention to an inscription on a marble fragment from the church of St. John in Ephesus.[25] To the left of the cross are the letters Ἰάκο/βος/ α΄ παπα, and the editors resolved the last line as πρωτοπαπα(ς). No date is offered for the inscription by the editors.[26] Given that it is in the church of St. John at Ephesus, a broad Byzantine dating is the best guess possible. No one questions that the inscription concerns James, the first bishop of Jerusalem. But why should such an inscription appear in Ephesus? It could be that the Eastern church submitted the name of James as the first pope in the face of growing claims of the primacy of Peter from the Western church in Rome. If this were the case the inscription might echo an earlier rivalry between the supporters of James and the supporters of Peter.

HE 2.1.3–5: Two Quotations from Clement

The first of two quotations from Clement that appear in *HE* 2.1.3–5 is introduced with the words "Clement puts it thus." Because the work quoted has been lost we cannot know if Eusebius has adapted and interpreted his source. Writing in the early years of the third century, Clement was defending Christianity against rampant Gnosticism in Alexandria. Like Origen after him, he daringly used gnostic language and approaches to overcome the gnostic ideology. What Clement has not drawn from the New Testament may come from gnostic sources such as the *Gospel of the Hebrews* and the *Gospel of Thomas*. Each of the two quotations of Clement speaks of a triumvirate.

The first triumvirate includes Peter and both of the sons of Zebedee (James and John). Their authority is implied by reference to their *choice* of James the

---

[24] For further information about the throne of James, in addition to 2.1.2, see 2.23.1; 3.5.2; 3.11.1; and especially 7.19.1 and the discussion below.

[25] "Jacobus der Herrenbruder—der erste 'Papst'?," in *Glaube und Eschatologie: Festschrift für W. G. Kümmel zum 80. Geburtstag*, ed. E. Grässer and O. Merk (Tübingen: J. C. B. Mohr [Paul Siebeck], 1985), 71–104.

[26] G. R. Horsley, ed., vol. 4, document 133, p. 266 ("James the First Pope").

Just as the bishop of Jerusalem. The gnostic tendency to elevate the authority of James is not rejected here but is brought under the overarching authority of Peter, James, and John. Given that Eusebius is purportedly quoting Clement, it is difficult to agree with Lüdemann who asserts that "the idea that James had been made the first bishop of Jerusalem by the apostles derives from Eusebian redactional work."[27] Not only does Eusebius quote Clement; he also had access to a traditional list of the bishops of Jerusalem in which James was named first bishop. The idea that James was the first bishop of Jerusalem is present in the quotation from Clement, and evidence of the relationship between tradition and redaction is found in redactional summaries.[28]

Lüdemann gives two redactional summaries of Eusebius as evidence of his view that Eusebius was responsible for introducing the role of the apostles in the appointment of James.

> [The Jews] turned against James, the brother of the Lord, to whom the throne of the bishopric in Jerusalem had been allotted by the apostles. (*HE* 2.23.1)

> Now the throne of James, who was the first to receive from the savior and the apostles the episcopate of the church at Jerusalem. . . . (*HE* 7.19.1)

Lüdemann argues that, with the exception of the quotation from Clement (*HE* 2.1.3), in passages where Eusebius is quoting tradition concerning the appointment of James, the apostles play no role. He does not contest the authenticity of the quotation from Clement. Thus it could be said that what Eusebius has done, if Clement is the source of his knowledge of the role of the apostles in the appointment of James, is to expand the triumvirate of Peter, James, and John into "the apostles" generally.

Clement tells only that the choice of James took place "after the ascension of the savior," which implies that James was the first to be chosen. The enumeration—"first," "second"—comes from the list of bishops mentioned above (see *HE* 4.5.1–5) and is not a redactional element from the pen of Eusebius.

The variety of ways in which the appointment of James is described suggests that the direct appointment of James by Jesus, a tradition found in the Nag Hammadi tractates, especially the *Gospel of Thomas* logion 12, and also in the *Gospel of the Hebrews* and the Pseudo-Clementines, is being opposed. There is no tradition in which the risen Jesus authorizes a successor other than James. While Eusebius is not responsible for making the appointment of James subject

---

[27] *Opposition*, p. 162.
[28] Ibid., p. 161. See *HE* 2.1.2; 3.5.2.

to the apostles, there is evidence that this was a secondary element in the tradition when it came to Eusebius. The leadership of James is not in question.

Eusebius appealed to Clement for information on a new configuration of the triumvirate of James, John, and Peter.[29] It is now James who is mentioned first, moving Peter from first to last. The James now in view is James the Just, the brother of Jesus. By mentioning him first his leadership even among the three "pillars" is implied. The same triumvirate is named by Paul in Gal 2:9 as the three "pillars" of the Jerusalem church. There James is named first, followed by "Cephas and John." The different order of the names and the use of "Peter" in the place of "Cephas" suggest that Clement is not here dependent on Galatians in naming the three. Leadership is expressed at a time described (in 2.1.4) as "after the resurrection," which is, presumably, before James was made bishop "after the ascension" (2.1.3).

Clement refers to James the Just to distinguish him from the son of Zebedee. Eusebius's language in the earlier summary (2.1.2) suggests that Clement was not the first to do so because the people of old had named James "the Just." He later quotes Hegesippus's account of the martyrdom of James, in which James is also called the Just. Hegesippus was not the first to use this title of James either. Our first evidence comes in a fragment of the *Gospel of the Hebrews,* a work known to Origen and Hegesippus. In the fragment, preserved by Jerome, it is said that the risen Jesus appeared to "James the Just" and addressed him as "My brother." The tradition, as it appears in Hegesippus, Clement, and Eusebius, has been subordinated to the interest and authority of the Great Church and lacks the note of intimacy between Jesus and James that is found in the *Gospel of the Hebrews.*

The conjunction of the two quotations from Clement raises a question. The first quotation indicates that, after the ascension of the savior, Peter, James, and John chose James the Just. The initiative for this choice was apparently theirs, and there is no hint that they did so on the instructions of the Lord. The second quotation signals that the risen Lord entrusted "the higher knowledge" to James the Just, John, and Peter. Presumably this development took place before the ascension. The problem is that James the Just, being mentioned first, is the implied leader of the triumvirate of which he was part. Yet the earlier quotation implies that until after the ascension James was subordinate to the triumvirate. Apparently Clement has taken over two independent traditions and has made no attempt to reconcile them. The second implies that James's priority came from the risen Lord, while the first asserts that Peter, James, and John chose James the Just.

The source of this tradition is suggested by the concentration on the higher

---

[29] Clement in book seven (ἐν ἑβδόμῳ) of the work already quoted, not book eight as in Williamson's translation, p. 72 [36].

knowledge. The tradition might well be associated with the Gnostics, a situation which is consistent with the focus on the priority of James. But in the quotation from Clement the Gnostic intent has been nullified by combining James's name with the apostles Peter and John. Because they too were the source of higher knowledge, a Gnostic tradition is transformed into an anti-Gnostic weapon. It has been modified also by asserting the transmission of the higher knowledge to and the control of it by the apostles and the seventy. Both the Gnostic and the anti-Gnostic traditions witness to the early leadership of James, although each tradition claims James for itself.

The death of James the Just is briefly described in a form that might be dependent on the earliest Christian report of that event.[30] We can deduce this because Hegesippus appears to be dependent on the same tradition, although he (or someone before him) has combined it with details reported by Josephus and perhaps with redactional comment. Clement's report is simple and unadorned. James was thrown down from the parapet (of the Temple) and beaten to death with a fuller's, or laundryman's, club. There is no mention of the stoning of James, common to Josephus and Hegesippus. While Hegesippus mentions the fuller's club, in his account James was dispatched by a single blow, whereas Clement's account (James was beaten to death) implies repeated blows. Clement makes no reference to any "judicial" action against James, such as is clear in Josephus.

The execution of James with a club rather than by stoning, which is a more usual form of Jewish execution (compare the stoning of Stephen in Acts), calls for some explanation. Given that Josephus's account mentions stoning, the absence of it in Clement may be intentional. Perhaps stoning implied a more lawful execution than Clement wished to portray. Alternatively, the omission may show that Clement was independent of both Josephus and Hegesippus. Even so, the use of the club is somewhat puzzling. Given that there is a tendency to portray James as a priest or even a high priest (see *HE* 2.23.6), it is possible that the punishment was specifically related to some supposed priestly offense. According to tractate *Sanhedrin* 81b, a priest performing Temple service while unclean was to be taken out of the Temple court by the young priests and his skull was to be split with clubs.[31] If the account in Josephus is regarded as historical, the historicity of the clubbing is put in question.

The juxtaposition of the two quotations from Clement (books six and seven) dealing with the two triumvirates, in which the James in question is variable, leads to the explanation of the two Jameses. The statement that there were two Jameses is interesting. Obviously there were more than two, but only two were notable enough in the early church to justify comment. It is unclear

---

[30] See Lüdemann, *Opposition,* p. 298 n.29.
[31] See Martin, p. lii.

whether the explanation that there were two comes from Clement or Eusebius. Eusebius used the two quotations together, and it may have been this positioning that called for the explanation that there were two Jameses. If this is the case then the account of the martyrdom of James might not be an exact quotation from Clement but a summary statement with which Eusebius has taken various liberties. This possibility seems to be excluded by 2.23.3, in which Eusebius refers to "the *words* of Clement already quoted" concerning the death of James and specifically mentions Clement's "narrating that he was thrown from the battlement and beaten to death with a club." This is unquestionably the account in our present passage attributed to Clement.

While most scholars accept that Clement was dependent on Hegesippus,[32] a good case can be made for his independence of both Hegesippus and Josephus. It could be that he was dependent on an earlier and simpler form of tradition now found in Hegesippus.

HE 2.1.5: EUSEBIUS APPEALS TO PAUL TO CLARIFY THE IDENTITY OF JAMES

Eusebius found it necessary to clarify the identity of James the Just. He does so by using a quotation from Paul's letter to the Galatians (1:19). He identifies this as a quotation from Paul but does not mention the letter to the Galatians. If in Eusebius's summary used prior to his quoting Clement there was a suspicion of the influence of Origen's *Commentary on Matthew*, so also there is here. In the passage dealing with "the brethren of the Lord" Origen also identifies James by reference to Galatians:

> And James is he whom Paul says in the Epistle to the Galatians that he saw, "But other of the apostles saw I none, save James the Lord's brother."[33]

There James is identified as the brother of the Lord but not called the Just. That title is not used of James by any of the New Testament authors. Eusebius expressed no doubts about this identification, nor does he in this instance provide any qualification to his description of James as the brother of the Lord. Because he had already qualified his understanding of James's relation to Jesus with regard to 1 Cor 15 (*HE* 1.12.5), Eusebius introduces no qualification when in the quotation from Galatians Paul calls James a brother.

---

[32] See F. S. Jones, "The Martyrdom of James in Hegesippus, Clement of Alexandria, Christian Apocrypha, including Hag Hammadi: A Study of the Textual Relations," *Seminar Papers Society of Biblical Literature 1990* (Atlanta: Scholars Press, 1990), 328 n.30.

[33] Origen, *Commentary on Matthew*, X.17, being the commentary on Matthew 13:54–56.

HE 2.23.1–25: The Martyrdom of James

When Eusebius deals specifically with the martyrdom of James, he repeats the details from the earlier quotation from Clement and adds the more detailed accounts of Hegesippus and Josephus.[34] At the same time he provides summary information without any indication of source. Following the pattern of his quotation of Clement, his account of the martyrdom begins with his own summary, which has points in common with the summary of 2.1.2.

HE 2.23.1–3: The Summary by Eusebius

When Paul appealed to Caesar and was sent to Rome by Festus the Jews were disappointed of the hope in which they had laid their plot against him and turned against James, the brother of the Lord, who had been elected to the episcopal throne of Jerusalem by the apostles. This is the crime that they committed against him. They brought him into their midst and in the presence of all the people demanded a denial of his belief in Christ. But when, contrary to all expectation, he spoke as he liked and showed undreamt of fearlessness in the face of the enormous throng, declaring that our savior and Lord Jesus was the son of God, they could not endure his testimony any longer, since he was universally regarded as the most righteous of men because of the heights of philosophy and religion which he scaled in his life. So they killed him, using anarchy as an opportunity for power since at that moment Festus had died in Judaea, leaving the province without governor or procurator. How James died has already been shown by the words of Clement already quoted, narrating that he was thrown down from the parapet and clubbed to death.

Eusebius has made use of Acts (25:11–12; 27:1); Josephus (*Ant.* 20.201–2); Hegesippus (*HE* 2.23.4–18); Clement of Alexandria (*HE* 2.1.3–5); and perhaps other unacknowledged sources. Here, in a summary passage (2.23.1), Eusebius does not qualify his reference to James as the Lord's brother. He says James "had been *elected* by the apostles to the episcopal throne at Jerusalem." But choice of James by the triumvirate differs from election by the apostles (2.23.2) or a wider body (which could be in view in 2.1.2). Indeed Hegesippus provides another alternative account (2.23.4–18).

The Jews brought James before all the people and demanded that he should deny "his belief in Christ." The language betrays its Christian origin, with "Christ" being used as an alternative name for Jesus rather than the Jewish "Messiah." In this summary Eusebius uses the Christian language of his day while drawing on the account from Hegesippus. The Jews expected a denial

---

[34] For Eusebius's account of the martyrdom of James, see Williamson, pp. 99–103 [58–61].

but, to their surprise, James declared fearlessly "that our savior and Lord Jesus was the Son of God." The testimony Eusebius gives here to the righteousness of James is also based on Hegesippus. He summarizes the basis for James's reputation for righteousness in terms of "the heights of philosophy and religion which he scaled in his life," a description which would appeal to his Graeco-Roman readers. It was because of the universal regard for James as "the most righteous of men" that his testimony to Jesus could not be allowed to pass unpunished.

Drawing on Josephus, Eusebius notes that the Jews took the opportunity to kill James provided by the anarchy following the death of Festus. For how James died he refers back explicitly to the account already given in the words from Clement.

HE 2.23.3–18: Hegesippus according to Eusebius

> But the most detailed account of him [James] is given by Hegesippus, who belonged to the first generation after the apostles.

A straightforward reading of this statement places Hegesippus in the first century, a detail which is in conflict with what Eusebius says elsewhere (HE 4.8.2; 4.12.1). Hegesippus refers to the building of a city in memory of the imperial slave Antinous by Hadrian in the year 134 and to his own residence in Rome in the episcopate of Eleutherus, during the reign of Antoninus Pius (138–161). Consequently we should take "the first generation after the apostles" to mean that Hegesippus was born about the time Eusebius thought that John the apostle had died, about the end of the first century. This would make Hegesippus roughly a contemporary of Justin (ca. 110–180). In the light of this dating, Clement might have made use of Hegesippus, but there is no positive evidence that he did so.

According to Eusebius, the *Memoranda* (*Hypomneumata*) of Hegesippus comprised five books (HE 2.23.3; 4.32.1), although Eusebius has preserved these in such fragmentary form that it is not possible to know precisely their date and place of composition or even their overall contents. Hegesippus made a succession list (*diadoche*) of the bishops of Rome down to Anicetus (died ca. 168) and was also interested in the episcopal succession of the See of Jerusalem (see HE 3.11.12). His motivation, like that of Irenaeus, was to show that the episcopacies of apostolic succession were a bulwark against heresies (see HE 2.23.9; 3.32.7–8). Like Eusebius, he was interested in the martyrs of the early church (HE 2.23.4–18; 3.32.6; 4.8.4). Eusebius may have learned of the list of the bishops of Jerusalem from Hegesippus, though he does not name his source. Broadly speaking, the work of Hegesippus should be dated between 150 and 180, at some distance in time from the events of the life and death of James.

Much then depends on the traditions at Hegesippus's disposal. About these we have no direct evidence, but we may construe certain hypotheses on the basis of the relation of Hegesippus to other writings that could be dependent on common sources.

Eusebius concluded that Hegesippus was a Jewish Christian (*HE* 4.22.8). The evidence he gives for this view is that Hegesippus names Jewish sects, draws on the *Gospel of the Hebrews*, on the Syriac Gospel, and on works in Aramaic/Hebrew, as well on Jewish oral tradition. If the *Gospel of the Hebrews* mentioned here is the same work known to Origen, Jerome, and others, it might add weight to Eusebius's conclusion and throw light on the tradition of the martyrdom of James transmitted by Hegesippus.

Eusebius describes Hegesippus's account of the death of James as the "most accurate" or "most careful" (2.23.3).[35] It is unclear whether he is putting in question details he has recorded from other accounts. Yet following the quotation of this long account, which he says Hegesippus has given "at length," Eusebius declares it to be in agreement with the briefer one of Clement set forth earlier (2.23.19). Only the account by Josephus is also quoted, and there is no reason to think that Eusebius questions its authenticity.

Martin Dibelius and Heinrich Greeven assert that "The narrative of Hegesippus reveals a large number of typical legendary motifs (not to mention some problems with regard to content), so that this narrative must already be viewed with scepticism as to its reliability."[36] The following points are noted. 1) The depiction of the Jews expecting James to give anti-Christian instruction is a legendary motif aimed at showing James as a Jewish hero, esteemed for his righteousness. 2) The influence of the LXX text of the Old Testament on the narrative is clear in the use of Isa 3:10 ("Let us take the just man . . .") in comparison to the cry of the opponents of James, "Let us stone James the Just." Other texts about the "righteous man" such as Wis 2:15 and Ps 33:16 have also influenced the narrative. 3) "This is one of the oldest martyr-legends in early Christianity." In addition to the Jewish tradition of the righteous sufferer there is evidence of the influence of the Jesus tradition and of hero motifs used in connection with saints. The prayer of James is derived from such tradition (also the prayers of Jesus and Stephen), and we may also add the motif of "the prayer of a *just* man" from James 5:16, 18. On the basis of such evidence Dibelius and Greeven rightly conclude that "This legend from Hegesippus cannot be considered a serious rival to the short, clear, and prosaic statement of Josephus."

---

[35] Williamson (p. 99 [58]) translates the term ἀκριβέστατα as "most detailed." He has been overly influenced by the fact that Eusebius commences his summary after the full quotation (2.23.19) by referring to the account given at length (διὰ πλάτους) by Hegesippus.

[36] *James: A Commentary on the Epistle of James,* rev. ed., Hermeneia (Philadelphia: Fortress, 1976), 16–17.

Since the work of Eduard Schwarz it has been commonly accepted that the text of Hegesippus known to Eusebius had been corrupted.[37] The evidence adduced in support of this is drawn from later accounts of the death of James that are thought to be dependent on Hegesippus but differ from what we find in Eusebius. The notion of a corrupted text of Hegesippus is only one solution to the problem. Alternatively, differences from Hegesippus in the later accounts could have arisen from critical and interpretative modifications made by authors to a text that did not differ from what we now find in Eusebius. We may also think of the continued existence and influence of the tradition used by Hegesippus. Hegesippus may not simply have quoted his source; he may have interpreted it. That he used more than one source is indicated by the portrayal of the opponents of James as Jewish sectarians in one place and scribes and Pharisees in another (HE 2.23.8–10); and the combination of three acts of violence against James (the casting down from the Temple, stoning, and the blow from the fuller's club) is a bringing together of irreconcilable motifs, perhaps achieved by Hegesippus,[38] although they could have been combined in the tradition he used.

The argument that tradition concerning the martyrdom of James survived only in Eusebius fails to explain the origin of the additional information in later accounts or the points of agreement in a number of accounts where they differ from Hegesippus according to Eusebius. Nevertheless it is likely that Eusebius accurately transmitted the early Christian tradition of the martyrdom of James that came to him from Hegesippus. That this tradition, as it appears in Eusebius, was the basis of all of the subsequent accounts—in the Nag Hammadi *Apocalypses of James,* as well as in the Pseudo-Clementine *Recognitions* and Epiphanius and in Clement of Alexandria's account—is improbable. Such a hypothesis presupposes a minimalist view of tradition and assumes that the simplest solutions must be correct.[39] It assumes that once the tradition had been adopted by Hegesippus, no other forms of the tradition continued to be transmitted. Differences between the later authors and Hegesippus are then explained as a consequence of modifications made by the later authors. This is the view of F. Stanley Jones, who dispenses with the need of otherwise unknown sources to explain features in later accounts of James's martyrdom, features not found in Hegesippus according to Eusebius.

It is unlikely that Hegesippus made use of all the traditions about the death of James or that those traditions ceased to exist once his account had been written. The nature of his work does not suggest that he simply copied his

---

[37] See Schwarz's "Zu Eusebius Kirchengeschichte, I. Das Martyrium Jakobus des Gerechten," *ZNW* 4 (1903): 48–66.

[38] See Dibelius, p. 15 n.36.

[39] See Jones, pp. 323, 331, 333, 334.

sources. Where later accounts differ from Eusebius's record, the differences could be a consequence of direct access to the source or sources used and redacted by Hegesippus. They could result from the influence of a source or sources independent of Hegesippus. Given that it is unlikely that Hegesippus knew and used all sources, it is argued that a wider tradition about James and his death continued to exist and to have an influence.

There is no good reason to argue that Clement, the Nag Hammadi *Apocalypses of James,* the Pseudo-Clementine *Recognitions,* and Epiphanius were all dependent on Hegesippus for their accounts of the death of James and that all except Clement were dependent on Eusebius's quotation of Clement. Rather the evidence suggests that a variety of groups had reason to preserve traditions about James, including accounts of his death. With Jones we can agree that we have no reason to think that the form in which Eusebius knew Hegesippus was corrupt. His quotation of Hegesippus may be taken as a fair account, though problems may be posed for the textual critic by the manuscript tradition of the Latin, Syriac, and Coptic versions of Eusebius's *History.* This is a separate problem. Eusebius quoted Hegesippus as follows (2.23.4–18):

> Control of the Church passed [presumably after the ascension of Jesus] together with the apostles, to the brother of the Lord James, whom every one from the Lord's time till our own has named the Just, for there were many Jameses, but this one was holy from his birth; he drank no wine or intoxicating liquor and ate no animal food; no razor came near his head; he did not smear himself with oil, and he took no baths. He alone was permitted to enter the Holy Place, for his garments were not of wool but of linen. He used to enter the Sanctuary alone, and was often found on his knees beseeching forgiveness for the people, so that his knees grew hard like a camel's from his continually bending them in worship of God and beseeching forgiveness for the people. Because of his unsurpassable righteousness he was called the Just and *Oblias*—in Greek "Bulwark of the people and Righteousness"— fulfilling the declarations of the prophets regarding him.
>
> Representatives of the seven sects [αἰρέσεων] already described by me asked him what was meant by "the door of Jesus," and he replied that Jesus was the Savior. Some of them came to believe that Jesus was the Christ: the sects mentioned above did not believe either in a resurrection or in one who is coming to give every man what his deeds deserve, but those who did come to believe did so because of James. Since therefore many even of the ruling class believed, there was an uproar among the Jews and scribes and Pharisees, who said there was a danger that the entire people would expect Jesus as the Christ. So they collected and said to James: "Be good enough to restrain the people, for they have gone

astray after Jesus in the belief that he is the Christ. Be good enough to make the facts about Jesus clear to all who come for the Passover Day. We all accept what you say: we can vouch for it, and so can all the people, that you are a righteous man and take no one at his face value. So make it clear to the crowd that they must not go astray as regards Jesus: the whole people and all of us accept what you say. So take your stand on the Temple parapet, so that from that height you may be easily seen, and your words audible to the whole people. For because of the Passover all the tribes have come together, and the Gentiles too."

So the scribes and Pharisees made James stand on the Sanctuary para-pet and shouted to him: "Just one, whose word we are all obliged to accept, the people are going astray after Jesus who was crucified; so tell us what is meant by 'the door of Jesus.' " He replied as loudly as he could: "Why do you question me about the Son of Man? I tell you, he is sitting in heaven at the right hand of the great power, and he will come on the clouds of heaven." Many were convinced, and gloried in James's testimony, crying: "Hosanna to the Son of David!" Then again the scribes and Pharisees said to each other: "We made a bad mistake in affording such testimony to Jesus. We had better go up and throw him down, so that they will be frightened and not believe him." "Ho, ho!" they called out, "even the Just one has gone astray!"—fulfilling the prophecy of Isaiah: " 'Let us remove the Just one, for he is unprofitable to us.' There-fore they shall eat the fruit of their works."

So they went up and threw down the Just one. Then they said to each other "Let us stone James the Just," and began to stone him, as in spite of his fall he was still alive. But he turned and knelt, uttering the words: "I beseech Thee, Lord God and Father, forgive them; they do not know what they are doing." While they pelted him with stones, one of the descendants of Rechab the son of Rechabim—the priestly family to which Jeremiah the prophet bore witness, called out: "Stop! what are you doing? the Just one is praying for you." Then one of them, a fuller, took the club which he used to beat the clothes, and brought it down on the head of the Just one. Such was his martyrdom. He was buried on the spot, by the Sanctuary, and his headstone is still there by the Sanctuary. He has proved a true witness to Jews and Gentiles alike that Jesus is the Christ.

Immediately after this Vespasian began to besiege them.

The account is detailed and lengthy,[40] but, unlike Eusebius, Hegesippus does not name his sources or quote them verbatim. It is likely that he has made

---

[40] See the introductory and concluding words of Eusebius in 2.23.3 and 2.23.19.

use of Josephus, who transmits the tradition of stoning, and the tradition known to us in the quotation from Clement, which says that James was beaten to death with a fuller's club, and attempts to reconcile these traditions. The stress on the righteousness of James, which runs through the account from beginning to end, marks its apologetic tone and purpose, suggesting that Hegesippus himself may have developed this.

Hegesippus claims that leadership in the post-ascension church "passed to James the brother of the Lord and the apostles." The focus of this statement is on James. This might be because he is the subject of the discussion rather than the dominant leader of the group mentioned. The passage quoted goes on to speak of the "legendary" righteousness of James. Lüdemann argues that Eusebius introduced the role of the apostles into accounts of the appointment of James.[41] In doing this Eusebius has made the statement by Hegesippus (*HE* 2.23.4) syntactically rough. It is improved by removing the words "with the apostles," which Lüdemann thinks are Eusebian redaction. He suggests that the quotation from Clement (*HE* 2.1.3) aided Eusebius in this development, which is found in "all other redactionally influenced passages . . . that speak of James's inauguration into office."[42]

Lüdemann also notes that, while Eusebius's summary concerning the appointment of Symeon (*HE* 3.11.1) mentions the apostles, they "play no role" in the account from Hegesippus (*HE* 4.22.4). The argument is then that, just as Eusebius introduced the apostles *into his summary* although they play no role in Hegesippus's own account of the appointment of Symeon, so he has introduced the apostles *into Hegesippus's account* of the inauguration of the leadership of James. There are flaws in this argument. What the precedent of the appointment of Symeon shows, given Lüdemann's case there is sound, is that Eusebius introduced the apostles into his summary while allowing the quotation to remain unchanged. Lüdemann has attempted to use this as evidence to argue that Eusebius modified his quotation of Hegesippus in relation to James. Further, his case depends on an overstatement of the differences between the summary and the quotation. According to Hegesippus (*HE* 4.22.4), "all determined that Symeon should be second" bishop after James, who was first. In that brief statement there is no room for the circumstances of that appointment to be set out. These are supplied in the summary (3.11.1). Three groups are mentioned: the apostles; the disciples; and the surviving members of the human family of the Lord. In the summary no special role is given to the apostles. Rather the stress is on the unanimity of the decision to appoint Symeon, which is consistent with the stress on "all" in the quotation.

The summary, dependent on Hegesippus, makes no claim to be exclusively

---

[41] *Opposition*, pp. 162–64.
[42] Ibid., p. 163.

dependent on him, which is consistent with Eusebius's general practice of drawing on other unspecified sources. There is no good reason for removing "with the apostles" from the quotation from Hegesippus in *HE* 2.23.4. Indeed, it should be recognized that, had Eusebius wished to modify Hegesippus, he would not have written "with the apostles" but that control of the church "passed to James *from* the apostles." Hegesippus associates the authority of James with the apostles but in a way different from Clement. Both Hegesippus and Clement developed traditions that probably reflect conflict with the Gnostic appeal to James. The Gnostic drive has been subordinated to the influence of the apostles but in different ways. Hegesippus links James with the apostles as the leaders. The prominence of James in the statement could imply that, of the leaders, he was the leader. This then would not be greatly different from the tradition in Clement that James was chosen by Peter, James, and John or, in the summary of Eusebius, that James was elected by the apostles because the apostles retained a leading role, even if James was the leader. The tendency to make James's appointment dependent on the apostles did not begin with Eusebius. It was already in the tradition that came to him. The wording of the statement by Hegesippus (*HE* 2.23.4) gives priority and prominence to James, especially because of Hegesippus's extended identification of James and the description of his martyrdom.

The epithet "the Just" distinguishes the Lord's brother from others named James. Its use of him is said to have been universally recognized and based on his saintly way of life. Hegesippus provides our earliest evidence of the use of the title in relation to James apart from the *Gospel of the Hebrews,* which could be dated as early as 140 CE. The support of the Nag Hammadi tractates confirms that Hegesippus puts us in touch with a widespread tradition. The surprise is that it is not attested in the New Testament. Perhaps that is because, apart from the Epistle of James, where 5:6 may suggest the title "the Just" or "Righteous," none of the other New Testament books is from a pro-Jamesian perspective. His manner of life is described by Hegesippus in terms which in part suggest the Nazirite rules of Num 4:1–5 (cf. Luke 1:15) and also indicate a rejection of Graeco-Roman ways, consistent with one who was a pillar of the mission to the circumcision. He did not smear himself with oil, he took no baths. Rejection of the Roman baths is what is at issue, not rejection of the Jewish rites of purification.

The piety of James is described in somewhat puzzling terms. Apparently Nazirite, priestly, and non-Jewish elements have been combined in this account. On the grounds that Epiphanius (*Pan.* 29.4) did not know of any Nazirite connection for James it has been suggested that the Nazirite elements were interpolated into the text of Hegesippus used by Eusebius.[43] But the evidence

---

[43] E. Zuchschwerdt, "Das Naziräat des Herrenbruders Jacobus nach Hegesipp (Euseb, h.e. II.23.5–6)," *ZNW* 68 (1977): pp. 276–87.

is inconclusive, and it is more likely that such elements would be removed in a non-Jewish context. What is more, it is not necessary to see the Nazirite elements in conflict with priestly piety because they are connected in Talmudic tradition.[44] The priestly portrayal includes reference to the linen garment (Lev 16:4–28 and Clement *Stromateis* 5.6) and James's exclusive role of the garment in relation to the sanctuary. Nevertheless there are non-Jewish elements that call for some explanation. That James did not anoint himself with oil or go to the baths might seem to be without Jewish precedent. The rejection of the use of oil does not look Jewish until it is seen in the context of the Roman baths. That James adopted a vegetarian diet is harder to explain. Irenaeus (*AH* 1.24.2; 1.28.1) and Epiphanius (*Pan.* 30.15) associate such dietary practice with deviant Jewish sects. It may be that the tradition came to Hegesippus via such a Jewish Christian group. While the historical James probably maintained a relationship to the Temple and was sympathetic to some of the priests, this account seems to have been shaped by transmission in later Jewish Christian groups.

Whether James was intended to be described as high priest is unclear because what is emphasized is his intercessory role which is based on the pattern of Jesus (and Stephen), who before him had prayed for those who killed them. That intercessory role was important for Hegesippus, who reports that so constant was James in his intercessions for the people that his knees became like those of a camel. The origin of the practice of kneeling in prayer, to which Hegesippus bears witness, is unclear. But the mention of James's linen garments and the assertion that he alone was permitted to enter the sanctuary add weight to the impression that the high priestly role is what is meant, even though the area described as the sanctuary was open to priests. The stress on the exclusive role of James implies that the sanctuary alluded to is the Holy of Holies, and in fact this is the reading of the Latin and the Syriac versions at this point. The question is, does this represent independent witness to the original reading,[45] or does it represent an early correction? Given that the Greek texts unanimously maintain the more difficult reading, it is probably right to accept it. The corrector was aware that what was described implied the Holy of Holies. If this conclusion is right, it raises questions about accuracy of the original source or perhaps about Hegesippus, who might be responsible for the actual wording. This need not have any implications about the Jewishness of Hegesippus or his source because the Temple had long been destroyed, and Hegesippus would have had no direct knowledge of it.

This description of James in high priestly terms allowed for the development of a tradition of episcopal succession in Jerusalem modeled on the tradition of the high priest. James was identified with priestly interests,[46] whereas

---

[44] See Martin, p. lii.

[45] Jones, p. 327.

[46] See Martin, p. l ("Introduction").

there has been a tendency, on the basis of a reading of Josephus, to associate James with the Pharisees in a way that excludes the priestly association.[47] This may be a mistaken conclusion based on an apparent but not actual contradiction.

Hegesippus says that, because of "his excessive righteousness," James "was called Just and *Oblias*," adding "in Greek 'Bulwark of the people' " (περιοχὴ τοῦ λαοῦ). The term *Oblias* is Hebrew or Aramaic and may support the claim that Hegesippus was himself a Jewish Christian. Lüdemann argues that Eusebius's conclusion that Hegesippus "had been converted from among the Hebrews" (4.22.8) was not based on adequate evidence.[48] The fact that *Oblias* may be an inaccurate transliteration of the Hebrew for "Bulwark of the people" does not demonstrate that Hegesippus was not a Jewish Christian. If it did, we would have to conclude that Philo's misuse of Hebrew proved that he was not a Jew either. The question of how James attracted the name "Bulwark of the people" finds a suggestive answer in a later passage (3.7.8),[49] in which the presence in Jerusalem of James and the other apostles is said to afford a strong protection (bulwark) to that place.

The notion that none of the seven sects believed in the resurrection or "the coming one to judge every one according to their deeds" until they were so convinced by James shows a lack of understanding of Judaism *before* 70 CE. But this need not be inconsistent with the understanding of a second-century Jewish Christian even of Palestinian origin. By the second century we need to allow for the changes brought about in Judaism as it defined itself over against emerging Christianity.

The question concerning "the door of Jesus"[50] is asked twice: first by representatives of the seven sects, then by the scribes and Pharisees. James also answers twice: first by saying that Jesus was the savior. The questions posed in these terms and James's answers do not appear in the quotations from Clement or Josephus but find a parallel in the *Second Apocalypse of James* (44.1–63.2) from Nag Hammadi. Here it seems that the report in the *Second Apocalypse* is secondary to the report of Hegesippus, though not necessarily directly dependent on it.[51]

---

[47] On the association of James with the Pharisees, see K. L. Carroll, "The Place of James in the Early Church," *BJRL* 44 (1961): 49–67; R. B. Ward, "James of Jerusalem," *RestQ* 16 (1973): 174–90; and also "James of Jerusalem in the First Two Centuries," *ANRW* II.26.1, 779–812.

[48] *Opposition*, pp. 166–67. See also K. Baltzer and H. Köster, "Die Bezeichnung des Jacobus als OBLIAS," *ZNW* 46 (1955): 141–42. For fuller bibliographical information pertinent to this discussion, see Dibelius, p. 15 n.37.

[49] Williamson, p. 118 [75].

[50] For the notion of Jesus as the "door" (θύρα) see John 10:7, 9; the image is probably associated with the motif of "the way" (John 14:6; see also Isa 40:3; Matt 7:13–14; Acts 9:2). On this association see my *The Quest for the Messiah: The History, Literature and Theology of the Johannine Community* (Nashville: Abingdon, 1993), 296.

[51] See Lüdemann, *Opposition*, pp. 171–73.

The strategy of those who were the traditional opponents of Jesus (scribes and Pharisees) was that James should stand on the parapet of the Temple and make his response to the pre-arranged question, "What is meant by 'the door of Jesus'?" This situation explains the precise location on "the parapet," not mentioned by Clement, from which James was thrown down. He was standing there giving his witness at the time.

The expectation that James would turn back those who had gone astray in following Jesus suggests James's good standing among the Jews of his day. Nevertheless the scenario is somewhat far-fetched. The scribes and Pharisees publicly tell James in advance that they will accept his ruling because he is the Just one. The effect of this is to display their bad faith when they reject his public response to their question, an answer which must be expected because James has already explained the meaning of "the door of Jesus."

James's second response to the question, now from the parapet of the Temple, is said to have been given at the time of Passover, with masses of Jews and Gentiles gathered. His response was a query: "Why do you question me about the Son of Man? I tell you, he is sitting in heaven at the right hand of the great power, and he will come on the clouds of heaven." The wording suggests a combination of Jesus' response to Caiaphas and the council (Matt 26:64) and Stephen's response at his martyrdom (Acts 7:56). These accounts have influenced the tradition of the martyrdom of James.

On each occasion after James expounds the meaning of "the door of Jesus," we are told that many believed. His witness was successful. This is in contrast to the responses to the witnesses of Jesus and Stephen. The scribes and Pharisees conclude that their strategy in using James was a mistake and determine to throw him down from the parapet. The reasoning expressed is that such an action will intimidate the hearers from believing in Jesus. In preparation for the action against James they call out, "Ho, ho! even the Just one has gone astray!" By way of commentary Hegesippus says that by their action they fulfill the scripture written in Isaiah: " 'Let us remove the Just one for he is unprofitable to us.' Therefore they shall eat the fruit of their works."[52] The motif of the fulfillment of prophecy confirms the righteousness of James and the significance of his role as a martyr.

Having thrown James down, the scribes and Pharisees call for his stoning. The stoning of James is in agreement with the account of Josephus. The role of the scribes and Pharisees, however, is not. Josephus attributes the death of James to the intervention of Ananus, the high priest. The suggestion that the scribes and Pharisees were responsible runs contrary to the tradition in Josephus that those people most strict in their observance of the law strongly protested against what they regarded as the lawless action of Ananus. Given the position

---

[52] See Isa 3:10, although the first part of the quotation comes from the Wisdom of Solomon.

of Josephus, the strict law observers almost certainly should be identified with the Pharisees. Hegesippus has introduced the traditional opponents of Jesus in the Gospels in his account of the opponents of James, producing some inconsistency because the tradition showed James in good standing with the scribes and Pharisees.

While they stoned James he interceded for them, praying for forgiveness of them in terms that echo the executions of both Jesus and Stephen. The motif of the intercession of James is doubly emphasized by having Rechab protest that the Just one is praying for them. The protest is probably a legendary addition to the tradition, a view that is confirmed by the fact that identifying Rechab the son of Rechabim as the speaker results from confusion because the Rechabites were a foreign tribe that intermarried with the Levites and so gained priestly status.

At this point the fuller's club is used on James's head to kill him, reconciling the testimony found in Clement with the tradition of stoning found in Josephus (although it will be recalled that James was killed with a single blow of the club according to Hegesippus, while the words of Clement suggest repeated blows). Hegesippus includes details about the usual use of the fuller's club, embroidering the account now found in Clement. This may suggest that the simpler account of Clement, although later, is independent of Hegesippus and manifests an earlier form of the tradition.

The grave and gravestone of James by the Sanctuary remained, according to Hegesippus, as evidence when he wrote. The location of the grave of James has also been identified as in that section of the Kidron valley known as the valley of Jehoshaphat.[53] Though not far from the old city, it hardly seems that this grave could be thought of as "by the Sanctuary." The quotation from Hegesippus in Eusebius gives every impression that Hegesippus knew the site: "and his headstone is still there by the sanctuary." Nevertheless, that precise position for the grave is unlikely, indeed impossible. Given that James died in 62 at the command of the high priest, we must presume that his burial conformed to Jewish law. Burials were not permitted inside the (old) city. While it is thought that Hegesippus was from Palestine and would have known Jerusalem, and there can be no doubt that Jerusalem was known to Eusebius, it must be remembered that neither of them knew the old Jerusalem with its Temple. Hegesippus describes James standing on the parapet of the sanctuary and being thrown down from there. This does not seem possible. If the account is historical at this point the reference should proba-

[53] K. Hintlian, *History of the Armenians in the Holy Land* (Jerusalem: Armenian Patriarchate Printing Press, 1989), 52. See J. Wilkinson, *Jerusalem Pilgrims before the Crusades, Revue Biblique* (1919): 480–99; *Palestine Exploration Quarterly* (1961), 101–13. The site is also identified in some tourist guides. See also R. H. Eisenman, *Maccabees, Zadokites, Christians and Qumran* (Leiden: Brill, 1983), 61 n.103.

bly be understood as to the parapet of the eastern wall of the Temple mount. If James had been thrown down from that point and then stoned and clubbed to death, this would have taken place adjacent to the burial place in the valley of Jehoshaphat. This seems to be the likely resolution to the puzzle.

"Immediately after this Vespasian began to besiege them." Either "Immediately" is used rather loosely, or Hegesippus has mistaken his chronology; the siege by Vespasian did not begin until 67 CE, while the evidence from Josephus would date the martyrdom of James in 62 CE. What is more, in *Chronicles* 2 Eusebius also dates the death of James in the year 62 CE.[54] It seems likely that Hegesippus used "Immediately" to emphasize the connection between the death of James and the siege of Jerusalem in causal terms. The martyrdom of James was the cause of the siege, and Hegesippus makes this point by stressing to the point of exaggeration the temporal closeness of the events. This causal connection was also made by Origen, perhaps in dependence on Hegesippus although he appeals to Josephus for support.

HE 2.23.19: Eusebius's Concluding Summary of Hegesippus

Eusebius concludes as follows:

> This account is given at length by Hegesippus, but in agreement with Clement. Thus it seems that James was indeed a remarkable man and famous among all for righteousness, so that the wise even of the Jews thought that this was the cause of the siege of Jerusalem immediately after his martyrdom, and that it happened for no other reason than the crime that they had committed against him.

According to Eusebius, the full account given by Hegesippus is in complete agreement with the briefer account in Clement. In saying this he implies that independent corroboration by these two accounts assures their reliability. Modern scholars have questioned whether Clement was dependent on Hegesippus,[55] though Schlatter argues that Clement was independent and clearer than Hegesippus and that Epiphanius (*Pan.* 78.14; 29.4.2) was dependent on Clement. There are significant merits in his arguments. The account in Clement is simple and unadorned when compared with that of Hegesippus, whose account might have been influenced also by Josephus. Recently F. Stanley Jones has argued that Clement was dependent on Hegesippus and so were the accounts of the

---

[54] See the Migne edition, *Patrologiae Cursus Completus* (Paris: Garnier, 1928–1967), vol. 19–G, p. 543.

[55] Thus E. Schürer, *The Jewish People in the Age of Jesus Christ*, rev. and ed. G. Vermes, F. Millar, M. Black, vol. 1 (Edinburgh: T & T Clark, 1973), 583.

martyrdom of James in the Pseudo-Clementine *Recognitions* and the *First* and the *Second Apocalypse of James,* as well as in Epiphanius.[56]

Jones argues that in each case comparison shows a sufficient number of parallels to justify the view that Hegesippus was the source and that appeal to an unknown source is both unnecessary and uncalled for by the evidence. Apart from the failure to give sufficient weight to differences, the underlying logic of his argument is questionable. He argues that if one known source (Hegesippus) can explain the subsequent developments, this view should be preferred to a theory involving an otherwise unknown source or sources. It is argued, again and again, that the simplest theory is to be preferred. The logic has much in common with arguments put forward in Gospel source criticism advocating dispensing with Q. In untangling these sources, however, there are other underlying assumptions that need to be questioned. It is unlikely that Hegesippus gathered all existing traditions about James. If he knew of Josephus's account of the death of James, there is much in it that Hegesippus does not use. The same is probably true for other sources. After Hegesippus used a source, it did not immediately disappear from the face of the earth.

The focus on similarities alone gives a distorted view of the likelihood of a direct literary relationship. For an adequate view attention must also be given to differences. While these might be due to redactional tendencies, one should not assume that this is the case just because it offers the simplest explanation. Variations need to be shown to conform to redactional tendencies, and even then it should not be assumed that a source cannot agree with redactional tendencies. To some extent conclusions will be influenced by assumptions about the distribution and dissemination of tradition. While traditions about James could go back to a couple of original sources—the tradition now in Josephus and a Christian source—it is likely that these traditions were taken up and used in a variety of contexts and for different purposes. Complex arrangements of agreements and differences are what we would expect to find. In addition there are traditions about James that come from sources earlier than Hegesippus and that remain independent of him, in particular the *Gospel of the Hebrews* and possibly the *Gospel of Thomas,* leaving aside the question of the sources of the Nag Hammadi tractates relevant to James and to the Pseudo-Clementines.

The fame and outstanding character of James are then attested by Eusebius. This is not something which he draws from either Clement or Hegesippus. Rather he is looking forward to the account in Josephus. Of the many things narrated by Josephus, Eusebius highlights the remarkable fame of James. He does not simply comment on the words from Hegesippus to the effect that the siege followed immediately on the death of James. He goes beyond this to assert that the more intelligent Jews thought that the siege immediately followed the

---

[56] Jones, pp. 322–35.

martyrdom of James because of this wicked crime. With this generalization Eusebius appears to make Josephus representative of these "more intelligent Jews."

HE 2.23.20: First "Quotation" of Josephus

According to Eusebius, Josephus confirms the assertion that the siege of Jerusalem was a consequence of the crimes against James:

> And indeed Josephus did not hesitate to write this down in so many words:
>
> > These things happened to the Jews to avenge James the Just, who was a brother of Jesus who is called Christ, for the Jews put him to death in spite of his great righteousness.

The major problem for us with this quotation is that it does not appear in our manuscripts of Josephus and, unlike Eusebius's next quotation of Josephus, from *Antiquities,* book 20, no reference is given for this quotation. While for Josephus we are dependent on a few manuscripts of rather late date, Eusebius had access to much earlier texts; the same quotation was apparently known to Origen, which would push the datable existence of the text back over half a century before Eusebius.[57] The text as Eusebius quotes it does not have the objectionable affirmation that Jesus was the Christ, which is found in the controversial reference to Jesus,[58] but only the report that Jesus was called the Christ. The expression is almost identical to the well-attested reference to James in *Ant.* 20.200, which Eusebius is about to quote. There James is described as "the brother of Jesus, who is called Christ, whose name is James." Such differences as exist are explicable in terms of the place of each identification in its own sentence. Indeed the differences are inconsistent with an interpolation by a copyist who is more likely to have reproduced the original reference exactly. In spite of this it is unlikely that the reference is original. The reference to James "the Just" and the affirmation that he was the most righteous of men are telltale Christian motifs in relation to James. Moreover, the omission from known manuscripts is unthinkable if the text was original.

The causal connection between the martyrdom of James and the siege of Jerusalem is to be seen as an early Christian apologetic motif which antedates

---

[57] See Williamson, p. 102 n.4. Origen apparently quotes from Josephus in his *Commentary on Matthew* X.17 (on Matthew 13:54–56) and in *Contra Celsum* 1.47; 2.13, and, like Eusebius, provides no reference for the quotation.

[58] *Ant.* 18.63–64. For a discussion of scholarly views on this and the following quotation, see Schürer vol. 1, pp. 430–32, 468, and J. P. Meier, *A Marginal Jew: Rethinking the Historical Jesus,* vol. 1 (New York: Doubleday, 1991), 59–60.

both Eusebius and Origen. The same motif was used in relation to the death of Jesus. Eusebius suggests that, "after the savior's passion . . . disaster befell the entire nation" (3.7.7–9). There is evidence in the works of Origen (*Contra Celsum* 1.47; 2.13; *Commentary on Matthew* X.17) that the destruction of Jerusalem should be seen as a consequence of what was done to Jesus rather than James. Eusebius was aware of this point of view and sought to provide a reconciling solution. The fact that both Origen and Eusebius find it necessary to relate James's death as the cause of the destruction of Jerusalem to the death of Jesus as the real underlying cause confirms that they found the tradition about James already in the tradition that came to them. The likelihood is that Eusebius derived the quotation from Origen.

The straightforward reference to James as the brother of Jesus in this tradition attributed to Josephus confirms its early date. In the quotation the qualification is made concerning the messiahship of Jesus in more or less the same terms as in the authentic reference to James which Eusebius quotes in 2.23.21–24. In each case the straightforward identification of James as the brother of Jesus is notable and the qualification of Jesus as "the one called Christ" has a ring of authenticity about it. It is not what we would expect from a Christian interpolator who would be expected to affirm the messiahship of Jesus. Further, if an interpolator were responsible for the passage in 2.23.20, an exact copy of the reference to James in 2.23.22 might have been expected. On the whole scribal copyists were not creative so that the variations in the two references look more like what we would find in the practice of an author rather than an interpolator. In spite of this the textual evidence counts too heavily against the supposed quotation in 2.23.20 for it to be considered authentic.

If 2.23.20 is a Christian formulation, its relation to the text of Josephus and the interpretation of Origen remains an open question. It was made at a time when James could be described as the brother of Jesus without any hesitation or qualification. The universally attested reference to James in *Antiquities*, if accepted as authentic, supports the view that James was accepted as the brother of Jesus in wider Jewish circles where he was known.

HE 2.23.21–24: Josephus and the Martyrdom of James

The unidentifiable quotation from Josephus leads Eusebius to the quotation from *Ant.* 20.197–203. From it Eusebius has taken up, in his own earlier summary, the reference to the anarchy that provided the opportunity for the unlawful act against James (2.23.2), a reference which is not to be found in the traditions quoted from Clement and Hegesippus.

The earliest account of the martyrdom is given by Josephus.[59] Eusebius

---

[59] For a complete collection of the extant sources concerning the martyrdom of James, see R. A. Lipsius, *Die apokryphen Apostelgeschichten und Apostellegenden*, II.2 (Braunschweig, 1884), 238–57.

records this passage in full though he places it at the end of his account of the martyrdom of James. His quotation from *Antiquities* agrees closely with existing manuscript evidence. He has given priority to the Christian witness, especially the account given by Hegesippus.

It is well known that the translations of Josephus into other languages include passages not to be found in the Greek texts. The probability of interpolations is thus established. But the passage in which the reference to James the brother of Jesus occurs is present in all manuscripts, including the Greek texts. Does this place the burden of proof on those who question its authenticity, as many older commentators were inclined to argue?[60] There is another reference to Jesus in *Ant.* 18.63–64 which many scholars now consider to be "too good to be true" from a Christian perspective.[61] This passage is present in all texts also. But then there are only three texts of this passage in *Antiquities,* and the earliest manuscript is from the eleventh century.[62] Because these texts were transmitted by Christian scribes there was ample opportunity for tampering with the text.

While earlier Christian writers knew the works of Josephus, Origen is the first to refer to them in a way relevant to our discussion.[63] Origen expresses surprise that Josephus, "disbelieving in Jesus as Christ," should write respectfully about James, his brother.[64] Thus there is no reason to doubt that Origen knew the reference to James, and, from what is said about Josephus not believing Jesus to be the Christ, he knew some form of the earlier reference to Jesus also. But it seems not to have been in the form now found in all extant texts. The majority of scholars today consider the extended reference to Jesus to have been subjected to Christian scribal modification but do not consider it to be a straightforward interpolation. Many attempts have been made to restore the original wording by excluding obvious Christian points of view and retaining those parts that maintain the style and wording which is common elsewhere in Josephus.

Given the questions raised about the authenticity of this reference to Jesus, similar questions inevitably have been raised concerning the second reference in book 20 which also mentions James. The second reference has not generated as much controversy, and many scholars who have doubts about or reject the first reference have no doubts about the second.[65] In book 20 Jesus is mentioned only as a means of identifying which James is in view and, because there were

---

[60] See Schürer, vol. 1, p. 432.
[61] G. Vermes has frequently expressed this view, for example in the TV documentary *"Jesus": The Evidence*.
[62] See Schürer, vol. 1, p. 432.
[63] See *Contra Celsum* 1.47; 2.13; *Commentary on Matthew* X.17.
[64] *Commentary on Matthew* X.17 and *Contra Celsum* 1.47. See Schürer, vol. 1, p. 432.
[65] Schürer, vol. 1, p. 430, esp. n.1.

many people named Jesus, Josephus adds, "Jesus who is called Christ." Here it seems Josephus has used "Christ" in its Jewish sense of Messiah and not as a proper name, as became common in later Christian use.[66] Further, it is noted that no Christian scribe would have been content to use the noncommittal phrase "who is called Christ" when a full affirmation of messiahship was possible. This has led many scholars to accept the authenticity of the account of the martyrdom of James in *Antiquities* and to regard it as "probably quite reliable."[67] Eusebius introduces the passage from Josephus by saying:

> The same writer [Josephus] also narrates his death in the twentieth book of the *Antiquities* as follows:
>
>> Upon learning of the death of Festus, Caesar sent Albinus to Judaea as procurator. The king removed Joseph from the high priesthood, and bestowed the succession to this office upon the son of Ananus, who was likewise called Ananus. . . . The younger Ananus, who, as we have said, had been appointed to the high priesthood, was rash in his temper and unusually daring. He followed the school [αἵρεσιν] of the Sadducees, who are indeed more heartless than any of the other Jews, as I have already explained, when they sit in judgement. Possessed with such a character, Ananus thought that he had a favourable opportunity because Festus was dead and Albinus was on the way. And so he convened the judges of the Sanhedrin and brought before them a man named James, the brother of Jesus who was called the Christ [τοῦ λεγομένου Χριστοῦ], and certain others. He accused them of having transgressed the law and delivered them up to be stoned. Those of the inhabitants of the city who were considered the most fair-minded and were strict in the observance of the law were offended at this. They therefore secretly sent to King Agrippa urging him, for Ananus had not even been correct in his first step, to order him to desist from any further such actions. Certain of them even went to meet Albinus, who was on his way from Alexandria, and informed him that Ananus had no authority to convene the Sanhedrin without his consent. Convinced by these words, Albinus angrily wrote to Ananus threatening to take vengeance upon him. King Agrippa, because of Ananus' action, deposed him from the high priesthood which he had held for three months and replaced him with Jesus the son of Damnaeus.[68]

---

[66] Ibid., p. 431.

[67] Lüdemann, *Opposition*, p. 62. H. Conzelmann (*History of Primitive Christianity* [Nashville: Abingdon, 1973], 111) regards the text of Josephus as a rare example of a non-Christian source which lends direct support to the writing of the history of the church.

[68] *Ant.* 20.197–203. There are minor differences in the text as quoted by Eusebius in book 2.23.21–24. See Williamson, pp. 102–3.

The death of James took place in a break in Roman administration. When the Roman procurator Festus died, Caesar (Nero) sent Albinus, who, because he had to travel to Judaea via Alexandria, took some time to arrive, probably three or four months. These events allow us to date the time of the execution of James with a fair amount of precision. Because Albinus arrived, at latest, during the summer of 62 CE, the death of James can be assigned with some certainty to that year.[69] In the interregnum there were some important developments. 1) King Herod Agrippa removed Joseph from the high priesthood and set in his place Ananus II, the son of Ananus. 2) Ananus II took the opportunity provided by the interregnum to convene the judges of the Sanhedrin and to bring before them "a man named James, the brother of Jesus who was called the Christ, and certain others. He accused them of having transgressed the law and delivered them to be stoned."

The appointment of Ananus is associated with the interregnum.[70] This might suggest that the appointment was not one that would have been favored by Roman rule. What follows suggests that this event is noted simply to provide the context for the next events in sequence. The first of these was "the execution of James . . . and certain others." The account is concerned also with the manipulation of the high priestly office by Herod Agrippa, who first replaced Joseph, then Ananus, then Jesus the son of Damnaeus. Throughout that succession Josephus shows how the influence of Ananus was maintained through bribery.

The death of James is dealt with in this context. He is described as the brother of Jesus who is called Christ.[71] It is interesting that the qualification concerns Jesus who is called the Christ and not James's being called the brother of Jesus, the latter qualification being common in Eusebius, reflecting later Christian sensitivity. This supports the authenticity of the text in *Antiquities*. Josephus notes that Ananus

> followed the school of the Sadducees, who are indeed more heartless than any of the other Jews, as I have already explained, when they sit in judgment.

Given that Josephus narrates the convening of the judges of the Sanhedrin by Ananus, to bring before them James and certain others, naturally we are led to think that the decision taken against this group was Sadducean in motivation.

The group of people executed by Ananus is anonymous except for men-

---

[69] See Schürer, vol. 1, p. 468 and n.50 and note c, p. 494; and *Ant.* 20.202.

[70] Reference to Ananus is to Ananus II.

[71] The text of Josephus quoted by Eusebius has a different word order, reading τοῦ Χριστοῦ λεγομένου rather than τοῦ λεγομένου Χριστοῦ.

tion of "a man named James." One of this anonymous group is significant enough to be named. But what was his significance for Josephus? That he was the most notable and influential of the group is supported by the fact that the group was significant enough to be targeted at the first opportunity by Ananus. But having named him as "James," it was necessary to indicate which James was in view because the name of the great patriarch Jacob was very popular among Jews of this period. Consequently Josephus goes on to identify this James as "the brother of Jesus who was called the Christ" (*Ant.* 20.200). The phrase neutrally reports what this Jesus is called by way of distinguishing him from others of the same name, such as the high priests Jesus the son of Damnaeus and Jesus the son of Gamaliel, both mentioned by Josephus in this context (20.203 and 20.213).[72] There is no implied evaluation of the ascription in 20.200. An alternative that cannot be ruled out is that James was named only because he was the brother of this Jesus. In this case the naming of him would not necessarily mark him out as a truly notable figure in his own right. Yet he was notable enough to be known as the brother of Jesus, and on balance that notability seems to have made him a target for violent action. Consequently the reference to James marks him out as a leader who was targeted by Ananus. Identification of him as the brother of Jesus implies an earlier reference to Jesus. Josephus identifies James by reference to a person he has already mentioned. This aspect of the evidence favors allowing that a Christian scribe "enhanced" the reference to Jesus in book 18 rather than treating the whole passage as an interpolation. On that basis scholars look for evidence of the stratum of genuine Josephus while identifying obvious Christian additions.

James and "the certain others" were accused (by Ananus) of "having transgressed the law" and were condemned to be stoned. It is perhaps natural (though not necessarily correct) to think that "the certain others" associated with James were other Christian Jews.[73] Alternatively, although Josephus associates James with Jesus, he also associates him with another group of citizens whom he describes as "the most fair-minded and strict in observance of the law." From the point of view of Josephus, the group of which James was part is to be understood more in relation to this strict group than to the Christian Jews of Jerusalem, whom he does not mention specifically. It is possible that "the certain others" like James were members of the other, "fair-minded" group (Pharisees)[74] and Christian Jews as well, and it might have been that particular combination that marked them out for attack by Ananus.

---

[72] For an extended list of people named Jesus mentioned by Josephus, see Schürer, vol. 1, p. 431 n.5.

[73] This is the position of M. Hengel, *The Charismatic Leader and His Followers,* trans. J. Greig (New York: Crossroad, 1981), 41.

[74] See Acts 15:1, 5.

James and "the certain others" were charged with lawlessness (παρανομη-σάντων). If "the certain others" were Christian Jews like James this reference can be taken to mean that the Jerusalem church did not keep the ritual law of Judaism and was considered lawless, thus contributing to the break from Judaism.[75] This hardly fits the understanding of the Jerusalem church derived from the letters of Paul and Acts. Allowing for the identification of "the certain others" with believing Jews, another reading of the situation seems probable. Josephus notes:

> Those of the inhabitants of the city who were considered the most fair-minded and were strict in the observance of the law were offended at this.

Precisely who these fair-minded citizens were is not indicated, just as the decision to stone James and "certain others" is not specifically identified with the Sadducees, though this is probably correct. The objection raised by this unidentified group is important because the charge against James and the others was of having transgressed the law. Yet those who objected are described as those considered to be the most fair-minded and strict in observance of the law. Here we need to allow for Josephus's own bias in this evaluation. His leaning toward the Pharisees scarcely needs to be argued, and the description of them as "the most fair-minded" lends itself to a calculated attempt to show them in a favorable light. We are probably right in identifying this group with the Pharisees. Their opposition to the sentence must bring into question the validity of the charge of "lawlessness." They appear to represent a Pharisaic position over against the Sadducean position of those responsible for the sentence.

Alternatively, it could be argued that their objection was purely formal and had nothing to do with support for James and the others because:

> They therefore secretly sent to King Agrippa urging him, for Ananus had not even been correct in his first step, to order him to desist from any further such actions.

and

> Certain of them even went to meet Albinus, who was on his way from Alexandria, and informed him that Ananus had no authority to convene the Sanhedrin without his consent.

---

[75] This is the position of R. Schnackenburg, "Das Urchristentum," in *Literatur und Religion des Frühjudentums,* ed. J. Maier and J. Schreiner (Würzburg: J. C. B. Mohr, 1973), 304.

According to this reading, the second point elucidates the first, even though the reports were made to two different people (Agrippa and Albinus), and the second was made by only some of the concerned citizens. The objection was simply that the proceedings in this condemnation and execution were technically illegal.

G. Schofield has raised the question of the legal grounds of the objection, suggesting not only that it was illegal to call the Sanhedrin in the absence of the governor but also that this act was compounded by executing the condemned men without the governor's fiat.[76] The second point depends on the dubious assumption that Rome withheld the power of life and death from the Jewish authorities. The assumption is based on John 18:31, in which we are told that the Jews had taken Jesus to Pilate, but Pilate responded by telling them, "You take him and judge him according to your law." The Jewish authorities asserted, "It is not lawful for us to put any one to death." Read straightforwardly, this text supports the view that the Jews were not permitted to put any one to death. This conclusion is put in question by a number of observations. The Jewish and Roman sources provide no evidence to support this view. The Gospels, which place the blame for the crucifixion of Jesus firmly on the Jews, must find some explanation for the indisputable fact that he was actually crucified by the Romans. Thus, for John, had the Jews been able to exercise the power of life and death they would have executed Jesus. Crucifixion, a Roman form of execution, was necessary to fulfill the word of Jesus (John 18:32).

Even in John the authority of the Jews to manage their own affairs is evidenced in the words of Pilate, "You take him and judge him according to your law." The probability is that the Jews retained authority in matters generally termed "religious," or dealing with their own customs. Had it been possible to convict Jesus on a charge of blasphemy, even broadly understood as an attack on the sanctity of the Temple, his execution by the Jews would probably have been possible. According to the Gospels, the witnesses could not agree in their testimony against Jesus, and hence the charges against him could not be sustained. In the end he was executed on a political charge in terms that had nothing to do with a breach of Jewish law or custom. The later execution of Stephen by the Jews was based on an attack on the Temple in which (according to Acts 7:48) Stephen denied that God dwelt in a temple made by hands. According to the Gospels, the cleansing of the Temple by Jesus manifests Jesus' respect for the Temple, whereas Stephen attacked the validity of the Temple itself.

The objections raised by the concerned citizens after the death of James were heeded in both appeals. Each of those to whom appeal was made took

---

[76] *In the Year Sixty Two: The Murder of the Brother of the Lord and Its Consequences* (London: Harrap, 1962), 11.

action. Albinus angrily wrote to Ananus threatening vengeance, and Agrippa deposed Ananus from the high priesthood. The order of these events is not clear. Did Agrippa act on his own initiative or only under pressure from Albinus subsequent to his angry letter? The narrated order suggests the latter.

It is unlikely that those citizens described by Josephus as "the most fair-minded" and "strict in the observance of the law" were completely preoccupied with a technicality of Roman law. Another way of reading the report to King Agrippa makes better sense of this situation. It was reported that "this was not the first time Ananus had acted unjustly,"[77] rather than that Ananus was not "correct in his first step," that is, in calling the Sanhedrin. In the report to Albinus, however, the technicality was used because the real concern, which involved a difference between Sadducees and Pharisees, was of no concern to a Roman procurator. According to this reading, we see a struggle between the Pharisees and Sadducees, with James and certain others caught up in it. There is no evidence here to suggest that the Jerusalem church had loosened ties with Judaism or that commitment to a strict observance of the law had weakened. The support of those who were "strict in observance of the law" makes that reading of the situation highly improbable.[78]

A further clue is given in the account of the continued activities of Ananus after he had been deposed. He bribed both Albinus and his own successor (Jesus the son of Damnaeus) so that he was able to take the tithes of the priests who now starved to death (*Ant.* 20.205–7). There are grounds here for seeing the exploitation of poor rural priests of Pharisaic inclination by the aristocratic Sadducean high priest. If this were the case, these events might be more intricately intertwined than is at first apparent. James and the fair-minded citizens were opposed to the exploitation of the poorer priests and this point of view led to the execution of James and others associated with him.[79]

The evidence of Paul and Acts associates the poor with the Jerusalem church, and there is reference to the conversion of many priests (Gal 2:10; Rom 15:22–32; Acts 6:7; 21:20). James's conflict with Ananus was a result of his opposition to the exploitation of the poor by the rich aristocratic ruling class and in particular the exploitation of the poor rural priesthood by the aristocratic urban chief priests.[80] If we allow that the poor rural priests serving in the Temple

---

[77] See *Ant.* 20.201 and note c pp. 496–97 in vol. IX LCL.

[78] Here M. Smith (*Jesus the Magician* [San Francisco: Harper & Row, 1978], 173) correctly concludes that the report by Josephus reveals Pharisaic sympathy for James.

[79] S. G. F. Brandon ("The Death of James the Just: A New Interpretation," in *Studies in Mysticism and Religion Presented to G. Scholem* . . . , ed. E. E. Urbach et al. [Jerusalem: Magnes Press, Hebrew University, 1967], 67) is probably right in seeing the exploitation of the poor priests as a factor in the situation but wrong in not also relating this to a struggle between Pharisees and Sadducees.

[80] See Josephus, *Ant.* 20.131–36, 180–81, 206–7, and E. M. Smallwood, "High Priests and Politics in Roman Palestine, *JTS* ns 13 (1962): 14–34; and Smallwood, *The Jews under Roman Rule: From Pompey to Diocletian. A Study of Political Relations* (Leiden: Brill, 1981), 272–84, 314.

were more closely aligned to the Pharisees than to the Sadducean aristocratic chief priests,[81] then we have a scenario in which to understand the conflict between James and Ananus, as described by Josephus. At this point Hegesippus has obscured the real opponent of James (the high priest Ananus) by portraying the scribes and Pharisees as responsible for his death. It may be that he simply transposed the traditional opponents of Jesus to the conflict with James.

Nothing in the passage in Josephus looks suspiciously like a Christian interpolation. The account of the execution of James in *Antiquities* 20 can be accepted as basically historical, allowing only for the tendencies within Josephus's own writing. The account reinforces our understanding of James and his association with believing Pharisees who affirmed the continuing relevance of the Jewish law. James and the Jerusalem church supported a mission to other Jews based on the continuing validity of the law, including circumcision. The execution of James by Ananus does nothing to undermine this understanding.

Perhaps Eusebius leaves the quotation from Josephus for last because he has given priority to the Christian tradition. The account by Hegesippus is featured and emphasized. It makes the points that are important for Eusebius concerning the righteousness of James and his courageous witness to Jesus in the face of martyrdom. In contrast to this, the account in Josephus, unless it is read with care, might be thought to cast doubt on the righteousness of James. It gives no hint of his witness to Jesus in the face of martyrdom.

By collecting together the brief quotation from Clement with the extended account of Hegesippus and the less detailed account of Josephus, Eusebius pointedly (if inadvertently) raises the question of the literary relationship among the three. The account of Josephus could have been used as a source by Hegesippus or elements from it could subsequently have been interpolated into Hegesippus's account. Some literary influence seems likely. This has been obscured by the ideological interpretation that has driven Hegesippus.

The grounds for thinking that Clement's brief account is dependent on Hegesippus are far from convincing. There is a case for thinking that Clement gives us access to an early independent Christian tradition of the death of James. In spite of obvious knowledge of Josephus, Hegesippus has produced his own account that has irreconcilable conflicts with Josephus. At every point of conflict it seems likely that the account of Josephus is to be preferred. The account of Hegesippus is ideologically driven and cannot be harmonized with Josephus.[82] On this matter modern scholarship tends to follow J. B. Lightfoot and Johannes Weiss.[83]

---

[81] J. Jeremias, *Jerusalem in the Time of Jesus*, trans. F. H. Cave and C. H. Cave (London: SCM, 1967), 256, asserts that "a large number of priests were Pharisees." Jeremias outlines the evidence upon which he bases his view on pp. 256–58.

[82] Contrary to R. Eisler, *The Messiah Jesus and John the Baptist* . . . (London: Methuen, 1931), 141–43, 182, 289, 518–20, 540–42, 596.

[83] See Lightfoot, *Saint Paul's Epistle to the Galatians* (London: Macmillan, 1874), 348–50, and Weiss, *Das Urchistentum*, ed. R. Knopf (Göttingen: Vandenhoeck & Ruprecht, 1917).

HE 2.23.24–25: Final Summary on James and Reference to the Epistle

Eusebius's quotation of Josephus concludes his narration of the death of James. Following the quotation he says only:

> Such is the story of James, to whom is attributed the first of the "general" epistles. Admittedly its authenticity is doubted, since few early writers refer to it, any more than to "Jude's," which is also one of the seven called general. But the fact remains that these two, like the others, have been regularly used in very many churches.

Important for our later discussion is the comment that the authenticity of the epistles of James and Jude was doubted because few early writers referred to them. Nevertheless, Eusebius asserts the widespread use of both epistles. Both epistles were late in gaining popularity and thus are not quoted by many early writers. While use of them had become widespread by the time of Eusebius, it was not universal.

HE 3.5.2–3: SUMMARY STATEMENTS CONCERNING JAMES AS FIRST BISHOP AND MARTYR

After his detailed account Eusebius makes only reflective and summary reference to James. In 3.5.2 Eusebius writes:

> After the ascension of our savior, the Jews had followed up their crime against him by devising plot after plot against his apostles. First they stoned Stephen to death; then James the son of Zebedee and brother of John was beheaded; and finally James, the first after our savior's ascension to be appointed to the bishop's throne there, lost his life in the way described, while the remaining apostles, in constant danger from murderous plots, were driven out of Judaea.[84]

In a passage probably dependent on 2.1.1–5, Eusebius commences his reference to James with the words "After the ascension of the savior," wording that is reminiscent of the quotation from Clement in 2.1.3. There the reference is to the choice of James the Just as the first bishop of Jerusalem by Peter, James, and John. Here James is linked with the series of martyrs going back to Jesus himself, and it is specifically said, like a recurring refrain, that James was the first bishop of Jerusalem after the ascension.[85] James's death is said to mark the driv-

---

[84] Williamson, p. 111 [68].

[85] Eusebius knows nothing of a tradition of the original leadership of Peter in the Jerusalem church, even though this way of reading Acts is popular today.

ing out of the other apostles from Jerusalem, and this observation may help to explain further the link made between the death of James and the siege of Jerusalem in 3.7.7–12. Because the siege is portrayed as a consequence of the martyrdom of both Jesus and James, the present reference telescopes these events so that it gives the impression that they occurred in quick succession. The plots against the apostles are only one explanation for the absence of the apostles from Jerusalem. Eusebius also goes on (3.5.3) to speak of the commission to evangelize the nations, which also took the disciples and apostles out of Jerusalem, and the prophetic warning to flee from Jerusalem to Pella before the outbreak of the Jewish war (see 3.11.1). This final point implies that all faithful believers abandoned Jerusalem prior to the siege.

In identifying James, Eusebius again (see 2.1.2) mentions that he was the first to be appointed to the bishop's throne in Jerusalem after the ascension. But here he makes no mention of James's reputed relationship with Jesus nor of his designation as "the Just." Given the earlier reference the one point of identification is enough to recall all of the details.

HE 3.7.7–9; 3.11.1; 3.12.1: THE DEATH OF JAMES AND THE SIEGE OF JERUSALEM

HE 3.7.7–9: The Delay of the Siege

The siege of Jerusalem is linked with the death of Jesus.[86]

> After the savior's passion . . . disaster befell the entire nation. . . . But . . . certain facts bring home the beneficence of all gracious providence, which for forty years after the crime against Christ delayed their destruction. All that time most of the apostles and disciples, including James himself, the first bishop of Jerusalem, known as the Lord's brother, were still alive, and by remaining in the city furnished the place with an impregnable bulwark.[87]

Eusebius goes on to indicate that in this way God gave the Jews time to repent and then appeals to "book 6 of Josephus's *Histories*" to support his views (3.8.1).

Eusebius characteristically writes of James as the one "known as" the Lord's brother and as the first bishop of Jerusalem. What is added here is the view that the presence of James and the other apostles and disciples held back the destruction impending after the "crime" against Jesus, thus modifying the tradition that the "murder" or martyrdom of James led to the destruction of

---

[86] Williamson, pp. 118–19 [75].

[87] Cf. 3.7.8 with 2.23.7 where the name "Bulwark of the people" (περιοχὴ τοῦ λαοῦ) is ascribed to James.

Jerusalem. Eusebius wished to make the death of Jesus the reason for the siege but was aware of the gap in time between the two events. The presence of James within Jerusalem then becomes the reason for the delay. With this modification of the causal link between the death of James and the siege, James is associated with a point of view expressed by Origen, whose views were drawn on by Eusebius.

The death of James marked the end of that protecting presence and "disaster befell the entire nation." Eusebius has reconciled the tradition that Jerusalem was destroyed because of the crime against Jesus with the tradition that the destruction followed immediately after the death of James. Naturally the "delay" following the death of Jesus invited some explanatory hypothesis, and this is now supplied by appealing to the safeguarding presence of James and the other apostles. While there is a delay following the death of James (before the destruction of Jerusalem), it is shorter than the one measured from the death of Jesus. For the idea of the presence of the righteous person providing protection for the wicked city, see Genesis 18:23–33 and Genesis Rabbah 30.7.

HE 3.11.1; 3.12.1: After the Siege

If, for Eusebius, the death of James marks the beginning of the siege of Jerusalem, there is a before- and an after-the-siege for the Jerusalem church:

> After the martyrdom of James and the capture of Jerusalem which instantly followed, there is a firm tradition that those of the apostles and disciples of the Lord who were still alive assembled from all parts together with those who, humanly speaking, were kinsmen of the Lord—for most of them were still living and they all took counsel together concerning whom they should judge worthy to succeed James and to the unanimous tested approval it was decided that Symeon son of the Clopas, mentioned in the gospel narrative, was worthy to occupy the *throne* of the Jerusalem see. He was, so it is said, a cousin [ἀνεψιόν] of the savior, for Hegesippus relates that Clopas was the brother of Joseph.[88] (3.11.1)

In 4.22.4 Eusebius quotes the passage from Hegesippus upon which the present account is based.[89] There Hegesippus says simply that Symeon was the cousin of the Lord, making no qualification such as "so it is said." Here (3.11.1) Eusebius provides evidence of a view that ill fits traditions that he has used earlier (3.5.2–3)[90] to offer reasons for a break in the continuity of the history of the Jerusalem church because: 1) after the death of James murderous plots

---

[88] Williamson, pp. 123–24 [79].

[89] Ibid., p. 181 [129].

[90] Ibid., p. 111 [68].

against the apostles drove them from Judaea; 2) the apostles went out from Jerusalem to every nation to fulfill the mission command of Jesus; 3) the faithful fled from Jerusalem to Pella before the outbreak of the war because an oracle from the Lord warned them and instructed them to flee from Jerusalem.[91]

Eusebius attempted to reconcile this tradition of catastrophe and discontinuity with one of continuity implied by the list of fifteen Hebrew bishops and the Hebrew character of the church until the time of the second siege (4.5.1–4). Eusebius makes the continuity explicit by asserting that the siege of Jerusalem followed instantly after the martyrdom of James, minimizing the time between the death of James and the appointment of Symeon. He also declares that the apostles and disciples who remained alive assembled, presumably in Jerusalem, from various parts of the world. They gathered with the human family of the Lord (γένους κατὰ σάρκα τοῦ κυρίου). Eusebius notes that of the apostles and disciples "many . . . were still alive." The family had previously (1.7.14) been referred to as δεσπόσυνοι because of their relation to the Lord, the despot. There is no indication that it was necessary for the human family of the Lord to regather in Jerusalem, there being no mention of their flight. In this way continuity before and after the siege is maintained. Finally, Eusebius has taken account of the flight of the apostles from Judaea and narrates their return after the war. But he assumes the continuity of the Jerusalem church because the purpose of the return of the apostles and disciples was to appoint a successor to James in a church that continued to be Hebrew in character.

The unanimous decision taken was that Symeon the son of Clopas[92] was worthy of the throne of Jerusalem.[93] In this case Eusebius has stressed the formal character of the decision. All of the surviving apostles, disciples, and members of the family of the Lord gathered in Jerusalem to take counsel together to judge who was worthy, and to the tested approval of all it was agreed that Symeon was worthy of the throne of Jerusalem. This unanimous decision to appoint Symeon is in contrast to the choice of James by Peter, James, and John in the tradition reported by Clement of Alexandria (HE 2.1.3), while the summary of Eusebius (HE 2.23.1) comes close in asserting that James was elected by the apostles. Apologetic tendencies are obvious.

Eusebius immediately goes on to bring out the family relationship of Symeon to Jesus, noting that he was said to be the cousin of Jesus according to Hegesippus, who indicated that Clopas was the brother of Joseph. In a later section (4.22.4)[94] Eusebius actually quotes from the passage of Hegesippus to

---

[91] This tradition is known to us in Epiphanius (Pan 29.7.7; 30.2.7 and Treatise on Weights and Measures 15), who might be dependent on Eusebius HE 3.5.3. See Lüdemann, Opposition, pp. 203–6.

[92] See John 19:25; Luke 24:18.

[93] See also 2.23.1 and the discussion of the throne in 7.19.1, Williamson, p. 302 [234].

[94] Williamson, p. 181 [129].

which he here refers, making clear that Symeon was appointed *because* he was the cousin of Jesus. The causal link is not clear in the summary made here by Eusebius, in 3.11.1. Hegesippus straightforwardly describes Symeon as the cousin of the Lord without Eusebius's qualification "so it is said," which appears in the summary. The qualification, consistently introduced by Eusebius, belongs to a later time and destroys the basis for the selection of Symeon.

In the summary Eusebius makes the surviving apostles, disciples, and family of Jesus responsible for the appointment of Symeon. Hegesippus affirms the unanimity of the decision without detailing the groups involved (4.22.4). While Eusebius named Hegesippus as the source of his knowledge of Symeon's relationship to Clopas, he names no source for his knowledge of those who made the decision. It is characteristic of Eusebius to express new views in his summaries, views that may or may not be dependent on sources. It may be that he has simply extrapolated the unanimity of the decision in terms of those he supposed would have been involved, though this seems less than likely because he appealed to "a firm tradition" to this effect. Compare the appeal to "an old and firm tradition" in 3.10.1. While the appeal to an anonymous tradition might be seen as an attempt to bolster the legitimacy of the succession to Symeon, there is probably more to it than this.

According to Eusebius, Hegesippus also recorded that after the siege of Jerusalem Vespasian instituted a search for members of the royal family of David and in so doing inflicted great persecution on the Jews (3.12.1).[95] This note follows immediately after the summary concerning the succession from James to Symeon (3.11.1). No explicit connection is made between these two events, but they are narrated one following the other. Symeon, said to be of the family of Jesus, succeeded James as bishop of Jerusalem. Vespasian ordered the rooting out of all descendants of the royal house of David. This comment prepares the way for a clearer statement about the royal status of the family of Jesus. At the same time Eusebius reinforces the idea of the punishment of the Jews for their *crimes* against Jesus (and James).

The compression of time is necessary to show that disaster befell Jerusalem as a consequence of what was done to James, and to Jesus. It was also necessary because, according to the tradition, Symeon succeeded James as bishop of Jerusalem but was not appointed until after the destruction of Jerusalem. His appointment was the first step in the reconstruction of the Jerusalem church. According to Josephus, James was martyred in 62 CE, a full four years before the outbreak of the Jewish war and eight years before the destruction of Jerusalem. We can only speculate concerning the leadership of the church between 62 and the outbreak of the war. The fate of the Jerusalem church itself in the war is also less than clear. Eusebius (*HE* 3.5.3) refers to the flight to Pella as an

---

[95] Ibid., p. 124 [79].

explanation of what happened.[96] Here he provides evidence of greater disruption of the continuity of the Jerusalem church than was comfortable for him to admit. Nevertheless he does not think that the Jerusalem church perished in the war. Rather, its leadership was reconstituted immediately after the war, and Eusebius appeals to a tradition of fourteen Hebrew bishops of the Jerusalem church up to the second major war in the time of Hadrian (*HE* 4.5.1–4).

Eusebius stresses the continuity of the Jerusalem church before and after the first Jewish war by playing down the gap between the leadership of James and of Symeon and by emphasizing that the first fourteen bishops were Hebrews. While apologetic tendencies are evident in his writing, he may have reported accurately because he makes no attempt to argue for a continuity of Jewish bishops after the second war. Continuity then is shown only by the veneration for the throne of James (see *HE* 7.19.1). But if the Jerusalem church after 70 CE maintained its Jewish character, there is no evidence that it maintained the kind of influence over the wider Christian movement that it had exercised in the time of James. Symeon may have had the support of all when appointed to succeed James, but we may doubt that he was able fill James's shoes. Those who followed James may also have been admirable in their own way, but none of them seems to have been able to dominate the development of Christianity by force of personality or leadership charisma. This failure contributed to the fading image of James. When after 135 CE the Jerusalem church became a Gentile church, the image of James was lost altogether from accurate memory.

HE 3.19.1–3.20.7: The Family of Jesus until the Reign of Trajan

In a passage dealing with the reign of Domitian, Eusebius tells how the emperor ordered the execution of all who were of the line of David.

> The same Domitian ordered the execution of all who were of the family of David, and there is an old and firm tradition that a group of heretics [αἱρετικῶν][97] accused the descendants of Jude—the brother, according to the flesh, of the savior—alleging that they were of the family of David and related to Christ himself. Hegesippus relates this as follows.
>
> > "Now there still survived of the family of the Lord the grandsons of Jude—who was said to be his brother according to the flesh—and they were informed against as being of the family of David. These the

---

[96] Many scholars, such as Lüdemann (*Opposition*, pp. 203–6), doubt the historicity of the account.

[97] Compare the role of the heretics as accusers of Symeon (3.32.3) and the representatives of the seven sects in the martyrdom of James (2.23.8).

evocatus[98] brought before Domitian Caesar. For he was afraid of the coming of Christ as Herod [had been] also. He asked them if they were descended from David and they admitted it. Then he asked them how much property they owned or how much money they controlled. They replied that they possessed only nine thousand *denarii* [99] between them, half belonging to each, and this, they said, was not available in cash but was the estimated value of only thirty nine *plethra* of land[100] on which they paid taxes and lived on by their own work."

They showed him their hands, putting forward as proof of their toil the hardness of their bodies. . . .

On hearing this Domitian did not condemn them but despised them as simple folk, released them, and decreed an end to the persecution against the church. When they were released they were the leaders of the churches, both because of their testimony and because they were of the family of the Lord and remained alive in the peace which lasted until Trajan. This we learn from Hegesippus.[101]

While Eusebius specifically drew on Hegesippus for his overall account of the incident, he names "an old and firm tradition" (3.19.1) as the source of the identity of those who accused the descendants of Jude. Compare the reference to "a firm tradition" in 3.11.1. We cannot rule out that this is simply an elaboration of Hegesippus, or even a confusion of the accusation against Symeon with an accusation against the descendants of Jude.

It is strange that here the qualification of the relationship of Jude to Jesus, "said to be his brother according to the flesh," appears in the quotation from Hegesippus (3.20.1), not in the summary introduction by Eusebius (3.19.1), where he is described as "the brother, according to the flesh, of the savior." We might suspect that Eusebius has inadvertently placed the qualification in the quotation rather than in his own summary, which was normally his practice. The "grandsons" (υἱωνοὶ) mentioned in the quotation are described generally as descendants (ἀπογόνους) by Eusebius (3.32.5). In the summary Eusebius says they were charged with being of the family of David and related to Christ whereas, according to Hegesippus, the charge related only to their belonging to the family of David, although there is dialogue about "the coming of Christ." Hegesippus makes the point that subsequent to their witness before Domitian

---

[98] The Greek ὁ ἠουοκᾶτος represents the Latin *evocatus*, meaning veteran, and apparently here names an official, though the precise use of the word is unknown.

[99] Estimating the value of a *denarius* is difficult. In the Gospels the wage of a laborer is calculated at one *denarius* a day (Matt 20:2).

[100] The Greek πλέθρον is not quite a quarter of an acre, but here the term is used for the Latin *iugerum*, which is more than half an acre.

[101] Williamson, pp. 126–27 [81–82].

the grandsons became leaders of the churches, leadership based on their witness and their place in the human family of the Lord.

HE 3.32.1–6: SYMEON IN THE TIME OF TRAJAN

This incident with the grandsons of Jude is again referred to briefly by Eusebius after dealing with Hegesippus's account of the martyrdom of Symeon.[102] In his summary Eusebius provides a context for the quotation that follows referring to the martyrdom of Symeon[103] the son of Clopas and second bishop of Jerusalem in the time of Trajan (3.32.1). He tells, purportedly basing his account on Hegesippus, of how Symeon was accused and tortured for being a Christian and suffered an end like that of the Lord. He then allows Hegesippus to tell, in his own words, how certain heretics[104]

> accused Simon son of Clopas of being descended from David and a Christian and consequently he suffered martyrdom [μαρτυρεῖ] at the age of one hundred and twenty, when Trajan was emperor and Atticus was consular governor.[105]

The grounds for Clopas's martyrdom are both that he was of the family of David and that he was a Christian. The grounds of the charge against Symeon appear to have been different from the charge brought against the grandsons of Jude. According to the quotation from Hegesippus, it was a single charge of being of the family of David, although reference to Domitian's fear of the coming of Christ might be thought to justify Eusebius in his summary account of a double charge of being of the family of David *and* related to Christ. Here (in 3.32.1–6), in the charge brought against Symeon, there is agreement about being of the family of David, but the other charge relates to being a Christian, a charge applicable more widely than simply to the family of Jesus. We know that in the time of Trajan it was a crime simply to be a Christian, and the use of this term (Χριστιανός) in relation to Symeon is consistent with the known correspondence between Pliny Secundus and Trajan.[106] While this remains the

---

[102] Ibid., pp. 142–43 [95–96].

[103] In this passage Eusebius varies the spelling of this name, sometimes using Συμεών and elsewhere Σίμων. The former is based on the Aramaic, but Eusebius uses it in a declinable form. See Συμεῶνα in 3.32.1.

[104] Compare the heretics (αἱρετικῶν) who accused the grandsons of Jude according to Eusebius in 3.19.1.

[105] While the dates for the office of Atticus are unknown, in his *Chronicles* Eusebius dates the martyrdom of Symeon in 106 or 107 CE.

[106] Eusebius makes reference to this in 3.33.1–3. For the correspondence between Pliny and Trajan see H. Bettenson, ed., *Documents of the Christian Church* (Oxford: Oxford University Press, 1956), 3–6.

most probable reading, so that Symeon died as a Christian, and not because of his human relationship as a member of the family of Jesus, it is just possible that the term should be understood in a more restricted sense of "the household of Christ," that is, a member of his family. But set in the time of Trajan, this interpretation seems unlikely, especially as the term had been used of Christians at least from the time of Acts and 1 Peter.[107] However the term is understood, Symeon is added to the list of martyrs and righteous sufferers, Jesus and James. It is a messianic family tradition of the bishops of Jerusalem to this point that they should die as righteous martyrs.

Ironically, Eusebius goes on to say that later, when members of the royal house of Judah were being hunted, Symeon's accusers were arrested also. Apparently Eusebius reintroduced discussion of the grandsons of Jude because they too were arrested, and Hegesippus combined his discussion of their role with his account of the martyrdom of Symeon. This was appropriate because the grandsons too were of the family of Jesus and are portrayed as leaders of the church and righteous sufferers. According to Eusebius, whose summary is based on Hegesippus,

> other descendants of one of the so-called brothers of the savior named Jude lived on into the same reign [of Trajan] after they had given, in the time of Domitian, the testimony in behalf of the faith of Christ already recorded of them.[108] He [Hegesippus] writes thus:
>
>> "Consequently they came and presided over every church, as witnesses and members of the family of the Lord, and since profound peace came to every church they survived until the time of Trajan Caesar, until the time of the son of the Lord's uncle, the aforesaid Simon the son of Clopas, was similarly accused by the sects on the same charge before Atticus the consular. He was tortured for many days and gave his witness so that all, even the consular, were astounded that at the age of one hundred and twenty he could endure it, and he was ordered to be crucified."

According to Hegesippus, Symeon "was similarly accused by the sects." This may imply that the descendants of Jude were also accused by the "sects," providing the basis for Eusebius's claim that there was "old and firm tradition" to the effect that the descendants of Jude were accused by heretics (3.19.1).

The continuing importance of the family of Jesus in the Jerusalem church and indeed in the churches at large is stated in Eusebius's summary and the quotation from Hegesippus. Leadership of the church depended on the recog-

---

[107] Acts 11:26; 26:28; 1 Peter 4:16.
[108] See 3.19.1–3.20.7, quoted above.

nition of members of the human family of Jesus. Reservations about leaders being part of the family belong more to the time of Eusebius, and qualification is normally present in those passages composed by him, even when he is summarizing sources from which it is absent. The qualification is generally absent from quotations from Hegesippus, and we might suspect that Eusebius was tempted to introduce such a qualification, as perhaps he did in 3.20.1. For the early church, two centuries before Eusebius, the important issue for leadership was membership in the family of Jesus, a position that would be destroyed by the denial of the reality of that relationship. The same tradition suggests that the civil authorities perceived that what was important was membership in the family of David because in the course of two wars with the Jews they had become familiar with messianic causes of unrest. According to the tradition, both issues came together in the family of Jesus. If this cause of conflict with the civil authorities came to rest for a while it re-emerged with new ferocity in the time of Trajan.

From Jesus to James to Symeon and the grandsons of Jude we have a succession of martyrs who might be considered *Zaddikim,* that is, notably righteous people. This view of James is consistent with our reading of the New Testament evidence. The link with the family of Jesus runs against the theological tendencies affirming his unique significance. The emerging orthodoxy of the early church tended to isolate Jesus from all but Mary, his virgin mother.

It is sometimes argued that the Davidic messianic motif fits the agenda of the early church and probably does not belong to the early tradition.[109] But there is independent evidence of messianic activity among the Jews, and, at least in the second of the two wars, Symeon bar Kochba was perceived by both sides to be a messianic leader. The distinguished rabbi Akiba supported him as the authentic Messiah and deliverer and was devastated by the failure of the rebellion.

He 4.5.1–4: THE TRADITIONAL LIST OF THE BISHOPS OF JERUSALEM

Eusebius appeals to a traditional list of the bishops of Jerusalem up to the time of the siege by Hadrian,[110] though he had no documentary evidence of their dates. Elsewhere he provided evidence of the conclusion of the reign of James in the account of James's death (2.23.1–25) and of the beginning and end of the reign of Symeon (3.11.1; 3.32.1–6; 4.22.4). But he claims to have documentary evidence that these bishops were short-lived and that there were fifteen of them prior to the siege of "the Jews" by Hadrian. Of these bishops Eusebius says:

---

[109] Thus Lüdemann, *Opposition*, p. 121.
[110] Williamson, p. 156 [107].

All are said to be Hebrews in origin, . . . at that time their whole church consisted of Hebrew believers who had continued from apostolic times down to the later siege in which the Jews . . . were overwhelmed in a full-scale war.

As this meant an end of the bishops of the circumcision, it is now necessary to give their names from the first. The *first* then was James who was called the Lord's brother; after whom Symeon was *second*; Justus third; Zacchaeus fourth; fifth Tobias; sixth Benjamin; John seventh; eighth Matthias; ninth Philip; tenth Seneca; eleventh Justus; Levi twelfth; Ephres thirteenth; fourteenth Joseph; and last, fifteenth Judas. Such were the bishops in the city of Jerusalem from the apostles down to the time mentioned; they were all of the circumcision.

After the siege Eusebius claims that Jerusalem became a Gentile city. The Jews were driven out, the city was populated by Gentiles, and the church was composed of Gentiles with a Gentile bishop named Mark (4.6.4). Thus there was a racial change in the character of the Jerusalem church after the second siege, in the time of Hadrian. That break in historical continuity modified the way the church came to perceive its earlier history.

For Eusebius the term "Jews" is used only of the unbelieving nation, while believers and bishops of Jerusalem up to the second siege are described as Hebrews and "of the circumcision." This use of "the circumcision" might reflect the dialogue and conflict between Paul and James, between Paul and the Jerusalem church, with its mission based on the requirements of circumcision. The circumcision mission continued to shape the Jerusalem church beyond the first Jewish war and lost its way only after the second siege. By the time Eusebius wrote the demand for circumcision and the keeping of the Jewish law had long since ceased, and he was unaware of the significance of the reference to the Jerusalem church as the circumcision. This fact adds weight to the view that here Eusebius is dealing with a traditional list of bishops in the Jerusalem church.

HE 4.22.4: THE JERUSALEM SUCCESSION AND THE BEGINNING OF HERESY

Eusebius tells how Hegesippus described the beginning of the heresies of his time, before which the church was a virgin.[111] According to Eusebius, Hegesippus wrote:

---

[111] Ibid., p. 181 [129].

After James the Just had suffered martyrdom for the same reason as the Lord, Symeon, the son of Clopas was appointed bishop, being a cousin of the Lord whom all determined that he should be *second*.

The word "second" can be taken as modifying "cousin," indicating "another" or "second" cousin. This reading of the text raises the question of who the first cousin is, the answer to which would be James because, according to this reading, Symeon would be the second cousin to be bishop.[112] Against this view is the evidence that Jerome nowhere appeals to this passage in Hegesippus to justify his view that the so-called brothers were actually cousins. Lightfoot rightly argues that Jerome's critical theory was without traditional precedent.[113]

Alternatively, the other implied noun to be read with "second" is "bishop," so that the statement may be understood as indicating that Symeon, "being a cousin of the Lord" was second (bishop of Jerusalem), James having been the first.[114] This latter interpretation is supported by Eusebius's account of the martyrdom of Symeon, in which Symeon is described as the second bishop of Jerusalem (3.32.1), and in the enumeration in Eusebius's list of the bishops of Jerusalem.[115] In ancient times no one, not even Jerome, read the passage as if it asserted that Symeon was the second cousin to be bishop.

Symeon was chosen because he belonged to the natural family of Jesus. In the earliest Jerusalem church the family of Jesus provided leadership. From the first, James was the natural leader in that church. When he was martyred he was succeeded by another, though more distant, member of the family, confirming the importance of the leadership of the family of Jesus in the Jerusalem church.

From Hegesippus Eusebius has picked up the theme of the righteous sufferers, identifying both Jesus and James as righteous martyrs. It is a theme developed further elsewhere. Here, as elsewhere when Eusebius is quoting Hegesippus, there is no qualification to the statement that Symeon was a cousin of the Lord. This relationship to the Lord is the basis for the universal demand

---

[112] This is the way R. B. Ward ("James of Jerusalem in the First Two Centuries," pp. 800–801) understands the text, as does R. P. Martin, p. l. "According to Hegesippus, James and Simeon are both ἀνεψιοί (kinsfolk) of the Lord (4.12.4), a designation indicating only near relationship."

[113] Lightfoot, pp. 252–53, 258–59.

[114] In his translation of Eusebius, Lake (vol. 1, p. 375) has adopted the former reading, while Williamson (p. 181 [129]) has adopted the latter. Williamson's reading is supported by A. Meyer and W. Bauer, "The Relatives of Jesus," in *New Testament Apocrypha*, vol. 1, ed. W. Schneemelcher, trans. R. McL. Wilson (Philadelphia: Westminster, 1963), 425.

[115] Ευμεῶνα τὸν τοῦ κλωτᾶ, ὃν δεύτερον καταστῆναι τῆς ἐν Ἱεροσολύμοις ἐκκλησιας ἐτισκοτον . . . See also the list of the bishops of Jerusalem (4.5.1–4; Williamson, p. 156 [107]), in which Symeon is named as "second" bishop.

that Symeon should be "second," that is, second bishop of Jerusalem after James.

He 7.19.1: The Throne of James

Eusebius's final reference to James concerns James's throne.[116]

> Now the throne [θρόνον] of James, who was the first to receive from the savior and the apostles the episcopate of the Jerusalem church and who was called [χρηματίσαι] a brother of Christ, as the divine books show, has been preserved to this day; and by the honour that the brethren in succession there pay to it, they show clearly to all the reverence in which the holy men were and still are held by the men of old time and those of our day, because of the love shown them by God.[117]

Here, in a passage for which Eusebius offers no corroborating sources, he shows his own veneration for James and the Jerusalem church. The veneration for the throne has implications for both James and Jerusalem. The account given by Eusebius asserts that this veneration was expressed not only by Eusebius but also by the succession of leaders in Jerusalem who preserved the throne down to Eusebius's day. This veneration continued after the line of "Hebrew" bishops had come to an end and a new line of Gentile bishops had been established. Reference to the honor given to the throne by the brethren in succession has been taken to mean that each in turn looked after the throne. Reference to the succession might mean that what was in mind was that succeeding bishops took their turns in caring for the throne, perhaps in their own homes.

It is claimed that the throne of James has been preserved in the Armenian Cathedral of St. James in Jerusalem. Kevork Hintlian gives evidence of the throne from the late seventeenth century:[118] "In the middle of the church is a pulpit made of tortoise-shell, and mother of pearl, with a beautiful canopy, or cupola over it, of the same fabric. The tortoise-shell and mother of pearl are so exquisitely mingled and inlaid in each other that the work far exceeds the materials." According to Hintlian, the throne was taken by the patriarch Cyril of Jerusalem into his house. Cyril was bishop of Jerusalem from about 350 to 386 CE. But there is no attempt in Hintlian, or elsewhere, as far as I know, to provide a history of the throne between the time of Cyril and the eighteenth century. This gap in evidence throws some doubt on the hypothesis that it is the throne of James. Suspicion is increased by noting that the doors to the shrine of James

---

[116] Williamson, p. 302 [234].

[117] In *HE* 7.32.29 there is a further reference to the preservation of the throne in which it is called "the apostolic throne." Williamson, p. 326 [255].

[118] Hintlian, p. 52.

the brother of John, which is in the same cathedral, are made of the same materials. Probability is that this throne comes from a somewhat later period than the episcopate of James. This throne is now used only once a year, on the feast day of St. James and at the investiture of a new patriarch.

The primary point of 7.19.1 is to demonstrate the love and honor shown to James, evidenced by the preservation of his throne, and the honor that continued to be shown to the throne in Eusebius's own day. No new sources are quoted. Nevertheless the summary gives new information for which no basis has been provided. Perhaps Eusebius intended that the reader would know that he had firsthand knowledge of the situation in Jerusalem in his own day. Such a position might imply that his knowledge of what had been done up until the present had come to him from the current representative of the succession of bishops.

Eusebius asserts that James "was the first to receive from the savior and the apostles the episcopate of the Jerusalem church." Much of this summary is a restatement of what has already appeared in earlier passages (2.1.2; 3.5.2; 4.5.1–5). It combines the implications of the two passages from Clement to combat the tradition that James was the first person to whom the risen lord appeared, authorizing him as leader.[119] Thus Eusebius asserts that James received the episcopate from the savior *and the apostles*. Eusebius, like Clement, was conscious of a tradition that elevated James the Just in order to subvert apostolic succession. That alternative tradition is found in the Nag Hammadi documents that honor James (the *Apocryphon of James* and the *First* and the *Second Apocalypse of James*), as well as in the works listed in the note 119 above. Clement and Eusebius were unwilling to give James up and attempted to reclaim him by placing him under the umbrella of apostolic authority.

One reason why James could not be given up to those opposed to apostolic authority is acknowledged by Eusebius. James was called a brother of Christ. Had this merely been a claim of the tradition of the opponents, Eusebius would have been able to deal with it simply by denial. His problem was that that designation was given to James in "the divine books," probably a reference to the Gospels. Almost certainly Eusebius was dependent on Origen's *Commentary on Matthew* (X.17), which deals with Matt 13:54–56 on the subject of "The brethren of Jesus." Origen, strangely, appears to be an unacknowledged source for Eusebius in his treatment of James. "Strangely" because Eusebius was an admirer of Origen. In his treatment of Matthew Origen refers to Paul's letter to the Galatians 1:19, in which Paul refers to James as the Lord's brother, and Eusebius makes use of this reference in 1.12.4–5; 2.1.2, 5. Thus there could be no dismissal of the significant role of James.

---

[119] See *Gospel of the Hebrews; Gospel of Thomas* logion 12; *Recognitions* 1.62.2; 1.68.2; 1.70.3; 1.72.1.

Eusebius also had to acknowledge the continued esteem with which James was held in the Jerusalem church. In spite of this veneration Eusebius continued to qualify James's relation to Jesus. He was called the brother of Christ, an expression that implies that he was not. Here we have a puzzle—that Eusebius uses tradition that unequivocally affirms the leadership of the Jerusalem church by the family of Jesus, brother and cousin, but himself qualifies those relationships. One reason for qualifying the relationships was to retain the influence and authority of the apostles over James. Consequently it is necessary to distinguish the view of James in the sources from the views adopted by Eusebius himself.

CONCLUSION: EUSEBIUS ON JAMES

The treatment of James by Eusebius highlights a number of themes and perspectives that call for further attention. In all of these it is important to keep in mind the distinction between the views expressed in Eusebius's summaries and those clearly derived from the sources collected on the subject. Where the summaries express views that are not derived from the sources quoted, we are left to decide whether Eusebius is simply stating his own views or drawing on an unspecified source. With regard to James there are strong grounds for thinking that Eusebius made use of Origen's discussion of "the brethren of the Lord" and his appeal to the works of Josephus.

James is portrayed as the brother of Jesus. Although Eusebius consistently qualifies the relationship as "so-called" or "supposed," that relationship is made a prominent reason for the leadership of James. The qualification is based on Eusebius's acceptance of the virginal conception of Jesus. As part of the wider family of Jesus, James exercised leadership in the earliest church, and members of the family continued to exercise leadership at least until the reign of Trajan. Membership in the family was an important reason for their rise to leadership. The more important the family relationship is perceived to be in the early church, the less convincing explanations are that suggest only a remote relationship or indeed no "natural" relationship between Jesus and James at all. Acceptance of the virginal conception of Jesus means that James and Jesus could not have had a common father, although they had a common mother. This situation would have made them brothers, even if they were only half-brothers. Eusebius himself apparently accepted a close family relationship but was sensitive to the need to qualify it because James had been claimed as an exponent of tradition opposed to the "apostolic tradition."

James is consistently referred to as the first bishop of Jerusalem, an enumeration which Eusebius probably derived from the list of the bishops of Jerusalem, most likely transmitted by Hegesippus. Mention of James's throne is a consistent feature of the description of James and his role in the church. This tradition goes back to a time before Clement of Alexandria and Hegesippus. But it is unclear at what point James's leadership in the Jerusalem church came to be seen in terms of episcopacy. Absolute confidence that "bishops" are a feature of the church only at the end of the first century has been eroded by the evidence of the Qumran Texts in which the term *"Mebaqqer"* and the role of the official indicated by it are now seen to provide a precedent for the role of bishop.

James is known as the Just (Righteous) and, although Eusebius explains this epithet in terms of the virtue of James, his narrative suggests that the term "Righteous" might also have been reinforced by James's martyrdom, through which he is presented in terms of a succession of righteous sufferers including Jesus, Stephen, and James the son of Zebedee (3.5.2–3).

Eusebius also describes the persecution of the wider family of Jesus (3.19.1–3.20.7; 3.32.1–6). Symeon himself was martyred in the reign of Trajan, and the grandsons of Jude were interrogated by Domitian and survived till the reign of Trajan, presiding over every church as "witnesses" (μάρτυρες) being of the family of the Lord. According to Hegesippus, their leadership was based on their relationship to Jesus, reinforced by the witness they bore. Interestingly, μάρτυρες can be translated "martyrs,"[120] though it appears that the grandsons bore witness but did not die. Earlier in the same narrative (3.32.3) Eusebius quoted Hegesippus's account of the martyrdom of Symeon, who was charged with being descended from David and being a Christian, and says that Symeon suffered martyrdom (μαρτυρεῖ)—or does this mean that he bore witness? This is certainly the meaning of ἐμαρτύρησεν in 3.32.6, in which the death of Symeon is revealed only in the statement that "he was commanded to be crucified." Thus in these statements the connection between bearing witness before hostile powers and suffering execution is what causes confusion and leads to the development of *"martyr"* as a technical term.

The earliest evidence of the death of James comes from Josephus, and there is no reason to be suspicious of ideological distortion through Christian editing in Josephus's presentation of James. Ananus is presented sympathetically in Josephus's account in *War* but is treated unsympathetically in *Antiquities*, where specific attention is drawn to his Sadducean position and the unlawful nature of the action he took against James and the others who were executed at the time. In this account Josephus is sympathetic to those fair-minded and meticulous law keepers, probably the Pharisees, who took exception to the unlawful action of Ananus. In his account of the war Josephus is sympathetic to Ananus in the high priest's opposition to those zealots whom he saw as responsible for plunging the Jewish nation into disaster. This different context explains the changed attitude toward Ananus.

---

[120] Williamson, p. 143 [96].

According to Josephus, the Sanhedrin condemned James and the others to be stoned. There are no christological charges brought against James. An inner Jewish conflict seems to have resulted in his death. While we do not know the source of Josephus's account, it is the earliest evidence of James's death we possess, and there are good reasons for thinking it is fundamentally historical. The earliest Christian account is to be found in the tradition transmitted by Hegesippus. Although Clement of Alexandria wrote after Hegesippus, it seems that Clement had access to an earlier form of the Christian tradition concerning James. In the light of this connection it can be seen that the form of the tradition in Hegesippus has joined the early Christian version with that of Josephus. In Clement James was thrown down from the pinnacle of the Temple and clubbed to death. According to Hegesippus, James was thrown down from the pinnacle, stoned, and then dispatched with a blow from a club. The reason for the execution of James is said to be the witness of James to Jesus and in particular the reference to "the door of Jesus." This is a distinctively Christian motif which has been added to exalt James. It is absent from both Clement and Josephus. In the light of this it is unlikely that the basis for the execution of James was his christological witness. Rather there is evidence of a conflict between the poorer rural priests and the rich aristocratic chief priests of Jerusalem. Because James sided with the poorer priests he and others were removed by Ananus. Historically, it seems certain that the Sadducean high priest Ananus was instrumental in bringing about the death of James, not the scribes and Pharisees as asserted by Hegesippus.

Eusebius leaves no doubt about the leadership of James in the Jerusalem church. There is no reason why James would have been portrayed in these terms had he not in fact been leader. The tradition is insistent that James was the first, and some attention is focused on his episcopal role and the throne he occupied. Focus on the episcopal role and the throne of James may be a legendary development based on the original tradition of the leadership of James.

CHAPTER 6

THE NAG HAMMADI LIBRARY

James as Successor to Jesus and Repository of Secret Tradition

In December 1945 peasants digging for fertilizer uncovered an earthenware jar on the south side of Jabal-al-Tarif, two hundred miles south of Cairo, forty miles north of Thebes, and on the eastern side of the Nile. In the jar were thirteen codices containing fifty-two works. This collection of works has become known as the Nag Hammadi library. Because the works were obviously Christian, being written in Coptic, and the discoverers were Muslims, no great care was taken of the codices. Part of one of the codices was used for lighting a fire in an oven, destroying most of one work. Eventually the codices found their way into the Coptic museum in Cairo. Much of the credit for the ultimate publication of a critical edition with translations and commentaries belongs to the Coptic Gnostic Library Project of the Institute of Antiquity and Christianity at Claremont, California, headed by James M. Robinson.[1]

Materials used to make the bindings confirm that the codices were produced locally, and receipts used as stiffening in the binding (cartonnage) of codex VII are dated between 333 and 348. Codex I mentions Chenoboskion, which was adjacent to the site where the codices were found. On the back of a piece of papyrus in codex VII there is a reference to "Father Pachom." While Pachomius was a common name, the reference to "my prophet and father Pachomius from Papnutius (Papnoute)" makes it probable that Father Pachom is Pachomius the founder of the monasteries because Papnoute the brother of Theodore was an important figure in the Pachomian *koinonia*.[2] Pachomius lived

---

[1] Texts are conveniently available in *The Nag Hammadi Library in English*, ed. J. M. Robinson (New York: Harper & Row, 1977, 1988).

[2] See A. Vielleux, trans., *Pachomian Koinonia, vol. 1: The Life of Pachomius and His Disciples* (Kalamazoo: Cistercian Publications, 1980). In these monasteries the monks lived in community (*koinonia*) under a rule that governed their life together.

from 290 to 346, and established eleven monasteries in Egypt. A Pachomian monastery and basilica in the region of Nag Hammadi are thought to be the likely origin of this library consisting of fifty-two works. The library was probably buried as a result of the Paschal letter of Athanasius in 367. The letter communicated Athanasius's decree against heretical books. Consequently, the books discovered in 1945 probably did not constitute the entire library but were only those books that had been "banned" recently by Athanasius.

While these works had probably been copied at Nag Hammadi by the middle of the fourth century, there is no reason to think that any of the works was actually composed there. Of the fifty-two works there are six duplicates, and six were previously known. Thus the discovery brought to light forty works previously not known in detail. The importance of the discovery for our knowledge of early Christianity and Gnosticism is difficult to overestimate. Certainly the collection and the probable date of its hiding suggest that there were more diverse forms of Christianity in Egypt prior to the episcopate of Athanasius.[3]

THE COPTIC *GOSPEL OF THOMAS:* APPOINTED BY THE RISEN LORD

Until the discovery of the Coptic Gnostic Library at Nag Hammadi this *Gospel of Thomas* was often confused with the *Infancy Gospel of Thomas.* Reference to it in patristic sources enables us to date the work as early as the beginning of the third century. Hippolytus (writing between 222 and 235) provides the earliest reference to the Gospel by name. The title is attested at the end of the Nag Hammadi text of this work, while the incipit (the opening words) suggests the name *The Secret Sayings of the Living Jesus.* The date of the Gospel can be pushed back by the identification of three fragments of the same work in Greek (P Oxy. 1, 654, 655), the earliest of which (P Oxy. 1) cannot be later than 200 CE. The first fragment contains sayings 26–30, 77, 31–33, in that order. The second includes sayings 1–7 and the third, sayings 36–40. The division of the Coptic *Gospel of Thomas* into numbered sayings is not original to the text but is a useful means of identifying sayings followed by most scholars. Each saying is identified by a formula introduction, generally "Jesus said . . . ," and contains dialogues with one or more disciples. A new saying is also identified by a new dialogue group and new subject. On the basis of comparison with the Synoptic sayings source (Q) some scholars would push the date of the earliest stratum of the *Gospel of Thomas* back into the mid-first century.[4] This dating is highly speculative and is opposed by many scholars who argue that *Thomas* is

---

[3] See C. W. Griggs, *Early Egyptian Christianity: From its Origins to 451 CE* (Leiden: Brill, 1991).

[4] See for example the work of J. D. Crossan, *The Historical Jesus: The Life of a Mediterranean Jewish Peasant* (San Francisco: HarperSanFrancisco, 1991).

dependent on the canonical Gospels. Without advocating an extreme early date it is possible to argue that the tradition about James is not later than the second century and did not suddenly appear from nowhere.

Like other works from Nag Hammadi, it appears that the *Gospel of Thomas* was composed in Greek and translated into Sahidic Coptic, although individual sayings might have been translated originally from Syriac or Aramaic. The finished Gospel is Gnostic in character, and this is immediately apparent in the authorship fiction. The Gospel is attributed to Didymos Judas Thomas. The precise form of this attribution suggests that the Gospel is derived from East Syrian tradition (Edessa) because only in this tradition was Thomas known as Judas Thomas.[5] In gnosticizing circles Didymos ("twin") was added because Thomas was known as the brother and twin of Jesus.[6] It is in this tradition that the *Gospel of Thomas* begins:

> These are the secret sayings which the living Jesus spoke and which Didymos Judas Thomas wrote down.

Reference to the living Jesus indicates the risen Jesus and the "secret sayings" imply Gnostic teaching. Thus, according to Robert McQueen Grant and David Noel Freedman: " 'Jesus the Living' who speaks the 'secret words' is undoubtedly the risen Lord who, according to various Gnostic sects, gave detailed instruction to chosen individuals or small groups after his resurrection."[7] Bertil Gärtner draws attention to a number of Nag Hammadi tractates that portray dialogue between the risen Jesus and one or more disciples, naming such dialogue a Gnostic motif.[8]

Contrary to this view, the recent *Dictionary of Jesus and the Gospels*[9] asserts that the *Gospel of Thomas* does not have a post-resurrection setting. One reason for thinking that the Gospel is a collection of sayings of the historical Jesus is that many of the sayings have parallels in the four Gospels of the New Testament, where they are presented as sayings of Jesus during his ministry. Sayings used in the *Gospel of Thomas* may have been derived from the ministry of Jesus. But they are here presented as "the secret sayings." While some of the sayings

---

[5] See *Acts of Thomas,* chapters 1 and 31, and the *Book of Thomas the Athlete.* Some Syriac manuscripts of John 14:22 suggest that the real name of Thomas was Judas, and this suggestion is consistent with the *Gospel of Thomas* 1. On Edessa, see J. B. Segal, *Edessa: The Blessed City* (Oxford: Clarendon Press, 1970), and H. J. W. Drijvers, *Cults and Beliefs at Edessa*, EPRO 82 (Leiden: Brill, 1980).

[6] See B. Gärtner, *The Theology of the Gospel of Thomas* (London: Collins, 1961), 97.

[7] *The Secret Sayings of Jesus,* p. 112.

[8] Gärtner, p. 98, and see also *The Encyclopedia of Early Christianity,* ed. E. Ferguson et al. (New York: Garland, 1990), 637.

[9] *Dictionary of Jesus and the Gospels,* ed. J. B. Green et al. (Downers Grove, Ill.: IVP), 287.

of Jesus in the canonical Gospels are presented to the disciples alone, they are not presented as secret sayings. Further, reference to the living Jesus is a reference to the risen Jesus. What would the point be otherwise? The dead Jesus does not speak, and words attributed to Jesus would be understood in terms of the historical Jesus unless otherwise indicated. Reference to the living Jesus is such an indication.

The name Didymos Judas Thomas refers to Judas the twin (Didymos in Greek = Thomas in Aramaic and means "twin"), that is, the twin brother of Jesus. He was in an ideal position to reveal the secret sayings. It may be that the portrayal of Thomas in the Gospel of John gave rise to his prominence in Gnostic gospels. In John, Thomas, who is identified as "the one who is called Didymos," is absent from the company of disciples in which the risen Jesus first manifests himself, and he is the focus of a later manifestation in which his doubts are overcome (20:19–23, 24–29). He is also named (again as Thomas who is called Didymos) among the disciples to whom Jesus appears in John 21:2.

In the Gospel venerating Thomas the revelations are not said to be made directly to Didymos Judas Thomas. Rather it is he who wrote down the secret words of the risen Jesus. It is also surprising that logion 12 names James as the leader of the disciples:

> The disciples said to Jesus, "We know that you will depart from us. Who is to be our leader?"
> Jesus said to them, "Wherever you are, you are to go to James the righteous, for whose sake heaven and earth came into being."

If Judas Thomas is understood to be the twin brother of Jesus, then naming James as leader maintains the priority of the family of Jesus. That this affirmation of the leadership of James is directed against Petrine leadership is supported by the responses of Peter, Matthew, and Thomas to the command of Jesus (in logion 13) to compare him with someone. The command is related to the dialogue of the Markan Jesus with his disciples at Caesarea Philippi (Mark 8:28–30). The responses of Peter and Matthew are shown to be inferior to the response of Thomas. Given the role of Thomas signaled at the beginning of the Gospel, this is not surprising.

In response to the inquiry by the disciples James is designated the leader of the disciples by the risen Jesus. The involvement of the disciples in the appointment of James in the *Gospel of Thomas* is in agreement with the reference in Eusebius (*HE* 2.1.3–5) attributed to Clement of Alexandria. There are differences: Clement restricts the group of disciples that chose James to Peter, James, and John and does not indicate that Jesus directed their choice of James. The *Gospel of Thomas* refers to James as leader, not first bishop, and makes clear that the choice of James was at the direction of Jesus. The James in question is specifically designated as James the righteous (the Just). Because Clement also uses this designation, it is the detail of the direction of Jesus that distinguishes the *Gospel of Thomas* from the tradition of Clement.

In this saying (logion 12) the outstanding importance of James is revealed. In the circles that produced the saying the leadership of James is justified by designating him "the righteous" and by the further explanation "for whose sake heaven and earth came into being"—an expression which is comparable to other sayings concerning "the righteous," including Abraham and the patriarchs generally, Moses, David, and the Messiah, as well as Israel as a whole.[10] The recognition of the leadership of James and the veneration of the family of Jesus signal that this tradition originated in a form of Jewish Christianity with a continuing memory of the role of James and the family.

Didymos Judas Thomas, introduced as the author, is Judas, the twin brother of Jesus. His authority underpins this Gospel. Logion 12 designates James as the leader of the disciples, giving him priority also over Didymos Judas Thomas.[11] Just how this tension between the authority of Didymos Judas Thomas and the leadership of James was resolved within the community for which the *Gospel of Thomas* was authoritative is unclear. The prominence of these two figures gives priority to the family of Jesus without signaling rivalry between James and Thomas. Rather the rivalry appears to be between Peter (and the twelve?) and the family of Jesus.

THE *APOCRYPHON OF JAMES:* JAMES AND THE SECRET TRADITION

Like so many books from the ancient world, the book which has come to be known as the *Apocryphon of James* is without formal title. It is pseudonymous, claiming to have been written by James.[12] Composed in the form of a letter, it is addressed to someone whose name has been eradicated from the beginning of the text, although the name Cerinthos has been reconstructed. The author, who identifies himself simply as James, tells that his work is in response to a request to send a "secret book" (*apocryphon*) that was revealed to him and to

---

[10] See Gen.R 1.7; 12.9; bSan 98b; and L. Ginzberg, *The Legends of the Jews* (Philadelphia: Jewish Publication Society of America, 1947), pp. 65–68, esp. 67–68. According to 2 Bar 14:19, "the world was created for the righteous," including the patriarchs (15:7; 21:24), and in 4 Esdr 6:55; 7:11, "for Israel." See the discussion on pp. 252–57 below.

[11] In addition to the collective reference to the disciples in logion 12, Thomas is mentioned in the prologue, logion 13, and the postscript; Peter in logia 13, 114; Matthew in logion 13; the two Marys in logia 21, 114; and Salome in logion 61.

[12] As part of the *Jung Codex* it was among the first documents of the Nag Hammadi Library to become known to the modern world. Because of Jung's well-known interest in Gnosticism, codex 1, when it was smuggled out of Egypt, was purchased for the Jung Institute and became known as the *Jung Codex*. It contains the *Prayer of the Apostle Paul,* the *Apocryphon of James,* the *Gospel of Truth,* and the *Treatise on the Resurrection.* This codex has now been returned to Egypt and is with the rest of the library at the Coptic Museum in Cairo.

Peter.[13] This might suggest that the book places Peter and James on the same level. This is not the case. James emerges in this work as the guardian of the higher knowledge and the leader of the disciples, with his authority centered in Jerusalem.

Soon after it was discovered scholars related the *Apocryphon* to Jewish Christian and Valentinian Gnostic influences.[14] The role of James as leader among the apostles was one key to the identification of the Jewish Christian influence, and the understanding of the period between resurrection and ascension as 550 days (2.19–21) broadly agrees with the Valentinian tradition of eighteen months (Irenaeus, *AH* 1.3.2; 1.30.14). Thus, like the documents in the *Jung Codex*, the *Apocryphon of James* is Gnostic, and the ending resembles the ending of the *Gospel of Truth*.

The sayings of Jesus in the *Apocryphon of James* have some relation to the sayings and parables of the Synoptic Gospels and the farewell discourses of Jesus in John. In the canonical Gospels the sayings are set in the ministry of the historical Jesus, even if in John the farewell discourses are situated in a private and secret context on the eve of Jesus' betrayal. The Gnostic tendency to develop secret teaching is taken a stage further than in John in the *Apocryphon of James*, in which the secret teaching of Jesus is given between the resurrection and ascension of Jesus. This placing is a mark of the Gnostic Gospels and in these writings led to the extension of the period in which the risen Jesus continued to appear and give secret teaching.

The James in question is not specifically identified as "the Just" or "the brother of the Lord," although he is associated with Peter and the twelve (1.10–15, 25–29). Because of this W. C. van Unnik has argued that the James in question is the son of Zebedee and not the brother of Jesus.[15] He denies the Jewish Christian or Gnostic origin of the work, arguing that susceptibility to Gnostic interpretation does not make the document Gnostic. Against the Jewish Christian connection based on the notion of the primacy of James, he argues that the James in question might not be the Lord's brother, and the document shows no connection with Palestine and no use of the Jewish scriptures. The primacy of this James does not prove Jewish Christian influence in a work that shows no connection with Palestine or the Old Testament. Further, van Unnik argues that the book is susceptible to Gnostic interpretation but is not itself Gnostic, having emerged from a small Christian community in Egypt not yet influenced by Gnosticism and without Jewish Christian ties.

---

[13] Hence the title given the book, *Apocryphon of James*.

[14] H.-C. Puech and G. Quispel, "Les Écrits gnostiques du Codex Jung," *Vigilae Christianae* 8 (1954): 1–51, esp. 7–22.

[15] "The Origin of the Recently Discovered 'Apocryphon Jacobi,'" *Vigilae Christianae* 10 (1956):149–56.

The leadership of James the son of Zebedee in the early church is unknown elsewhere, but the leadership of James the Lord's brother is widely attested.[16] The notion of secret or restricted revelation to James the son of Zebedee after the resurrection of Jesus is also unknown, but it is affirmed to James the Lord's brother.[17] Perhaps for these reasons scholars today accept that the James in view is the Lord's brother and treat this as uncontroversial. This conclusion fits in with the presentation of this James and of his importance in other works from Nag Hammadi and elsewhere where he is clearly identified.

The *Apocryphon of James* seems to have had a complex history. It was developed from an original apocalyptic revelation text. This text has been incorporated into the present letter. Having identified himself as James in the opening lines, the writer goes on to speak of the request for a secret book and explains why he has written his letter and what it contains.

> Since you asked that I send you a secret book [*apocryphon*] which was revealed to me and Peter by the Lord, I could not turn you away or gainsay you; but I have written it in the Hebrew alphabet and sent it to you, and you alone. . . . and take care not to rehearse this text to many—this that the Savior did not wish to tell to all of us, his twelve disciples. . . . I also sent you, ten months ago, another secret book which the Savior had revealed to me. Under the circumstances, however, regard that one as revealed to me, James; but this one. . . . (1.9–35)

The secret book was revealed to James and Peter, but it was James who wrote it down and who then revealed it to his now unknown correspondent. Reference to the *Apocryphon* being written in the Hebrew alphabet may be no more than a claim to authenticity, but it is possible that it reveals the Jewish Christian origin of this tradition. This possibility would have been strengthened had James been called the Just and the brother of the Lord.

The restricted scope of the revelation is stressed. The book was revealed to James and Peter but not to the rest of the twelve, and James exhorted his correspondent not to reveal the contents of the book to many. Thus the esoteric nature of the teaching is emphasized. If this seems to place James and Peter on a common level, above the rest of the twelve, what follows sets James apart and on a level of his own.

That there is something competitive in the presentation of James and Peter is confirmed when James responds to Jesus' exhortation, "Remember my cross and my death, and you will live." James reports, "But I answered and said to him, 'Lord, do not mention to us the cross and death, for they are far from

---

[16] Acts, Clement of Alexandria, the *Gospel of Thomas*, Pseudo–Clementines, and so forth.
[17] Clement of Alexandria in Eusebius.

you' " (5.33–6.1). This dialogue appears to be built on the dialogue between Jesus and Peter in Matt 16:22. It is James who speaks the words that Mark (10:28) puts on the lips of Peter, "Behold we have left everything and followed you"; see James's words in the *Apocryphon*, "for we have forsaken our fathers and our mothers and our villages and followed you" (4.25–28). Thus James replaces Peter in Peter's prominent role in the Synoptics. While it is true that 1 Cor 15:5–7 names only Peter and James among the witnesses to the risen Lord, it is hardly likely that the author of the *Apocryphon* constructed his work recording the revelation to James and Peter simply on the basis of that text. There is no evidence of the influence of 1 Corinthians in this work.

James also reminds his correspondent that he had, ten months earlier, sent another secret book that the savior had revealed to him alone. Then, in dealing with the circumstances in which the secret book was revealed to himself and Peter, James tells how the savior, five hundred and fifty days after his resurrection, had taken him and Peter aside from the rest of the twelve (2.30–40). What follows is a set of dialogues between Jesus and Peter and James. In these dialogues James is singled out when Jesus recalls "And I have commanded you [singular and therefore referring to James alone] to follow me, and I have taught you what to say to the archons" (8.30–39), and "moreover, I have revealed myself to you [singular], James, and you [plural] have not known me" (13.39–14.1). The dialogues conclude with Jesus taking final leave of James and Peter.

> "But I have said (my) last word to you, and I shall depart from you, for a chariot of spirit has borne me aloft, and from this moment on I shall strip myself that I may clothe myself." (14.32–36)

Jesus' words conclude with an exhortation and blessing, and James narrates, "Having said these words, he departed." No doubt this is meant to indicate the final departure and ascension of Jesus.

At the ascension of Jesus, James and Peter bend their knees, give thanks, and send their "hearts"(15.8) upward to heaven, where they experience what Jesus said was awaiting him (14.20–31). The verses of 15.15–16 refer to the ascent of their *minds*. When later they wish to send their spirits upward again to the "Majesty," the other disciples interrupt them, wanting to know what the master said to them and where he has gone. It appears that the accounts of the ascent of the heart, mind, or spirit are alternative descriptions of the heavenly journey that appears to be a Gnostic variation on an apocalyptic theme. In response to the inquiry of the disciples James and Peter answer:

> He has ascended, and he has given us a pledge and promised life to us all and revealed to us children who are to come after us, after bidding [us] love them, as we would be [saved] for their sakes. (15.35–16.2)

The disciples believe the revelation but are displeased about the children to be born because they are given prominence over the disciples. Because of this James sends out each one of the disciples to another place, while he himself goes up to Jerusalem[18] praying for a "portion among the beloved, who will appear" (16.5–11). This is a request for the fulfillment of the prediction of 15.1–5. Finally James prays that the beginning of the fulfillment of this prediction may come through the recipient of his letter, that he may be the first of the children to appear, having been enlightened through James and his faith. James concludes with the assertion that the revelation was restricted and was made for the sake of the sons who were yet to come. Their salvation, and that of James also, depends on the effectiveness of the proclamation made by James.

The importance of James in this document is clear and is reinforced by the cluster of documents that focus attention on James. From Nag Hammadi, in addition to the *Apocryphon*, there are the *First* and *Second Apocalypse of James*, the *Gospel of Thomas*, and the *Gospel of the Egyptians*. Outside of Nag Hammadi there are the canonical Epistle of James, the *Protevangelium of James*, the *Ascents of James*, and the *Kerygmata Petrou* in the Pseudo-Clementines, and the prominence of James in the writings of Hegesippus, Clement of Alexandria, Eusebius of Caesarea, and Epiphanius.

The focus on the primacy of James is signaled not only by the leading role he plays in the *Apocryphon* but also by his acknowledged authority in sending each of the other disciples to another place while he himself went up to Jerusalem (16.5–11).[19] This is in no way diminished by the recognition that the resentment of the disciples was the reason for James's decision. The case for Jewish Christian influence would be stronger had the *Apocryphon* called James "the brother of the Lord" and used the epithet "the Just" of him. But the absence of these features does not remove the probability of Jewish Christian influence, even if there is evidence of Gnostic veneration of James the Lord's brother (Hippolytus, *Ref.* 5.2). Nor does the evidence suggest that later Gnostic elements are pushing against stubborn Jewish Christian tradition. There is now much evidence to suggest that some forms of Jewish Christianity were susceptible to Gnosticism, perhaps even inclined to it. Hence there is no necessity to think that the *Apocryphon* was successively Jewish Christian and then Gnostic because it might have been simultaneously Jewish Christian and Gnostic.

The Gnostic influence in the *Apocryphon* is evident in the stress on the secret teaching to particular disciples occurring between the resurrection and ascension of Jesus.[20] Apart from the duration of the appearances prior to the

---

[18] Compare the *First Apocalypse of James* 42.20–22.

[19] For Clement of Alexandria also James was both the leader of the apostles (and the Jerusalem church) and the recipient of the higher knowledge from the risen Lord (*HE* 2.1.3–4).

[20] Compare the opening of the *Gospel of Thomas* with the *First Apocalypse of James* 32.13–42.19 and Clement of Alexandria according to Eusebius (*HE* 2.1.4).

ascension there is nothing to connect the Gnostic motifs with Valentinianism. The motifs are common to Christian Gnosticism and are evident even in the writings of such teachers of the Great Church as Clement of Alexandria and Origen. The argument that the teaching of the *Apocryphon* 4.23–6.21, in which Jesus advocates that his followers seek death and not resist it, is contrary to the Valentinian attitude of avoiding persecution and martyrdom[21] runs up against the suspicion that this section of the *Apocryphon* is a redactional insertion. The Gnostic tendencies of the *Apocryphon* are dominant, although the links with Clement and Origen are worthy of note.

The Gnostic *topoi* of the document make clear that it must be considered Gnostic. These can be listed as the identification of sapiential fullness as a trait of the pneumatic; sobriety as opposed to sleep and drunkenness; the stress on the role of knowledge; salvation of the psyche through spirit; psyche as the cause of sin; depreciation of the flesh. Gnostic terminology is amply present, with references to "men of light," "alien," "light and life," "brightness." The force of the argument for Gnostic influence is in the cumulative impact of this evidence.[22] The evidence of the James tradition of the *Apocryphon* suggests a Jewish Christian Gnostic tradition that became accessible to other Gnostic movements without losing earlier Jewish Christian features.

THE *FIRST APOCALYPSE OF JAMES:* THE BROTHER OF THE LORD AND THE CHAIN OF SUCCESSION

The manuscript names this work the *Apocalypse of James* both at the beginning and the end but it is called the *First Apocalypse of James* to distinguish it from the work that follows it in Nag Hammadi codex V which bears the same name and has been called the *Second Apocalypse of James*. The *First Apocalypse*, a Coptic translation from Greek, is recognized as Valentinian by the cult formulae of 33.5–36.11 which appear to be a late form of those in Irenaeus (*AH* 1.21.5; and see Epiphanius, *Pan.* 36.3.1–6). Other Valentinian (not necessarily exclusive) motifs are Docetism (24.12–16; 36.15–16, and compare Irenaeus, *AH* 1.6.1; 1.7.2; 1.21.2); the union of James with "He who is"(27.8–10; and compare the *Gospel of Truth* 42.25–28); the doctrines of *Achamoth* and *Sophia* (36.2–4); indeed a case could be made for Valentinian additions in 24.18–25.5; 33.5–36.11. On this basis it seems that the final work should be dated at the beginning of the third century. In three passages the story is told from James's point of view (24.10; 25.12; 27.18), but for the rest the words of James are

---

[21] According to Irenaeus (*AH* 4.33.9), Clement of Alexandria (*Strom* 4.4.16–17), and Tertullian (*Scorpiace* 10).

[22] See J. Zandee, "Gnostische trekken een Apocryphe Brief van Jacobus," *Nederlands Tijdschrift* 17 (1963): 401–22, and K. Rudolph, "Gnosis und Gnosticizismus: ein Forschungsbericht," *ThR* ns 34 (1969): 172–75.

introduced with the words "But James said." This distinction might help to identify two stages of development, but it is unclear which idiom indicates the earlier stratum.[23] There is a general consensus that the *First Apocalypse* was based on an earlier Jewish work. An openness to Gnosticism is suggested by the ease with which the Valentinian elements have been introduced, though it needs to be recognized that some anti-Valentinian elements have survived the transformation, in particular the focus on the role of James and the necessity of his facing persecution and martyrdom (e.g., 25.13–14; 27.16–17; 28.29–30; 32.10–11, 17–18) against the Valentinian avoidance of persecution.[24] Probably this focus antedates the Valentinian influence.

There is a good case for identifying the origin of the tradition used by the *First Apocalypse* with Syria and in relation to Jewish Christianity. The naming of Addai as the successor to James in the chain of revealers is decisive, as Addai is linked with the foundation of Christianity there (Eusebius *HE* 1.13).[25] This raises the question of the influence of Jewish Christianity on the earliest form of the *First Apocalypse*. The post-resurrection dialogues are set on Mount Gaugela, which is located in Syria;[26] and like the dialogues of the *Gospel of Thomas* and the *Apocryphon of James*, these signal a Gnostic milieu.

Alexander Böhlig has argued that there are eleven points of evidence in favor of associating the *Apocalypse* with Jewish Christianity: 1) The presentation of James as the brother of the Lord (24.12–16); 2) the presentation of James as the true prophet (39.18); 3) the identification of James by the epithet "the Just" (31.30; 32.1–3, 12; 43.19–21); 4) the opposition to sacrifice (41.7ff); 5) the focus on the second coming of the Lord (30.16–17); 6) the use of the intimacy of James with the Lord as an anti-Pauline motif (31.1–5; 32.7) (though the anti-Pauline motif is evident only through a knowledge of the Pseudo-Clementine *Homilies* 17.14–19, in which the visionary perception of Jesus by Paul is shown to be inadequate); 7) false pericopes in Scripture (26.2ff); 8) the use of the *syzygy* motif (36.2–6); 9) the exoneration of the Jews (31.21f); 10) the exodus of James (the Jerusalem church) to Pella (25.15); 11) the presentation of James's authority over the twelve (and the early community) (42.20ff).[27] While not all of these points are equally persuasive, together they present a prima facie case for the Jewish Christian origin of the *First Apocalypse*. The earliest use of the

---

[23] Compare the *Protevangelium of James*.

[24] See Tertullian, *Scorpiace* 10; Irenaeus *AH* 4.33.9; Clement of Alexandria *Stromateis* 4.4.16–17.

[25] See G. Howard, *The Teaching of Addai*, SBL Texts and Translations 16; ECL Series 4 (Chico, Calif.: Scholars Press, 1981), and the discussion of *HE* 1.13.1–22 above.

[26] See Salaminius Hermias Sozomen, *Historae Ecclesiasticae*, NPNF 2d series, vol. 2, ed. P. Schaff (Grand Rapids: Eerdmans, 1957), 3.14.

[27] "Der Jüdische und Judenchristlichen Hintergrund in gnostischen Texten von Nag Hammadi," in *Le Origini dello Gnosticismo: Colloquio di Messina*, ed. U. Bianchi (Leiden: Brill, 1967), 109–40, esp. 130–40.

image of James was in Jewish Christian traditions, and without the preservation there the image would not have survived to have been used in later Gnostic and Catholic traditions. The Gnostic and Catholic use of the image of James, then, needs to be explained.

James appears in a wide range of early Christian literature, suggesting his relevance in Catholic and Gnostic Christianity as well as Jewish Christianity. There is good reason, however, to think that the image of James first became significant in Jewish Christianity and was taken up by other groups that found particular emphases in the Jewish Christian image relevant to their own understandings, even if this meant that the image was transformed by its new contexts. The *First Apocalypse* is in three parts:

1) 24.10–30.13: dialogue between the Lord and James on the Tuesday prior to the Lord's death (25.7f); 2) 32.13–42.19: second dialogue a few days after the Lord's resurrection; 3) 42.20–44.6: James's death foretold.

The first two sections make the point that James was with the Lord before and after his passion. In the *Gospel of the Hebrews* Jesus and James are together on the Thursday evening before the passion. In the *First Apocalypse* they are together on the Tuesday before the passion. This is implied by Jesus' words to James at the beginning of the first set of dialogues: "For they will seize me the day after tomorrow" (25.7–8). In terms of the Jewish reckoning of days this could imply either Tuesday evening or Wednesday before sunset. Both works assume that James was already a follower of the Lord before the passion. The *First Apocalypse* makes use of the Gnostic dialogue genre. What is Gnostic about the dialogues here is that they are secret dialogues; they take place between the Lord and an individual disciple; and the second series of dialogues is set between the resurrection and the ascension. This is the period for the disclosure of true *gnosis,* although John's farewell discourses to the disciples on the eve of the crucifixion are already a development in this direction.

At the beginning of the *First Apocalypse* James reports:

> It is the Lord who spoke with me: "See now the completion of redemption. I have given you a sign of these things, James, my brother. For not without reason have I called you my brother, although you are not my brother materially."

The Lord addresses James as "my brother." Thus from the beginning there is no doubt at all as to which James is in view. The identification is confirmed by the later references to James using the epithet "the Just." That James is the brother of the Lord is made the basis of the special relationship between them and for the revelation of secret knowledge that is made to him (29.4–13, 20; 32.27-33.1). In spite of these established links the precise nature of the relationship is put in question immediately by the qualification "you are not my brother materially." This could be read in terms of the hypothesis that James was a son of Joseph by a marriage prior to that with Mary and thus, in view of the virgin birth, no blood relation of the Lord at all. But this is clearly not the meaning, as is clear from the use of the term "materially." What is denied is the material being of the Lord. The *First Apocalypse* manifests a docetic christology. Thus the Lord says: "James, do not be concerned for me . . . I am he who was within me. Never have I suffered in any way, nor have I been distressed. And this people has done me no harm . . ." (31.15–24). This description raises the question of the nature of James's kinship to the Lord without impinging on the question of the parentage of James.

In the opening set of dialogues the Lord foretells his passion and the suffering and death of James. This is the Gnostic assimilation of the motif of the redeemer and the redeemed. In 24.19–24 the Lord identifies himself with the unnameable One Who Is in the beginning, and James is told that, through casting away the bond of flesh and ascending to Him Who Is, he will no longer be James but the One Who Is (27.1–10). James thus *returns* to the place from whence he came. The crucifixion of Jesus and the death of James are treated as complementary in the victory over the powers of darkness that was brought about by the fall of Jerusalem, the seat of the archons (that is, the powers of darkness) (25.15–19).

The dark powers are associated with Jerusalem and Judaism (25.15–29), and for this reason James is bidden to leave Jerusalem, a command that reflects the flight of Jewish Christianity from that city. The problem concerning the historicity of the flight of the Jerusalem church to Pella is well known.[28] It is not necessary to solve this problem for our purpose. All that is necessary is an early tradition concerning this flight to explain the existence of Jewish Christians in Pella, a tradition to which they appealed for the basis of their perceived self-importance. That James's death is understood as the defeat of the archons implies that the destruction of Jerusalem is a consequence of his death because war breaks out when he departs (36.16–19).[29] But because of the assimilation of the death of James and the death of Jesus the destruction can also be seen as a consequence of Jesus' death. In this way the *First Apocalypse*, like Eusebius, harmonizes what appear to be two independent traditions about the cause of the destruction of Jerusalem.[30]

According to this reading, the twelve are to be distinguished from the

---

[28] The tradition is known in Eusebius *HE* 3.5.2f.; cf. Epiphanius *Pan* 29.7.7–8. See S. G. F. Brandon, *The Fall of Jerusalem and the Christian Church* (London: SPCK, 1957), 168–72; L. W. Barnard, "The Origins and Emergence of the Christian Church in Edessa in the First Two Centuries AD," *Vigiliae Christianae* 22 (1968): 61–75. G. Lüdemann, *Opposition to Paul in Jewish Christianity* (Minneapolis: Fortress, 1989), 200–13.

[29] See Eusebius *HE* 2.23.18, 20; Origen, *Contra Celsum* 1.47.

[30] Origen, *Contra Celsum* 2.13; Eusebius *HE* 3.7.7–9; 3.11.1.

archons and identified as the children of Achamoth, the lesser Sophia (34.1–36.14), that is, the femaleness that was not first (24.26–31). The twelve were born without any participation of Him Who Is and are alien, but not completely alien, because she (Achamoth) is from above (34.1–15), although female from female. The superiority of male over female is implied in the *First Apocalypse,* although, like the *Gospel of Thomas* (logion 114), the inferiority of the female is overcome in the Gnostic process of redemption. In this sense these documents can be seen as reactions against the devaluing of the female principle, even if it is revalued only by transformation. The feminine is not placed outside the realm of transforming possibility, but untransformed it is inferior. James is seen to be superior to the twelve whom he rebukes (42.20–24), showing his greater authority. The primacy of James is asserted on the basis of his kinship with the Lord, whom he embraces and kisses and from whom he alone receives the revelation of redemption.

What has been outlined looks very much like the tripartite division of humanity by the Valentinians. The state of the text of the *First Apocalypse* is fragmentary, and it may be that the distinctions are not as clear-cut in the document as in this analysis. There is a conflict between James and the twelve because, in the *First Apocalypse,* the twelve form no part in the chain of revelation that is passed on from the Lord through James to Addai and Addai's younger son (36.15–38.10). This chain of succession is presented as exclusive and esoteric, obviously in competition with the tradition of the twelve which represents emerging Catholicism.

In the *First Apocalypse* the Lord apparently gave some account of why James is called "the Just" (31.31–32.24). Unfortunately, the text is fragmentary at this point, but the following seems to be relevant to the explanation given in this passage. When Jesus reappears to James after the resurrection James is alone in prayer on Mount Gaugela. It is here he embraces and kisses the Lord. It is likely that the text read "The Just is his servant. Therefore your name is James the Just," and that this is linked by the Lord with "Now since you are a just man of God you have embraced and kissed me." What follows then is an account of the way James's actions have stirred up anger against him, leading to his own suffering and martyrdom and in turn to the destruction of Jerusalem. The epithet "the Just" is most clearly linked to the intimate relationship between James and Jesus and manifest in the embrace and kiss. It also appears in the assertion that "the Just is his servant." The martyrdom of James is evidence of the Just one as righteous sufferer, linking him with the Lord. As a consequence of this treatment of the Just one and of Jesus, Jerusalem falls. Therefore we have a play on separate traditions concerning the fall of Jerusalem, linking them with the epithet "the Just" as applied to James.

The *First Apocalypse* is made up of Jewish and anti-Jewish tradition. The

Jewishness is reflected in James's repeated reference to Jesus as rabbi (25.10; 26.2, 14; 28.5; 29.14; 31.5; 40.4; 41.20). In contrast, that Jerusalem should be seen as full of the archons is anti-Jewish. But while the piety of James is portrayed as a rebuke to the twelve (42.20–24), it would be a mistake to see the twelve in relation to Jerusalem. Rather the interpretation given Jerusalem is a consequence of its having been destroyed and under the influence of the tradition that interpreted the destruction as a consequence of what was done to James. This tradition has been subjected to Gnostic influence, so that the Jewish capital has become the seat of the archons.

The comparison of traditions concerning the chain transmitting the revelation by the risen Lord in Clement of Alexandria (Eusebius, *HE* 2.1.4), the *Apocryphon of James,* and the *First Apocalypse of James* is worthy of reflection. In Clement there is a transmission through four levels: 1) James the Just, John, and Peter; 2) other apostles; 3) the seventy (naming Barnabas); 4) the Church. In the *Apocryphon* the transmission is through three levels: 1) James and Peter, though mainly James; 2) the recipient of the *Apocryphon,* perhaps Cerinthos; 3) the "beloved ones" who are yet to be manifest. This is an altogether more esoteric chain of transmission than the one manifest in Clement. The naming of Peter with James at the beginning is a bit of a puzzle. Very likely the text implies the inferiority of Peter in this relationship. The attribution of the work to James signals this perspective as does the reference within the text to an earlier secret book from James alone. In the *First Apocalypse* the revelation is made to James alone, and he is given precise instructions about the chain of transmission by the Lord. This includes: 1) transmission to Addai, who is instructed under what conditions the book is to be written down; 2) oral transmission by Addai to his younger son. In this text there is no mention of the disciples/apostles as part of the chain of transmission, though it is possible that Addai is to be identified with Thaddaeus who is named as one of the seventy. This identification is probably coincidental and not intended within the text.

From this comparison we can chart a trajectory in the development and use of the image of James. The historical James "the Just" epitomized conservative Jewish Christian values. Even though James, John, and Peter were pillars of the "circumcision mission," there are reasons why the name of James should have become synonymous with it. One reason for this is his leadership role in the Jerusalem church and his martyrdom in Jerusalem. Then, as a traditional recipient of a post-resurrection revelation, James was a ready made revealer figure in a gnosticizing situation. The gnosticizing tendency can be seen at various levels, some of which identify the tradition with more or less "heretical" figures such as Cerinthos and Addai. Finally, James, as a colleague of the apostles (as in Clement), becomes a bastion of "orthodoxy" in a catholicizing milieu.

THE *SECOND APOCALYPSE OF JAMES:* THE REVELATION DISCOURSE OF JESUS TO "THE JUST ONE"

At the beginning of the manuscript this work is titled the Apocalypse of James; as we noted above, it is called the *Second Apocalypse of James* to distinguish it from the preceding work in the Nag Hammadi codex V. Also a Coptic translation from Greek, it was placed deliberately after the *First Apocalypse* by the scribe who ordered codex V. The *First Apocalypse* deals with James and Jesus before the crucifixion and Jesus' prediction of James's suffering and death which was given to James by Jesus after his resurrection. The *Second Apocalypse* recounts a revelation of the risen Jesus to James that James reported to Mareim, the priest who wrote it down and reported it to Theuda, the father of James and Mareim's own relative (44.13–20). According to Hippolytus (*Ref.* 5.2), the Naassenes attributed the revelation embodied in numerous discourses, the heads of which are listed, to James the brother of the Lord, who handed them down to Mariamne. While there is in this a formal parallel to the idea of James handing down the revelation to Mareim, it should be noted that the names of the recipients of the revelation differ, and the revelation reported in the *Second Apocalypse* does not fit the description supplied by Hippolytus.[31]

Hippolytus lived from ca. 179 to 236. Though known as a leader (bishop) of the church of Rome, Hippolytus represents the Greek tradition. He probably was not a native of Rome. His authorship of *Refutation* has been questioned. That work has been attributed to Origen. But Origen showed no inclination to write a work tracing the plethora of heresies back to Greek philosophy, refuting them. It is more likely that the account of the Naassenes is correctly attributed to Hippolytus.

The revelation reported through James to Mareim is not clearly distinguished from Mareim's account of the trial and martyrdom of James, which reveals that Mareim was a priest and a juror at the trial. Here Jewish Christian traditions, known to us in the *Memoirs* of Hegesippus, have been incorporated in the tractate. The figure of James has been developed beyond the stereotype suggested by the epithet "the Just" (44.13–14; 49.9; 59.22; 60.12–13; 61.14) and the recognition of his leadership of the Jerusalem church. James is the heavenly guide of those who pass through the heavenly "door" and are his (and the Lord's). He is the "illuminator and redeemer" (55.17–18), and of him it is said:

> You are he whom the heavens bless (55.24–25);
> For your sake they will be told [these things], and will come to rest.
> For your sake they will reign [and will] become kings.

---

[31] See T. V. Smith, *Petrine Controversies in Early Christianity Attitudes towards Peter in Christian Writings of the First Two Centuries,* WUNT 2/15 (Tübingen: J. C. B. Mohr [Paul Siebeck], 1985), 107–8.

For [your] sake they will have pity on whomever they pity. (56.2–6)

The saying is reminiscent of logion 12 of the *Gospel of Thomas,* where Jesus speaks of James as the one for whom heaven and earth were made. It goes further by assimilating the role of James to that of Jesus as redeemer.

The *Second Apocalypse* is introduced as the discourse which James the Just spoke in Jerusalem. When it is set in the context of the trial and martyrdom of James, a comparison with the account of Hegesippus is suggested. One difference is that in the *Second Apocalypse,* James's discourse recounts the words of Jesus to him and is therefore a revelation discourse. In both accounts James's discourse concerns "the door" (55.5–14 and *HE* 2.23.8, 12–13), but the interpretation of the door in the *Second Apocalypse* is generally Gnostic. The discourse is much extended, manifesting Gnostic influence. The motif of James's speech at the Temple prior to his death is known from Hegesippus and *Recognitions* 1.68.3–70.8. In the *Second Apocalypse* the speech is built upon the basis of the martyrdom narrative. It embodies distinctively Jewish Christian characteristics and invites comparison with the accounts of Josephus and Hegesippus, as well as with the prediction of the event found in the *First Apocalypse.* There is also the account of *The Ascents of James,* now found in Pseudo-Clementine *Recognitions.*

Even in the discourse of the *Second Apocalypse* there are traditional elements which draw attention to Jewish Christian perspectives. Jesus is reported as calling James "my brother" (50.16–17), continuing the tradition of referring to James as "the brother of the Lord." The Gnostic interpretation is then brought out by James's report:

> my mother said to me, "Do not be frightened, my son, because he said 'My brother' to you [singular]. For you [plural] were nourished with this same milk. Because of this he calls me 'My mother.' For he is not a stranger to us. He is your [. . .] (50.15–22)

James is here thought to be no actual brother, nor, it is implied, is the mother of James also the mother of the Lord. Jesus calls her "My mother" and James "My brother" only because he was nourished by the same milk as James. Three main conclusions are justified on the basis of the explanation to James by his mother. 1) The mother of James also fed Jesus with her own milk, leaving no room for the theory that James was the child of Joseph by a first marriage while Jesus was the child of Mary. That the one who fed both Jesus and James was actually the mother of James is not in question here. 2) There is no room for the view that James was a cousin of Jesus. 3) The apparent mother of Jesus was not actually his mother. There is no suggestion that some other woman was his mother. Rather, what the saying does is to put in question that Jesus

had any earthly mother at all. This is confirmed by the *First Apocalypse*. There
the Lord says to James,

> I have called you my brother although you are not my brother *materially*.
> (V.24.14–15)

A further explanation is given by the Lord, who explains to James that he has
not suffered.

> James, do not be concerned for me or for this people. I am he who was
> within me. Never have I suffered in any way, nor have I been distressed.
> And this people has done me no harm. (V.31.15–23)

This interpretation of the Jewish Christian motif of the distinctive relationship
of James to Jesus is an expression of Jewish Christian Gnosticism. As in the *First
Apocalypse* the interpretation of James as brother is made the basis of the teaching of the intimacy between James and the Lord. Whereas in the *First Apocalypse*
James took the initiative by embracing and kissing the Lord when he revealed
himself to James after the resurrection (31.4–5; 32.7–8), in the *Second Apocalypse*
it is Jesus who embraces James and kisses his mouth. This intimacy is made the
basis of the revelation the Lord makes to James.

> And he kissed my mouth. He took hold of me saying, "My beloved!
> Behold, I shall reveal to you those (things) that (neither) [the] heavens
> nor their archons have known. . . . Behold I shall reveal to you every-
> thing, my beloved. (56.14–57.5)

The appearance of the Lord to James, with all its intimacy, is made the
basis of a commissioning. In this respect the *Second Apocalypse,* like the *First,* as
well as the *Ascents of James* (*Rec* 1.43.3)[32] and the *Kerygma Petrou* (*Cont* 5.4),
affirms a direct revelation to James, not shared with any apostles as claimed by
Clement (*HE* 2.1.3). This claim of a direct revelation is also the basis of the
claim to succession of the authority of leadership from Jesus to James (47.23–25;
49.9–11; 55.6–14, 17–22).

James is characteristically "the Just One" (44.13; 49.9; 59.22; 60.12–13;
61.14). Here (60.12–23) James predicts the destruction of the Temple because
the jurors (priests) intend to kill him, and there is a case for understanding the

---

[32] With *Recognitions* 1 the *Second Apocalypse* shares the motifs of the prediction of the destruction
of the Temple (R 64.2 and A 60.13–22); James's secret ally in the Council (R 65.2; 66.4 and A
61.9–11); the speech of James (R 68.3; 69 and A 46.6–60.24); given on the steps of the Temple
(R 70.8 and A 45.24); James's fall (R 70.8 and A 61.25f.); and the tumult (R 70.4–8; 71.1 and A
61.1–5).

use of this epithet of James in relation to the fall of Jerusalem as a result of his death as a righteous martyr.

With the *Second Apocalypse* we are reminded of traditions of the martyrdom of James that became important for various groups in the early church. The complexity of the evidence raises questions about the streams of tradition and their sources. The earliest source is Josephus, who was present in Jerusalem in the year of James's death. The other early sources known to us through Euseb- ius are Hegesippus and Clement. With Hegesippus the *Second Apocalypse* uses the "righteousness" of James and his martyrdom in relation to the fall of Jerusa- lem, situating the trial and speech of James at the Temple and including in the speech the theme of the "door," though each treats this theme in a different way. In each only James is accused and is thrown down from the pinnacle of the Temple, and stoning follows. According to Josephus, others were executed with James.

The final prayer of James (62.14–63.29) is in the tradition of the prayer of the righteous sufferer, although Gnostic motifs have had an influence even here. While the ascription ("the Just") draws attention to the piety of James, it is doubtful that it would have been applied to him had he not suffered martyr- dom. The concluding prayer is both a sign of the piety of James and a part of his righteous suffering.

According to Josephus, James was stoned, and those responsible were asso- ciated with the high priest and the Sanhedrin. They should be identified as priests and Sadducees. Here the *Second Apocalypse* agrees with Josephus against Hegesippus, who identifies those responsible for the death of James as the scribes and Pharisees. But the *Second Apocalypse* emphasizes the Jewish legal elements of the trial, making use of traditions now known to us in *Mishnah* tractate *Sanhedrin* 6.4, 7.4. The complexity of the tradition suggests that the *Second Apocalypse* is drawing on a tradition about James independently of Jose- phus, Hegesippus, or Clement, and it could be that this stream flows through an early form of Jewish Christian Gnosticism.

CONCLUSION

These four Nag Hammadi tractates—the *Gospel of Thomas,* the *Apocryphon,* and the *First* and *Second Apocalypse*—name James as the successor to Jesus and the first leader of the Jerusalem church. He is also named as the primary recipient of the esoteric revelation from the risen Lord. Inasmuch as Peter is also named in the *Apocryphon of James,* it is to assert the superiority of James and of the revela- tion made to him. We are reminded of the subservient role played by Peter in relation to the Beloved Disciple in the Fourth Gospel. Many scholars see in that account a struggle between the Johannine community, for whom the Beloved Disciple was the ideal leader, and emerging "Catholic" Christianity represented by Peter. As the fictive author, the Beloved Disciple is also portrayed as the repository of secret tradition, although this was delivered by Jesus in his farewell discourses, not as secret teaching between the resurrection and the ascension. The Johannine picture is made more complex by the claims concerning the Paraclete/Spirit of Truth. From this perspective Jesus continues to teach after the resurrection and in a way not limited by the ascension. No doubt the evangelist claims that this teaching is embodied in the Fourth Gospel. The Johannine tradition was harnessed by the Great Church through the reconciliation of the roles of Peter and the Beloved Disciple in the epilogue to the Gospel and through acceptance of John as one of four canonical Gospels, thus accommodating it within a broader context.

There is evidence, in the tradition from Clement transmitted by Eusebius, of an attempt to harness the authority of James to the benefit of the emerging Catholic Church by rooting his authority in that of the apostles and by making him a co-recipient of the revelation with Peter and John. The probability is that the latter tradition has grown out of Paul's reference to the Jerusalem pillars in his letter to the Galatians. The naming of James as first of the three pillars (Gal 2:9) and the reference to Peter's submission to the authority of James in Gal 2:12 imply the leadership of James.

Pauline opposition to the authority of James, the disappearance of the Jerusalem church, and the emergence of Peter as a more ecumenical transformation of the James tradition seem to have led to the suppression of James in the emerging Catholic tradition. This was made easier by Luke's attempt to obscure the conflicts within the early church in his accounts in Acts. His harmonization obscured the leadership of James by assimilating the roles of Peter and James, but the cracks in this treatment appear when his account is read in the light of the letters of Paul.

From the letters of Paul we also learn of the appearance of the risen Lord to James. While there are grounds for suspicion, the evidence does not assert the priority of the appearance to James or refer to any esoteric teaching communicated at that appearance. The Nag Hammadi tractates affirm both the leadership priority of James and his superiority as a recipient and transmitter of esoteric revelation. Here there is no hint of any dependence of James on the apostles for his authority or for the esoteric revelation.

The authority of James was developed on the basis of the tradition that the appearance to James was the first of a series, thus confirming James's priority. The priority of the appearance was based on James's intimate relationship to Jesus as the brother of the Lord. The *Gospel of Thomas* reflects a later stage of the development concerning the leadership of James. There it is the disciples who are instructed by the risen Jesus to acknowledge James as their leader. The form of this tradition already reflects the transformation of it by the emerging Catholic church, where the authority of James is authorized by the disciples ("the twelve"), even if the authorization is carried out at the instruction of Jesus. But in the *Gospel of Thomas* James is not made the recipient of any esoteric teaching. His authority is, however, linked with that of Didymos Judas Thomas, whose esoteric account of the secret sayings of the risen Jesus is given in this work. In the other three works from Nag Hammadi it is the esoteric teaching communicated by James more than his leadership that is in view. While this tradition is later than that which asserts the leadership of James based on the first resurrection appearance of Jesus, it is earlier than the tradition that makes the authority of James dependent on the recognition of the apostles or associates the revelation made to him with them also.

Historically it is likely that James's authority was independent of the (twelve) apostles and that his supporters affirmed his priority both in terms of his special relation to Jesus, as the brother of the Lord, and in terms of the priority of the appearance of the risen Lord to him. It is not likely that in the earliest period an esoteric revelation was claimed on this basis. Rather, after the destruction and dispersal of the Jerusalem church, the priority of James, based on his special relation to Jesus and on the resurrection appearance, was made the basis for the advocacy of a tradition of esoteric revelation. To add to the authority of this tradition its supporters also appealed to James as a righteous martyr, referring to him not only as the brother of the Lord but also as "James the Just." Esoteric revelation is the focus of the Nag Hammadi tractates, and there is reason to think that this developed in a Jewish Christian context where Gnostic tendencies were also present.

Recently F. Stanley Jones has argued that both the *First* and the *Second Apocalypse of James* are dependent on Hegesippus.[33] Perhaps even more important, he has argued the same case for the Pseudo-Clementine *Recognitions* 1.27–71, thus dispensing with the hypothetical source, The *Ascents of James*. His argument concerning the dependence of the *First Apocalypse* is illuminating. Recognizing that scholars dispute whether the mutilated ending preserved an account of the martyrdom, he nevertheless asserts "that there is no reason for denying that the *First Apocalypse of James* is dependent on Hegesippus." In a note attached to this statement he says, "Brown, *James*, 108–9, denies direct dependency without cause."[34] This is a strange argument by which the onus of proof seems to be shifted to those who deny dependence on the grounds that "a simple explanation of the Christian tradition of James' martyrdom seems to be the best one."[35] Yet the only point of contact that he adduces in favor of

---

[33] "The Martyrdom of James in Hegesippus, Clement of Alexandria, Christian Apocrypha, including Nag Hammadi: A Study of the Textual Relations," *Seminar Papers Society of Biblical Literature 1990* (Atlanta: Scholars Press, 1990), 331–34.

[34] Ibid., p. 334, including n.56. See below, n.38, for details of Brown's contribution.

[35] Ibid., p. 334.

dependence on Hegesippus is "the statement that the war will come immediately after James' departure (36.16–18; compare *HE* 2.23.18)."[36] At the same time he acknowledges that the same connection is to be found in the text that Origen ascribes to Josephus, although Jones fails to note that Eusebius refers to this text also (*HE* 2.23.20).

That this is a Christian interpolation is signaled both by textual evidence—it is not in known texts of Josephus—and the reference to James as "the Just." It is shown to be an early interpolation by the straightforward way in which James is named the brother of Jesus. Thus it is likely that this tradition linking the death of James with the siege of Jerusalem antedates Hegesippus. Certainly the one point of contact is insufficient to show that the *First Apocalypse* was dependent on Hegesippus, especially when other differences between the two works are given due weight.

Jones argues that the second part of the *Second Apocalypse*, which begins at 61.12, is dependent on Hegesippus. He accepts the theory that the first part is dependent on a source different from the second part.[37] Apparently he is unaware that evidence of tradition, independent of Hegesippus, concerning James in the first part of the *Second Apocalypse* weakens his case for a simple single line of dependence on Hegesippus.

Jones notes the comparisons made between Hegesippus and the *Second Apocalypse* by a number of scholars.[38] He lists what he thinks are the four most important points of contact.

Second Apocalypse	Hegesippus
"Come let us stone the Just One," 61.13–15	"Let us stone James the Just," *HE* 2.23.16
The play on Isaiah 3.10 LXX	Citation of Isaiah 3.10 LXX
"pinnacle of the Temple," 61.21–22	"pinnacle of the Temple," *HE* 2.23.12
"You have erred," 62.7	"Even the Just One erred," *HE* 2.23.15[39]

Jones, however, fails to note the differences pointed out by the scholars from whom he has drawn the parallels. He says that "Lüdemann, for example,

[36] Ibid.

[37] Here Jones appeals to the analysis of W.-P. Funk, *Die Zweite Apokalypse des Jacobus aus Nag-Hammadi-Codex V* (Berlin, 1976), 173, 197.

[38] S. K. Brown, *James: A Religio-Historical Study of the Relations between Jewish, Gnostic, and Catholic Christianity in the Early Period through an Investigation of the Traditions about James the Lord's Brother,* Ph.D. dissertation, Brown University (Ann Arbor: University Microfilms, 1972), 173; Lüdemann, *Opposition*, pp. 171–72; W. Pratscher, *Der Herrenbruder Jacobus und die Jacobustradition* (Göttingen: Vandenhoeck & Ruprecht, 1987), 239–40, 248–51.

[39] Jones, p. 332.

fails to list a single reason for not assuming that the *Second Apocalypse of James* is directly dependent on Hegesippus."[40] In Lüdemann's presentation it is clear that the first speech fails in the *Second Apocalypse* but succeeds in Hegesippus; the opponents of James are the priests in the *Second Apocalypse,* not the scribes and Pharisees, as in Hegesippus; there is no mention of the blow by the fuller's club in the *Second Apocalypse* and Wilhelm Pratscher notes that the "stairs," mentioned in both the *Second Apocalypse* and *Recognitions* 1, are absent from Hegesippus. Pratscher also notes that Isa 3:10 is not cited in the *Second Apocalypse,* although it is in Hegesippus. With this observation we note how even a point of contact can contain an important difference. If we knew that the *Second Apocalypse* was dependent on Hegesippus we would be able to explain this but, because we do not know this, the differences cast doubt on the theory of direct dependence. Both Lüdemann and Pratscher provide complex descriptions of the transmission of the tradition of the martyrdom of James.[41] After we have discussed the Pseudo-Clementines some further suggestions will be made concerning the development of the Christian tradition of the martyrdom of James.

For the moment it is of interest to note the variety of ways in which the James tradition was employed. All traditions stress the piety of James, although there are various ways in which this piety is understood. All traditions recognize the importance of his suffering, although it was in Jewish Christianity that his suffering was interpreted in the tradition of the Wisdom heroes, the righteous sufferers. As such, James is seen to be a defender of Jewish institutions and piety, and his suffering was in defense of that piety. He is thus an example for Jewish believers. Gnostic tradition was able to build on this view by stressing the special relationship of James to Jesus, who addresses him as "brother." As the brother of the redeemer, James himself tends to take on a parallel role as a helper and revealer. At the same time he becomes the model of Gnostic piety.

Against these ways of understanding James, the emerging Great Church adapted the traditions by subjecting James to the authority of the apostles while making him the first bishop of the Jerusalem church. The principle of apostolic succession was asserted, making James the exponent of orthodoxy. A struggle over the authenticity of the Epistle of James emerged, especially in relation to other books attributed to him. For orthodoxy, James the Just had become the model moral character and the model martyr, showing that the church needed to find its own heroes in addition to the heroes of Jewish scriptures. In this context there was a complex problem raised by the memory of the serious conflict between Paul and James. Rooted in historical reality, this conflict was exploited and developed in some later forms of Jewish Christianity, especially in a strand that found its way into the Pseudo-Clementines.

---

[40] Ibid., p. 332 n.49.
[41] See Pratscher, *Jacobus,* p. 255, and Lüdemann, *Opposition,* p. 177.

CHAPTER 7

THE APOCRYPHA AND LATER CHRISTIAN EVIDENCE
Bishop of Bishops and Bulwark of Truth

Because there is no natural collection of works known as the New Testament Apocrypha there is need to say something about the collection of works treated here under that title. We are speaking of works that competed for recognition as authoritative. This is true of the Apostolic Fathers and the Nag Hammadi Library. While works belonging to the former were considered "orthodox," the latter is a collection deviating from emerging "orthodoxy." The main reason why that library is not included in the Apocrypha is that it was discovered after the scope of the Apocrypha had been defined; in addition the value of maintaining the integrity of the Nag Hammadi Library, coming as it did from one place, probably one community or group, was recognized. Yet it is not true to say that the Apocrypha is a collection of heretical works. Such works as the *Protevangelium of James* were popular in their time and, for a while, continued to maintain a widespread influence. Only the influence of Jerome brought about the suppression of the *Protevangelium of James* in the West. His influence did not dampen the popularity of that work in the eastern part of the Roman Empire. It is also clear that such works as the *Gospel of the Hebrews* were widely used in certain areas of the empire. So, then, we could say that the Apocrypha includes works that gained local but not universal acceptance. Although this is generally true of the works collected in *The Apostolic Fathers*, the latter continued to be influential in the West as well as the East.

Views that emerged in the writings of Origen in the East and Ambrose, Augustine, and Jerome in the West have a bearing on the subject of James. The writings of these scholars were not considered to be canonical and they were not apocryphal or apparently secret works. Rather they were perceived to be commentary and interpretation of authoritative texts. Such scholars gave expression to the emerging Western perspective while there were others, such as

182

Epiphanius and Helvidius, whose views expressed a tradition of an earlier age that continued to be maintained in the East.

In the later period, attention moves from James in his own right to the problems raised by the so-called brothers and sisters of Jesus to the growing ascetic ideal of virginity and the perception of both Mary and Joseph as the ideals for human (women and men) virginity. The importance of the perpetual virginity of Mary was also driven by the perception of her as "the mother of God" (*Theotokos*). While it can be argued that one reason for this affirmation was the importance of recognizing Jesus as uniquely both human and divine,[1] there was an independent focus on Mary and her significance as the model virgin. The title mother of God or God bearer may have christological implications. It is far more significant for the development of the cult of Mary.

THE *GOSPEL OF THE HEBREWS:* THE BROTHER OF JESUS AS THE FIRST WITNESS

The *Gospel of the Hebrews* is the title modern scholars have given to a number of fragments surviving in the quotations of several writers down to the time of Jerome. In these quotations four different designations are used: "Gospel of the Hebrews," "Gospel written in the Hebrew speech," "Hebrew Gospel," "Gospel called according to the Hebrews."[2] There are various other references to what appears to be a Jewish Gospel or Gospels. The important witnesses are Papias, Hegesippus, Irenaeus, Clement of Alexandria, Origen, Eusebius, Epiphanius, and Jerome. From these quotations and the way they are introduced scholars conclude that a work or works known as the "Jewish Gospel" circulated from the first half of the second century. Uncertainty remains as to whether this designation referred to one, two, or three Gospels. From inconsistencies in the naming and description of the Jewish Gospel, as well as ideological differences in the quotations, a good case can be made for the recognition of three separate works:[3]

1) The *Gospel of the Nazaraeans* is identified as a Synoptic-type Gospel written in Aramaic and probably dependent on canonical Matthew. It is distinguished from Matthew by translation into Aramaic and by fictional develop-

---

[1] Because medical views of the time regarded the mother's womb as the place in which the seed, implanted by the male parent, developed until the baby was ready for birth, the notions of the virginal conception and Mary as a God bearer were dangerously close to a docetic view of Jesus that made no room for his genuine humanity.

[2] See the fragments collected by E. Hennecke in *New Testament Apocrypha*, vol. 1, ed. W. Schneemelcher, trans. R. McL. Wilson (Philadelphia: Westminster, 1963), 163–65, and *The Apocryphal New Testament: A Collection of Apocryphal Christian Literature in an English Translation Based on M. R. James,* ed. J. K. Elliott (Oxford: Clarendon Press, 1993), 3–16.

[3] For a useful discussion of the issues see A. F. J. Klijn, *Jewish Christian Gospel Tradition* (Leiden: Brill, 1992), and the same author's contribution in *ANRW* II.25.2, pp. 3997–4033.

ment of the tradition. Evidence for the existence of this Gospel is found in Origen's commentary on Matthew, in Eusebius, and in the Latin of Jerome.

2) The *Gospel of the Ebionites* is related to Matthew also but is distinguished from the *Gospel of Nazaraeans* in that it is written in Greek and is in ideological tension with Matthew, omitting the infancy narrative and affirming the union of a heavenly being with the man Jesus. This Gospel is cited by Epiphanius in his *Panarion*.

3) The *Gospel of the Hebrews* is quite distinct from these, being a non-Synoptic type of Gospel. Written in Greek, it manifests a Gnostic, mythical perspective. Because evidence is provided by Clement of Alexandria and Origen and is lacking elsewhere, this Gospel is frequently located in Egypt and dated in the first half of the second century. It is argued that the *Gospel of the Egyptians* and the *Gospel of the Hebrews* were two gospels from the same place, the first from Egyptian Gentile-Christians and the second from Egyptian Jewish-Christians.[4] The conception of Jesus as the Holy Spirit is also found in the Coptic Epistle (*Apocryphon*) of James, perhaps supporting an Egyptian locale. Reference to the *Gospel of the Hebrews* by Hegesippus supports a date not later than the first half of the second century. The Gospel was also known to Jerome who preserved the fragment under discussion here.

The hypothesis of three Jewish Gospels, of which the *Gospel of the Hebrews* is one, is now widely accepted. But no example was found in the Coptic library of Nag Hammadi. Although a Coptic *Gospel of the Egyptians* was found, this work is to be distinguished from the Greek *Gospel of the Egyptians*. In spite of this lacuna the probable existence of the *Gospel of the Hebrews* should be accepted. The inclination to attribute the origin of this Gospel to Jewish Christianity in Egypt is supported by the use of the epithet "the Just" in relation to James, reference to him as "My brother" by Jesus, and the portrayal of him as the first witness of the resurrection, thus supporting the notion of the primacy of James.

The quotation important for our study is fragment no. 7 which was preserved by Jerome.[5]

> The Gospel called according to the Hebrews which was recently translated by me into Greek and Latin, which Origen frequently uses, records after the resurrection of the Savior:
>
>> And when the Lord had given the linen cloth to the servant of the priest, he went to James and appeared to him. For James had sworn that he would not eat bread from the hour in which he had drunk the cup of the Lord until he should see him risen from among them that

---

[4] See *New Testament Apocrypha*, vol. 1, p. 163.

[5] *De vir. inl.* 2, which appears in *New Testament Apocrypha*, vol. 1, p. 165.

sleep. And shortly thereafter the Lord said: Bring a table and bread! And immediately it is added: He took the bread, blessed it and brake it and gave it to James the Just and said to him: My brother, eat thy bread, for the Son of Man is risen from among them that sleep.

Although Jerome mentions that Origen frequently used the *Gospel of the Hebrews*, there is no indication that this passage was used anywhere by Origen. Jerome's claim to have translated this Gospel into Greek and Latin is generally questioned because the Gospel is thought to have been composed in Greek, not Aramaic, and it is uncertain that Jerome knew and used the whole Gospel. The passage quoted has clear implications for the study of James beyond what is specifically said about him. It is implied that James was present at the last supper, partaking of "the cup of the Lord." There is no doubt that this is James the brother of Jesus because not only does Jesus address James as "My brother," a designation that can be used figuratively, but also it is said of Jesus that he gave bread to "James the Just," an epithet used as well in *Gospel of Thomas* logion 12. Thus this Gospel elevates the significance of James by placing him in this context. James is addressed by Jesus as "My brother" only here and the *Second Apocalypse of James* 50.13.

The point of the passage quoted is to place James in a preeminent place among the disciples of Jesus. His oath not to eat bread until he had seen the Lord risen from among them that sleep depicts James in relation to a particular kind of piety. The portrayal of the last supper is apparently dependent on the canonical Gospels, and it may be that the oath of James was suggested by Jesus' statement at the supper that he would not drink the fruit of the vine again until he drank it anew in the kingdom of God (Luke 22:18). Already this sets James apart from all others, although the information is given to explain why, when Jesus had risen from the dead, he first went to James and appeared to him. Jesus took bread, blessed it and brake it, and gave it to James the Just. Not only does this fulfill the oath of James not to eat bread until he had seen the risen Jesus; Jesus risen now also provides him with bread, and the provision is described in terms that suggest the first *commemoration* of the last supper. There can be no doubt that in this tradition James is portrayed in terms that imply his priority and leadership. The words of Jesus spoken to James are also important: "My brother, eat thy bread, for the Son of Man is risen from among them that sleep." Self-reference by Jesus to the Son of Man suggests dependence on early tradition. According to Hegesippus (*HE* 2.23), reference to the Son of Man is part of the witness of James prior to his martyrdom.

This fragment is important for the study of James because it portrays James as belonging to the circle of the disciples of Jesus during his ministry and those present at the last supper. It puts in question the notion that James joined the believing community only after the resurrection of Jesus and the appearance of

Jesus to him. Recognition of the ideological stance adopted by the canonical Gospels puts in question the reading that concludes that the brothers of Jesus did not, during his ministry, believe in him (John 7:5). Although the Gospels do not present the brothers in a positive relationship to Jesus, they are portrayed in the company of Jesus and his disciples (John 2:12; 7:1–9). Nevertheless, the tradition of the first appearance to James runs contrary to the witness of the Gospels.

The *Gospel of the Hebrews* asserts that James was the first witness to see the risen Lord on the first day, on which he rose "from among them that sleep." It has been argued that the focus of the narrative is not on the appearance itself but on the resolution of the problem caused by James's vow not to eat bread until he had seen Jesus risen.[6] Certainly the appearance resolves that problem. But why is James portrayed in this way? Was it merely to manifest one aspect of his piety in the solemn vow? Is it not rather that the vow gives a necessary basis for the first appearance of the risen Jesus to James? The need to give some basis for the claim of the first appearance implies that the claim itself was controversial. Thus, while the appearance resolves a personal problem for James, it also gives him priority, and this priority is emphasized by the use of the epithet "the Just" and by Jesus' form of address, "My brother." Martin Dibelius notes the affinity of the motif of the vow to John 20:24–29, in which Thomas, absent from the first appearance of the risen Lord to the disciples, vows he will not believe until certain conditions are fulfilled.[7] But differences should be noted. For example, while Thomas was unbelieving, James is stubborn in belief. Really, there is little evidence that the Gospel of John has been influential at this point.

When 1 Corinthians 15 is read in the light of the *Gospel of the Hebrews* it may seem that the supporters of James are asserting the priority of the appearance of the risen Lord to James and in so doing implying his leadership rather than Peter's. That rivalry developed at some stage is likely, but it is unclear where the *Gospel of the Hebrews* fits into this history.

The motif of the risen Jesus giving the "shroud" to the servant of the high priest is strange because it means that, technically, Jesus appeared to someone prior to his appearance to James. Because the point of this passage is not to elevate the servant of the high priest above James it must be assumed that another point is being made. Most likely this detail gives expression to a Gnostic motif in which the shroud represents the body, so that in this action Jesus gives up his body appropriately to the servant of the high priest (see the *Gospel of Thomas* logion 21 and, also in the Nag Hammadi Library, the *Treatise on the Resurrection* 45.15–40).

---

[6] Thus W. Pratscher, *Der Herrenbruder Jacobus und die Jacobustradition* (Göttingen: Vandenhoeck & Ruprecht, 1987), 46.

[7] M. Dibelius, *James: A Commentary on the Epistle of James*, revised edition, revised by H. Greeven, Hermeneia (Philadelphia: Fortress, 1976), 13.

THE PSEUDO-CLEMENTINES: BISHOP OF BISHOPS IN THE CHURCH OF THE HEBREWS

In their present form the Pseudo-Clementines are not earlier than the late fourth century. They are in two main parts, the *Homilies* and the *Recognitions*. The *Homilies* are preserved in Greek in two codices, along with two epistles to James, one by Peter (*Epistula Petri,* or *Ep. P.*) and the other by Clement (*Ep. C.*), and with instructions as to the right use of the book (*Contestatio*). The Greek of the *Recognitions* has not survived, but the work has been preserved in the Latin translation of Rufinus. Both the *Recognitions* and the *Homilies* were soon translated into Syriac, and a manuscript from Edessa dated to the year 411 gives evidence of a collection of texts from the *Homilies* and the *Recognitions*. There is an overlap between the *Homilies* and the *Recognitions* which can be set out roughly as follows:[8]

Recognitions	Homilies	Recognitions	Homilies
I	I, II	VI	XI
II, III	III	VII	XII, XIII
—	IV–VII	VIII–IX	XIV XV
IV	VIII–IX	—	XVI–XIX
V	X, XV	X	XX

First the one and then the other seem to preserve the original text, suggesting that the two works are dependent on a common *Grundschrift*. On the basis of the identification of the *Epistula Petri* and the *Contestatio,* which follows, Georg Strecker proposed that the *Grundschrift* made use of earlier works, including *Kerygmata Petrou*. This hypothetical source should not be confused with the *Kerygma Petrou* referred to by Clement of Alexandria in his *Stromateis*. At one time these works shared the identical designation *Kerygma Petrou*, but the title for the hypothetical work was changed to *Kerygmata Petrou* by R. A. Lipsius (1872), thus breaking the suggested connection between the work referred to by Clement of Alexandria and the source of the Pseudo-Clementines. Strecker identified the source of the Pseudo-Clementines as Gnostic, Jewish, Christian, and located it in Syria around 200 CE. He also identified the *Ascents of James,* a source underlying *Recognitions* 1.33–71 which he dated in the second half of the second century. A work known as *Ascents of James* (᾽Αναβαθμοὶ ᾽Ιακώβου), referred to by Epiphanius, was first associated with *Recognitions* 1.36–71 by K. R. Köstlin in 1849. While F. J. A. Hort (1894) agreed with this identification, he also noted that in the understanding of "ascents" in the source for *Recognitions,* James's ascent of the Temple steps was in view, while Epiphanius

---

[8] See *The Ante-Nicene Fathers,* vol. 8, ed. A. Roberts and J. Donaldson (Edinburgh: T & T Clark, 1989), 71, which refers to the "books" into which the two works are divided.

referred to the ascent in the steps of instruction. Strecker thinks that the two documents are related but not identical and postulates a common archetype and suggests that the source of *Recognitions* 1.33–71 was written in Pella between 150 and 200 CE by the Jewish Christian community that saw itself as the successor to the Jerusalem church.[9] Some relationship is postulated with the Jewish Christian community at Pella in Transjordan where the veneration of James was part of a distinctive ethos. Robert E. Van Voorst[10] supports this consensus view on the date and place of origin of the *Ascents of James,* and there is a wide consensus among scholars, although it is challenged by S. K. Brown.[11]

The Pseudo-Clementines take their name from Clement of Rome, in whose name they are written and whose story they tell. Clement was bishop of Rome at the end of the first century. According to Tertullian, Clement was appointed by Peter, but Eusebius (*HE* 3.4.8; 3.15; 3.21; 3.34; 5.6)[12] says that Clement is the third bishop after Peter (and Paul), following Linus and Anencletus. Tertullian dates Clement's death in the third year of Trajan's reign so that his episcopacy can be dated from 92 to 101 CE.

According to the story in the Pseudo-Clementines, Clement belonged to an aristocratic family in Rome which underwent great misfortunes when the mother of the family, directed by a vision, secretly left the city with Clement's two older twin brothers. When they did not return the father went in search of them. Eventually Clement also left Rome and in his travels met Peter and joined his company as a believer, traveling with him on his missionary journeys to cities of coastal Syria. This narrative provides the context for the preaching of Peter, which the *Homilies* contain, and the setting for Peter's confrontation with Simon Magus known to us in Acts 8:9–24. The figure of Simon becomes far more sinister in the Pseudo-Clementines because Paul stands barely cloaked behind him and Peter's confrontation with and triumph over Simon is to be seen as his victory over Paul. Much of this material appears to have been drawn from the *Kerygmata Petrou.*

The Ascents of James *and the Martyrdom Tradition*

The *Ascents of James* deals with James's ascent of the steps of the Temple (*Recognitions* 1.66–71) to continue a public disputation over the messiahship of Jesus. This dispute had been initiated by Peter and Clement with Jewish oppo-

---

[9] See his *Das Judenchristentum in den Pseudoklementinen,* TU 70/2 (Berlin: Akadamie, 1981), 137–254. See also R. E. Van Voorst, *The Ascents of James: History and Theology of a Jewish-Christian Community,* SBL Dissertation Series 112 (Atlanta: Scholars Press, 1989).

[10] Van Voorst, p. 180.

[11] *James: A Religio-Historical Study of the Relations between Jewish, Gnostic, and Catholic Christianity in the Early Period through an Investigation of the Traditions about James the Lord's Brother,* Ph.D. dissertation, Brown University (Ann Arbor: University Microfilms, 1972).

[12] See Williamson, pp. 110, 124–25, 127–28, 145, 208–9.

nents. It is from the key event of James's ascent of the steps that the hypothetical source takes its name. It should be remembered that, although we speak of this section as if it were the source, we are actually dealing with *Recognitions* 1 on the assumption that it is based on an earlier source. In the first instance the chief of the opponents is named Caiaphas (1.68), but, at the point at which James has persuaded the multitude to accept baptism, Clement reports that, "one of our enemies, entering the Temple," intervened, and, although James was able to refute him, he created a tumult and there was great bloodshed through the ensuing violence. The "enemy" threw James down from the top of the steps and left him for dead. From there James was rescued by his friends and support-ers (1.70). The account of the throwing down of James from the Temple steps appears to have some relation to the account of the martyrdom of James in Hegesippus. There are major differences. In *Recognitions (Ascents of James)* the top of the Temple steps replaces the pinnacle of the Temple in Hegesippus; Saul is introduced into the narrative in *Recognitions*; James does not die in *Recognitions*.

The "enemy" who threw James down is identified as Saul in a marginal note in one of the manuscripts, and this identification is confirmed by 1.71. There we are told that Gamaliel, who has already been identified as a secret believer and secret supporter among the opponents (1.65, 67), brought news that the "enemy" had received a commission from Caiaphas to go to Damascus in pursuit of believers because it was thought that Peter had fled to this city. There is no doubt that this is a reference to Saul of Tarsus in Acts 9:1–2. There is no hint of his conversion. The motif of the secret supporter among the oppo-nents of James is also found in the *Second Apocalypse of James*, although there the supporter is the priest Mareim.

The Kerygmata Petrou *and the* Epistula Petri *on Peter, Paul, and James*

The *Kerygmata Petrou* is introduced by the *Epistula Petri* in which we learn that Moses had made known the true teaching that Jesus had confirmed (*Ep. P.* 2.2, 5). This, the "lawful proclamation" of Peter, is opposed to the "lawless doctrine" of the "hostile man" (*Ep. P.* 2.3). The *Kerygmata Petrou* teaches the reincarnation of the true prophet, first in Adam (*Recognitions* 1.47), also in the lawgiver Moses (*Homilies* 2.52.3), and then in Jesus (*Homilies* 3.17–19 and *Ep. P.* 2.5). The opposition between true and false prophecy is manifest in the pairs (*syzygy*) in which the false feminine form is first (Eve is the first example), followed by the true and masculine form (Adam is the first example). The last pair in the series of *syzygy* is Paul (the feminine) antagonist of Peter (*Homilies* 2.17.3). Here the portrayal of Simon Magus is a veiled reference to Paul, and it is said that the false prophet to the Gentiles appears before the true (Peter).

Peter's lawful proclamation is opposed to Paul (*Homilies* 2.15–17; 11.35.3–6 = *Recognitions* 4.34.5–4.35.2.; *Homilies* 17.13–19). The conflict at Antioch between Paul and Peter (Gal 2:11–14) is in view in *Homilies* 17.19. There is a polemic against visions such as Paul's (Acts 9; Gal 2:2; 1 Cor 15:8; 2 Cor 12:1–10) that are in contrast to the commission of Peter by Jesus (Matt 16:17; *Homilies* 17.18–19). It is argued that Paul cannot have been given the teaching of Jesus in a vision because he does not agree with the teaching of Peter and James. Nor can Paul be an apostle because he is not one of the twelve (*Recognitions* 4.35). His lawless gospel is false doctrine that cannot be approved by James (*Homilies* 11.35.4–6; *Ep.P.* 2.3–4). Here the motif of the primacy of James has an anti-Pauline intent. But it is Peter who takes the true law-based gospel to the Gentiles. Thus we have confirming evidence of the role of James in the law-based mission to the circumcision/Jews, which is perhaps expressed in the "M" tradition in Matthew, and of the role of Peter as the proponent of the circumcision, law-based mission to the nations expressed in the final composition of Matthew. These positions make sense of a nuanced reading of Acts and Galatians. Here also Paul is portrayed as the opponent of James and Peter.

In the *Ascents of James* Paul is identified as the enemy Saul, a representative of high priestly authority persecuting James, causing his fall from the top of the Temple steps. He is also seeking to persecute Peter, pursuing him to Damascus. Thus his role as persecutor is recalled (Acts 8:3; 9:1–2) but without any reference to his conversion. In the *Kerygmata Petrou*, in the persona of Simon Magus with his lawless gospel, it is actually Paul who is the opponent of Peter. The picture is of James as the bishop of bishops in charge of the Jerusalem church (*Ep.C.* Preface), the judge of true teaching (*Recognitions* 1.68.2–1.70.1; 1.70.3; 4.34–35; *Homilies* 11.35.3–5) and Peter as the apostle and missionary of the true and lawful proclamation to the Gentiles. Here the role of Paul the convert is recalled, and to make clear the corrupt nature of his gospel he is portrayed in terms of Simon Magus (Acts 8:9–24). The *Ascents of James* is concerned with the primacy of James (*Recognitions* 1.43.3; 1.66.2, 5; 1.68.2; 1.70.3; cf. 1.72.1); as is the *Kerygmata Petrou (Contestatio* 5.4; *Homilies* 11.35.3–5). This concern goes beyond the interest in James as the first bishop, asserting that Jesus himself ordained James as head of the Jerusalem church, presiding over the twelve (*Ascents of James, Recognitions* 1.44.1; 1.66.1; cf. 1.72.1, and *Kerygmata Petrou,* Preface to *Ep.P.; Homilies* 1.20.2–3/*Recognitions* 1.17.2–3; *Homilies* 11.35.3–5/ *Recognitions* 4.34–35) and overseeing their missionary labors *(Recognitions* 1.17.2–3; 1.44.1; cf. 1.72.1; *Ep.P.* 1.1; *Homilies* 1.20.2–3).

Some aspects of this description appear to echo historical reality. James and Peter are representative of a law-based gospel of the circumcision, with James based in Jerusalem while Peter is involved in a mission to the Gentiles. Yet James had authority to veto teaching and action even in the mission situation outside Jerusalem. It could be that Acts was responsible for the presence of these elements. The authority of James over members of the mission from Jerusalem is also attested by Paul in Gal 2:11–14.

The Pseudo-Clementines and Jewish Christianity

The Pseudo-Clementines provide evidence of a Jewish Christian Gnosticism opposed to Paul. Strangely Paul takes on the persona of Simon Magus, who, in terms of "Catholic" tradition is the father of heresy. That a Jewish Christian Gnostic text should portray Paul in this way is ironical, showing that issues related to keeping the Jewish law have become paramount. Only sacrifice is no longer relevant for the gospel of the circumcision, which is not surprising after the destruction of the Temple.

References to James in the Pseudo-Clementines are illuminating. In *Recognitions,* narrating what leads up to the incident in the Temple, where James is thrown down from the top of the steps by "that enemy," Saul, Peter refers to James on a number of occasions, as "our James" and twice as "James the bishop" (1.66). In the process James encounters Caiaphas, who is referred to as "the chief of the priests," while James is called "the chief of the bishops" (1.68) and "our James" (1.69). Then, after being thrown down the steps, James is rescued and sends Peter to Caesarea to confront Simon and requires him to send back to him an account of his sayings and doings at regular intervals (1.72).[13] This incident shows the authority of James both in Jerusalem and in the mission beyond. On arrival in Caesarea Peter reports that he was welcomed by "our most beloved brother Zacchaeus" who inquired "concerning each of the brethren, especially concerning our honorable brother James." Peter then informed him of the way the priests and Caiaphas the high priest had called them to the Temple, and how "James the archbishop, standing at the top of the steps," convinced the people that Jesus was the Christ (1.73). Simon's challenge to Peter follows. When Peter has spent three months in Caesarea, ordaining Zacchaeus as bishop, he instructs Clement to record and to send to James an appropriate account. In his report Clement addresses James as "my Lord James" (3.74). Then (in 3.75) Clement reports to James, summarizing the ten books of the teaching of Peter. It is not possible to say if this summary refers to some source used in the writing of the *Recognitions.* Naturally the teaching is consistent with the *Recognitions,* in particular with the emphasis on the law of Moses and the role of the true prophet.

Having confronted Simon in Caesarea, Peter and his mission proceed to Tripolis. Books 4–6 of *Recognitions* are set in Tripolis, which is also the setting of *Homilies* 8–11, books 4–7 treating the journey from Caesarea. In his discourse Peter cautions his hearers concerning false apostles: "believe no teacher,

---

[13] In the *Epistle of Clement* to James, Clement indicates that he has sent an Aepitome of Peter's preaching and is about to send the full text, apparently referring to *Homilies.*

unless he brings from Jerusalem the testimonial of James the Lord's brother, or whosoever may come after him" (*Recognitions* 4.35). Not only does this saying recognize the authority of James (and his successors) beyond Jerusalem; it is also anti-Pauline in intent. Paul denied his dependence on Jerusalem, even if he did, on his own admission, go up to Jerusalem to lay his gospel before "the pillars" (Gal 2:1–10). The conflict between Paul and the Jerusalem pillars is also a matter of contention for Paul (Gal 2:11–14). *Recognitions* ascribes to James the authority to authenticate the credentials of all teachers. With the description of James as "our bishop," "the chief of the bishops," and "the archbishop," this authenticating role sets James as the supreme authority in the early church.

Two epistles have been attached to the *Homilies*, the first attributed to Peter and the second to Clement. To the *Epistle of Peter* is attached the *Contestatio*. Peter addresses his letter "to James, the lord and bishop of the holy Church" and addresses him as "my brother." The stated purpose of the letter is to request that James not reveal the teaching/preaching of Peter to any untried and uninitiated Gentile or Jewish teachers but that he follow the practice of Moses, who delivered his books to the seventy who succeeded him (see Num 11:16, 25). The stated reason for this concern is that "some from among the Gentiles have rejected my lawful preaching, attaching themselves to certain lawless and trifling preaching of the man who is my enemy." This strong anti-Pauline motif is related to the special tradition in Matthew often designated "M." In the words of the epistle:

> some have attempted while I am still alive to transform my words by certain various interpretations, in order to teach the dissolution of the law; as though I myself were of such a mind, but did not freely proclaim it, which God forbid! For such a thing were to act in opposition to the law of God which was spoken by Moses, and was borne witness to by our Lord in respect of its eternal continuance; for thus he spoke: "The heavens and the earth shall pass away, but one jot or one tittle shall in no wise pass away from the law."

The quotation is from Matt 5:18, which is from the special M material, a tradition which represents James and Jerusalem and is here affirmed by Peter. The difference between Peter and James in the Pseudo-Clementines is that James maintains the Jewish mission centered in Jerusalem, while Peter extends the law-based mission to the Gentiles. That Peter affirms a law-based mission against the Pauline law-free mission is clear. The role of the seventy is also important, linking this text with other works related to James.[14] Here the ex-

---

[14] See especially Clement of Alexandria (*HE* 2.1.4) and the *First Apocalypse of James*, in which Addai, identified with Thaddaeus, is named in the chain of transmission of higher knowledge.

plicit link with Moses is spelled out in terms of safeguarding the law-based mission. A consequence of the instruction not to reveal the preaching/teaching openly is that there is an explanation for the late appearance of the pseudonymous apocryphal work attributed to Peter.

In the *Contestatio* the conditions requested by Peter are formalized by James, who, when he had called the elders, instructs them to maintain a six-year proving of those to whom the instruction is to be transmitted. Those receiving the teaching are to be required to agree to strict rules of further transmission.

The letter of Clement to James provides a rationale for the *Homilies* that follows. The letter is addressed

> to James, the lord (probably "the Lord's brother"), and the bishop of bishops, who rules in Jerusalem, the holy church of the Hebrews, and the churches everywhere.

Here Clement acknowledges the leadership of James, not only in the Jerusalem church, which is described as the church of the Hebrews, but also in the churches everywhere. One of the purposes of the letter is to report the martyrdom of Peter in Rome and to authenticate Peter's choice of Clement as his successor and bishop in that place. One of the justifications for the choice is that Clement had traveled with Peter from beginning to end, had heard all of his homilies, shared all of his trials, and been proved worthy to succeed to the chair of Peter. The letter reports Peter's homily on the occasion of the installation of Clement; at the end of the homily Peter charges Clement with communicating to James something of Clement's own biography, including his hearing of the discourses of Peter and his knowledge of the circumstances of Peter's death. At the end of the record Clement adds that he has already sent to James his epitome of the popular preaching of Peter but will now set forth those sermons as he has been ordered. No doubt we are to think of the homilies that follow as the fulfillment of this obligation.

Historically it is unlikely that Peter's martyrdom preceded that of James in 62 CE, though the time of the death of Peter, which tradition locates in Rome, cannot be fixed with any certainty. But it was important that Clement, in whose name these works were published, should have the explicit approval of Peter and also the implicit support of James, who, according to the Pseudo-Clementines, was the bishop of bishops with authority over the churches in every place.

The primacy of James was recognized in the Jerusalem Church until the time of his death. The tradition of his primacy must have its origin in the history of the Jerusalem community. It is unclear whether any formal succession continued from James or if those who succeeded to the leadership of the Jerusalem Church enjoyed the same authority as he had beyond the boundaries of Jerusalem. Certainly that is the position portrayed and advocated by the

Pseudo-Clementines. These works are not only Jewish in character but also Gnostic. What is likely is that the form of Jewish Christianity of which they are an expression became increasingly Gnostic after the disappearance of any Jewish Christian community in Jerusalem.

James emerges, especially in the section dependent on the *Ascents of James*, as the bishop and leader of the Jerusalem church (*Recognitions* 1.62.2; 68.2; 70.3) whose authority derived directly from the risen Lord and encompassed the twelve (1.44.1), including Peter (1.72.1). While not denying the leadership of James, the tradition of the Great Church was eager to couple the apostles with the Lord as the source of the authority of James, as can be seen in Eusebius (*HE* 7.19). But in the *Ascents of James* James also has responsibility for the early Christian mission, and he is depicted as an apologist to the Jews, seeking their conversion (1.70–71). Characteristically James is opposed by Saul of Tarsus (1.70–71), and this motif has played an important role in the history of research concerning a distinctive Jewish Christianity, becoming one of the defining characteristics of what is meant by Jewish Christianity. While this motif is un-ambiguously present here, it must be recognized as having its roots in earlier, probably historical, tradition.

There are puzzling features concerning the *Ascents of James*. On the one hand its identification as a Jewish Christian source suggests that it might provide access to early and reliable information about James and the early church. On the other there are features that put in question the Jewishness of the source. Robert E. Van Voorst notes that the *Ascents of James*, in locating the Temple debates, grossly overestimates the size of the Temple sanctuary and overlooks the fact that the space identified was restricted to priests and Levites. The depic-tion of the Temple as open to the public, including Samaritans, confirms "that the Temple debates ([*Recognitions*]1.55–71) have no good claim to historicity."[15] Of course the *Ascents of James* is from the second half of the second century, a time when memory of the Temple was remote. But this need not mean that no tradition relating to debates located in the Temple precincts underlies the work.

Van Voorst also rejects as unhistorical the attack on Paul in which he is blamed for the failure of the mission to the Jewish nation. To substantiate his view Van Voorst appeals to Acts 21:17–26 and Romans 9–11.[16] While he ac-knowledges that Acts 21 refers to the rumor that Paul had taught Jews in the diaspora not to observe the law, he notes that James does not blame Paul for the failure of the mission to the Jews and in fact affirms that the mission in Jerusalem had been successful. Such conclusions arise from a partial, "face value" reading on the part of Van Voorst. No attempt is made to raise any question about the historicity of the Acts account or the tendencies of its author

---

[15] Van Voorst, pp. 170–71.
[16] Ibid., pp. 171–72.

to obscure conflicts. Indeed such evidence of conflict as remain in the Acts account are obscured by Van Voorst. For example, did the Jerusalem community accept the collection brought by Paul? Why does Acts not refer to this? Why is there no mention of any advocacy on behalf of Paul by the Jerusalem church after his arrest? Thus even the Acts account reveals real tension between Paul and the Jerusalem church.

Paul's account shows that he was anxious about his reception in Jerusalem and was uncertain of how, and even if, the collection would be received (Rom 15:22–32). He asked the Romans to pray that he might be delivered from the unbelievers in Jerusalem and that his service (the collection referred to in 15:25–27) might be acceptable to saints, the believers or Jerusalem church. Subsequent events showed that Paul's anxiety was well founded, probably on both counts. Paul's account of the mission to Israel is also at odds with Van Voorst's reading of Acts, in which the success of the mission of the Jerusalem church is stressed to show that Paul would not have been blamed for failure because the mission was a success.

Paul acknowledges "the overwhelming failure of the mission to Israel."[17] Although Van Voorst recognizes this, he does not allow the observation to cast doubt on the historicity of his reading of Acts. Instead he responds by arguing that Paul did not blame himself and his law-free mission for the failure. Rather the failure is attributed to "the mysterious purposes of God (9.6–33)." There is no doubt that this is true to Paul's argument in Romans. This is Paul's expressed point of view. This does not mean that his point of view was shared by all others, including James and the Jerusalem church. Indeed, in Romans there are clues that suggest Paul was arguing against those who accused him of disloyalty to his own people, of lacking natural affection for them (9.1–5; 10:1). What is more, his answer shows that he was sensitive to this charge, and much of Romans is well understood as Paul's answer to it. It was necessary for him to show the continuing place of Israel in his understanding of the plan and purposes of God from the perspective of a law-free mission to the Gentiles. Thus, contrary to Van Voorst, the evidence of both Acts and Romans suggests that Paul was accused of threatening the mission to the Jewish nation. That Paul repudiates the charge does not mean that it was not made or that he did not feel the force of it. On the contrary, his repudiation tends to confirm such a view.

Van Voorst also argues that in the *Ascents of James* the "portrait of the pre-eminence of James . . . is not historical."[18] He rightly notes the inconsistency of referring to James as the "head bishop" and the "only bishop" and the anachronism of referring to James as bishop at all. Granted that the title of bishop is anachronistic, what of the claim that James was appointed leader of the Jerusa-

---

[17] Ibid., p. 172.
[18] Ibid.

lem church by Jesus himself (*Ascents* 1.43.3)? Here Van Voorst argues that James was not the first leader, that Acts and Paul depict the shared leadership of James with the twelve and that this is confirmed by Hegesippus according to Eusebius (*HE* 2.22.1).[19] This reference is obviously a mistake, as there is no reference to either Hegesippus or James here. In *HE* 2.23.1 there is a reference to the election of James by the apostles to the throne of the bishopric of Jerusalem. This summary by Eusebius fits his view of the pattern of leadership transmission in the early church, in which Jesus chose the twelve and the twelve ordained the first bishops. Thus 1 Clement 42; 44.1–2; and Irenaeus in *AH* 3.3.2–4. But Eusebius does not attribute this view to Hegesippus or to anyone else for that matter. It may be that Eusebius thought that he was drawing on the tradition quoted from Clement of Alexandria in *HE* 2.1.3, which says "After the ascension of the savior Peter, James and John chose James the Just as bishop of Jerusalem." Contrary to Van Voorst, this implies that James was leader from the first. The other tradition reported from Clement (*HE* 2.1.4) asserts a direct link with the risen Lord and James the Just, asserting that "After the resurrection the Lord gave the tradition of knowledge to James the Just and John and Peter. . . ." By naming James first this tradition already implies his leadership, prior to the ascension and perhaps prior to the recognition of his leadership by Peter and the sons of Zebedee. That recognition is associated with the ascension of Jesus.

Thus, contrary to Van Voorst, the *Ascents of James* confirms the original leadership of James. The depiction of that leadership in terms of the bishop's throne and the appointment of James by the twelve is to be seen as an expression of the ideology of the emerging Great Church. While the leadership of James could not be denied, being too firmly entrenched in a wide variety of traditions, his leadership could be made dependent on the authority of the twelve as mediators of the authority of Jesus.

Van Voorst rightly argues that the *Ascents of James* exhibits a positive view of the observance of the Mosaic law, including circumcision (1.33.3–5; 1.35.2; 1.43.2). Only sacrifice is excluded from observance, and this position was developed in relation to the teaching of Jesus, the prophet like Moses. While the teaching of the prophet like Moses does not appear outside the *Ascents of James*, the teaching of the true prophet provides a similar basis in the rest of the Pseudo-Clementines. Overall the Pseudo-Clementines insist on law observance while being anti-sacrificial and anti-Pauline. On this basis Van Voorst argues that the church of the *Ascents of James* "is Jewish in ethnic origin; it promotes an identification with the Jewish people as 'our people.' In practice, the community of the *AJ* is composed of law-observant Jews. They keep Jewish feasts and customs; they may practice circumcision. In belief, they are Jewish-Christian as well. Their christology, that of the Mosaic Prophet, is rooted in Jewish

---

[19] We have argued that Acts and Paul actually reflect the leadership of James.

belief. . . . [A]side from its acceptance of Jesus as Messiah and what follows from it, the community of the *AJ* is one with Judaism." Nevertheless it is clear from 1.44.2; 1.62; 1.70–71 that the community of "*AJ* underwent persecution at the hands of the Jewish authorities."[20]

Given that this form of Jewish Christianity was manifest in the second half of the second century, the question is raised as to its relationship to the original Jewish Christianity of the Jerusalem church. Johannes Munck and S. G. F. Brandon have argued that authentic Jewish Christianity did not survive the fall of Jerusalem in 70 CE.[21] Against this absolute break Van Voorst argues for some continuity between Stephen and the Hellenists as depicted in Acts.[22] This is surely mistaken, overlooking the fact that, according to Acts, it was the scattered Hellenists who began to preach a law-free gospel in Antioch (Acts 11:20). A greater continuity exists between James and the Pharisaic believers of Acts 15:1, 5 and the Jewish Christians of the Pseudo-Clementines.

The Tradition of the Martyrdom of James

Studies have shown that the account of the martyrdom of James in Hegesippus has some sort of relation to the *Ascents of James*. But was Hegesippus dependent on the *Ascents,* or the *Ascents* on Hegesippus, or were both dependent on a common source? Similarities are stressed by F. Stanley Jones in his argument that *Recognitions* 1 was dependent on Hegesippus.[23] Jones notes that the dominant view is that *Recognitions* 1 and Hegesippus were dependent on a common, now lost, source. His purpose is to argue the dependence of *Recognitions* on Hegesippus. To this end he lists thirteen points of similarity but fails to note important differences. Lüdemann also lists points of contact but notes differences.[24] Three important differences suffice to show that the case for direct dependence has not been made. In the *Ascents* James ascends the Temple steps; in Hegesippus it is the pinnacle of the Temple. In the *Ascents* the opponents are not the scribes and Pharisees, as in Hegesippus, but the high priest and the one known as "the enemy." In Hegesippus James is martyred while in the *Ascents* he is not killed. There are other important differences also, some of them at the very point where contact seems to be indicated. Thus while the issue of Jesus' messiahship is at stake in each of these documents it is not presented in the same terms.

---

[20] Van Voorst, p. 177.

[21] Munck, "Jewish Christianity in Post-Apostolic Times," *NTS* 6 (1960): 103–16, and S. G. F. Brandon, *The Fall of Jerusalem and the Christian Church* (London: SPCK, 1957).

[22] Van Voorst, p. 180.

[23] "The Martyrdom of James in Hegesippus, Clement of Alexandria, Christian Apocrypha, including Nag Hammadi: A Study of the Textual Relations," *Seminar Papers Society of Biblical Literature 1990* (Atlanta: Scholars Press, 1990), 328–31.

[24] *Opposition to Paul in Jewish Christianity* (Minneapolis: Fortress, 1989), 175–77.

The *Ascents* does not deal with the martyrdom of James but with a serious point of conflict. Given that Josephus provides evidence of the death of James, the early Christian traditions have been embroidered by an account or accounts of the exploits of James in Jerusalem that focused on his witness to Jesus. Josephus suggests that James died because of a serious intra-Jewish problem which was not specifically Christian. Those who regarded James to be a righteous martyr reworked this tradition to portray James as a witness to Jesus, making use of the tradition of the righteous sufferer, the tradition of the trial of Jesus, and tradition concerning the martyrdom of Stephen. The *Ascents of James* brings to light the fact that the early Christian tradition concerning the death of James was combined with tradition dealing with the witness of James to Jesus in a conflict with Jewish authority that did not lead to James's death. In Hegesippus this view becomes joined to the tradition now found in Josephus.

THE *PROTEVANGELIUM OF JAMES:* JAMES THE SON OF JOSEPH

The document known as the *Protevangelium of James* gains its title partly from the conclusion, where the author names himself as James (25.1) and partly from its content. The first clear evidence of the work is provided by Origen in his *Commentary on Matthew* book X.17, although the *Protevangelium* was probably used by Clement of Alexandria in *Stromata* 7.16.93. The earliest manuscript evidence is Bodmer Papyrus V, dated to the third century and already showing secondary developments. Translations were made into Syriac, Ethiopic, Georgian, Sahidic, Slavonic, Armenian, and Latin although no Latin manuscripts have survived. Following rejection of the *Protevangelium* by Jerome, it ceased to have wide appeal in the West. Jerome rejected it because it portrayed the brothers (and sisters) of Jesus as children of Joseph by a marriage prior to his marriage to Mary.

This work appears to be composite, changing from third person to first person narration by James at the end.[25] James is identified as Joseph's son who led the she-ass upon which the pregnant Mary rode while Joseph followed behind (17.2). This scene is often depicted in art, for example in the crypt of the Benedictine Dormition Abbey in Jerusalem and in the refectory of a monastery outside Jericho, though it is modified to the extent that in those scenes Mary, riding on the ass, carries the baby Jesus in her arms. The scene in these murals is the flight into Egypt with James leading while Joseph brings up the rear, following the donkey bearing Mary and the infant Jesus.

The *Protevangelium* is dependent on the infancy stories of both Matthew and Luke, although in this document attention has turned from a concentration on the circumstances of the birth of Jesus to the virginity of Mary. Her own miraculous birth is first narrated, based on the model of the births of Isaac and

---

[25] Compare the *First Apocalypse of James*.

Samuel rather than on the later doctrine of the immaculate conception. Following the pattern of the story of Samuel, Mary is made a child of the Temple (7.1). When she attains the age of twelve her presence in the Temple becomes problematic, probably because of the onset of puberty, making her presence in the Temple a purity hazard. Joseph is chosen by lot to receive Mary as his virgin ward (9.1). As a virgin, she conceives (9.1) and bears Jesus (18.1–20.1). What is more, after the birth of Jesus, the test conducted by the midwife proves that her virginity has remained intact. Because the teaching of the continuing virginity of Mary had become important, the *Protevangelium* develops the teaching of the earlier marriage of Joseph to account for the supposed brothers and sisters of Jesus. Of those children James is by far the most prominent and gives his name to this Gospel, which is probably the earliest and most influential of the infancy Gospels. By postulating an earlier marriage and a number of children as the fruit of that marriage the picture is painted of Joseph as an older man, though no actual age is mentioned, nor are the children in addition to James named. In the description of Joseph's son leading, the pregnant Mary riding the she-ass while Joseph follows behind, the image of a youthful James seems to be implied. The artistic presentation of James leading the ass in the scene of the flight to Egypt is of a preadolescent boy. In this way the *Protevangelium* of James became the model for the understanding of the family of Jesus in Eastern Christianity.

Building on the infancy stories of Matthew and Luke, the *Protevangelium* manifests tradition from the second century in which the continuing virginity of Mary was important. Origen in his *Commentary on Matthew* X.17, which discusses Matt 13:54–56, associates the *Protevangelium* with the *Gospel of Peter*. There are no grounds for thinking that traditions asserting that Mary bore no other children after Jesus are historically reliable. Rather they are preoccupied with the preservation of the virginity of Mary. Once Mary's perpetual virginity had been accepted, it was necessary to find an alternative understanding of those who were spoken of as the brothers and sisters of Jesus. While developing out of the Matthean and Lukan infancy stories, according to which those called brothers and sisters were actually half-brothers and sisters, the *Protevangelium* teaches that these people were not blood relations at all. The brothers and sisters were children of Joseph by a first marriage, while Jesus was the child of Mary without a human father. Given that Joseph was the legal father, it is not impossible that all might be described as brothers and sisters. It is just that there is no hint of this complex web of relations in the earliest evidence, and when the tradition does emerge it has a strongly apologetic character. The intent was to establish the perpetual virginity of Mary and to venerate her virginity. We are not able, with any confidence, to identify evidence of this tradition any earlier than the middle of the second century. The earliest tradition, which can be traced back to the middle of the first century (Paul and Mark), shows no knowledge of the virginal conception of Jesus, let alone the continued virginity of Mary. From these sources we have no reason to think anything but that Jesus and his brothers and sisters were children of Joseph and Mary.

ORIGEN: THE BROTHERS OF JESUS AND JAMES
IN PSEUDO-JOSEPHUS

Origen, a native of Alexandria, was born circa 185 CE and died in 254 CE. During his lifetime he was the outstanding scholar. His reputation was later damaged by the Arian controversy when it was wrongly thought that his views gave support to Arius. By the time of Jerome, Origen had become a controversial figure and Jerome, who had at first been an admirer of Origen, adopted a polemical position in relation to him. With Jerome one has the suspicion that this change of heart was dictated more by political than theological considerations.

Yet Origen was a controversial figure even in his own day. Like Clement before him, Origen adopted the language of the Gnostics, whom he opposed by giving their language his own distinctive meaning. He also dared to speculate and develop mythical hypotheses which challenged the Gnostic cosmologies. For those of lesser theological acumen than he it might have been difficult to distinguish the views of Origen from the Gnostics he opposed. But whereas the Gnostic cosmology supported the notion that human life was determined within a creation that was the consequence either of an inferior or evil god, Origen affirmed that human beings were morally responsible and free in a creation designed by a positively good, benevolent God to enable them freely to find their way back to him.

Origen was a controversial figure also because of his conflicts with the bishop of Alexandria. As a lay head of the catechetical school he was independent of the authority of the bishop. His prestige was great in the universal church, where his authority was often sought by those seeking to settle disputes. His relationship with his bishop was not helped when, without consulting the bishop, Origen was ordained in Caesarea, where he settled for the latter part of his life. There he left an intellectual legacy that influenced Eusebius, who was first librarian, caring for the archives of Origen, and then bishop of Caesarea. Origen's influence on Eusebius is not surprising. What is surprising is that Eusebius fails to acknowledge Origen's influence on his own account of James. Here, it seems, Origen is a significant but unnamed source.

In Caesarea Origen was in close contact with Palestinian Judaism. Here he wrote his *Commentary on Matthew* and *Contra Celsum* between 244 and 249 CE. In these two works there are important references to James and the family of Jesus. Here too there are clues that might enable us to solve the problem of the unidentified appeal to Josephus to the effect that what the Jews did to James brought about the destruction of Jerusalem.

Commentary on Matthew *X. 17*

Here Origen discusses Matt 13:54–56 with reference to the kinsfolk of Jesus. Origen is sensitive to the Matthean description of the carpenter as the father of Jesus. In addition to supplying Joseph's name, Origen explains that those who ascribed paternity to Joseph were either ignorant that Jesus "was the son of a virgin," or, having been told this, they did not believe it. Origen shows sensitivity where Matthew does not.

Origen notes that Jesus' apparent wisdom was put in question by the people of Nazareth by "depreciating the whole of what appeared to be his nearest kindred." This position is qualified by Origen: "They thought, then, that he was the son of Joseph and Mary." Origen has already explained that Jesus "was the son of a virgin"; thus the assumption of Joseph's paternity is taken to be an error. This much is clear from Matthew. Origen wished to go further.[26] To do so he appealed to tradition found in the *Gospel of Peter* and the *Protevangelium of James*. The *Gospel of Peter* was known from the reference in Origen and in Eusebius *HE* 3.3.2; 6.12 but was encountered directly when a fragment was discovered in the late 1880s in the excavations of Akhmim. Most scholars regard the work to be dependent on the canonical Gospels and date it in the second half of the second century though John Dominic Crossan names it as one of his early Gospel sources.[27]

The Brothers of Jesus

From the two named sources Origen mentions the view that the brothers of Jesus were children of Joseph by a marriage prior to his marriage to Mary. Origen notes that this view comes from those who "wish to preserve the honor of Mary in virginity to the end." Consequently Origen admits that this view is not found in the canonical sources and that it is put forward by those who wish to preserve the virginity of Mary. Nevertheless he shows himself to be in harmony with this view. "And I think it in harmony with reason that Jesus was the first-fruit among men of the purity which consists in chastity, and Mary among women; for it were not pious to ascribe to any other than to her the first-fruit of virginity." This argument reveals an awareness of no traditional evidence for the view. The argument arises from what is fitting. That Origen knows no earlier evidence than the sources he cites for the view places a serious question over the argument for the historical reliability of the tradition that seeks to establish that the brothers and sisters of Jesus were children of Joseph

---

[26] Likewise in *Commentary on John. Frag. 31.* A. E. Brooke, *The Commentary of Origen on St. John's Gospel,* vol. 2 (Cambridge: Cambridge University Press, 1896), 244.

[27] *Four Other Gospels: Shadows on the Contours of Canon* (Minneapolis: Winston, 1985), 125–81. Crossan was answered by R. E. Brown, "The Gospel of Peter and Canonical Gospel Authority," *NTS* 33 (1987): 321–43.

(but not Mary) by a previous marriage. Nevertheless this is the position adopted by Origen.[28]

Origen then goes on to speak of James, identified by reference to Paul's letter to the Galatians (1:19), which names him as "the Lord's brother."

> And James is he whom Paul says in the Epistle to the Galatians that he saw, "But other of the apostles saw I none, save James the Lord's brother."

It is likely that Eusebius drew his own quotation of Paul (*HE* 2.1.5) from Origen's quotation, and the same quotation might have influenced *HE* 1.12.4–5. Origen then goes on to mention James's reputation for righteousness.

> And to so great a reputation among the people for righteousness did this James rise, that Flavius Josephus, who wrote the *Antiquities of the Jews,* in twenty books, when wishing to exhibit the cause why the people suffered so great misfortunes that even the Temple was razed to the ground, said that these things happened to them in accordance with the wrath of God in consequence of the things which they had dared to do against James the brother of Jesus who is called the Christ.[29] And the wonderful thing is, that, though he did not accept Jesus as Christ, he yet gave testimony that the righteousness of James was so great; and he says that the people thought that they had suffered these things because of James. And Jude, who wrote a letter of few lines, it is true, but filled with the healthful words of heavenly grace, said in the preface, "Jude, the servant of Jesus Christ and the brother of James." With regard to Joseph and Simon we have nothing to tell; but the saying, "And his sisters are they not all with us," seems to me to signify something of this nature—they mind our things, not those of Jesus, and have no unusual portion of the surpassing wisdom as Jesus has. And perhaps by these things is indicated a new doubt concerning him, that Jesus was not a man but something diviner, inasmuch as, he was, as they supposed, the son of Joseph and Mary, and the brother of four, and of the others—the women—as well, and yet had nothing like to any one of his kindred, and had not from education and teaching come to such a height of wisdom and power.

Because he is dealing with Matt 13:54–56, where the brothers of Jesus are named but the sisters are not, Origen goes on to speak of Jude, about whom he has no more information than is given at the beginning of the letter in

---

[28] See also his comments in *Joann.* ii.12 and *Hom. in Luc.* 7.

[29] The supposed reference to Josephus apparently ends at this point.

Jude's name. There the author identifies himself as the brother of James. Origen assumes that this must be James the brother of Jesus, so that the Jude in question must also be the brother of Jesus. Origen provides us with the first *evidence* for this interpretation although this identification was probably commonly understood even if not always accepted as true.

Origen has nothing to add concerning the other two brothers, perhaps because nothing more is said of them in the New Testament. Very likely his conclusion concerning the sisters, who are unnamed by him as they are in the Gospel text, is simply a deduction from the statement of the unbelieving citizens of Nazareth: "Are they not all with us?" That is apparently understood by Origen as separating the sisters from Jesus because he says of the sisters, "they mind our things, not those of Jesus, and have no unusual portion of surpassing wisdom as Jesus has." It is just possible that this difference is meant to relate to the brothers (perhaps only the unelaborated ones) as well as to the sisters. Origen then, rather strangely, implies that the mystification of the unbelieving citizens of Nazareth led them to think that "Jesus was not a man but something diviner" because he had so little in common with those supposed to be his natural family.

Of Jesus Origen wrote: "He was, as they supposed, the son of Joseph and Mary, and the brother of the four, and of the others the women—as well, and yet had nothing like to any one of his kindred." The untutored wisdom of Jesus, as in the text of John 7:15, is also made the basis of the comparison of Jesus with his family and the townsfolk.

James in Pseudo-Josephus?

Origen refers to the twentieth book of the *Antiquities*, in which Josephus deals with the death of James. What he has to say at this point is, however, not to be found in extant texts of Josephus. No precise reference is given by Origen, and the quotation cannot be found in Josephus, nor does its form suggest that it is a precise quotation. The first part of the statement sets the context in which the reported statement was supposedly made. The context is the misfortunes of the people (the Jews) which included the destruction of the Temple. This statement has the appearance of being Origen's own summary. In relation to these unfortunate events Origen writes that Josephus

> said that these things happened to them in accordance with the wrath of God in consequence of the things which they dared to do against James the brother of Jesus who is called the Christ.

Just as the circumstances of the statement appear to be Origen's own summary, so does the form of the reported words, although reference to James as the brother of Jesus who is called the Christ retains the idiom of Josephus in the genuine reference to James. Josephus is, then, with the Gospel text under consideration, part of the basis for reference to James as the brother of Jesus. The other evidence referred to by Origen comes from Paul's letter to the Galatians.

If Origen has worked loosely with Josephus, giving Josephus's views rather than his words, a possible explanation of the supposed quotation emerges. Josephus adopted a providential view of history in which the judgment of God was visited on those opposed to his will, those who practiced evil. Thus, in principle, it is consistent with the views of Josephus that the wrath of God should be turned against those who martyred James if the righteousness of James is acknowledged. Certainly this is Origen's assumption, for he prefaces his appeal to Josephus by reference to James's great reputation for righteousness. But this is precisely what is missing from the evidence of the genuine reference to James in *Ant.* 20.197–203 the objection to the execution of James is not based on his righteousness but on the lawless manner in which Ananus had dealt with his opponents.

Origen continues in a way that suggests a reporting of the views of Josephus rather than direct quotation.

> And the wonderful thing is this, that, though he did not accept Jesus as the Christ, he yet gave testimony that the righteousness of James was so great; and he says that the people thought that they had suffered these things because of James.

The recognition of the righteousness of James is clearly stated, but it is not clear that Origen is asserting that Josephus spoke of the righteousness of James. Josephus said "the people thought that they had suffered these things because of James." Recognition of the righteousness of James may have been implied to Origen by this statement. We may further ask whether Origen thought that Josephus made two independent statements attributing the destruction of Jerusalem and Temple to the wrath of God in response to the death of James or whether the two expressions were thought to be based on a single statement. Given that neither of the statements seems to be a direct quotation, being reported in the third person, it is likely that Origen intended to state and restate what he thought Josephus had said and to draw out the most favorable reading of this concerning James.

Contra Celsum *1.47; 2.13*

Origen makes similar claims about Josephus in two passages in *Contra Celsum*, which was written shortly after his *Commentary on Matthew*.[30]

> For Josephus in the eighteenth book of the *Jewish Antiquities* bears witness that John was a baptist and promised purification to people who were

---

[30] See *HE* 6.25.32.

baptized. The same author, although he did not believe in Jesus as the Christ, sought for the cause of the fall of Jerusalem and the destruction of the Temple. He ought to have said that the plot against Jesus was the reason why these catastrophes came upon the people, because they had killed the prophesied Christ; however, although unconscious of it, he is not far from the truth when he says that these disasters befell the Jews to avenge James the Just, who was a brother of 'Jesus the so called Christ,' since they had killed him who was a very righteous man. This is the James whom Paul, the true disciple of Jesus, says that he saw, describing him as the Lord's brother, not referring so much to their blood relationship or common upbringing as to his moral life and understanding. If therefore he says that the destruction of Jerusalem happened because of James, would it not be more reasonable to say that this happened on account of Jesus the Christ? (*Contra Celsum* 1.47)[31]

As in the first passage Origen affirms that Josephus did not accept/believe in Jesus as the Christ. The importance of this statement is that it makes Josephus independent and therefore more effective as a source of evidence for those who did not believe. In the *Commentary on Matthew* Origen also refers to Paul's reference to James in Gal 1:19. The same reference is in view in the present passage, although Galatians is not specifically cited. In both passages reference to Jesus is qualified by noting he is "the one called Christ." In both passages Origen twice asserts that Josephus said that the destruction of Jerusalem occurred because of what was done to James. The argument is that the destruction was a consequence of divine retribution because of what was done to James. Whereas in the *Commentary on Matthew* Origen appeals to the righteousness of James as a basis for what befell Jerusalem, only in *Contra Celsum* 1.47 does he refer to James the Just. The statement suggests that this is in a quotation from Josephus, but Origen may be paraphrasing the evidence of Josephus. The title "James the Just" appears to be distinctively Christian and was used by Origen to sum up the recognition of James by Josephus.

In *Contra Celsum* 1.47 Origen makes a significant modification to Josephus by saying that "He ought to have said that the plot against Jesus was the reason why these catastrophes came upon the people, because they had killed the prophesied Christ;" and "would it not be more reasonable to say that this happened on account of Jesus the Christ?"

In *Contra Celsum* 2.13, after telling of Jesus' prophecy of the destruction of Jerusalem, citing the text of Luke 21:20, Origen indicates that the siege began while Nero was emperor and continued until the rule of Vespasian, whose son Titus captured Jerusalem. He continues:

---

[31] For the text of *Contra Celsum*, see H. Chadwick, ed., LCC (Philadelphia: Westminster, 1980), 43.

so Josephus says, [that the siege was] on account of James the Just, the brother of Jesus the so-called Christ, though in reality it was on account of Jesus the Christ of God. (*Contra Celsum* 2.13)[32]

This report also refers to "James the Just," suggesting at least Christian redaction of the Josephan text. The form of the statement provides no confidence that Origen was intending to give a verbatim quotation. In all three instances where Origen appeals to Josephus to elaborate on the consequences of the martyrdom of James he gives no precise reference, and the form of the statements suggests a loose summary rather than verbatim quotations.

The prediction by Jesus of the destruction implies, in the mind of Origen, that the siege was a consequence of what was done to Jesus. Because Origen wished to assert that the siege was a result of the martyrdom of Jesus there is no reason to think that he was responsible for the tradition that what happened to James was the cause. Therefore the tradition antedates Origen. He attributes the tradition to Josephus but without providing an exact reference. When Eusebius quotes the same tradition he also ascribes it to Josephus (*HE* 2.23.20), but, contrary to his frequent practice, he gives no precise reference (see *HE* 2.23.21–24). According to Eusebius, Josephus did not hesitate to write this down in so many words:

Josephus according to Origen	*Josephus according to Eusebius*
[he says that] these disasters befell the Jews to avenge James the Just, who was a brother of Jesus the so-called Christ, since they killed him who was a very righteous man.	These things happened to the Jews to avenge James the Just, who was a brother of Jesus the so-called Christ, for the Jews put him to death in spite of his great righteousness (*HE* 2.23.20)

Eusebius claims to give the views of Josephus "in so many words," supposedly quoting Josephus. Origen reports in the third person what Josephus wrote. This evidence provides us with a puzzle concerning the relationship of Eusebius to Origen.

Conclusions

Eusebius was in a good position to draw on the works of Origen. Finding a reference to Josephus there, someone more or less contemporary with James, Jesus, and the siege, he had a suitable witness for his case. Perhaps Eusebius looked for the text in Josephus and, failing to find it, used the quotation in Origen on the assumption that it was faithful to Josephus and correct.

---

[32] Chadwick, p. 80.

At the conclusion of the extract from Hegesippus on the martyrdom of James Eusebius quotes Hegesippus as follows: "Immediately after this Vespasian began to besiege them" (*HE* 2.23.18). The assertion of the sequence, first the death of James and then, *immediately*, the siege, might be thought to imply a causal relationship. The explicit assertion could be Origen's interpretative contribution. Hegesippus also attests James's reputation for righteousness, which Origen draws on explicitly to show that the sequence of the death of James followed immediately by the siege was a manifestation of the judgment of God because of what was done to righteous James.

But how could a scholar as careful as Origen mistake Hegesippus for Josephus? Origen appeals to the same quotation on three separate occasions. Perhaps having used it once, he simply made use of his own quotation. This possibility is suggested by the association of Gal 1:19 with the supposed quotation in both the *Commentary on Matthew* and *Contra Celsum* 1.47. There must, however, be more to the explanation than this. There is evidence of a philosophy of history in some passages of Josephus that provides a basis for both Origen and Josephus. For example, in *Ant.* 11.297–305 Josephus tells of the retribution of God for the killing of another Jesus in the Temple with the result that the people were made slaves and the Temple defiled by the Persians. This sequence provides an example of the causal connection between a crime done against a righteous person and the consequent judgment of God.

Eusebius develops the thesis (which both he and Origen attribute to Josephus) that the judgment of God was a consequence of the crimes against James. He develops further Origen's view that Josephus should really have attributed the cause of the siege to the death of Jesus. According to Origen, viewing the death of James as the cause was *almost correct*. Eusebius took this line of thought further, reconciling the two views. He argued that the siege of Jerusalem was delayed because of the presence of James and other apostles in Jerusalem. With the martyrdom of James the bulwark protecting Jerusalem against the judgment of God was removed, and the city was destroyed, the Temple with it (see *HE* 3.7.7–9; 3.11.1). In this way Eusebius reconciles in a more complete way the tradition which both he and Origen attribute to Josephus with the conviction that actually the crimes against Jesus were the direct cause of the siege. Reconciling the tradition with that conviction has the advantage of helping to bridge the gap between the death of Jesus (circa 30 CE) and the destruction of Jerusalem (70 CE). Yet the death of James occurred in 62 CE, some years before the siege. It was, however, an event somewhat closer in time to the siege than the death of Jesus. The motif of the delay of judgment because of the presence of James enables the primary focus on Jesus to be maintained without losing sight of the significance of James as a righteous martyr and of the relationship of his death to the siege also.

That both Origen and Eusebius should appeal to Josephus as the source of the view that the siege was a consequence of what was done to James and that both should in a way accept and yet modify this view to take account of the death of Jesus suggests strongly that Origen was the source used by Eusebius at this point. Origen then seems to have been an unacknowledged source for Eusebius in his treatment of James. In the summaries provided by Eusebius Origen makes a larger contribution, probably supplying the quotation from Gal 1:19 and his qualification of the relationship to Jesus of those known as Jesus' brothers and sisters.

THE *PANARION* OF EPIPHANIUS: THE ROYAL AND PRIESTLY ROLE OF THE FIRST SON OF JOSEPH

Epiphanius was born in Palestine between 310 and 320 CE. Around 366 he was chosen as bishop of Constantia (Salamis) in Cyprus. During a long episcopate, ending with his death in 402, he wrote the three books of the *Panarion*, the medicine chest that provided the antidotes to the false teaching of the eighty sects which had existed down to his time.

In his first reference to James (28.2.3) he identifies Cerinthus as

> one of those . . . who caused a disturbance against the apostles when those of James' group wrote a letter to Antioch, saying, "We have discovered that some from our group have come to you and upset you by what they said, although we gave them no instructions."

Epiphanius is making use of Acts 15:24, where, at the conclusion of the Jerusalem assembly, those of James's group sent a letter to accompany "the decree" conveyed by the two envoys.[33] What is added in the account of Epiphanius is that Cerinthus was in the group of those who troubled the believers at Antioch. Epiphanius acknowledges the dualism of Cerinthus while noting his insistence on the keeping of the law and opposition to Peter visiting the uncircumcised (Gentile) Cornelius. The circumcised Cerinthus opposed uncircumcised believers and took the opportunity to stir up the circumcision controversy. What this treatment does, building on Acts, is to exonerate James from any responsibility for the circumcision controversy, attributing the responsibility for this to the "heretic" Cerinthus. Paul provides no support of this view.

The second reference to James (29.3.8–29.4.4) asserts that the royal and high priestly roles were united and passed on by Jesus to the church in the person of

---

[33] The envoys could be identified with the messengers from James mentioned by Paul in Gal 2:12. In Epiphanius's account eating with uncircumcised believers is precisely that to which Cerinthus is supposed to have objected. According to Paul, that was also the point of contention with the messengers from James. This is probably the first attempt to distance James from the messengers from James mentioned in Gal 2:11–14.

James, having been ordained at once the first bishop, he who is called the brother of the Lord and apostle, Joseph's son by nature and spoken of as having the place of the brother of the Lord due to having been reared with him. For James was Joseph's son from Joseph's [first] wife, not from Mary, as we have said in many places and treated of more clearly.

Epiphanius goes on to say that James was of David's stock, being Joseph's son, and as his firstborn, dedicated as a Nazirite, exercising the priestly role, entering the holy of holies once a year as the high priest was permitted to do, wearing the "plate" on his head. Eusebius (*HE* 3.31.3) refers to the sacerdotal (high priestly) plate or diadem (πέταλον) worn by John. See Exodus 28 (LXX). The precise meaning of the term is unclear but may have some reference to what was to become the bishop's mitre. For his authority Epiphanius appealed to Eusebius, Clement, and others. Consequently the royal and priestly "throne" is claimed for James as the first bishop of Jerusalem. Eusebius consistently re ferred to the "throne" of the Jerusalem church and of no other church did he use this term.

In dealing with the Ebionites he names Ebion the founder, asserting that he broke away from the Nazaraeans and argues that Ebion was inconsistent, at first taking pride in "virginity because of James, the brother of the Lord" (30.2.6) but subsequently forbidding virginity and continence. Here, then, we have a clear assertion that James did not marry, that he was a virgin (but see 1 Cor 9:5). The account goes on to assert that the Ebionites began in Pella and in a village called Cocaba, after the capture of Jerusalem. This etymology and history is unconvincing.

Epiphanius also mentions the *Ascents of James* (30.16.7), in which James is supposed to have spoken against the Temple and sacrifices and a number of inanities. He asserts that the Ebionites were against Paul, accusing him of being born of pagan parents. The Ebionites are also accused of producing pseudonymous works in the names of apostles, including James (30.23.1). Whether this is James the brother of Jesus is unspecified but likely. It has already been noted that the Ebionites venerated him and works were produced in his name.

When Epiphanius is speaking of the passing away of the apostles, James is named again as the first bishop of Jerusalem, and his relationship to Jesus, Mary, and Joseph is more fully elaborated, giving expression to the view that remained common in the East (66.19.7–66.20.1). This might have been derived from the *Protevangelium of James,* in which it found classical expression. James is identified not only as the first bishop of Jerusalem but also as one

called the Lord's brother although he was Joseph's child, born of his own wife with the rest of his brothers, with whom the Lord Jesus Christ, born of Mary ever virgin according to the flesh, was brought up and [whom] he had as brothers, so that he was called their brother.

In what follows Epiphanius tells that when James was martyred he was succeeded by his cousin Symeon, the son of Clopas, Joseph's brother. He briefly tells that James was martyred in Jerusalem during the reign of Nero and that he died when he was struck with a club. Here he is dependent on Clement of Alexandria and Hegesippus, perhaps through Eusebius. There follows a list of the thirty-seven bishops of Jerusalem, in correlation with the emperors, down to the reign of Aurelian; the first fifteen were from the circumcision, and those that followed were Gentiles.

Epiphanius denounces those who argued that, after the birth of Jesus, Mary had sexual relations with Joseph (78.1.3). The continued virginity of Mary is further explained and defended in 78.7.1–78.8.2. Epiphanius is dependent on the *Protevangelium of James,* appealing to the fact that Mary "the virgin was given to Joseph, to whom the lots compelled her to go; she was not given to him for the purpose of sexual relations . . . because he was a widower." He asserts that the purpose of this arrangement was to preserve evidence of the incarnation because the aged Joseph was given the virgin as a wife many years after his wife's death. Joseph's first wife was from the tribe of Judah, and they had six children, four boys and two girls, as the Gospels of Mark (6:3) and John (19:25) tell.

> The firstborn was James, surnamed "Oblias," meaning "wall," and also surnamed "Just," who was a Nazirite, which means a holy man. He was the first to receive the bishop's chair, the first to whom the Lord entrusted his throne upon earth. He was called the brother of the Lord, with whom the apostle [Paul] [34] too agrees when he says, "I saw no other apostle except James, the brother of the Lord," and so on. He was called the Lord's brother because he was reared with him, it was a matter not of nature but of grace. . . . He [Joseph] became the father of James, then, when he was about forty years old, more or less. After James the boy called Joses was born, after him Simeon, then Judas, and the two daughters called Mary and Salome, and then his wife died. After many years he took Mary when he was a widower, being over eighty years old.

Epiphanius appears to be using the *Protevangelium of James,* but he has developed the argument in two ways to heighten the circumstances of Mary's continuing virginity. First he stresses Joseph's advanced age at the time Mary was allotted to him. Second he asserts that the relationship was not intended to be

---

[34] See Gal 1:19.

a consummated marriage. While the argument is introduced in terms of preserving evidence of the incarnation, only Mary's virginity prior to the birth of Jesus is necessary for this. The assertion of the perpetual virginity of Mary elevated her in her own right. In Epiphanius's exposition the ages of Joseph and James at the time of the birth of Jesus are indicated. Joseph is said to be over eighty, which means that James would have been over forty, given that Joseph was said to be about forty when he was born. By this reckoning James would have been more than seventy-three at the time of the crucifixion and over one hundred at the time of his martyrdom in 62 CE. But in the following quotation Epiphanius indicates that James died at the age of ninety-six, twenty-four years after "the Savior's Ascension." This dating cannot be reconciled with the specific evidence provided by Josephus by means of which the death of James is fixed at the year 62 CE.

In 78.14.1–6 Epiphanius repeats and develops some of the earlier themes. It is again said that James wore the "plate" on his head, and stress is placed on his piety.

> And once during a drought he lifted his hands to heaven and prayed, and at once heaven sent rain.[35] He never wore woollen clothing. His knees grew hard as a camel's from his continual kneeling before the Lord out of his excessive piety.[36] Thus they no longer called him by his name; his name was "The Just." He never washed in a bath, did not partake of animal flesh, as I have explained above, and did not wear sandals. And there is much else that one could say about the man and his virtuous way of life. You see then that this house was in every respect most noteworthy. For if Joseph's sons revered virginity and the Nazarite life, how much more did that elderly and honorable man guard with reverence the holy virgin and honor the vessel in which the salvation of the human race dwelt! "Does not nature itself teach you" that the man was elderly, greatly advanced in age, grown great among men, faithful in his ways, and reverent in appearance? For the Gospel now says that "the God-fearing man sought to divorce her secretly."[37] But James, the brother of the Lord and son of Joseph, died in Jerusalem, having lived twenty-four years, more or less, after the Savior's Ascension. He was ninety-six years old when he

---

[35] See James 5:16–18. There it is said that the fervent prayer of a righteous man avails much, and the example of Elijah is mentioned as a man who prayed so that it did not rain, and when he prayed again "the heaven gave rain."

[36] Here Epiphanius is dependent on the witness of Hegesippus to the martyrdom of James now found in Eusebius HE 2.23.4–18, where, as in this quotation from Epiphanius, James is called "the Just," and it is said he wore no wool, that his knees grew hard like a camel's through kneeling before the Lord, that he took no baths.

[37] See Matt 1:19.

was struck on the head by a fuller with his club, flung from the pinnacle of the Temple and cast down, and he who had done no wrong knelt and prayed for those who had thrown him down, saying: "Forgive them, for they do not know what they are doing."[38] Thus even Simeon, his cousin, the son of Clopas, who was standing at a distance, said, "Stop, why are you stoning the just one? Behold, he is uttering the most wonderful prayers for you." And thus he was martyred.

The virtue of James is stressed and recognized: in his prayer, in the name "the Just," in his rejection of the Hellenistic bathhouse, his ascetic rejection of meat, and his and his brothers' virginity. The aim of this emphasis is to stress even more the virtue and virginity of Mary. The argument runs: if in Joseph's house such virtue is to be seen in the sons, how much more is the virtue to be seen in Mary the virgin. Much of the credit for this goodness is given to Joseph, "greatly advanced in age, grown great among men, faithful in his ways, reverent in appearance."

The account of the martyrdom of James is dependent on Hegesippus, although elements are added, including the indication of when this took place and the age of James at the time. The account does not mention stoning because in the Jewish context this signals a legal execution, an element which is played down in the Christian accounts. In the account of Epiphanius the blow from the fuller's club precedes the casting down of James from the pinnacle of the Temple. Epiphanius maintains, "and he who had done no wrong knelt and prayed for those who had thrown him down." This motif is also found in the account of Hegesippus. But in his account it is Rechab the son of Rechabim who appeals to those who stone James to stop, whereas in Epiphanius it is Simeon, his cousin, the son of Clopas. Epiphanius already has an eye to the succession of the bishop's throne in Jerusalem from James to Simeon.

With Epiphanius many of the concerns and motifs of the earlier Jacobean tradition are gathered together. There is reference to the martyrdom of James and the use of the epithet "the Just" or "the Righteous" in relation to him. James is referred to as the first bishop of Jerusalem, and there is reference to his "throne" and the succession. His piety—his prayer and his ascetic practices— are emphasized. There is also a new stress on the virginity of James. It turns out that this focus has another purpose. James is not himself the focus, but his virginity tends to direct attention to the greater virginity of Mary.

The view that Mary conceived the infant Jesus while she was a virgin is developed, so that Epiphanius maintains the perpetual virginity of Mary. He explains those known as the brothers and sisters of Jesus by arguing that they

---

[38] See the words recorded of both Jesus and Stephen at their executions in Luke 23:34 and Acts 7:60.

were the children of Joseph but not of Mary, being the children of Joseph by a previous marriage. Joseph, he says, was a widower when he married Mary. This view was not original to Epiphanius; it was widespread in the East long before his time and found expression in the *Protevangelium of James,* which he used. Since the time of J. B. Lightfoot this has been known as the Epiphanian view of those known as the brothers and sisters of Jesus. As we noted above, Lightfoot chose to name the different views of exactly who these people were after the outstanding fourth-century exponents of each view: "I shall call them respectively the Epiphanian, the Helvidian, and the Hieronymian theories, from the names of their most zealous advocates in the controversies of the fourth century when the question was most warmly debated."[39]

There is no reference in Epiphanius to James as the recipient of a significant post-resurrection revelation, either in reference to his call or in terms of an ongoing secret tradition. From the perspective of Epiphanius, the fighter of heresy, this theme gave too much away to the enemy to be taken on board in his own treatment of James.

JEROME AND HELVIDIUS: JAMES AS THE COUSIN OR BROTHER OF JESUS

Jerome was born in Stridon circa 347, educated in Rome, where he was baptized in 366, and dedicated himself to the ascetic life. He set out for the East circa 372, staying first in Antioch, and then lived as a "hermit" in Chalcis in Syria. There he studied Hebrew and began to lay the foundation for his later work as translator of the Jewish scriptures into Latin. In Antioch he was later ordained, and although he did not function as a priest he was embroiled in ecclesiastical intrigue. At the Council of Constantinople in 381 he became acquainted with Gregory of Nazianzus and Gregory of Nyssa. On returning to Rome he became the secretary of Pope Damasis I, but at the death of the pope in 384 he returned to the East because of opposition to him in Rome. Opposition was provoked by his censorious and polemical attitudes, especially in relation to the clergy, and by what was perceived as his extreme asceticism. Alongside this was his attraction to younger women, both widows and virgins. As long as Damasis was alive Jerome was safeguarded by this protective relationship but with his death the scarcely hidden antagonisms emerged, and Jerome fled to the East.

Jerome was an advocate of forms of asceticism which had come to Rome from the East, where the virginity of Mary, the mother of Jesus, had become an important symbol for a movement which advocated the superiority of virginity. This movement by no means had a smooth passage in Rome, where

---

[39] "Appendix II: The Brethren of the Lord," in *Saint Paul's Epistle to the Galatians. A Revised Text with Introduction, Notes, and Dissertations* (London: Macmillan, 1874), 254.

many Christians were suspicious of what seemed to be extreme asceticism and pagans were diametrically opposed to it. It had the support of Pope Damasis, the great Ambrose of Milan, and Augustine of Hippo. In Rome the support of Damasis was critical. Jerome craved the company of noble women and the recognition of the rich and powerful in the church. His rapid development of a favorable relationship with Pope Damasis was frustrated when, after only a few years, the pope died, leaving Jerome without strong support in Rome and with a host of enemies.

The ascetic arrogance of many monks found expression in a pamphlet circulated by a monk named Carterius. It was probably this pamphlet that provoked Helvidius, a layman,[40] to respond, taking up the cause of those who were not persuaded by arguments concerning the superior state of virginity, especially those based on the ideal of the perpetual virginity of Mary. From Gennadius, who continued Jerome's work,[41] we learn that Helvidius was a sincere and pious person, although he was ridiculed by Jerome, whose invective ensured that the work of Helvidius did not survive. We know his work only through a reconstruction from Jerome's refutation of it. Indeed from this evidence alone his case seems to have been ordered and impressive.

Helvidius seems to have made five main points. 1) He argued that Matt 1:18, 25 imply that subsequent to the birth of Jesus Joseph and Mary had other children. Reference to Mary's being found to be pregnant through the action of the Holy Spirit "before they [Joseph and Mary] came together" ($\pi\rho\grave{\iota}\nu$ $\mathring{\eta}$ $\sigma\upsilon\nu\epsilon\lambda\theta\epsilon\hat{\iota}\nu$) was taken by Helvidius to mean that subsequently they came together, just as the assertion that Joseph did not "know" Mary "until she bore a son" ($\mathring{\epsilon}\omega\varsigma$ $o\mathring{\upsilon}$ $\mathring{\epsilon}\tau\epsilon\varkappa\epsilon\nu$ $\upsilon\acute{\iota}\acute{o}\nu$)[42] was taken to mean that he did "know her," that is, have sexual intercourse with her, subsequently.[43] 2) He appealed to Luke 2:7 which refers to Jesus as Mary's "firstborn son" ($\tau\grave{o}\nu$ $\upsilon\acute{\iota}\grave{o}\nu$ $\alpha\mathring{\upsilon}\tau\hat{\eta}\varsigma$ $\tau\grave{o}\nu$ $\pi\rho\omega\tau\acute{o}\tau o$-$\varkappa o\nu$), arguing that it implied subsequent children.[44] 3) He listed the various passages in which the evangelists mention and sometimes name the brothers and sisters of Jesus.[45] 4) He appealed to older Western tradition[46] in which the brothers and sisters of Jesus had been mentioned in a way consistent with his

---

[40] The fact that Helvidius was a lay person has been contested by G. Jouassard, "La personnalité d'Helvidius," *Mélanges J. Saunier* (Lyon, 1944), 139–56.

[41] *De vir. ill. 33*, which was completed about 480 CE, was a continuation of Jerome's book of the same title.

[42] The variant $\tau\grave{o}\nu$ $\upsilon\acute{\iota}\grave{o}\nu$ $\tau\grave{o}\nu$ $\pi\rho\omega\tau\acute{o}\tau o\varkappa o\nu$ is obviously a secondary reading under the influence of Luke 2:7.

[43] See *Against Helvidius (Adv. Helvidium de Perpetua Virginitate B. Mariae) 3*.

[44] See Ibid., p. 9.

[45] See Ibid., p. 11.

[46] See Ibid., p. 17.

views and specified Tertullian[47] and Victorinus of Pettau.[48] 5)He argued that it was no dishonor that Mary was a real wife to Joseph since all the patriarchs had been married men and that child-bearing was a participation in the divine creativity.[49]

Because Helvidius was the most notable exponent of the view that the brothers and sisters of Jesus were the later (after the birth of Jesus) children of Joseph and Mary his name has become inseparably associated with this view, which J. B. Lightfoot called the Helvidian theory.[50]

Jerome's response was to ridicule the literary deficiencies of Helvidius but without dealing adequately with his arguments. He attempted to nullify Helvidius's appeal to tradition by asserting that Tertullian was a schismatic and that Victorinus did not support Helvidius, while at the same time asserting that the majority of the fathers accepted the perpetual virginity of Mary.

That Jerome conceded Tertullian to the opposition implies that Helvidius was correct in his claim of support. This tends to be confirmed, as Lightfoot notes: "though he [Tertullian] does not directly state it, his argument seems to imply that the Lord's brethren were His brothers in the same sense in which Mary was His mother (*Adv. Marc.* iv.19, *De Carne Christi* 7). It is therefore highly probable that he held the Helvidian view. Such an admission from one who was so strenuous an advocate of asceticism is worthy of notice."[51] The evidence of Victorinus cannot be settled because his works are lost, and it is the word of Jerome against Helvidius. Jerome's appeal to tradition in this matter provides no grounds for any confidence in his word against that of Helvidius.

Jerome claimed the great weight of tradition in support of his own position against Helvidius. On the point of the perpetual virginity of Mary he could make use of all who adopted what has been called the Epiphanian position. This he did, but he failed to note that they did not support his own distinctive position. His appeal to Ignatius, Polycarp, Irenaeus, Justin, and many others was not relevant to his own theory. As Lightfoot has shown, in the case of Ignatius Jerome has seriously misconstrued his meaning. Not only does Ignatius not support Jerome's theory; he nowhere maintains the perpetual virginity of Mary. Where he does refer to the virginity of Mary, which he does in a passage quoted several times by later writers (*Eph.* 19), it is with reference to the conception of Jesus.[52] This careless use of sources to his own advantage gives no confidence in Jerome's appeal to others on this issue.

---

[47] See his *Adv. Marc.* 4. 19; *De Carne Christi* 7; *De monog.* 8.

[48] The reference was apparently to his now lost commentary on Matthew which was referred to by both Origen (*Homilies on St. Luke,* preface) and Jerome (*Commentary on St. Matthew,* preface).

[49] See *Against Helvidius* 18.

[50] "The Brethren of the Lord," p. 254.

[51] Ibid., p. 279.

[52] Ibid., p. 278 n.1.

As Lightfoot has shown, Jerome's view that those called brothers were actually cousins was a novel hypothesis, unsupported by any traditional sanction.[53] The theory is built on a new critical reading of the New Testament evidence, but the motivation for this reading was to preserve not only the virginity of Mary but that of Joseph also.[54] Essential to his view is the argument that the terms "brothers" and "sisters" need not refer to those who were strictly brothers and sisters but could also be used of other relatives in a more general sense—in this case, cousins. To make this argument he had to produce evidence that would provide precedent for the broader understanding of the terms. He showed that the term "brothers" was used in the scriptures in four different senses: of actual brothers; of kinsmen; of those of common nationality; and of those related by friendship or sympathy, that is, "natura, gente, cognatione, affectu." Those called the brothers of Jesus were kinsmen, not brothers in the strict sense but in the same sense that Abraham called his nephew Lot "brother" (Gen 13:8) and Laban called his nephew Jacob "brother" (Gen 29:15). There is no doubt that the term "brother" can be used in extended senses. The question is whether the indications favor such a reading of the references to the brothers and sisters of Jesus.

Jerome notes that, in the Gospels, the list of the twelve apostles contains the names of two who are called James, the son of Zebedee and the son of Alpheus. Elsewhere (e. g., Gal 1:19) James the Lord's brother is mentioned. There he is referred to in such a way as to suggest that he was an apostle. If this is so he must be the son of Alpheus because he obviously was not the son of Zebedee who was dead at the time the brother of the Lord was mentioned. To further support this conclusion Jerome makes or implies several other deductions. 1) The Gospels name both James and Joseph as brothers of the Lord and elsewhere name Mary as the mother of James "the less" and of Joseph or Joses (Matt 27:56; Mark 15:40). The title "the less" is said to imply one greater and to confirm that only two Jameses were in view, one of which was "the less," that is, the brother of the Lord. 2) Thus Mary, the mother of James "the less," must be the wife of Alpheus, the father of the second James named among the twelve apostles. As Lightfoot notes, the identification of James "the less" with the son of Alpheus is necessary to Jerome's hypothesis. 3) In John 19:25 the sister of the mother of Jesus is named Mary of Cleophas (Clopas). She is thus to be identified with the mother of James and wife of Alpheus. Thus Alpheus is Cleophas.

This intricate set of relations was the result of Jerome's deductive detective work. It leads to the conclusion that the so-called brothers and sisters were the

---

[53] A fragment, "On the Twelve Apostles," attributed to Hippolytus, says: "James the son of Alpheus, when preaching in Jerusalem, was stoned to death by the Jews, and was buried there beside the Temple." This is probably a reference to the "brother of the Lord." It was unknown to Jerome and is likely to be authentic.

[54] Ibid., pp. 252–53, 258–59, including p. 252 n.1.

children of the sister of the mother of Jesus, who was also named Mary. They were cousins. So far we have the response of Jerome to Helvidius in 383 CE. His position was not yet fully developed in some respects, and in others he did not maintain a consistent position. For example, as J. N. D. Kelly notes, at this stage (383 CE) "Jerome was not yet ready to support the view soon to be accepted in the West that she [Mary] had retained her virginity in the process of parturition, i.e., that the act was a miraculous one involving no opening of her womb."[55]

What this shows, in addition to the developing position of Jerome, is that he was motivated by concern for the virginity of Mary. He came to accept a position common to the Epiphanian theory although he had rejected the *Protevangelium of James*, in which this view found classical expression. Even in his initial work against Helvidius Jerome showed that his main concern was for the perpetual virginity of Mary. He was not firm in his resolve concerning the identity of Mary of Cleophas with Mary the mother of James and Joses, although his own theory presupposes this. Thus in his commentary on Galatians, written in 387, and commenting on 1:19, he remarks more vaguely on the relation of James as a brother of Jesus.

> Suffice it now to say that James was called the Lord's brother on account of his high character, his incomparable faith, and extraordinary wisdom: the other Apostles also are called brothers (John xx.17; comp. Ps. xxii.22), but he preeminently so, to whom the Lord at His departure had committed the sons of His mother (i.e., the members of the Church of Jerusalem).[56]

Here Jerome asserts a broadened (symbolic) sense of "brother" which includes members of the Jerusalem church ("the sons of His mother"). James was singled out and called brother because of his high character, incomparable faith, and extraordinary wisdom and because the risen Lord had committed the leadership of the Jerusalem church to him. The order of the statements might imply that James was entrusted with the leadership because of the virtues already listed. Certainly there is no indication that his leadership had anything to do with a special family relationship between James and Jesus. Rather the name brother is applied especially to him because of his appointment as leader.

Reference to the Lord committing the church to James at his departure can only be understood as the direct commissioning of James as leader by the

---

[55] *Jerome: His Life, Writings and Controversies* (New York: Harper & Row, 1975), 106. In note 10 Kelly refers to *Against Helvidius* 18 and *Letters* 22, 39. He notes that "Many years later . . . influenced by Augustine and Ambrose . . . Jerome came to teach the virginity of Mary *in partu*." He refers to Jerome's *Dialogue against the Pelagians* 2, 4.

[56] Quoted by Lightfoot, "The Brethren of the Lord," p. 260.

risen Lord. Just what tradition Jerome was drawing on here is unclear except that it is distinct from the tradition which subordinates James to the apostles, whether Peter, James, and John (as in the tradition known in Clement of Alexandria) or to the apostles generally (as asserted by Eusebius). The direct commission of James by the risen Lord is implied in the *Gospel of the Hebrews* and finds expression in the *Gospel of Thomas*. But it is unlikely that Jerome was dependent on these as he disparages such works, referring to "the ravings of the apocryphal writings."

In his *Commentary on Matthew* (398 CE) and his *Lives of Illustrious Men* (*De viris illustribus,* 392 CE) Jerome maintains his original position and denounces those who hold the Epiphanian view. In a later work again (407 CE) he allows for the distinction of Mary of Cleophas, as the maternal aunt of Jesus, from Mary the mother of James and Joses. Yet, as Lightfoot notes, the identification of these two as one person is essential to Jerome's view.[57] Thus there is a strange ambivalence about the way Jerome holds to his theory which Lightfoot suggests might have been a result of Jerome's long residence in Bethlehem, where he must have encountered the Palestinian (Epiphanian) tradition at firsthand.

Jerome's position depends on a synthesis of Mark 15:40 with John 19:25. He identifies Mary the mother of James "the less" with the sister of the mother of Jesus. This James, he argues, is also named, in the list of the twelve, as the son of Alpheus. A possible problem for that identification is found in John 19:25, in which Mary is identified as either the wife of Clopas or the mother of Clopas. If the reading "the mother of Clopas" is accepted no problem exists for the acceptance of Mary as the wife of Alpheus.

Most scholars have adopted the understanding that Mary was the wife of Clopas and noted that the Hieronymian theory therefore involves identifying Clopas with Alpheus.[58] Lightfoot attributes the first recognition of this identity to Chrysostom and after him to Theodoret and suggests that this identification is a strengthening of the theory. The argument is that both names are derived from the Aramaic *Chalphai* which, when produced in Greek, could omit the Aramaic guttural *cheth,* as in Alpheus. While this is possible, it is a complex solution to a problem that exists only because Jerome sought to identify several persons bearing the same names as the same persons, in this case a Mary, James, and Joses.

In his later works Jerome acknowledged other apostles in addition to the twelve. He did not see this as a loophole in his argument that if James the Lord's brother was an apostle he must be James the son of Alpheus because he was not the son of Zebedee and there were but two Jameses among the twelve. His observation meant, however, that although James was an apostle (Gal 1:19),

---

[57] Ibid., p. 261.
[58] Ibid., pp. 256–57.

he need not be numbered among the twelve. Once the necessity of seeing this James as one of the twelve has been removed there is no reason to identify James as the son of Alpheus. Further, the stress on "the less" implying that this James was one of two is unjustified. Nowhere is there any reference to "the greater" James. Further, τοῦ μικροῦ probably means "the small" rather than the comparative sense "the less." By rejecting this comparative sense, pressure to identify this James with the son of Alpheus, one of the twelve, is removed. That James "the less" had a brother named Joses is insufficient evidence to identify them with the brothers of Jesus by those names.

Relatively few Jewish names were in use in the period, and the names of the brothers—James (Jacob), Jude (Judah), Simeon, Joseph—include the names of notable patriarchs, and both Jude and Simeon were the names of notable Maccabaean heroes. These were among the most popular names in the period, and pairs of these names were common in different families. The coincidence of names is not adequate evidence on which to base a theory of the identity of the persons. This observation is also true of the use of the name Mary.

It has been suggested that others named as brothers of Jesus (see Mark 6:3) were numbered among the twelve, in particular Jude and Symeon. In Luke's list of the twelve (Luke 6:16; Acts 1:13) "Judas of James" is found, and the writer of the epistle of Jude identifies himself as the brother of James (Jude 1). In Luke's list of the twelve (Luke 6:15–16) three names appear together, James of Alpheus, Simon called *Zelotes*, and Judas of James. If these were three brothers it would be natural to group them together. This is quite speculative and without any early supporting evidence, even from Jerome. That three of the brothers of Jesus could have been numbered among the twelve is most unlikely. In spite of the ingenuity of Jerome, his theory creates and leaves unresolved many loose ends. The distinction between the family of Jesus and the twelve in early tradition counts against his theory, as does Paul's reference to the apostles and the brothers of Jesus in 1 Cor 9:5.

The suggestion that the sister of Mary was also called Mary is necessitated by the use of Mark 15:40 in relation to John 19:25–27, an association crucial to Jerome's theory. This is also most unlikely. To nullify this problem Richard Bauckham has suggested the rather desperate strategy of modifying the relationship to that of sister-in-law.[59] He suggests that Jerome's hypothesis is strengthened if Mary the wife of Alpheus (Clopas) was married to the brother of Joseph. That overcomes the difficulty of two sisters bearing the same name but it does not fit the description of John 19:25. Who would have guessed, without knowing, that sister meant sister-in-law?

Conclusively against Jerome's theory is the fact that the brothers and sisters are consistently associated with the mother of Jesus, Mary, and her husband

---

[59] *Jude and the Relatives of Jesus in the Early Church* (Edinburgh: T & T Clark, 1990), 21.

Joseph. They are never referred to as the brothers and sisters of Jesus in relation to any other parents. While the term "brothers" can be used in a metaphorical or broader sense, such a use would be extraordinary in the contexts in which they are mentioned in the Gospels. There Mary is mentioned as the mother of Jesus and they as his brothers (and sisters), while Joseph is referred to as father. In this context the suggested meaning of cousins or some other affiliation is totally unconvincing. In Matthew and Luke only the paternity of Joseph in relation to Jesus is qualified. The reader knows this, so that it is not misleading to the reader when Joseph is called the father of Jesus. The reader knows that, according to Matthew and Luke, this is his "legal" or "supposed" status, whether or not this is actually the case. Jerome's reconstruction suggests a puzzle of his own making into which the pieces of evidence have been forced even where they are a poor fit. The suspicion is strong that no such reconstructions would have occurred had Jerome not wished to preserve the virginity of Mary.

Concern for the perpetual virginity of Mary motivated Jerome and was a significant and growing factor in the Western church. Through Augustine Jerome came to adopt the view, found in the *Protevangelium of James,* which provided an account of the birth of Jesus in which the midwives gave evidence that the virginity of Mary remained intact even in the act of giving birth. This modified version of Jerome's theory became the dominant view in the West. It had the advantage of elevating the virginity of Mary and at the same time maintaining the virginity of Joseph. It resulted in the relegation of James, along with the other brothers and sisters of Jesus, to a secondary position. James the brother of Jesus ceased to be a point of focus or concern in any Western tradition.

CONCLUSION

Opposed tendencies concerning James have emerged. In the *Gospel of the Hebrews* and the Pseudo-Clementines the leading role of James is developed. He is the leader of the apostles, of the Jerusalem church, and of the church at large. In the *Protevangelium of James,* Origen, Epiphanius, and Jerome there is a distancing of James from any natural relationship to Jesus. The position of Origen is less clear on this matter than are those of the others mentioned. For the rest it is clear that Mary is the mother only of Jesus and not of those designated his brothers and sisters. For them there is a growing preoccupation with the perpetual virginity of Mary, which Jerome also extends to Joseph. Clearly the need for ascetic models in the church has begun to drive this exegetical and interpretative exposition. Consequently there was a lessening of interest in James and his contribution to the leadership of the church.

The role of James was not immediately obliterated. Origen notes that such was the righteousness of James that once he had been murdered Vespasian began his siege of Jerusalem. Even Jerome acknowledges the leadership of James in Jerusalem. He notes that James was called the brother of Jesus "on account of his high character, his incomparable faith, and extraordinary wisdom" but "preeminently" because "the Lord at his departure had committed" the leadership of the Jerusalem church to him. Unlike earlier accounts of the succession of authority in which James was appointed leader, at least in part, because he was the brother of Jesus, here he is called brother preeminently because he was appointed leader. The earlier tradition did not overlook the "righteousness" of James and other members of "the family," and James's relationship to Jesus was treated as an independent ground for his appointment. This was true also in the tradition of the succession of Symeon.

Although Jerome attempted to dissolve the natural relationship of James to Jesus, he made no direct attempt to obscure the leading role of James in the earliest church. Indeed, in his *Lives of Illustrious Men* James is listed second, following only Peter, and Jerome's account is about twice as long as his "life" of Peter. The complete text, which can be considered a summary of the traditions received by Jerome, is reproduced here.

> James, who is called the brother of the Lord, surnamed the Just, the son of Joseph by another wife, as some think, but as appears to me, the son of Mary sister of the mother of our Lord of whom John makes mention in his book, after our Lord's passion at once ordained by the apostles bishop of Jerusalem, wrote a single epistle, which is reckoned among the seven Catholic Epistles, and even this is claimed by some to have been published by someone else under his name, and gradually, as time went on, to have gained authority. Hegesippus who lived near the apostolic age, in the fifth book of his *Commentaries*, writing of James, says:
>
> > After the apostles, James the brother of the Lord surnamed the Just was made head of the church at Jerusalem. Many indeed are called James. This one was holy from his mother's womb. He drank neither wine nor strong drink, ate no flesh, never shaved or anointed himself with ointment or bathed. He alone had the privilege of entering the Holy of Holies, since indeed he did not use woolen vestments but linen and went alone into the Temple and prayed in behalf of the people, insomuch that his knees were reputed to have acquired the hardness of camels' knees.
>
> He says also many other things too numerous to mention. Josephus also in the 20th book of his *Antiquities* and Clement in the 7th of his *Outlines* mention that on the death of Festus who reigned over Judaea, Albinus was sent by Nero as his successor. Before he had reached his province, Ananias the high priest, the youthful son of Ananus of the priestly class, taking advantage of the state of anarchy, assembled a council and publicly

tried to force James to deny that Christ is the Son of God. When he refused Ananias ordered him to be stoned. Cast down from a pinnacle of the Temple, his legs broken, but still half alive, raising his hands to heaven he said, "Lord forgive them for they know not what they do." Then struck on the head with a club of a fuller, such a club as fullers are accustomed to wring out garments with, he died. This same Josephus records the tradition that this James was of so great sanctity and reputation among the people that the downfall of Jerusalem was believed to be on account of his death. He it is of whom the apostle writes to the Galatians that "No one else of the apostles did I see except James the brother of the Lord," and shortly after the event the Acts of the Apostles bear witness to the matter. The Gospel also which is called the *Gospel according to the Hebrews*, and which I have recently translated into Greek and Latin and which also Origen often makes use of, after the account of the resurrection of the Savior says, "but the Lord, after he had given his grave clothes to the servant of the priest, appeared to James (for James had sworn that he would not eat bread from that hour in which he drank the cup of the Lord until he should see him rising again from among those that sleep)" and again, a little later, it says, " 'Bring a table and bread,' said the Lord." And immediately it is added, "He brought bread and blessed and broke and gave to James the Just and said to him, my brother, eat thy bread, for the son of man is risen from among those that sleep." And so he ruled the church in Jerusalem thirty years, that is until the seventh year of Nero, and was buried near the Temple from which he had been cast down. His tombstone with its inscription was well known until the siege of Titus and the end of Hadrian's reign. Some of our writers think he was buried in Mount Olivet, but they are mistaken.

In his preface to this work Jerome acknowledged Eusebius's *Church History* as his main source. Indeed, apart from his own analysis of the Gospels, which is assumed, and his use of the *Gospel of the Hebrews* (discussed above), all is drawn from Eusebius. Like Eusebius, Jerome combines Hegesippus, Clement, Josephus, and the reference to James as "the brother of the Lord" in Paul's letter to the Galatians. He also makes use of the appeal to the spurious text attributed to Josephus which asserted that the destruction of Jerusalem was because of what had been done to James. What Jerome adds to Eusebius's account is his awareness of the Epiphanian view and his own theory concerning the brothers of Jesus. He also tells that the fall broke James's legs. This detail may have come to Jerome, adding color and making clear that the fall did not kill James. He was dispatched with a single blow from a fuller's club, agreeing with Hegesippus against Clement, who implies repeated blows. While Josephus is used to date the death of James, Jerome uses Clement and Hegesippus for his account of

James's death. From Josephus he calculates that James ruled the Jerusalem church for thirty years, more or less from the time of Jesus. At the beginning Jerome implies, generally following Clement, that James was appointed by the apostles, though his quotation from the *Gospel of the Hebrews* suggests an appointment of James as his successor by Jesus.

Jerome gets wrong the name of the high priest, which is in Josephus. He notes the tradition of the tombstone from Eusebius and adds that it was known until the siege of Titus, which he seems to equate with the end of the reign of Trajan! What this means is that Jerome could no longer find the stone. Though he does not say so, his reference to other writers mistakenly thinking that James was buried in one of the tombs on Mount Olivet is probably evidence that they too could not find the tombstone. This detailed account shows that Jerome recognized the greatness of James, and no doubt this was reinforced for him by the ascetic ideal which had come to be associated with James. But by breaking the bonds of the family relationship he helped to ensure that awareness of the significant and distinctive leadership of James would not endure.

Part III

JAMES AND
JEWISH CHRISTIANITY

CHAPTER 8

JEWISH CHRISTIANITY, THE RIGHTEOUS SUFFERER, AND THE EPISTLE OF JAMES

From the beginning of our study of the historical James and all along the trail of tradition concerning him in the history of early Christianity we have encountered the question of the relationship of James to Judaism and especially to Jewish Christianity. While all of the earliest Christians were Jewish, there were those who intended to maintain their Jewish identity while at the same time adopting the messianic faith in Jesus. The complexity of this subject is clear from the study of the evidence concerning Paul and James.

The portrayal of James as the just or righteous one arises from Jewish tradition. This ascription is fundamentally related to the martyrdom of James and should be understood in terms of the tradition of the righteous sufferer. This tradition is intimately linked with a particular understanding of God that emotionally (or psychologically) sustains the faith of the righteous sufferer and of those who perceive righteous suffering to be a problem while at the same time magnifying the intellectual challenge of the problem.

In this context the Epistle of James emerges with an unexpected force. After the first two chapters, the epistle appears to be a loose collection of paranetic material.[1] There is, however, an underlying unity of thought, and this has been emphasized by a number of recent studies. It is thus necessary to distinguish the collection of tradition on formal grounds and the unity of thought, which can be seen by concentrating on the content. From these perspectives, the formal and the "essential," the Epistle of James emerges as a work with much to contribute to our study of Jewish Christianity and the role of the righteous sufferer. Various important aspects within the epistle must now be brought into sharp focus. What does the epistle reveal of the relationship of

---

[1] Thus M. Dibelius, *James: A Commentary on the Epistle of James*, revised edition, revised by Heinrich Greeven, Hermeneia (Philadelphia: Fortress, 1976).

James and Jesus, James and Paul? What kind of Judaism or Christianity is it that the epistle advocates, and within which identifiable group is it likely that the letter of James was produced?

JEWISH CHRISTIANITY

The notion of Jewish Christianity is fraught with difficulties.[2] Two important aspects can be identified immediately. First, time makes a difference. Initially all of the followers of Jesus were Jewish. Somewhat later there is no evidence of any distinctive and exclusively Jewish form of Christianity. Again, the earliest stage of the Christian movement reflected the varieties within Judaism. Later Christianity was differentiated by other factors, and there were pressures toward a more monolithic uniformity. Second, geography makes a difference. At first all of the followers of Jesus were from Judaea and Galilee. By the end of the first century the vast majority of Christians were located outside these regions and were differentiated from each other by geographical location. In due course pressures were brought to bear, seeking to impose the synthesis of one geographical locality on all. Such pressures did bring about an accord in the West that lasted more or less until the Reformation, although it had already begun breaking down before then. A different kind of solution emerged in the East. The study of James can be used to clarify these matters.

The precise definition of Jewish Christianity is somewhat arbitrary. There is no single *correct* understanding. Persuasion of appropriate meaning depends largely on the usefulness of the definition. Various definitions have had their appeal in the study of different periods of history, in which a number of perspectives emerge. Nevertheless the most useful definition is one that is meaningful in a wide range of contexts.

To define Christianity as a Jewish sect makes sense of the beginnings of Christianity. Within a century the complexity of the Christian movement proved this to be an oversimplification because, by the middle of the second century, Christianity had become a dominantly Gentile phenomenon. Continuity with Judaism could still be perceived by concentrating on Jewish themes and motifs in the Christian writings of the period. That no distinction is made between dominant and secondary themes and motifs is a weakness in this view in that those who attempt to show continuity fail to ask about whether the identifying, defining Jewish elements are retained by Christianity. No attention is given to the question of whether circumcision and food and purity laws are observed. What makes these important is that they are continuing boundary markers of Jewish identity. By the middle of the second century what is per-

---

[2] See F. J. A. Hort, *Judaistic Christianity* (London: Macmillan, 1904); A. F. J. Klijn, "The Study of Jewish Christianity," *NTS* 20 (1973–74): 419–31; J. Danielou, *The Theology of Jewish Christianity* (London: Darton, Longman and Todd, 1964).

ceived as Jewish Christianity was distinguished by these markers and essential beliefs. Belief in the messiahship of Jesus formally linked all Christians, but in Jewish Christianity messiahship lacked developments common to Christianity elsewhere. This phenomenon is frequently referred to as Ebionism, the belief that Jesus was Messiah but not divine.

This summary might suggest that the fundamental distinction is between Jewish Christianity and Gentile Christianity. These categories obscure the recognition that in the beginning there was only Jewish Christianity. Some form or forms of this had the potential to bring about the emergence of Gentile Christianity, while other distinctively Jewish forms did not long survive the two cataclysmic Jewish wars. Those forms of Christianity that survived were less like the Judaism that emerged (Rabbinic Judaism) than the distinctive Jewish Christianity that failed to survive. Quite a wide range of identifiably Jewish positions can be recognized prior to the first of the Jewish wars. These also found expression in the nascent Christian movement. Above we have discussed this variety in terms of the six factions of the two missions of the circumcision and the uncircumcision.

By the second century only those factions that maintained Jewish identity were perceived to be Jewish, and the name of James was associated with them. In the process the Jewish Christians became isolated from other Jews because of the confession of Jesus as the Messiah and isolated from other Christians because of their adherence to the Jewish law. Perhaps because of this isolation Jewish Christianity failed to follow developments in the broader Christian movement. The most notable of these developments is to be seen in terms of christology. Jewish Christians maintained belief in Jesus as Messiah and looked to his speedy return as judge of the ages. There was a reticence about ascribing divine attributes to Jesus. A connection between early Jerusalem Christianity (the Hebrews) and the later Ebionites is probable. Ebionism failed to follow the interpretative option of identifying Jesus with the divine Wisdom and became separated from what was to become mainstream Christianity. In this growing isolation Jewish Christianity and emerging Gnosticism have an intimate relationship, and the name of James remains prominent.

Syrian Antioch was a storm center in the early struggles of the Jesus movement. There the followers of the Way achieved a recognizable identity and were first called Christians (Acts 11:26). Antioch is now something of a storm center of modern scholarship. Perhaps because more work has been done on Antioch than on most of the other important cities of the time, there is a temptation to locate the origin of much of the early Christian literature with that place—not only Matthew but also Luke and the *Didache*. While a plausible case can be made, the state of the evidence falls short of establishing as probable the Antiochene origin of these books. To say that a better case can be made for Antioch than for elsewhere may sound convincing, until it is recognized that none of these books gives any indication of its place of origin. Nevertheless, there is no doubt that Matthew came to have an important influence in Antioch.

Antioch was a storm center in the struggle between the two missions, as can be seen from the book of Acts and especially from Paul's letter to the Galatians. Most scholars assume that Gal 2:11–14 indicates that Paul lost the struggle there, that Peter won, and that Paul had little to do with Antioch from that point onward. There is little evidence to support this view. We have argued that Paul maintained his role as a missionary of the Antioch church. His mission strategy was an extension of the strategy of the Hellenist mission that had laid the foundation in Antioch, where Paul had been a recognized leader from quite early days.

What happened after the final departure of Paul is another question. The execution of James took place in 62 and the first Jewish war had broken out by 66. Somewhere between these two events it is likely that members of the Jerusalem church migrated to Antioch, taking with them the tradition of the teaching of Jesus associated with James, the tradition we now perceive as Matthew's special tradition, "M." While this body of material may seem to reflect the redactional position of the finished Gospel, there are points at which it is more narrowly Jewish, particularly in the way the mission of Jesus is categorically restricted to Israel. The final Gospel represents a modification of this position and should be associated with Peter. While James and Peter each represented the circumcision mission, Matthew reflects important modifications in line with Petrine tradition and provides strong advocacy of Petrine leadership. This was seen with clarity by Streeter. The position of James could only have been in bitter conflict with the dominant faction of the Antioch church. Consequently the modification of this position in Matthew, whether or not that Gospel was written in Antioch, can only have been welcomed by the community of believers there.

James and his supporters intended to maintain the integrity of the Jesus movement as an authentic Jewish movement. Robert H. Eisenman argues that James the Just needs to be understood in relation to the Qumran Teacher of Righteousness.[3] He argues that "it was a comparatively easy task to link the events and teachings of the Righteous Teacher in the Habakkuk Pesher to those of James the Just in the early 'Jerusalem Community.' "[4] To come to this conclusion it was necessary to reject the common dating of the main activities of the Qumran Community and the Righteous Teacher. He does this by: 1) putting in question the single-line reconstruction based on paleographic evidence that he associates particularly with Frank Moore Cross;[5] 2) asserting that a vari-

---

[3] In particular see his *Maccabees, Zadokites, Christians and Qumran* (Leiden: Brill, 1983) and *James the Just in the Habakkuk Pesher* (Leiden: Brill, 1986).

[4] *James the Just*, pp. vii, viii, xii, 38.

[5] *Maccabees*, p. xvi.

ety of terms identified different individuals and groups known by other names in the evidence of Jewish history outside the Qumran Texts;[6] 3) claiming that the *pesher* interpretation was not common until the mid-first century CE.[7]

In an article entitled "Playing on and Transmuting Words: Interpreting Abeit-Galuto in the Habakkuk Pesher,"[8] Eisenman sets out his method of identifying historical people and events from the indirect (symbolic) references of the texts. His method, though less elaborate, is similar to the so-called *pesher* method of interpretation employed by Barbara Thiering.[9] What Thiering does not acknowledge is that this kind of commentary (the *Habakkuk Pesher*) was written in order to make relevant the meaning of a book from the past (Habakkuk) to the time of the Qumran sect. The *Habakkuk Pesher* itself was not written in "code." Rather, it purported to "decode" the book of Habakkuk. The term "pesher" does not concern writing books in code. It is a method of decoding made necessary by the belief that books from the past had a direct meaning for the history of the sect. There is no evidence here of authors writing works in which the intended meaning is hidden and can only be "recovered" by a *pesher* method of interpretation. Such a construct is the product of a free flight of fantasy. The arbitrary nature of it can be shown by the irreconcilable conclusions drawn by Thiering and Eisenman. Equally serious is the fact that, using their methods, there is no way the relative virtues of their views can be evaluated, and they are not open to critical dialogue.

Eisenman argues that the *Habakkuk Pesher* gives the impression of being recorded soon after or even at the time of the events of 68 CE and "almost every turn-of-phrase in the Habakkuk pesher . . . can . . . [be] put into real historical settings relating to real and important people contemporary with the fall of the temple about 70 CE.[10] Eisenman therefore argues that the events relating to the Righteous Teacher and the writing of the *Habakkuk Pesher* belong to the mid-first century and are likened to the events surrounding James the Just in the early "Jerusalem Community." While Eisenman's earlier works stop short of explicit identification of the Righteous Teacher with James the Just, there seems to be no other reasonable conclusion to draw from his argument, and his later article is more to the point.[11] Certainly the journalists who have popularized his views have not drawn back from the explicit identification.[12] Crucial in this is

---

[6] *Maccabees,* pp. xi–xii; *James the Just,* p. vii.

[7] *James the Just,* pp. 37–38.

[8] In *Papers on the Dead Sea Scrolls in Memory of Jean Carmignac,* ed. Z. J. Kapera (Cracow: 1991), 177–96.

[9] *Jesus the Man* (Garden City, N.Y.: Doubleday, 1992).

[10] *James the Just,* pp. 49, 75.

[11] "Playing on and Transmuting Words: Interpreting Abeit-Galuto in the Habakkuk Pesher," in *Papers on the Dead Sea Scrolls,* pp. 184, 188, 189, 191, 196.

[12] See M. Baigent and R. Leigh, *The Dead Sea Scrolls Deception* (New York: Summit Books, 1991).

the identification of the "Wicked Priest" with the high priest Ananus and the "spouter of lies" with Paul.[13]

To accomplish this interpretation references to Damascus are interpreted in terms of Qumran. Paul's journey to Damascus in pursuit of Christians is understood to take him to Qumran, where James presided. In all of this Paul is understood to be an agent of the Romans.[14] Undergoing a conversion experience, Paul submitted to the authority of James at the Jerusalem council.[15] Nevertheless he is presented as the real creator of Christianity because, unlike Jesus, who was faithful to the law, Paul turned the new movement into a mystery cult in which Jesus was worshiped as a dying and rising God, thus appealing to pagans.[16] The hypothesis reflects long-discredited views about the beginnings of Christianity, views that hang on only in circles that are critical of Christianity for other reasons. The identification of Qumran with Damascus is also wrong. It had long been known from Josephus that the Essenes had communities in the townships, but until recently this fact had not been confirmed in the Qumran Texts. The texts now show that it is likely that members of the sect lived in Damascus, and the so-called *Damascus Document* appears to be a rule appropriate to their circumstances.

Eisenman is right in his assertion that the "main stream" hypotheses make only fragmentary identifications from the Habakkuk *Pesher* with events and persons of known contemporary history. Given the fragmentary nature of the sources of the period, his complete set of identifications is somewhat surprising. Is it reasonable to suggest that, with all the gaps in the evidence, no gap falls at a point that has bearing on the identification of persons and events in the Qumran Texts?

The critique of the paleographic evidence by itself has some weight. But the dating and interpretation of the history of the Qumran sect are not done on the basis of paleography alone. The dating is the consequence of complex and cumulative evidence: the reconstruction of the history of the sect from the archaeology of the site; the history of its occupation, taking account of coins and pottery; the carbon dating of the material of the scrolls; the identification of historical figures and events in the scrolls; and paleographic evidence. What is more, the literary evidence places the Righteous Teacher near to the beginning of the history of the sect,[17] a history that begins around the time of the Maccabean revolt.

What then are we to make of the parallels Eisenman has drawn between the Righteous Teacher and James? First, he has been selective in his use of the

---

[13] See Baigent and Leigh, pp. 286–87.

[14] R. H. Eisenman and M. Wise, *The Dead Sea Scrolls Uncovered* (Shaftsbury, Dorset, and Rockport, Mass.: Element Books, 1993), 273, and Baigent and Leigh, p. 320.

[15] Baigent and Leigh, p. 266.

[16] Ibid., p. 267, and Eisenman, *Maccabees,* p. 59 n.99.

[17] *CD* I.9–11.

James traditions. Because the account in the Pseudo-Clementines (*Recognitions* 1.70) fits his hypothesis, he argues that the account given there of an attempt on James's life is historical. The use of source material about James demands careful critical attention, and it will not do simply to choose those elements that fit into a hypothesis. Eisenman makes an interesting suggestion about the tradition in 1 Corinthians 15. Harnack suggested that the tradition of the appearance to James and all the apostles was expressed using a rivalry formula challenging the leadership of Peter that was established on the basis of the tradition of the appearance to Peter and the twelve. Eisenman argues that the tradition of the appearance to James and all the apostles is original and the appearance to Peter and the twelve a later intrusion.[18] Just when Eisenman thinks this "later" intrusion took place is unclear, although the reason for suggesting that the appearance to Peter looks suspiciously late is that it is linked with an appearance to "the twelve," although only eleven remained after the defection of Judas. The unhistorical character of the witness in relation to Peter is what makes Eisenman think it to be later. Eisenman does not even raise the question of whether "the twelve" might be a technical term that continued to be used of the group, even if there were only eleven at the time.

The notion of the intrusion of a rivalry formula must take account of the relatively early date of 1 Corinthians. On Harnack's view the rivalry implicit in the James formula implies the original authority of Peter, challenged by James. This view can make sense of Acts 12:17 if it is read as implying a transition of authority from Peter to James. There is, however, no clear evidence of the original leadership of Peter. On Eisenman's reading, the authority of James is prior to and was challenged by the authority of Peter at a later stage. His view of the original authority of James fits in with traditions from the early church recorded by Eusebius, texts in the Nag Hammadi Library, and the Pseudo-Clementines, in all of which James is named as the first bishop of Jerusalem, appointed by Jesus or the apostles or by Peter, James, and John. What is common to these traditions is that James is portrayed as the original leader of the Jerusalem church. A tradition of the first appearance of the risen Jesus to James is supportive of this position and is clearly affirmed in the *Gospel of the Hebrews*. James's authority was from the first based on his relation to Jesus and the appearance of the risen Jesus to him.

Second, why Eisenman is able to find parallels between the Righteous Teacher and James is that each of them is portrayed in terms of the genre of the righteous sufferer. Eisenman recognizes this and even outlines a tradition of righteous sufferers from the time of the Maccabees to James and beyond:[19] "It

---

[18] *Maccabees*, p. xii.

[19] See *James the Just*, p. 75, and also *Maccabees*, p. 52 nn.70 and 71, and our discussion of this motif below.

is possible to identify a series of martyred *Zaddikim* beginning with Onias the son of Simeon the *Zaddik*. Judas Maccabee, Honi the Circle-Drawer, his grand-son Hannan the Hidden, John the Baptist (if not identical with Hannan the Hidden), Jesus, James, etc. . . ."

But this weakens his case for identifying the two figures on the basis that they share elements of the righteous sufferer *genre*.

He also links James with the "rainmaker" tradition.[20] Consequently the case for identifying the Righteous Teacher of Qumran with James is greatly overrated by Eisenman. It is not that the two have nothing in common, as we have seen. Both advocate positions of zeal for the law. Had they not, the attri-bute of righteousness would hardly have been applied to them. There is, how-ever, no evidence of a direct relationship of James to the Qumran Righteous Teacher. Indeed, as good a case can be made for the identification of Jesus with the Righteous Teacher[21] as can be made for James, and it has even been argued that the identification should be made with John the Baptist.[22] What makes the case for such identifications possible is that all of these figures fit the genre of the righteous sufferer.

For all the difficulties in identifying the precise history of the Qumran sect, the chronology of the beginnings and the role of the Teacher of Righteousness rule out any identification of that figure with James. There is no reason to think that the wicked priest should be identified with Ananus, the opponent of James, or that the "spouter of lies" refers to Paul. There is, moreover, no good reason for identifying James or Paul with any figures in the texts, where it may be that the references to the "spouter of lies" and the "wicked priest" should be identi-fied with one and the same person. Certainly James is not the Qumran Righ-teous Teacher, although this description may well fit his role within the Jerusalem church and the perception of it more broadly in Jewish Christianity. There too, as can be seen in the Pseudo-Clementines, Paul was perceived as "the enemy" of Peter and James and of the truth.

THE EPISTLE OF JAMES

At the conclusion of his extended account of the martyrdom of James Eusebius writes:

> Such is the story of James, whose is said to be the first of the epistles named Catholic. It is to be observed that its authenticity is denied, since few of the ancients quote it, as is also the case with the epistle called

---

[20] See *James the Just*, pp. 34, 75 nn.2 and 3; *Maccabees*, pp. xiv, 52 nn.70 and 71.

[21] See A. Dupont-Sommer, *The Essene Writings from Qumran* (Oxford: Blackwell, 1961).

[22] This has been argued by B. E. Thiering in *Jesus the Man*. For Thiering, Jesus is to be identified as the Wicked Priest.

Jude's, which is itself one of the seven called Catholic; nevertheless we know that these letters have been used publicly with the rest in most churches. (*HE* 2.23.24–25)

Eusebius was reticent about attributing the epistle to James. Nowhere does he venture his own opinion, although he notes the basis upon which doubt is cast on its authenticity. Few early writers refer to it. The subsequent acknowledgment that by the time of Eusebius the Epistle of James was used publicly in most churches shows that its canonical status was still in question. It is said to be the first of those called Catholic, a reference to the canonical order of the Catholic Epistles, not to the order in which these epistles were written.

What counts most strongly against the recognition of the epistle as a work of James the brother of Jesus is that it is unattested until 180 CE when Irenaeus quoted James 2:23 in *AH* 4.16.2. Not until the mid-third century is the work appealed to as scripture. Origen quoted the work, showing that he believed he was quoting scripture, but he cited it in such a way as to show that he was aware that his view did not enjoy universal support.[23] Such evidence as there is suggests that Origen did not identify the author of the Epistle with James the brother of Jesus. In his *Commentary on Matthew* X.17 Origen deals with Matthew 13:54–56 on the subject of "the brethren of Jesus." There he mentions Paul's reference to James as the Lord's brother in Galatians and James's reputation for righteousness. He then goes on to speak of Jude "who wrote a letter of a few lines" and "said in the preface, 'Jude the servant of Jesus Christ and brother of James.'" No mention is made here of any letter written by this James. Had Origen thought the Epistle of James had been written by this James he would have said so at this point. Nothing he says of the Epistle of James suggests that it was written by the brother of Jesus.

James was not among the canonical works listed at the Council of Nicaea in 325 CE. Its canonical status was given a decisive boost when Athanasius, in section 8 of his Easter Festal Letter of 367 CE, set out the order of the Catholic Epistles as James, 1 and 2 Peter, 1, 2, and 3 John, and Jude. Athanasius also asserted the apostolic status of James and his letter. The views of Alexandria were adopted in Caesarea and found champions in the Cappadocians, especially Basil and Gregory Nazianzus. In 379 CE Jerome visited Constantinople and came under the spell of Gregory Nazianzus. Not only did Jerome include the Epistle of James in his Vulgate translation; he quoted from the epistle 128 times. Thus the influence of Origen and Athanasius—the influence of Alexandria— was carried to Rome and the West. Augustine followed the canon of Jerome.[24]

---

[23] *Commentary on John. Frag. 6.* See A. E. Brooke, *The Commentary of Origen on St. John's Gospel*, II, p. 216.

[24] *Christian Instruction*, 2.18.13.

Augustine attempted to write a commentary on James but had to make do with an inaccurate Latin translation. Jerome's translation was not published until 383. Augustine quoted from James 389 times, showing his acceptance of its authority. Thus James was included in the canon of the Synod of Hippo in 393 CE, which led to the adoption of the same canon at the third council of Carthage (397 CE) and the fourth council of Carthage (419). It was also adopted in the canon of the Council of Rome (382 CE). Thus, through the influence of Origen, Athanasius, and the Cappadocians, the place of James was secure in the Greek churches and the West.

The Syrian church was slower in acknowledging the canonical status of James. Such recognition eventually came through the influence of the Greek-speaking church of Syrian Antioch. John of Antioch persuaded Rabbula, bishop of Edessa (411–35), to commission a Syrian translation of James. Thus James also became part of the Syrian scriptures. The leading influence of the Greek-speaking churches in this process is clear. It is likely that the acceptance of James, first at Antioch and then in Edessa, was a consequence of the influence of John Chrysostom (died circa 407 CE). Chrysostom identified the author of the Epistle as James the Lord's brother, "God's brother," and refers to him as rabbi and bishop of Jerusalem.[25] Chrysostom was a clear advocate of the canonical status of James. Thus James finally achieved clear canonical status in East and West. It remained undisputed until the Reformation. Luther questioned its canonicity, referring to it as "an epistle of straw" and as "deuterocanonical."[26] He also rejected attribution of authorship to James the Lord's brother. His views were shared by Erasmus.[27] While the reasoning of neither Luther nor Erasmus is consistently persuasive on this issue, modern scholarship has tended to be persuaded by their conclusion that the epistle does not come from the hand of James the brother of Jesus.

The main argument in favor of attributing this letter to James the brother of Jesus is that there is no other James in the early church who could expect to be recognized simply by the use of the name James.[28] While he identifies himself neither as the brother of Jesus nor as an apostle, the simplicity of his address is taken to be supportive of this view. James identifies himself simply as "a servant (δοῦλος) of God and of [the] Lord Jesus Christ." This may seem to be a humble description, but it should not be forgotten that the scriptures characteristically refer to God's servants the prophets, and Israel is ideally the servant

---

[25] *Homilies on Penitence* 2; *Commentary on the Epistle to the Galatians* 2.9; *Homilies on the Acts of the Apostles* 46.

[26] See W. J. Kooiman, *Luther and the Bible* (Philadelphia: Muhlenberg Press, 1961), 110ff., esp. p. 226 n.2.

[27] See A. Rabil, *Erasmus and the New Testament: The Mind of a Christian Humanist* (San Antonio: Trinity University Press, 1972), 115.

[28] Thus J. B. Adamson, *James: The Man and His Message* (Grand Rapids: Eerdmans, 1989), 9–11.

of the Lord, an unfulfilled vocation that led Isaiah to portray the ideal servant of the Lord in the celebrated "Servant Songs." Against this background the author's reference to himself as "James the servant of God and the Lord Jesus Christ" should be seen as noble rather than humble. In addressing the church at Rome Paul also refers to himself as "a servant of Christ Jesus," though he there adds, "called to be an apostle." His address in Philippians is more straight-forward: "Paul and Timothy servants of Christ Jesus." Paul's frequent assertion of his apostleship is a signal of the controversial nature of his claim. Nowhere is that clearer than in the opening of his letter to the Galatians. That no claims of apostleship are associated with the James of the epistle need not mean that he was not so perceived. Rather it may indicate that, in the circles for which the epistle was intended, his apostolic status was not in question.

No one doubts that, whether the epistle is authentic or pseudonymous, the author intended that it should be understood as the epistle of James the brother of Jesus. Against the pseudonymous view it is argued that such an author would have made clear that the James in view was the brother of Jesus and would have used a more exalted title than "a servant of God." But "servant" has an exalted history in Jewish tradition. Yet no other James is of sufficient note to be recognized without further elaboration. This observation is a double-edged weapon. Certainly it supports the view that the reader is intended to identify this James. Thus if the work were pseudepigraphical, the author could expect the readers to recognize which James was in view. There was no need to make this clear elaborately, especially if the letter, in some way, represented or re-flected tradition coming from James.

Adamson thinks that the simple form of address by means of which James identifies himself supports the identification of the actual author with the brother of Jesus. "If the document had been forged, we would expect a more sophisticated effort to stress his authority."[29] The assumption that only James the brother of Jesus had no need of anything but a simple form of address leads to a conclusion unforeseen by Adamson, that a pseudepigraphical work attributed to James might well adopt a straightforward form of address.

Adamson reveals a modern evaluative perspective when he refers to pseud-epigraphical works as "forged." Pseudepigraphy in the ancient world was not treated in the way we treat forgery. There is also a modified pseudepigraphy by which tradition emanating from an eminent person was written up by another person in a new and later situation and presented straightforwardly as the work of the eminent person. This process has been suggested as a solution to the problem of the Pastoral Epistles in relation to Paul[30] and is suggested here as a way of approaching the puzzle of the Epistle of James.

---

[29] Ibid., p. 39.

[30] Thus J. N. D. Kelly, *A Commentary on the Pastoral Epistles* (New York: Harper, 1963), and C. K. Barrett, "Pauline Controversies in the Post-Pauline Period," *NTS* 20/3 (1974): 229–45.

Adamson's argument that it makes more sense to attribute a masterpiece like James to the known brother of Jesus than to some unknown author is not persuasive.[31] James is the only composition that might have been written by James. It is thus impossible to say whether it is the sort of epistle James could or would have written or that he is more likely to be the author than some other person unknown to us.

At the same time arguments to the effect that James could not have written such a book are not persuasive either. The book is written in good Hellenistic Greek, but the literary quality is not such that James could not be the author. Greek was widely spoken in Galilee and Judaea[32] and both Jesus and James were almost certainly bilingual. Too much stress should not be placed on the humble Galilean peasant origin of James. We need to allow for the influence of the Jesus mission, the educative effect of the Jesus tradition, and more than thirty years as the leader (effectively as first bishop, even if the title is anachronistic) of the Jerusalem church.

The ascription "the (our) Lord Jesus Christ" (James 1:1; 2:1) is not exactly what we would expect to find in an early Palestinian Jewish Christian document. James Adamson, aware of this problem, notes that "Christos" was used "first as an appellative and then as a proper name."[33] Adamson, wishing to argue that the Epistle of James should be seen as an early Christian Jewish document by the brother of Jesus, has to cope with the apparent use of "Christ" as a name in James. Without directly discussing the ascription in James, Adamson argues: "In Acts *Christos*, used singly or in "Jesus Christ" or "Christ Jesus," is always an appellative, and used only in addressing a Jewish audience (except, *possibly*, by Philip, to Samaritans, and notably, by Paul before Agrippa II). Perhaps it was not yet a proper name; certainly the evidence is that in Acts *Christos* is usually employed as a title. It is so elsewhere in the NT in addressing Jews; except perhaps in Mt. 1.1, 18, all the 14 uses indicate a title or designation, not a name."[34] Adamson's intention was to conclude that in James the use is also appellative, not a name. This is hardly clear. Rather it seems that what we have is the use of "Christos" as a name, a use that seems to signal that James is a more complex composition than Adamson would like to think. R. P. Martin acknowledges that debate continues over whether the origin of the full confessional formula, which occurs frequently in the introductory section of Pauline correspondence, is of "Jewish Christian or hellenistic provenance."[35] Adam-

[31] *James: The Man and His Message*, p. 9.

[32] See M. Hengel, *Judaism and Hellenism,* 2 vols. (London: SCM, 1974); S. Freyne, *Galilee from Alexander the Great to Hadrian 325 BCE to 135 CE: A Study of Second Temple Judaism* (Wilmington, Del.: Michael Glazier, 1980).

[33] *James: The Man and His Message*, p. 28.

[34] Ibid., pp. 28–29.

[35] *James*, Word Biblical Commentary 48 (Waco, Tex.: Word Books, 1988), 7.

son's confidence that the use in James conforms to early Christian Jewish practice appears to have influenced his reading of the evidence. It did not occur to him, for example, that the evidence of the use of "Christos" he has produced from Acts might reflect Lukan redaction and not provide evidence of early Christian Jewish use.

More seriously, however, we need to recognize that James belonged to the group within the Jerusalem church known as the Hebrews and that he concentrated his attention on the Jerusalem church. After the death of Jesus, the only incident concerning a situation outside Jerusalem where James is mentioned (in the New Testament) is the incident at Antioch (Gal 2:11–14). There his intervention is via messengers, and it is to call on Jewish believers to conform to the practice of the circumcision mission of Jerusalem. Nowhere in the New Testament is there evidence to suggest that James traveled outside Jerusalem to spread the mission to Jews of the diaspora or to Gentiles. This role seems to have been undertaken by Cephas/Peter, who visited Antioch, and the evidence of the Cephas party at Corinth suggests that he traveled to that city also. Tradition later places Peter and Paul in Rome, which might suggest an ongoing rivalry between the two missions. The identification of James with the Hebrews mentioned in Acts and James's own concentration on the affairs of the Jerusalem church raise serious questions for the straightforward attribution of the epistle to James.

The vast majority of modern scholars question the authenticity of the letter, although its authorship by James the brother of Jesus is not without significant defenders.[36] A mediating approach, which has some recent advocates, can be described as the secretary hypothesis.[37] Although Adamson allows that what he has called James's letter to Gentile Christians (Acts 15:23–29) might have been composed by Luke while conveying the message of James,[38] he rejects the secretary hypothesis in relation to the Epistle of James, saying that it "raises more problems than solutions."[39] Adamson has in mind the model of Peter and Silvanus with 1 Peter, a model which is not useful in relation to James. Yet Adamson shows that there is a significant word statistical relationship between James and Luke-Acts.[40] He shows that the vocabulary of James is closer to Luke than to Matthew or Mark. This evidence supports the recognition of James as a Hellenistic composition by a native Greek speaker and perhaps supports the view of the use of (Christian) Jewish tradition by a native Greek-speaking author.

---

[36] See W. Pratscher, *Der Herrenbruder Jacobus und die Jacobustradition* (Göttingen: Vandenhoeck & Ruprecht, 1987), 209 nn.2, 3.

[37] Thus G. Beasley-Murray, F. F. Bruce, G. Kittel, W. Khmmel, B. Mitton, F. Mussner, and most recently R. P. Martin.

[38] *James: The Man and His Message*, pp. 22–23.

[39] Ibid., p. 37.

[40] Ibid., pp. 173–78.

Theories concerning the situation in which James was written are often closely related to authorship. An attempt to analyze the different positions has been made by Richard Prideaux in his work on James. What follows is a modified summary of his research[41]

1) James was originally a Jewish document. This thesis is found in three forms:
   a) James is a Jewish document with minor Christianization— the insertion of the name of Jesus in 1:1; 2:1[42]
   b) the Christian author in writing James made use of a Jewish document such as *The Testament of Jacob*[43]
   c) James is a Christian midrash on Jewish scripture such as Psalm 12:1–4.[44]

2) James was a very early Christian composition—
   a) the composition of pre-Pauline Galilean Christianity[45]
   b) the composition of James the Just and from the Jerusalem church.[46]

3) James was written in two stages. Theories that take this point of view seek to address the problem of Jewish material expressed in cultured Greek style and allow for authorship by James at the level of the first stage.[47]

4) James is a pseudonymous composition. This approach is expressed in a number of ways that are differentiated by the supposed place of composition: a) Palestine;[48] b) Alexandria;[49] c) Rome;[50] d) an undeter-

---

[41] See his unpublished M. A. thesis, "The Place of the Epistle of James in the Growth of the Primitive Church, La Trobe University, Melbourne, 1985, pp. 8–102.

[42] Thus L. Massebieau, "L'Epître de Jacques: est-elle l'oeuvre d'un chrétien?" *RHR* 32 (1895): 249–83, and F. Spitta, *Der Brief des Jacobus untersucht* (Göttingen: Vandenhoeck & Ruprecht, 1896). Massebieau and Spitta apparently independently reached similar conclusions about the same time.

[43] Thus A. Meyer, *Das Rätsel des Jacobusbriefes* (Giessen: Topelmann, 1930); H. Windisch, *Die Katholischen Briefe*, HNT 15 (Tübingen: J. C. B. Mohr [Paul Siebeck], 1951); and B. S. Easton, "The Epistle of James," *Interpreters Bible,* vol. 12 (New York Abingdon, 1957), 9–11.

[44] Thus M. Gertner, "Midrashim in the New Testament," *JSS* 7 (1962): 283–91.

[45] Thus L. E. Elliott-Binns, *Galilean Christianity* (London: SCM, 1956).

[46] Thus J. B. Mayor, *The Epistle of St James*, and Adamson, *James: The Man and His Message.*

[47] Thus W. L. Knox, "The Epistle of St James," *JTS* 46 (1945): 10–17; P. H. Davids, *Commentary on James*, NIGNTC (Grand Rapids: Eerdmans, 1982); and more recently, *James.*

[48] J. H. Ropes, *The Epistle of St James*, ICC (Edinburgh: T & T Clark, 1916).

[49] S. G. F. Brandon, *The Fall of Jerusalem and the Christian Church* (London: SPCK, 1957), 238–39.

[50] S. Laws, *A Commentary on the Epistle of James* (London: A & C Black, 1980). Laws argues for a Roman provenance because of the evidence of a connection between James and the *Shepherd of Hermas*, in which a Roman context is accepted. Laws thinks that the many examples of verbal similarity are enough to show that the author of *Hermas* knew and used James, and because James was a literary letter it was likely to be used first in its place of origin (p. 25). The major flaw with this argument is that most scholars consider that the similarities do not show that the writer of *Hermas* knew and used James, especially as similarities occur in conflicting ways.

mined place in the diaspora where a Hellenistic Christian community had developed out of a liberated diaspora Judaism.[51]

The view of James Hardy Ropes is that a post-Pauline, post-Jewish war author in Palestine, perhaps in Caesarea or Tiberias, has made use of Jewish devotional and Wisdom tradition in writing this letter. The author was in some isolation from other Christian groups and untouched by controversy over Jewish law. There is evidence, however, of encounter with a misunderstanding of the Pauline teaching in relation to justification by faith. Ropes has impressively gathered evidence within the epistle to show that it moves in a characteristically first-century-CE Jewish world of thought and for which *The Testament of the Twelve Patriarchs* is an important example of devotional literature. Ropes takes the absence of mention of such important early Christian teaching on the death of Jesus and the Holy Spirit to be instructive of the position of James. In Jewish Wisdom literature "Wisdom" had taken over the role of the Spirit of God. The absence of reference to such matters as idolatry, slavery, and lax moral standards is taken to be indicative of the context of James in a Jewish community.[52] Ropes's argument is impressive in showing both the Jewish and Hellenistic provenance of James. Location in Palestine, rather than some place in the diaspora, such as Alexandria or Rome, is also impressively argued. Jerusalem is ruled out because Ropes sees James as a post–Jewish war composition. This might be modified if a different kind of two-stage theory of composition were put forward. If the Jewish tradition postulated by Ropes actually came from James of Jerusalem then Ropes's theory is given an added dimension. The letter would then not be strictly pseudepigraphic and would provide some justification for the use of the name of James as its author.

Interestingly, although Ropes and Dibelius recognize in James a synthesis of Jewish and Greek characteristics, neither of them finds any reason for proposing a two-stage composition hypothesis. Of course neither of them relates James of Jerusalem to the Jewish elements, and it may be that it is this assumption that necessitates the development of such a hypothesis. If that is the case we need to look carefully at the evidence which leads us to associate James with the epistle. There is the self-identification of the author which, no one doubts, was intended to be understood as a reference to James of Jerusalem. But this proves nothing because it was the nature of pseudepigraphical works to create such literary fictions. What, then, suggests that more than the name of James has been taken up into this epistle?

---

[51] Thus Dibelius, who allows for a variation on a two-stage theory involving diaspora Judaism and Hellenistic Christianity but allows no connection with James, thus asserting the pseudonymous nature of the epistle.

[52] See Ropes, pp. 28–31, 33, 49.

Dibelius asserts that James stands in relation to "an early Christian development which did not directly derive from Paul." Nevertheless he rejects the
view that *James* is pre-Pauline because the author's "*remarks in 2.14ff are still
inconceivable unless Paul had previously set forth the slogan 'faith, not works.'* "[53] This
point will need to be discussed in more detail in order to address the question
of whether and in what sense James might be considered anti-Pauline. But it is
precisely at this point that we need to recognize, if not tradition from James
himself, then at least what a later writer supposed would have been appropriate
to James. Not only is the epistle inconceivable without Paul; it is in a tradition
that needed to respond to Paul and did so in a manner appropriate to the situation after the Jewish war. In what follows the case for a two-stage theory is
advocated in a way that takes account, in particular, of the positions of Ropes
and Dibelius.

Although he offers only an outline, a persuasive alternative to the standard
two-stage hypothesis has been put forward by R. P. Martin.[54] He suggests that
tradition from James reflecting Jerusalem in the 60s was subsequently carried by
refugees from Jerusalem to bilingual Antioch. He seems to have in mind a
situation subsequent to the Jewish war. In Antioch the tradition was edited to
make it relevant to the new situation. It is this situation that is thought of as
providing the second stage of the process of composition. Martin draws attention to a comment by Jerome to the effect that "James wrote a single epistle
and some claim that it was published by another under his name."[55] While this
might support a two-stage composition theory, it is more likely that Jerome was
indicating that the authenticity of the epistle was questioned by some who
suggested that the epistle was not written by James but, being published in his
name, was a pseudepigraphic work.

If we accept the viability of this two-stage theory, it remains unclear
whether the tradition now in the epistle was written down at all prior to its
publication in the present epistle. In what form was the tradition carried from
Jerusalem to Antioch? Even if we are dealing with a written tradition, the suggested process is quite different from that covered by the normal secretary hypothesis, because if we think of the final editor as the secretary he completed
his work after the death of the named author. Nevertheless this hypothesis has
the virtue of acknowledging that the economic critique of the epistle makes
sense in Judaea and Galilee before the Jewish war, while the Greek of the epistle
and the focus on the diaspora make better sense in a later situation in the diaspora.

Whether the letter was penned by James or, as is argued here, was inten-

---

[53] Dibelius, p. 179.
[54] Martin, pp. lxxii–lxxviii, cviii.
[55] Martin, p. lxxii, quoting *De vir. ill.*, 2.

tionally attributed to him, there are three important indications that the intention was to spread his views beyond Jerusalem. First, the letter was written in Greek, the language most suited to the wider dissemination of ideas. Consistent with this is the author of the epistle's undoubted use of the LXX as his bible.[56] Second, the letter is addressed to "the twelve tribes of the diaspora." Third, the letter uses a characteristically Greek greeting, χαίρειν. Helmut Köster rightly sees the epistle as evidence of the continuing tradition of the Jerusalem church in the Hellenistic world.[57] The letter should be seen as an expression of Jerusalem tradition, indeed originating from the powerful influence of James. In all probability this letter was issued some time after the Jewish war and after the dispersal of the Jerusalem church.

In writing a letter as if from James at least two important transformations had to be made to James's point of view. His concentration on Jerusalem was no longer possible. Hence the Petrine perspective on the circumcision mission to the diaspora became a stronger influence. This was inevitable. The mission, as understood by Peter, was concentrated on "the circumcision," that is, the Jews; but it also took in Gentiles if they would submit to circumcision and the requirements of the Mosaic law. With Peter the mission spread into the diaspora, to Corinth, and, it would seem likely, to Rome. Now, after the Jewish war, it became clearer than ever that any concentration on mission to the Gentiles jeopardized the mission to the Jews. Here the Jamesian perspective was reasserted and became the stance of Christian Judaism. Paradoxically, although this involved the transformation of Petrine tradition within Christian Judaism, the name Peter became synonymous with the mission of the Great Church and even the Gospel of Matthew was interpreted in these terms rather than as a document from the mission of the circumcision. The evidence suggests that the same fate befell the Epistle of James.

James is addressed to "the twelve tribes of the diaspora." The problem with this expression is that it is found nowhere else in the early Christian or contemporary Jewish literature, though aspects of the address are found in the LXX and early Christian literature. Reference to the "twelve tribes" is rare in the LXX but see Matt 19:28 = Luke 22:30; Acts 26:7; Rev 7:4–9; 21:12. For reference to the diaspora see James 1:1; 1 Peter 1:1; John 7:35; and the verb (διασπείρω) in Acts 8:1, 4; 11:19. The expression "the twelve tribes of the diaspora" has been broadly understood in three ways.[58]

---

[56] See Dibelius, p. 27.

[57] *Introduction to the New Testament, vol. 2* (New York: Walter de Gruyter, 1982), 157.

[58] Adamson, *James: The Man and His Message*, p. 11 n.64, lists five ways of understanding the reference. He distinguishes unconverted Jews from the Jewish nation, which we have included under 1); and Gentile Christians from the church as the new Israel, which we have included under 3). References to these three positions are given in nn. 59–63 below (see nn. 59–61 on position number one).

1) The reference may be to all Jews in the diaspora which, when the letter was written, might be thought to encompass all Jews. This is broadly the position of A. Meyer, who argues that the epistle was pseudonymously attributed to the patriarch Jacob and that the name "Jesus Christ" in 1:1 and 2:1 was inserted later in an attempt to Christianize a Jewish document.[59] J. B. Mayor proposes a more straightforward address to the Jewish nation.[60] Martin Dibelius correctly observes that diaspora "is a technical expression, and it is not really possible to interpret it as a reference to the situation of the Jewish people in general."[61] After the Jewish war, however, there was a growing tendency to perceive all Jews in diaspora, and, if the Epistle of James were to be dated after 135 CE, the case is even stronger for viewing this as an address to all Jews.

2) The reference may indicate all believing Jews in the diaspora.[62] At the time of the Jewish war the Jerusalem church was scattered, and the address might be considered to include all believing Jews.

3) The reference may be to all believers, Jews and Gentiles.[63]

The third approach, the so-called symbolic understanding of the twelve tribes, was probably adopted by the early church in recognizing the Epistle of James as apostolic and canonical, the first of the Catholic Epistles. Yet it presupposes a very late date of origin because there is no early evidence of the symbolic use of the twelve tribes of the diaspora.[64] Such an interpretation is unlikely; in fact, there is no indication that such an interpretation is in mind. Thus the epistle, like the mission of the historical James, was oriented toward the Jewish people. It is not possible to decide whether all Jews or only believing Jews are in view. Adamson argues: "James is addressing Jews in Jerusalem and throughout the Dispersion, converted and unconverted, at a time when Christianity was still simply a Jewish sect. . . . It is addressed to the Christian Jews of the Diaspora, and we suggest that here is evidence of their attitude to Christianity in the early Apostolic Age."[65]

Evidently for Adamson the question of audience, all Jews (including those of Jerusalem) or only Christian Jews of the diaspora, remained unresolved. Why Adamson should say that James was addressing "Jews of Jerusalem" as well as "throughout the Dispersion" is unjustified, given that the epistle is explicitly addressed to "the twelve tribes which are in the diaspora." No doubt Adamson's interpretation is driven by his view that James wrote while the Jerusalem church was the leading exemplar of Christian Judaism and would not have been over-

---

[59] See Meyer's *Das Rätsel des Jacobusbriefes*.

[60] *The Epistle of St. James*, p. cxliii.

[61] *James: A Commentary on the Epistle of James*, p. 66 n.15.

[62] Thus Martin, pp. 8–10.

[63] This is the position of Dibelius, pp. 20, 66–67.

[64] Thus correctly Adamson, *James: The Man and His Message*, p. 13.

[65] Ibid., pp. 29, 33.

looked by James. His interpretation is a subtle assertion of a pre-70 CE date, but, contrary to the explicit reference of the epistle itself, to a diaspora audience.

Certainly the author, from the beginning, openly states his commitment to Jesus. This need not mean that he has restricted the scope of his epistle to those who share his views. The letter is addressed to Jews, or Christian Jews, in the diaspora.

The epistle can be seen as a "quasi-encyclical" letter to Jews (or Christian Jews) just as the so-called Jerusalem decree can be seen as a "quasi-encyclical" letter from James (Acts 15:23–29) to Christian Gentiles. Adamson provides a summary analysis of the 230 words of Acts 15:23–29, making a comparison with the Epistle of James. He concludes that the affinities are too numerous and nuanced to be coincidental.[66] His conclusion is that both letters come from the hand of James the brother of Jesus. There are some problems with this view. 1) Some of his comparisons fall outside Acts 15:23–29, suggesting that the comparison is between the Epistle of James and Acts. 2) The letter is not said to be from James but from the apostles and elders (Acts 15:23).

Of course on the one hand it can be argued that James wrote on behalf of all. On the other hand it may be that the author of Acts is more responsible for the wording of this speech/letter than is the supposed author(s). Such a view opens an interesting possibility concerning the authorship of James. Could it be that the Epistle of James owes something of its present form to the author of Acts? Or is it more likely that the author of Acts has composed a speech for James in what he has supposed to be the idiom of James? To assert such is to take a step further than Adamson: "Luke may have composed the version of the speech James doubtless made on this occasion; but we think that the style is that of James himself; . . . we definitely see James of the Epistle of James. . . . We believe that Luke may have been like, e.g., Thucydides, who put speeches in the mouths of his generals and politicians, as he himself says: 'Keeping as far as possible the general tenor of what was actually said' (*Peloponnesian War*, Bk.1, sec. 22)."[67] But Adamson wishes to maintain that both in the substance and language of the speech in Acts "we definitely see *the* James of the Epistle of James."

Whether the author of Acts had a hand in the shaping of the Epistle of James or shaped the speech of James in what he supposed to be the idiom of James is a moot point. The latter seems to be the more likely; it allows scope for the introduction of Luke's own ideological point of view in the speech but fails to take account of the similarities with James that go beyond the letter from the "council." If we recognize that the Epistle of James is the subsequent editing of Jamesian tradition, perhaps from Antioch after the Jewish war, it is possi-

---

[66] Ibid., pp. 18, 19 n.111.
[67] Ibid., p. 23, including n.112.

ble to allow that both hypotheses can be accepted. Luke was responsible for James's speech in Acts and perhaps was the editor or final author of the Epistle of James.

While this hypothesis cannot be proved, it has some merit. Luke was capable of writing good Hellenistic Greek such as we find in James. The author of Acts did not, however, adopt the position of Christian Judaism, even if he shows a distinct sympathy for the Jerusalem church. Rather his position presupposes the mission to the nations without the demand of circumcision and submission to the law of Moses. While insisting on a certain continuity between Judaism and the church, part of which may be seen as a concession, if Luke is responsible for the fiction of the demands of the Jerusalem decree, Luke has no doubts about the centrality of the Gentile mission.

Consequently, what we suppose is that the final author of James was a person who, like Luke, spoke Greek as his first language. Nevertheless, like James, this author was committed to the continuing mission to the Jews. At the time of writing this issue had ceased to be controversial among continuing Christian Jews because they could see, as James had much earlier, that survival of a mission to the Jews was threatened by the Gentile mission. After the Jewish war this was more true than in the time of James. The crisis of the war, with the destruction of Jerusalem with the Temple, left the Jews struggling to find the marks of their identity as Jews. Although the experience of a long history of diaspora Judaism was helpful in this task, it was not by itself sufficient because it was no longer possible even to look to Jerusalem and the Temple, let alone travel there on pilgrimage to the festivals. Because of this sensitive situation Christian Jews concerned to maintain their own identity as Jews and to develop a mission to other Jews could not even consider developing a mission to the Gentiles.

The author of James was a Jew of the diaspora for whom Greek was his "mother tongue." This would explain how the epistle has come to be expressed in a way that is suggestive of paranesis and diatribe and makes use of the characteristic Greek greeting, χαίρειν. Dibelius stresses that the author of James "writes Greek as his mother tongue" and gives as evidence the way he employs rhetorical devices[68] and that the epistle is to be understood in terms of paranesis which makes use of elements of diatribe.[69] Here the Epistle of James is analyzed in terms of a series of sayings loosely strung together using such literary techniques as catchwords (Stichworte). This favorite device is observed in "1.4 and 5; 1.12 and 13; (1.15 and 16–18?); 1.26 and 27; 2.12 and 13; (3.11f and 13f?);

---

[68] *James: A Commentary on the Epistle of James*, p. 17, 34–38.

[69] Ibid., pp. 1–11. But Dibelius (p. 2 n.12) rejects the view that these elements of diatribe mean that the whole epistle can be understood as diatribe, as Ropes argued in *A Critical and Exegetical Commentary on the Epistle of James*.

3.17 and 18; 5.9 and 12; 5.13ff, 16ff and 19f " (p. 7). These catchwords depend on being written in Greek and are used so frequently that any notion that the epistle might have been composed originally in some other language is untenable. The author uses the Greek bible, which is consistent with the other evidence that the author was a native Greek speaker. According to the analysis of the epistle as paranesis, "the entire document lacks continuity in thought" (p. 2). "By paranesis we mean a text which strings together admonitions of a general ethical content. Paranetic sayings ordinarily address themselves to a specific (though perhaps fictional) audience" (p. 3).[70] "Suffice it to say that even those warnings and admonitions do not reveal a specific occasion for the letter and, consequently, do not disclose an actual epistolary situation" (p. 2).

While accepting the paranetic analysis, it is argued that there is significant thematic continuity and development in James. Contrary to Dibelius and in agreement with R. P. Martin[71] it is argued that the tradition in James is best understood against the background of the issue of poverty within the Jerusalem church before 66 CE. P. J. Hartin also argues against Dibelius's tendency "to see paranesis arising in isolation from the *Sitz im Leben* of the community."[72] What Dibelius asserted is a context in literary history. "Therefore, at least through the agency of Judaism, nascent Christian paranesis was subject to Greek and Hellenistic influence. In this respect Christianity is also the heir of a long literary development which—as one can observe in Judaism—leads from poetry to prose" (p. 4). The process is also described as one of "a pervasive *eclecticism* . . . [in] the transmission of an ethical tradition" in which the transmission is more important than any creative composition by the author (p. 5). "The absence of continuity, the scarcity of continuous trains of thought, distinguishes Jas even from diatribe. Therefore I cannot concur with Ropes . . . , who attempts to characterize Jas as diatribe. The presence of brief diatribes . . . and the occasional use of devices common in diatribe style do not make a text as a whole a diatribe" (p. 2 n.6). The analysis of Dibelius is consistent with the transmission of Christian Jewish tradition by a native Greek-speaking editor.

Hartin rightly acknowledges the contribution of Dibelius in correcting Ropes's emphasis on the direct Greek stylistic influence on the Epistle of James by asserting the importance of the Jewish paranetic tradition.[73] Hartin is at pains to set paranesis in the context of the Jewish Wisdom literature, thus extending in detail an aspect of the thesis put forward by Dibelius. But Hartin has not given sufficient attention to the second part of Dibelius's thesis: that the paranetic tradition of James was transmitted by a Greek-speaking editor.

---

[70] See Dibelius, pp. 26–34.
[71] *James*, pp. lxvii–lxviii.
[72] *James and the Q Sayings of Jesus*, p. 20.
[73] Ibid., p. 21. See Dibelius, p. 26.

Luke's own perspective was broader than that of James and the Christian Judaism of Jerusalem, and his editorial work would explain the way the distinctively Jewish emphases are played down in the epistle, although the language and content suggest, to the sensitive reader, that these emphases lie not far below the surface of what is written. In other words, distinctively Jewish emphases are expressed in ways that suggest points of contact with the Hellenistic world. The distinctive Jewish understanding remains a possibility for those with eyes to see. On the other hand, it may be that, at the level of the Greek transformation of the tradition of James, it was hoped that the letter, addressed by James to the twelve tribes in the diaspora, would be seen as a letter to the churches generally, even if that form of address was intended to maintain awareness of the role of the historical James in relation to Christian Judaism.

Historically we are faced with the question of whether James was himself concerned with the mission beyond Jerusalem and Judaea. The evidence concerning this matter is ambiguous. While Acts portrays James as leader of the Jerusalem church, there is more or less silence concerning his responsibility for mission beyond Jerusalem. There are hints of his concern in regard to the participation of the circumcision mission in situations with Gentiles (Gal 2:11–12). The *Apocryphon of James* 16.5–11 implies James's overall responsibility for mission in depicting him sending the other apostles to various destinations, although he himself remained in Jerusalem. A similar picture is given in the Pseudo-Clementines, although there is more stress on the mission. James directs the strategy from Jerusalem, while Peter is the chief exponent of mission beyond Jerusalem.

James was not directly involved in mission beyond Judaea and Galilee. The way he is made responsible for the direction of the mission through the other apostles, including Peter, is suggestive of later development. In contrast, Galatians supports the view that James was concerned about maintaining the rules of the circumcision mission in the regions beyond his own direct concern. If James was not directly involved in the wider mission, then the addressees in the epistle are part of the attempt to communicate the tradition of James to a wider audience. While it is likely that this was restricted to a Jewish audience initially, and that was what was intended, the transition of the tradition of James from Jerusalem to the diaspora proved to be the means by which the Epistle of James became a truly catholic epistle, an epistle for the whole church.

The Teaching of the Epistle of James

The epistle is written in good Hellenistic Greek, and many facets of it suggest an author of Greek background. Yet there is something essentially Jewish about its implied social setting and fundamental message. This begins with the distinctive understanding of God, which is related to essential elements of what might be called theodicy and the role of the righteous sufferer, and treats the question of faith and works. Here it is necessary to ask about the relationship of the message of the Epistle of James to both the teaching of Jesus and to the teaching of Paul. James also raises the question of the nature of true religion. Thus we cannot agree with Dibelius when he asserts that "Jas has no 'theology.' "[74]

Social Setting Reflected in Ethical Teaching in the Epistle of James

One of the aspects of James that offers some support for the view that the epistle has its context in Judaea and Galilee before the Jewish war is the focus on the exploitation of the poor by the rich. While this problem must have been perennial within the Roman Empire, the manner in which it is characterized in James seems to have relevance to "Palestine" before 66 CE. One complicating factor in making this judgment is the influence of the biblical tradition on James,[75] in particular the teaching of the prophets. Because of this influence it is not possible to be sure that the teaching is a consequence of the influence of the first-century context rather than the tradition of the great prophets, although it is most likely a consequence of the interaction of these two factors.

The poverty of the early Jerusalem church is well attested by Paul and the author of Acts. In Gal 2:10 Paul recalls that, in agreeing to a two-missions policy, James, Peter, and John had required "only that we should remember the poor." The poor of the Jerusalem church are in mind. The issue of poverty was significant enough for it to emerge in settling the two-missions policy. In Galatians Paul indicates that he and Barnabas, as leaders of the mission to the nations, are keen to "remember" the poor. Consequently we should be aware that Paul's preoccupation with "the collection" has this agenda in view. (See 2 Corinthians 8–9; Rom 15:22–29; Acts 11.29. The reason that poverty is a more than usually difficult problem might be signaled in Acts 2:44–45; 5.1–11.) In Jerusalem the believers experimented with an early form of "communism," that is, of giving up the private ownership of land and resources to provide resources for all. In a land-based economy such a policy was shortsighted, as it meant giving up the means of producing income. While resources were produced in the short term, this was a recipe for long-term poverty. The Jerusalem church might be forgiven for an error of judgment if they believed that the Lord would soon return, revolutionizing socioeconomic issues. The Epistle of James provides evidence of a firm belief in the imminent end of the age (James 5:9).

Josephus (*Ant.* 20.180–81) provides evidence of conflict between the aristocratic Sadducean high priestly party and the poorer priests, who sided with

---

[74] Dibelius, p. 21.
[75] See Adamson, *James: The Man and His Message,* pp. 230–39.

the disadvantaged peasants. This particular conflict began in 59 CE and led to the chief priests ordering that the tithes be withheld from the poorer priests. While the conflict can be analyzed in socioeconomic terms, characterizing it as a struggle between the aristocratic rich and the poor peasants, it can be viewed in other terms as well. The aristocratic rich were probably closely associated with the Sadducean chief priestly party, while the poor peasants and poorer priests identified more closely with the Pharisees. The former were closely associated with and supported by Roman power and can be seen as the establishment, while the latter harbored dissidents and even gave support to revolutionary groups.[76] Because the chief priestly party was supported by the Roman establishment, questions concerning the legitimacy of the high priestly succession were rampant, and this was obviously a factor leading to the dissent and separation from establishment Judaism of the Qumran sect.

According to Acts 6:7 many priests became obedient to the faith. Almost certainly they were recruited from the poorer priests. Thus when the author of James affirms the option for the poor it may be that he is not only following a prophetic precedent but also taking the side of the believing priests against the rich Sadducean chief priestly faction. According to Josephus, in the year 62 CE, when the Roman procurator (Festus) died, King Herod Agrippa took the opportunity to remove Joseph from the high priesthood and to put Ananus II in his place.[77] While the new procurator (Albinus) was en route, Ananus took the opportunity to convene the Sanhedrin to condemn and oversee the execution of a group that included James the brother of Jesus. The most likely scenario for this action is the conflict between the poorer priests with the high priestly party. Because Ananus was acting against a group with anti-Roman sentiments he might have hoped that he would have had the tacit support of the new procurator, although he had overstepped his own authority. If that were the case, in this instance he miscalculated the Roman concern for law and order, and his rash action led to his own replacement as high priest.

The Epistle of James has as its central concern a deep sympathy for the poor and persecuted (2:1–9; 5:1–6). It advocates the rights of widows and orphans (1:27) while offering a stern critique of the rich merchants (4:13–17) and rich farmers (5:1–6). This is perhaps the most sustained perspective in the book and seems to throw light on the historical context of the tradition in James. If we are right in suggesting that James threw in his support for the poorer priests we may well have gained some insight into the implications of Josephus's ac-

---

[76] See E. M. Smallwood, "High Priests and Politics in Roman Palestine," *JTS* ns 13 (1962): 14–34; Smallwood, *The Jews under Roman Rule: From Pompey to Diocletian: A Study in Political Relations* (Leiden: Brill, 1981), 272–92, 314; R. A. Horsley with J. S. Hanson, *Bandits, Prophets, and Messiahs* (Minneapolis: Winston, 1985), 61, 72.

[77] *Ant.* 20.197–203 and see Eusebius, *HE* 2.23.21–24.

count of the martyrdom of James. That Ananus selected James, among a group of otherwise unnamed victims, would make sense if these victims were perceived to be the leaders of the "recalcitrant" priests. If this hypothesis is correct, then Ananus might have expected to have had Roman support, even if he violated regulations concerning the constitution of a meeting of the Sanhedrin.

God in the Epistle of James

It is frequently noted that there is little in James of what might be called distinctive Christian theology. Without the two specific references to the lord Jesus Christ (1:1; 2:1) a reader might be forgiven for thinking that this was a Jewish rather than a Christian Jewish document, and A. Meyer regarded these references to Jesus as redactional additions to a Jewish document.[78] They are strangely incongruous with the rest of the letter. Reference to "the (our) lord Jesus Christ," not simply reference to Jesus as lord or Jesus as Christ, looks more like an ascription from Gentile Christianity than from early Christian Judaism. The epistle as a whole fits more happily with Christian Judaism than the sort of Christianity that seems to be promised by the opening ascription. The epistle as a whole is focused on God rather than on Jesus. But then James has identified himself as "a servant of God and the lord Jesus Christ." The teaching about God in James is drawn from the riches of the Jewish tradition, rooted in an understanding of creation which finds itself confronted by evil and suffering.

Richard Prideaux has summarized what Ropes has to say about the teaching of James and its relation to such Jewish works as *The Testament of the Twelve Patriarchs.*[79] What emerges is not only a very Jewish theology without distinctive Christian developments but also a remarkably complete theology for such a short document which is supposedly untheological and practical in orientation. An abbreviated form of this summary follows. James teaches:

1) belief in one God as creator of the universe and father of all people; who cares for all people; who is holy, the giver of good gifts, and the source of all goods; who gives wisdom; who is merciful, hears prayers and forgives sins;
2) belief in a coming judgment upon all people; the need to strictly obey God's law which is the basis for judgment and justification; the privilege of possessing God's law which can lead to salvation, eternal life, the inheritance of the kingdom of God;

[78] See Meyer, p. 123. Meyer was building on the earlier work of Massebieau in "L'Epître de Jacques: est–elle l'oeuvre d'un chrétien?," and of F. Spitta, "Der Brief Jacobus," in his *Zur Geschichte und Litteratur des Urchristentums*, II (Göttingen: Vandenhoeck & Ruprecht, 1896), 1–239, who had, independently, come to this conclusion.

[79] "The Place of the Epistle of James in the Growth of the Primitive Church," p. 56.

3) belief that sinful desires are the cause of human downfall; that death and future torment arise from unforgiven sin; that riches are a mark of the ungodly.

4) belief that God requires complete devotion and faithfulness in the face of trials that characterize the world which is opposed to God.

5) belief that true religion involves caring for the poor, sick, and needy, correcting those who err, treating all people with fairness, gentleness, peaceableness, self-control especially in relation to speech.

The key to James's understanding of God is found in 1:16–18. "Every good and every perfect gift is from above," that is, from God. The affirmation is rooted in the understanding of the goodness of the creation and thus, by implication, of the creator, who is described here as "the father of lights." While in Jewish thought God is understood to be the lord of all creation, his sovereign control over the heavenly lights was especially thought to manifest his power.[80] The idea is quite fundamental to Judaism, going back to the archetypal creation story of Genesis 1 in which God creates light by his all-powerful word, "Let there be light" (compare Ps 33:6, 9; 136 [135]:7). James extends the principle of creation to ongoing life in the world. God is the *giver* of every *good* and every perfect *gift*. James stresses the unchangeable, constant, goodness of God. James 1:17 asserts the constant goodness of God in contrast to the fleeting and changing light of the sun in its journey across the sky. God remains constantly good and only gifts of goodness come from him. The understanding of God as absolutely benevolent is suggestive of the later teaching of Origen. It is precisely this understanding of God that poses a problem in confronting all forms of evil.

Theodicy in the Epistle of James

The specific form in which evil is confronted is in "temptations" or "testings" (πειρασμοῖς 1:2, cf. 1:12). Part of the complexity of this discussion is that the same term is capable of these two quite different meanings. The idea of temptation implies attraction which arises from one's own desires, while "testing" implies hostile external circumstances. What connects these two apparently different issues is that either by attraction or by hostile forces the believer is under pressure to deviate from the will and purpose of God. It may even be that the author of James was not conscious of the clear-cut distinction our analysis has revealed. Certainly James has not dealt with "testing" in 1:2–8 and "temptation" in 1:12–16. Indeed, the reference to "a double-minded man" in 1:8 fits more appropriately in a discussion of temptation, although it cannot be said to be irrelevant to the theme of testing.

---

[80] See *Testament of Abraham* 7.6 and the ascription "the prince of lights" in *CD* 5.17–18; *I QS* 3.20.

The reference to "a double-minded man" has generated an interesting discussion concerning the milieu of the expression, which occurs only here and in 4:8, where it appears without "man." There is little merit in the suggestion that the expression is the manifestation of Essene psychology,[81] or that I QH 4.14 shows that what is in mind is a Hellenistic-Gnostic dualistic view of man as a combination of body and soul.[82] An excellent comparison of Hebrew thought with the Greek of James is found in rabbinic comment on Deut 26:16: "When you make your prayer to God, do not have two hearts, one for God and one for something else."[83] We need to allow for the transformation from an Hebraic setting, in which "heart" is the appropriate term, to a genuinely Greek way of thinking where we would expect to find "double-minded" using δίψυχος or some alternative. From this perspective it seems right to treat 1:2–8 and 1:12–16 as two aspects of the one theme, that testing is a form of temptation and temptation is a particular kind of test.

Even though James exhorts his readers to "Count it all joy whenever you fall into many and varied temptations," the notion that such temptations come from God as part of his purposeful creation is rejected. Rather, in James, gratitude in falling into temptation is a case of seeking to join in God's work of bringing good out of evil. Thus the testing of faith is the opportunity for the development of endurance, and in the process of testing those who lack are to ask God for what is needed, and God, who is positively good, gives freely and without recriminations.

James declares the person who endures in faith in the face of temptation to be blessed (1:12). The blessedness consists in that such a person is perceived as one who loves God and who will receive a crown of life. Again, this might appear to suggest that temptation is part of the strategy of God. This James explicitly denies, "Let no one who is tempted say, 'I am tempted by God', for God is not tempted by evil, nor does he tempt anyone." Not only does the author of James reject the notion that God is responsible for this testing; in addition no suggestion is made that the devil is the source of this testing. Rather he asserts that the source of testing comes from each one's own "desire" and that sin is the result of giving in to "desire" (ἐπιθυμία).

Here we have no reference to the two inclinations between which each person is called to choose, such as we know from the Qumran Texts and the rabbinic literature. Rather it would seem that "desire" is an essential part of the make-up of every person, and there is no mention of a balancing inclination to

---

[81] Thus W. I. Wolverton, "The Double-minded Man in the Light of Essene Psychology," *ATR* 38 (1956): 166–75.

[82] See O. J. F. Seitz, "Antecedents and Significance of the Term δίψυχος," *JBL* 66 (1947): 211–19; and "Afterthoughts on the Term 'Dipsychos'," *NTS* 4 (1958): 327–34.

[83] See *Taánit* 23b in H. L. Strack and P. Billerbeck, *Kommentar zum Neuen Testament aus Talmud und Midrasch*, vol. 3 (Munich: C. H. Beck), 751.

good. Such evil desire "lures" and "entices." The imagery is suggestive of the way the baited hook lures the fish so that the fish is dragged off. Thus there is a sense of entrapment, so that "desire" takes those who are enticed into situations in which they have no desire to be. Because "desire" is a feminine noun the lure may be thought of as the "allure" and seduction of the person. The close, though not exclusive, relationship of "desire" to sexual desire suggests this line of thought. The consequence of this liaison then is that "desire" conceives and brings forth sin, and sin, when it is fully grown, brings forth death. The closest parallel to this notion of "desire" is found in the Pauline understanding of "the flesh" (σάρξ). Here in James, as in Rom 7:17–23 and Gal 5:16–21, "desire" has the negative sense of an evil desire or lust.[84]

Given that desire is part of the human make-up, this seems to imply that God is responsible for the source of temptation and ultimately responsible for evil. Just how James can deny this is unclear, but deny it he does. Responsibility for sin does not belong to God but to the human person who gives in to desire. The reason for introducing teaching about desire is to assert the human responsibility for sin and to provide instruction on the way to overcome it. This defense of the goodness of God could be called the argument from human responsibility, which is not the same as "the free-will defense." Whether the human person subject to desire has free will in any meaningful sense is open to serious question, though it can be argued that the will subject to desire submits to the allure rather than being unwillingly overpowered. To enter such a discussion is, however, to become more philosophically inclined than James had any intention to be. His aim was to place the responsibility for sin firmly on the head of the sinner and in so doing to affirm the unwavering goodness of God.

The Righteous Sufferer and the Epistle of James

Given this scenario of testing and temptation, it must be expected that the righteous person will suffer (5:6), although it may come as a surprise to find that there is a righteous person.[85] Apparently, then, it is possible to resist the allure of desire, to resist temptation and through this process to be righteous. Endurance (ὑπομονήν [1:3] and ὑπομένει [1:12]) is necessary in the face of severe testing. Those who endure will suffer. Righteousness is a virtue of those who suffer in enduring testing. In this context James appeals to his readers to pray for one another that they may be healed because "the prayer of the righteous person [δικαίου] is strong, being powerfully effective" (5:16).

The righteous person is condemned and killed by the rich (5:6) and is

---

[84] See R. Jewett, *Paul's Anthropological Terms: A Study of Their Use in Conflict Settings* (Leiden: Brill, 1971), 114–16.

[85] On the theme of the righteous sufferer see especially K. T. Kleinknecht, *Der leidende Gerichtfertige*, WUNT 2/12 (Tübingen: J. C. B. Mohr [Paul Siebeck], 1984).

mentioned again in the context of sin and sickness (5:16). Thus, even though the righteous person is portrayed in a context of suffering, in relation to God, the prayer of such a person is seen to be powerfully effective. There is something of an anomaly in this position. If the prayer of the righteous person is so mightily effective, how is it that the righteous so often are portrayed as suffering at the hands of the rich and the wicked? This question calls for a treatment of the theme of the righteous sufferer in Jewish tradition.

The role of prayer in relation to the righteous sufferer is illustrated in the early Christian tradition of the martyrdom of James, transmitted by Hegesippus, and also in the accounts of the martyrdoms of Jesus and Stephen. In these three cases the martyrs Jesus, Stephen, and James are depicted as praying for their adversaries. This portrayal goes further than the tradition of nonresistance in the face of violence, which is part of the Jewish tradition of the righteous sufferer that has undoubtedly influenced the traditions about James. The brief outline that follows attempts to show the chronological development of the theme. As far as possible the most important documents for the theme are discussed in their probable order of composition.

Gen 6:9 depicts Noah as a righteous man, the original *Zaddik,* and Genesis Rabbah 30:7 portrays the primary role of the righteous man as providing a warning to others. Isaiah 53 positively combines the role of the righteous servant with suffering. The Psalms of the righteous sufferer deal with the motif in relation to both the individual and the righteous community. See for example Psalms 15; 24; 35. The prophets also provide a basis for associating the poor with the righteous, especially Amos in his critique of the rich "because they sell the righteous for silver and the needy for a pair of shoes; that trample the head of the poor into the dust of the earth, and turn aside the way of the afflicted" (Amos 2:6–7) Here Yahweh's prophet takes the side of the righteous poor, a tradition important for the Epistle of James.

Sirach 44–50 contains the praise of the ἔνδοξοι. It parades the famous men of the history of Israel before the eyes of the reader. What constitutes their glory is described more in terms of their righteousness than in suffering and death, and righteousness is understood in terms of law-keeping and piety. The Maccabaean crisis threatened the distinctiveness of Judaism, and the vision of 1 Maccabees is enshrined in the manifesto uttered by Mattathias to his sons (1 Mac 2:49–69).

> Arrogance now stands secure and gives judgment against us; these are days of calamity and raging fury. Now, my sons, be zealous for the law, and give your lives for the covenant made with your forefathers. If you keep in mind the deeds they did in their generations, great glory and everlasting fame will be yours. Did not Abraham prove faithful under trial, and so win credit as a righteous man?

The succession of the valiant righteous runs from Abraham to Daniel, whose story was recycled at the time of the Maccabaean revolt. But whereas the Daniel cycle was used to advocate a nonviolent resistance to the forces of evil, that is, the forces contrary to the law of God, thus maintaining righteousness, the manifesto of Mattathias was a call to arms of all zealous for the law, and Judas and his brothers and his father's supporters "carried on Israel's campaign with zeal." Of Judas it is written, "He enhanced his people's glory. Like a giant he put on his breastplate and girt himself with weapons of war. He waged many a campaign from a camp well guarded with the sword . . ." (3:1–9). When eventually Judas fell in battle "the people mourned him for many days, saying, 'How is our champion fallen, the savior of Israel!' " (9:21–22). In 2 Maccabees this militant tradition is given a new turn with Onias the priest as the model of the righteous sufferer who refuses to offer violent resistance (3:1; 4:30–38), but was nevertheless the protector of the people (4:1–2; 15:12).

In the Hellenistic period, while there was tension between Hebrew and Hellenistic values which led to increased emphasis on law-keeping as the mode of righteousness, there was also an increasing variety of expressions of righteousness. Naturally resistance to the corruption of hellenization is featured, but as we have seen, resistance takes two forms: violent resistance (Judas) and nonviolent resistance (Onias). The call for violent resistance offers its own solution. Nonviolent resistance accentuates the problem of the righteous sufferer, whose refusal to fight is an expression of faith in God. In 1 Enoch the problem of the suffering righteous is resolved in the affirmation of eschatological vindication. Another common development (in *Jubilees*) in the period is the universalization of righteousness by depicting virtue and piety in terms of universal morality. Wisdom is understood in terms of morality in Sirach.

The sectarian texts from Qumran provide a distinctive body of evidence. The Damascus document (*CD*), coming from the early first century BCE, features the righteous sufferer (columns 1, 4, 6, 12), but it is in the *Hymn Scroll* (*1 QH*) and the *Habakkuk Pesher* (*1 Q pHab*) that distinctive Qumran themes appear. The *Hymn Scroll* shows how the motif of the righteous sufferer is taken up in the portrayal of the Teacher of Righteousness.[86] Some of the hymns are apparently to be understood as autobiographical reflections from the life of the Teacher. But it is *1 Q pHab* that specifically deals with certain aspects of the life of the Teacher. In this work צדיק is used only of the Teacher.[87] What is featured is the crisis of the opposition of the Wicked Priest, probably also known as the Man of Lies, to the Teacher of Righteousness. The document predicts the overthrow of the wicked priest because he opposed the Teacher of Righteousness.[88]

---

[86] See *1 QH* 1.1–2, 19; 2.20–30, 32–39; 3.19–36; 4.5–5.4; 5.20–6.2.

[87] *1 Q pHab* 1.13; 5.10; 7.4; 8.3; 9.10; 11.5.

[88] See *1 Q pHab* 9.9–11 and *1 QH* 2.32.

Because the role of the righteous sufferer is concentrated on the Teacher of Righteousness it is not surprising to find a heightened awareness of eschatological fulfillment. The events described in the sectarian documents belong to the last time, in which the suffering of the righteous will be inevitable but vindication is assured when history has run its course. In that vindication it is unclear whether the sect expected the return of the Teacher or the appearance of new messianic figures, the prophet and the messiahs of Israel and Aaron.

The *Wisdom of Solomon* 10–11, like Sirach and 1 Maccabees, acclaims the heroes of Israel as models of virtue. There is, however, a tension in chapters 6–9 over the question of how the works of wisdom relate to the law. This is a manifestation of the influence of universalizing tendencies in the Wisdom tradition, which was committed to the position that the way of wisdom was both virtuous and, practically, the most "successful" way of living. While commending the way of wisdom, it was impossible to avoid the problem of the righteous sufferer, and this problem is featured in chapters 1–5. In 2.10–3.6 the "deluded" attitude of the wicked in relation to the "just" person is set out:

> For us let might be right! Weakness is proved to be good for nothing. Let us set a trap for the just man; he stands in our way, a check to us at every turn; . . . he says that the just die happy, and boasts that God is his father. Let us test the truth of his claim, let us see what will happen to him in the end; for if the just man is God's son, God will stretch out a hand to him and save him from the clutches of his enemies. . . .

The narrator continues:

> So they argued, and how wrong they were! Blinded by their own malevolence, they failed to understand God's hidden plan; they never expected that holiness of life would have its recompense, never thought that innocence would have its reward. But God created man imperishable, and made him the image of his own eternal self; it was the devil's spite that brought death into the world, and the experience of it is reserved for those who take his side.
>
> But the souls of the just are in God's hand; no torment will touch them. In the eyes of the foolish they seemed to be dead; their departure was reckoned as defeat, and their going from us as disaster. But they are at peace, for though in the sight of men they may suffer punishment, they have a sure hope of immortality; and after a little chastisement they will receive great blessings, because God has tested them and found them worthy to be his. He put them to the proof like gold in a crucible, and found them acceptable like an offering burnt whole on the altar. . . . They

will be judges and rulers over nations and peoples, and the Lord will be their King for ever. . . .

A number of interesting developments are clear in this passage. Death is attributed to the devil, and it is implied that all of the ills that befall people come from him. This view is modified by asserting that death is reserved for those who take the devil's side, while no torment can touch the just because they are in God's hand. The death of the just person is acknowledged by saying that "in the eyes of the foolish they seemed to be dead," but that position is modified by asserting the immortality of the just beyond death. The suffering of the just is not denied but it is minimized, being described as "a little chastisement." Beyond this the just are promised "great blessing." Thus the blessing outweighs the chastisement, making it negligible. Although the devil is made responsible for death, the sufferings of the just, viewed as chastisements, are attributed to God "who has tested them and found them worthy to be his." The *Wisdom of Solomon* takes a road rejected by the author of James, who makes no room for the devil in the temptation and suffering of the just and totally rejects the view that any one is tested or tempted by God. James, with its recognition of imminent judgment (5:9) acknowledges that the righteous who suffer in this life will be vindicated by God, though this theme is not treated explicitly. It is assumed in the treatment of the theme of the rich and the poor in which the Epistle of James takes the side of the poor.

In the book of Daniel, set in a "pagan" Babylonian context, the author has portrayed the challenge to Daniel's fidelity to the law. This theme is repeated in a Persian context in the book of Esther. The same themes are apparent in the *Additions to Daniel*. A variant on this theme is found in Judith. Here the sufferings of the people of Israel are attributed to testing by God, and it is stressed that the purpose and manner of the testing by God are inscrutable to the human mind (Judith 8:11–17). In all of these cases we have stories in which God extricates the righteous from the situation of testing. There is righteous suffering in keeping the law but also vindication in this life. The themes of wisdom and righteousness are here more nationalistic and cultic than universal and ethical.

Further important developments can be seen in 4 Maccabees. The nationalistic ideology of the Maccabaean tradition is maintained in the inseparable connection between righteous suffering and fidelity to the Jewish law. Indeed it seems that keeping the law inevitably involves suffering (6:22, 27, 30; 7:22; 9:6, 7, 29, 30; 11:2; 13:27, and so forth). In this context the older theme of the role of the righteous minority in relation to the nation reemerges.[89] Thus the

---

[89] See the role of the suffering servant in Isaiah 53.

question of the efficacy of vicarious suffering becomes important, and the theme is justified by precedents from the past, Abel (18:11); Joseph (2:2–3; 18:11), and Daniel and his three friends (16:21). The role of the righteous sufferer is now taken a step further so that it is interpreted in terms of the efficacy of the death of the martyr. Now it is asserted that the death of the martyr expiates the sins of the community.

In the Rabbinic literature Judas Maccabaeus is depicted as one of those whose existence prevented the destruction of the world (*Sanh.* 97a–b; *Suk.* 45b). In such a context we may understand the tradition, known to Eusebius (*HE* 3.7.7–9), about the presence of James preserving Jerusalem from destruction. According to logion 12 of the *Gospel of Thomas,* it was for the sake of James that heaven and earth were made.

A wide and rich tradition of the righteous person had developed in Jewish literature by the first century. Josephus treated every prominent Jewish figure as "righteous" (δίκαιος), but this portrayal is out of step with the tradition of the righteous sufferer, and perhaps led Josephus to develop a high view of martyrdom. In the case of the Epistle of James the traditions of righteous sufferer and martyr are combined in a way that owes something to the Christian Jewish tradition. The teaching that righteousness is the way of wisdom, which is rooted in the recognition that, in God's creation, wisdom is in harmony with the creation, that therefore righteousness "pays off," is modified by the recognition of the righteous sufferer. The way this theme is handled depends on context; whether there is an aggressive suppression of the Jewish law or a more general oppression of the poor by the rich, of the weak by the powerful, of the righteous by the wicked. In such contexts the righteous can appear as the heroes of the faith raised up to overthrow the wicked or as those who suffer and will be vindicated beyond death.

This tradition sheds light on the Epistle of James, which recognizes that the believer faces adversity (1:12) just as the succession of righteous people—the prophets (5:10), Job and Elijah (5:17)—had in the past. The case of the righteous man in 5:6 is very likely intended to be understood as an autobiographical statement by the author. This suggestion gains force if the epistle gathers together tradition originating with James the Just, presenting it in a way relevant to a new and later situation. In other words, the reference of James 5:6, "You have condemned and murdered the righteous one, who offers no resistance," would be understood in relation to the martyrdom of James the Just if the epistle appeared subsequent to that event, as we have suggested. The righteous sufferer is now understood as the martyr, and the fate of James as depicted in the early Christian tradition is closely associated with traditions such as those in the *Wisdom of Solomon* 2.10–3.6. Eschatological vindication is also the hope of James (5.7–9).

True Religion in the Epistle of James

James's presentation of religion is nearer to Matthew than to the other Gospels. Attention is often drawn to the literary relationship between Matthew, especially the Sermon on the Mount, and James. James 1:26–27 provides an important insight into the epistle's teaching about religion.

> If anyone thinks that he is religious and does not bridle his tongue, he is deceiving himself; this person's religion is vain. Pure and faultless religion before God the father is this: to look after the orphans and widows in their tribulations and to keep himself unspotted by the world.

Religion (θρησκεία) is normally understood in terms of cultic obligations, but James has a prophetic interpretation. There is no doubt that there is a burning ethical concern in the Epistle of James. Control of the tongue is featured, and, with that, traditional, in prophetic terms, concern for the weakest and most unprotected members of society, widows and orphans. Both of these groups were without traditional protectors, husbands and parents. Thus here, as elsewhere, James affirms that God is on the side of the poor. Nevertheless James is also concerned with purity, "to keep himself unspotted from the world."

The Epistle of James and the Jesus Tradition

Dibelius is of the view that such parallels with the Gospels as have been noted show only James's familiarity with the Jesus tradition rather than any knowledge of the Gospels themselves.[90] James is to be compared therefore with the collections of the Jesus tradition that we have come to know as Q and M. Ropes argues that "James was in religious ideas nearer to the men who collected the sayings of Jesus than to the authors of the Gospels."[91] Thus, while James has drawn on the Jewish Wisdom tradition, including the tradition of the righteous sufferer, the Jesus tradition, especially as drawn together in what is now Matthew's Sermon on the Mount (Matt 5–7), has made a manifest impact on the Epistle of James.

As suggested above, James's presentation of religion is nearer to Matthew than to the other Gospels.[92] Adamson has interpreted this point of contact in terms of an understanding of the true fulfillment of the law (see above, pp. 90–95, for treatment of the law in Matthew). He also draws attention to vocabulary and content links between Matthew and James:

---

[90] Dibelius, pp. 28–29.

[91] Ropes, *A Critical and Exegetical Commentary on the Epistle of James*, p. 39.

[92] Adamson, *James: The Man and His Message*, p. 188.

	James	Matthew
"perfect"	1:4	5:48; 19:21
"righteousness"	1:20; 3:18	3:15; 5:6, 10, 20; 6:1, 33; 21:32
beatitudes on the poor	2:5	5:3
the merciful	2:13–14	5:7
ambitious teachers	3:1	23:8
the peacemakers	3:18	5:9
anxiety for tomorrow	4:13–14	6:34
"church"	5:7	16:18; 18:17
"parousia"	5:7	24:3, 27, 37, 39
"oaths"	5:12	5:33–37

Adamson goes on to insist that such similarities need to be carefully evaluated. James is hostile to riches, while Matthew is more conciliatory. Matthew is hostile to Judaism, while James promotes a form of Christianity uncritical of and firmly grafted onto Judaism. Thus James has a conciliatory attitude to Judaism.[93] From this evidence it appears to be right to conclude that James and Matthew independently use something like the same tradition but in different situations.

R. P. Martin also sees a relationship between James and the tradition found in Matthew, drawing attention to twenty-three allusions, while P. J. Hartin concentrates on James's relation to Q.[94]

	James	Matthew	Source and Luke
1. Joy in trial	1:2	5:11–12	Q (Luke 6:22–23)
2. Call to perfection	1:45:48	M	
3. Asking and being given	1:5, 17; 4:2–3	7:7, 11,7–8	Q (Luke 11:9, 13, 9–10)
4. Faith and doubting	1:6		Mark 11:23
5. Enduring and being saved	1:12	24:13	Mark 13:13 (Luke 21:19)
6. Against anger	1:20	5:22	M
7. Doers of the word	1:22–23	7:24, 26	Q (Luke 6:46–47, 49)
8. Blessing of the poor	2:5	5:3, 5; [11:5]	Q (Luke 6:20; [7:22])
9. Warning against the rich	2:6–7	19:23–24	Q(Luke 19:24)

continued on next page

---

[93] Ibid., pp. 189–90.

[94] The following table is based on the list given by R. P. Martin (pp. lxxiv–lxxvi), combined with another from P. J. Hartin (pp. 141–42), who notes twenty-six points of contact between James and the Synoptics, mainly Q in the form represented by Matthew.

	James	Matthew	Source and Luke
10. Law of love	2:8	22:39–40	Mark 12:38–44 (Luke 10:27)
11. To work sin (lawlessness)	2:9	7:23	Q (Luke 13:27)
12. Royal law of love of neighbor	2:10–12	22:36–40	Q (Luke 10:25–28)
13. Obligation to keep whole law	2:10	5:17–19	M Q (Luke 16:17)
14. Do not kill . . .	2:11	5:21–30	M
15. The merciless will be judged	2:13	5:7; 6:14–15; 7:1	M Q (Luke 6:36)
16. Against lip service	2:14–16	7:21–23	M
17. Help to the poor	2:15–16	25:34–35	M
18. Fruit of good works	3:12	7:16–18	Q (Luke 6:43–44)
19. In praise of meekness	3:13; contrast 4:6, 16	5:3, 5	M
20. Meek . . . peacemaking	3:17–18	5:5, 9	M
21. Against divided loyalty	4:4	6:24	Q (Luke 16:13)
		12:39	Q (Luke 11:29)
22. Pure in heart	4:8	5:8	M
23. Mourn and weep	4:9		L (Luke 6:25)
24. Humility and exaltation	4:10	18:4; 23:12	Q? (Luke 14:11; 18:14)
25. Against slander	4:11	5:22; 7:1–2	M Q (Luke 6:37–38)
26. Weep	5:1		L (Luke 6:24–25)
27. Against hoarding	5:2–3	6:19–21	Q (Luke 12:33–34)
28. Do not condemn	5:6	(7:1)	Q (6:37)
29. Eschatological imminence	5:9	24:33	Mark 13:29 (Luke 21:31)
30. Example of the prophets	5:10	5:11–12	Q (Luke 6:23)
31. Prohibition of oaths	5:12	5:33–37	M
32. Elijah as example	5:17		L (Luke 4:25)
33. Relation to sinful brother	5:19–20	18:15	Q? (Luke 17:3)

The parallels are more than interesting, and some are closer than others. Nothing compels acceptance that James knew and used Matthew. Rather the allusions to common themes and motifs—it is often no more than this—show that Matthew and James are independently working out of a common pool of tradition that can be identified as Wisdom tradition and Jesus tradition, perhaps Q, and Hartin thinks that James is likely to have some contact with Q in the form in which it was used in Matthew.[95] Importantly, when dealing with Q, Hartin quotes J. P. Meier who asserts that "M was the living sea of oral tradition in which Mark and Q floated and were steeped."[96] Hartin continues: "M would exert an influence upon Mark and Q before Matthew began the writing of his Gospel. I have argued consistently that the Q source, once accepted into the Matthean community, underwent a development through the incorporation of other Q sayings as well as the insertion of the M material. This was evident in the development of the Sermon on the Mount and, in particular, in the growth of the Beatitudes. Ultimately a written form of Q, which we term Q^{Mt}, emerged within the Matthean community and was used by Matthew in the construction of his Gospel."[97] This is the form of Q (Q^{Mt}) that Hartin thinks influenced James, Q floating on and saturated by the living sea of M. While Hartin thinks of M as the living sea of oral tradition in the Matthean community, I am more inclined to accept a modified form of Streeter's position. The core of M is tradition emanating from James that may well have attained written form after the death of James. Whether written or oral, this body of tradition, more than any other, shaped the ideological position of Matthew. This means that the orientation of Matthew is determined to a large extent by M, even when Q material is being used. Q brought to Matthew an openness to mission to the Gentiles, which was accepted on terms appropriate to the ideology of M. Thus, in the words of I. Havener: "for a Gentile convert to become a member of the Q community probably meant, in effect, a Christian Jew, following the Jewish law and customs like the rest of the community. It is precisely this kind of Gentile mission that Paul was adamantly opposed to but one which the Q community could hardly have conceived in any other way."[98] While Havener has expressed this in terms of the Q community, I take it to be true of the Q^{Mt}. In all probability both Q and M emanated from the Jerusalem church. M may well emanate from James, while it is likely that Q is a Petrine tradition.

Relating this understanding of the composition of Matthew to the Epistle of James draws attention to the relation of the epistle to what Hartin designates

---

[95] Hartin, pp. 214, 233, 240, 243.

[96] *Antioch and Rome*, p. 55.

[97] Hartin, p. 233.

[98] I. Havener, *Q: The Sayings of Jesus: With a Reconstruction of Q by Athanasius Polag* (Wilmington, Del.: Michael Glazier, 1987), 103.

Q^{Mt}. Recognition of the influence of M on the formation of Q^{Mt} reveals the influence of James of Jerusalem in this process. Thus it is argued that, although the epistle emanates from James, it is not directly from him but, like Q^{Mt}, reflects a later situation and the influence of the more moderate tradition of Peter. Here "moderate" signals commitment to a Gentile mission. This was not true of James of Jerusalem or of the epistle known by his name, which reflects his burning ethical concern for the poor even though it is directed to the twelve tribes in the diaspora, to an exclusively Jewish audience.

Martin sets out the common viewpoints on key matters shared by James, Matthew, and the *Didache*.[99] The purpose is not to show direct literary dependence among any of the documents but to confirm the Antiochene locale of James. Reference should be made to B. H. Streeter's *The Primitive Church*, chapter 5. Streeter's contribution has been discussed concerning the relationship of the Gospels to each other, not only in literary terms but also in relation to factional struggles in the church and the relevance of geographical locale to these struggles. The identification of Antioch as the origin of James may be correct. That does not mean that Paul was embarrassed and defeated there, leaving the field open for James. Rather the influence of the Epistle of James in Antioch must be located at the time of or after the Jewish war. Refugees belonging to the Jerusalem church fled to Antioch, bringing with them tradition from James now embodied in the epistle and directed, by an editor, to the twelve tribes of the dispersion. In this way the tradition of James was broadened both in content and perspective. One important influence in this broadening was tradition coming from Peter.

The conflict in Jerusalem between the poorer priests and the rich aristocratic chief priests was representative of a more general socioeconomic problem in which masses of powerless poor were exploited by a rich and powerful minority. That this conflict should have given a focus to the Jamesian tradition is to be expected, especially as James's intervention in it contributed to the situation that led to his martyrdom. Then the martyrdom tradition has been influenced by the tradition of the righteous sufferer, in which an identification has been made between the poor and the righteous. Finally, after the Jewish war, the tradition was gathered together and addressed to the twelve tribes in the diaspora at a time when Formative Judaism[100] was working out a new interpretation of Jewish identity. In this context, general ethical concerns were overshadowed by the need to focus on those things that were distinctive and marked out Jewish identity. Thus there was a need to emphasize the essential nature of

---

[99] Martin, pp. lxxiv–lxxvii.

[100] On the use of this term to describe that phase of Judaism in which a new Jewish identity was shaped on a design formulated for survival in the diaspora in the Roman Empire, see Jacob Neusner, "The Formation of Rabbinic Judaism: Yavneh from AD 70–100," *ANRW* II.19.2, pp. 3–42.

such ethical issues as the exploitation of the poor. There is, however, no sign in the Epistle of James to indicate any relaxation of the Jewish law. Thus there is no reason to think that circumcision and the food laws were abandoned by those who were responsible for the reformulation of the James tradition in the epistle or by those to whom it was addressed.

James and Paul

Because from Acts and the letters of Paul we know of a degree of conflict between Paul and James, it is natural that, once the Epistle of James was identified with James the brother of Jesus, evidence of that conflict should be sought in the epistle.[101] We now need to assess whether the evidence actually justifies the identification of the conflict in the epistle. The situation is complicated by two opposed inclinations. There is an inclination toward a dismissive attitude in relation to James, particularly since the time of Luther, who wrote: "Therefore St. James' epistle is really an epistle of straw, compared to these others, for it has nothing of the nature of the gospel about it."[102] Many who have noted these critical remarks have gone further than Luther, who retained James in his New Testament. His remarks about James were comparative, in relation to certain other works ("these works"), which he named as "St. John's Gospel and first epistle" and Paul's letters to the Romans, Galatians, and Ephesians, as well as 1 Peter. This interpretation is consistent with other remarks Luther makes about James. Certainly the focus in James on the law rather than on the gospel did not commend itself to Luther, even though he saw this as a strategy to deal with those who relied on faith without works. "In a word, he [James] wanted to guard against those who relied on faith without works, but was unequal to the task. He tries to accomplish by harping on the law what the apostles accomplish by stimulating people to love. Therefore I cannot include him among the chief books, though I would not prevent anyone from including or extolling him as he pleases, for there are otherwise many good sayings in him."[103] Luther's critical attitude toward James has left its mark on critical scholarship.

Alternatively, a tendency to view scripture uniformly, harmonizing conflicting positions, characterizes some other scholars. Although James B. Adamson's work is careful and helpful, there is a predisposition to reconcile apparently different positions without first exploring the significance of the differences. For example, while recognizing that they worked in different situa-

---

[101] See especially the commentary by Dibelius, pp. 151–80; Martin, pp. 75–101; and Adamson, *James: The Man and His Message*, pp. 195–227.

[102] Preface to the New Testament of 1552, *Word and Sacrament* I, vol. 35 of *Luther's Works,* ed. E. T. Bachmann (Philadelphia: Muhlenberg Press, 1960), 362.

[103] Ibid., p. 397.

tions and circumstances, he says "Paul and James, each in the best way possible, were working for the same gospel and the same Christ."[104] We are dealing with an emotive issue, with scholars on one side likely to be denigrated as "Lutheran" and those on the other regarded as "uncritical." This situation makes more difficult the task of providing a careful and nuanced understanding of the relation of the Epistle of James to the thought of Paul as expressed in his epistles.

The crucial passage for discussion is in James 2:14–26. Here James seeks to set out his understanding of the appropriate relationship between faith and works. There is no attempt to deny the importance of faith. What is denied is that a person is justified by faith alone (ἐκ πίστεως μόνον, 2:24). This terminology is significant. We must suppose that James would not deny this position unless it was affirmed, at least by someone. Further, this denial comes at the end of the first and longer of two illustrations of the principle of justification by works. The second concerns Rahab, but the first and more important of the two is introduced by the words,

> Will you not learn, you foolish person, that faith apart from works is useless? Was not Abraham our father justified by works when he offered Isaac his son on the altar? You see that faith was working with his works and from his works faith was completed, and the scripture was fulfilled which says, "Abraham believed God, and it was reckoned to him for righteousness" and he was called a friend of God. See that from works a person is justified and not from faith alone. (2:20–24)

Two points of focus in this passage are diametrically opposed to the teaching of Paul, at least in the words in which they are formulated. First, James has asserted that Abraham was justified by works and has quoted Gen 15:6 to make his point. Second, on the basis of this illustration the principle of justification by works is asserted against the position of justification by faith alone.

In Rom 4:2 Paul rhetorically asserts that Abraham was not justified by works:

> For if Abraham was justified by works, he has a basis upon which to boast, but not in relation to God.

He continues by quoting Gen 15:6 to the effect that "Abraham believed God and it was reckoned to him for righteousness." The whole of the chapter is developed by Paul to show that Abraham was justified as a consequence of his belief and not on the basis of his works. In Rom 4:6 Paul summarizes the teaching of Ps 32:1–2, which he attributes to David.

---

[104] *James: The Man and His Message*, p. 195, and see pp. 195–227.

> Even as also David speaks of the blessedness of the man to whom God reckons righteousness apart from works [χωρὶς ἔργων].

Here Paul teaches justification by believing (faith) apart from works. In the development of the theme, the focus turns to the situation in which this occurred, and it is important for Paul to show that Abraham was reckoned righteous while he was uncircumcised. The reason for this is that, in Paul's time, the demand for circumcision had become the symbolic marker for Jewish identity expressed in the demand to keep the whole of the Mosaic law (see Acts 15:1, 5).

James, in contrast, also in rhetorical mode asserts that Abraham was justified by works! The question "Was not Abraham our father justified by works?" implies the answer "Yes!" as is clear from the use of οὐκ in the formulation of the question. James then goes on to quote Gen 15:6 to make his point, quoting the text in exactly the same words as Paul did in Rom 4:3. Paul twice quotes the same text in a more fragmentary way later in the argument (Rom 4:9, 22) and again in Gal 3:6. Obviously both authors are making use of the LXX. James's choice of text is peculiar because it says, "Abraham *believed* God and it was reckoned to him for righteousness." Yet James concludes, "See then that a person is justified by works and not by faith alone." In Romans Paul, having quoted from Gen 15:6, continues: "To the one who works the payment is not reckoned as a gift but as a debt. . . ." It seems that James's use of Gen 15:6 to show that Abraham was justified by works is directly opposed to the language of the teaching as formulated by Paul.

Two lines of approach unsuccessfully attempt to deflect this conclusion. The first argues that in Rom 4:2, 6, although Paul has written that Abraham was reckoned righteous apart from works, he really meant "works of the law."[105] But this is to miss the point, as Rom 4:4 shows. It is not that Paul devalues works. He asserts that a person is not *justified* by works, works of the law or any other kind of works that build up credit as a basis for standing before God. Paul does not use the term "justified" in Romans 4. Because of the influence of the wording of Gen 15:6 he uses the terms "reckoned" and "righteousness." The language of justification is not far away, however. We find it in Rom 3:28—"For we maintain a person to be justified by faith apart from the works of the law"—and in Rom 5:1: "Therefore, being justified by faith. . . ."

Why has James 2:21 used the language of justification (ἐδικαιώθη)? It is not in the text of Genesis, quoted to prove that Abraham was justified by works.

---

[105] Thus J. A. Fitzmyer, "The Biblical Basis of Justification by Faith: Comments on the Essay by Professor Reumann," in *Righteousness in the New Testament*, by J. Reumann, J. A. Fitzmyer, and J. D. Quinn (Philadelphia: Fortress, 1982), 220.

What is more, James 2:18 is concerned to refute the validity of faith apart from works (τὴν πίστιν σου χωρὶς τῶν ἔργων; compare Rom 4:6 and 3:28). An attempt is being made to refute what is understood to be the Pauline teaching of justification by faith alone, which is James's way of summing up the Pauline teaching in an attempt to refute it. That is not to suggest that the author of James had read and understood Romans.

A pervasive tradition of Jewish teaching focused on Abraham as an example of the faithful Jew.[106] His story provided excellent examples of obedience under all sorts of constraints. Abraham provided evidence of one who acted faithfully, who obeyed God. But James chose to quote Gen 15:6 in a similar context to that used by Paul and to prove exactly the opposite, at least in linguistic terms, to the conclusion Paul sought to establish. On face value, the text quoted supports Paul's position. Why did the author of James use this text, especially when it was the offering of Isaac (Gen 22:9, 12) that provided the evidence he wanted? James was responding to a use of Gen 15:6 that asserted that Abraham was justified by faith. Consequently he used the same text but tapped into the characteristic Jewish teaching about the faithfulness of Abraham as the archetypical Jew. It was precisely this tradition, that was known to Paul, that led Paul to use the primary example of Jewish piety to demonstrate his distinctive teaching of justification by faith apart from works, and he found, almost made to order, the text of Gen 15:6. All that was missing was Paul's precise and characteristic terminology, in place of "faith," "believed"; and in place of "justified," "reckoned . . . for righteousness."

James's answer (in 2:14–17) to the Pauline teaching of justification by faith alone, as he perceived it, was to respond in terms of a hypothetical person. Such a person says that he has faith but has no works. James asks, "Surely faith is not able to save him is it?" This question, introduced by μὴ, implies a negative answer. No! Faith cannot save him. Apparently faith without works is equated with words without actions, to say to the naked and starving brother or sister, "Go in peace, be warmed, and filled," but to do nothing effective. Such faith is worthless. Faith without works is dead. Of course this critique is very wide of the mark if it is aimed at Paul's teaching. That is not the point. Rather it is clear that the critique is aimed at what is perceived to be that teaching. The beginnings of the critique may come from a time contemporary with Paul, but the formulation in this letter reflects a time long after Paul and the context of continuing Christian Judaism.

The critique continues (2:18–26) with another hypothetical person (2:18; see 2:14). As in 2:14 we would expect to find the position of the opponent. "But someone will say, 'You have faith and I have works; show me your faith apart from works and from my works I will show you my faith.' " This, how-

---

[106] See especially the excursus "The Abraham Example" in Dibelius, pp.168–74.

ever, appears to be the position advocated by James. The point of the argument was then made by using the case of the offering of Isaac by Abraham to show that faith was operative in his works (James 2:22). The quotation of Gen 15:6 appears to be intended to lead logically to the conclusion that a person is justified by works and not by faith alone (2:24), that as the body without the spirit is dead, so faith apart from works is dead (2:26).

Certainly Paul would have agreed that faith was active in the performance of good works. So far Paul was in agreement with the Jewish tradition concerning faithful Abraham. Where he parts company radically with James is in the assumption that a person is justified by the works performed, however those works are understood. Paul also rejected the notion that faith is a justifying work. Rather faith in Paul is essentially the recognition of God as the one who justifies the ungodly and the grateful acceptance of that justification freely given. Works involve payment, justification is the gift of grace, freely given to those who have no grounds to deserve this (Rom 4:4). Thus, while Paul and James are not as far apart as the author of James supposed, they have radically different understandings of justification.

JUST JAMES

Our journey with James is almost at an end. Unfortunately the story ends with just James. All the promise that first surrounded the figure of the one who, from the beginning of the story of the church in Jerusalem, was known as "the brother of the Lord," failed to be realized. The first of a series of reasons for this is that the mother church of Christendom, the Jerusalem church, suffered the fate of the city, and its members either dispersed before the war or were decimated with the city. Either way, there was a significant break in the history of that church, and it seems likely that it never again attained the leading role which it had played prior to the war. While this may be true, Eusebius gives a list of the bishops of Jerusalem that suggests a continuous history down to the second revolt and destruction at the beginning of the second third of the second century. While not attaining the heights of the earlier church of Jerusalem, according to Eusebius's account Jerusalem did retain a leading role.

What followed was a transformation in Jerusalem from a Jewish to a Gentile church. Even in this context, according to Eusebius, James and his throne were honored. Nevertheless, this historical process diminished the awareness of both the role of James and the significance of his role in the life of the earliest church. That diminution was reinforced by the scriptures adopted by the church; references to James were few, and even in these the significance of his role was obscured. One reason for this lack of emphasis is that the documents that became the New Testament expressed the position of those who advocated interpreting the mission of Jesus in terms of a mission to the whole world, to the nations, the Gentiles. Not surprisingly, what emerged was a Gentile church in which the roots connecting it to Judaism were precariously attached. Even those roots were subject to a point of view that, when read from a non-Jewish perspective, could be seen as anti-Jewish. Criticism which should have been understood in terms of a family quarrel between siblings, Formative Judaism and the nascent Christian church, came to be seen as the stuff of a war between two incompatible religions.

The route traversed by the church would have been different had the way of James prevailed. James's approach, restricting mission to Jews in Palestine, was consistent with the practice of Jesus, who did not go outside "Israel" and for whom contact with Gentiles was exceptional. James's way did not prevail because of the fate of the Jerusalem church. His way was concerned with maintaining the mission to fellow Jews, especially Jews in Jerusalem. Had the way of James prevailed it is unlikely that Christianity would have emerged as a religion separate from Judaism. Rather James looked to winning Jews to faith in Jesus the Messiah, who was to come again in judgment. This understanding of the position of James is supported by the account in Acts and the letters of Paul, as well as by the evidence of Hegesippus and the Pseudo-Clementines.

What prevented James's influence from spreading more widely was the unintended consequence of another development. The Gospels of Matthew and Luke proclaim that Jesus was conceived by Mary while she was a virgin. For both Gospels the story of Jesus' conception was understood to be a sign of his messiahship. Neither of those Gospels seems to envisage a continuing role for Mary as a virgin, and it is natural to read the Gospels, Matthew and Luke included, as referring to the brothers and sisters of Jesus as if they were children born later to Joseph and Mary. The virginity of Mary was a more powerful symbol than either Matthew or Luke envisaged. Thus there emerged the vision of the perpetual virginity of Mary, so that, predominantly in the East, the brothers and sisters of Jesus were understood to be children of Joseph by a marriage prior to his "relationship" with Mary, who remained a perpetual virgin. In the West Jerome went further, affirming that the so-called brothers and sisters were actually cousins, so that the virginity of both Mary and Joseph was preserved. The consequence of this teaching was to diminish the significance of the relationship of James to Jesus, and it became customary to refer to James as "James the less," the son of Zebedee being the greater James.

What became an increasingly dismissive attitude to James is now linked to the fact that no contemporary tradition looks back to him as a foundation figure, as is the case with Peter and Paul and, to a lesser extent, Thomas. One of the most difficult problems to be dealt with by a contemporary historian, in search of the role and significance of James, is the bias of the modern reader. The task has been complicated by the fact that the earliest sources contain few references to James. Martin Hengel has described this situation as one-sided and tendentious. His judgment is strongly supported by the present study. That is to say, James is unjustifiably ignored in the New Testament sources.

From the earliest sources, dismissive though they may be, it is clear that attempts to remove James from the closest of family relationships to Jesus are unjustified. There Jesus and James are shown to be brothers, even if the birth stories of Matthew and Luke suggest that they are half-brothers, sharing only a common mother. The tradition, beginning with Jerome, that makes them cousins is without historical credibility, and the alternative that James was the child of Joseph by a marriage prior to his marriage to Mary does not have much more in its favor.

The treatment of James in the New Testament is already one-sided and tendentious. In the early centuries we find tradition that corrects this bias and tradition that extends it. In the long run the tradition that extended the bias triumphed, and the modern reader interprets the evidence of the New Testament from this point of view. Attention needs to be given to tradition that corrects this bias. A beginning has been made by reinstating James as the brother of Jesus. A further step can be taken by attending to the traditions in which James looms large, as the first bishop of Jerusalem and leader of the church, including the apostles. We may then ask how the New Testament evidence reads in the light of these traditions.

The negative view of the family of Jesus during the ministry of Jesus is unjustified. This conclusion becomes secure when we separate tradition from the redactional views that, in the case of Mark and John, show some negative attitudes to the family of Jesus. This comment must be qualified because both Mark and John are also critical of the twelve. Whatever negative conclusions are drawn concerning the family must also be drawn concerning the twelve. Mark is critical of both the family and the twelve in order to elevate whoever does the will of God, and may well have Paul in mind. On the other hand John idealizes the Beloved Disciple, whom he elevates at the expense of the twelve, and the brothers of Jesus, while Mary too is portrayed as an ideal disciple. Consequently it is no more justified to dismiss James and the brothers of Jesus than it is to dismiss Peter and the twelve. The tradition of reading the New Testament that has prevailed until modern times is dominated by the legitimating authority of Peter and the twelve. Consequently the negative attitudes to them in Mark and John tend to be moderated. This has not been the case for James. The grounds upon which the case for thinking that James was opposed to the mission of Jesus during his lifetime will not bear the weight of scrutiny. There is no more reason for thinking that James was a convert only after the resurrection of Jesus than for thinking that this was true of Peter.

The view that James only came to leadership after the forced departure of Peter is groundless. Nevertheless the cumulative and psychological effect of this view is to imply that James was a leader of second quality only, who came to his leadership position only when the man of first quality was forced to leave. But nowhere in the sources is it said that Peter was leader. This conclusion is drawn from texts that make no explicit comment on the leadership question (Acts 12:17 and Gal 1:19) and that, when they are analyzed concerning this matter, are open to quite a different reading. Indeed, it is possible to read these texts as implying the leadership of James rather than Peter. Given that all explicit statements about the leadership of the Jerusalem church, even though these statements are later than the New Testament documents, assert that James was leader from the first, this conclusion is the more secure of the two.

The fortunes of James, and his influence in the church at large, were largely bound up with the fate of the Jerusalem church. All of the evidence suggests that James focused his attention and energies on the life and growth of that church, although this did not preclude the impact of his influence from extending beyond those borders. Consequently when that church dispersed, at the time of the Jewish war, those who bore the tradition and memory of James were scattered, and his influence ceased to be a concentrated force. Whereas, during his lifetime, the circumcision mission had been regarded as legitimate—indeed it was the uncircumcision mission that had then been questioned—a specific mission to Jews now became increasingly questionable. The tradition of James was now forced into increasingly marginalized Christian Jewish communities and forced to adapt to new situations.

The Epistle of James is an attempt to deal with the marginalized situation of Christian Jews in the diaspora. That is not to say that it was addressed only to Christian Jews, even if their marginalized situation is a major reason for the publication of the letter. Realistically, though addressed to all Jews in the diaspora, it is likely that the readers were mainly Christian rather than unbelieving Jews. The concern of the epistle is that Christian Jews should make their lives meaningful in relation to the Jewish community. There is nothing in James to suggest or encourage mission to other Jews. After the Jewish war this task became too sensitive, especially in the face of the growing mission of a church that was dominantly Gentile in constituency. The epistle can be understood as a Christian interpretation of the law, without any polemical attitude toward the ritual elements that would have emerged had Gentiles been involved. On the one hand, for Christian Jews in the tradition of James these elements were not controversial, and the issues of significance lay elsewhere. On the other hand, the impact of the Pauline teaching of justification by faith could not be ignored because of the consequences of such a teaching within the Jewish community at large. In Acts (21: 17–36) this is dramatically illustrated by the Jewish reaction to Paul on his return to Jerusalem.

The Epistle of James is a Christian interpretation of God and the appropriate response to him which is in complete harmony with the burning ethical concern of the Jewish prophetic tradition. That is not to say that James is a comprehensive summary of the teaching of the prophets. Rather, James provides a specific interpretation that is completely at home within the Jewish tradition. God as the creator is understood to be the giver of every good and perfect gift. The response to him for which James calls is absolute faithfulness in the midst of the mystery of suffering, by which the righteous person is tested. That testing, though not attributed to God, leads to the good of the righteous person who continues in faithfulness to God. An essential element in affirming the good purposes of God is to be found in the eschatological perspective of the epistle. Judgment is impending, coming soon, and the righteous will be vindicated and the wicked punished. James, then, provides a profound understanding of God and the role of the righteous person as the model for the Christian Jew.

As a document of Christian Judaism the fate of the Epistle of James was in the balance. Only by becoming recognized as a "Catholic" epistle, an epistle for the whole church, could James become acceptable to that church as a part of its scriptures. This fate was to obscure the Jewish character of the letter and the essentially Jewish character of the fount from which it sprang. Christian Judaism, in spite of the Epistle of James, became increasingly marginalized from Judaism as well as from the emerging Great Church. The fate of the tradition of James and the memory of him were bound up with Christian Judaism, and with its demise his fate was sealed.

The memory of James was, however, embedded within the Christian scriptures. Even if this memory was one-sided and tendentious, the Great Church had to come to terms with it. In the first instance this had to be done in competition with the memory of Christian Judaism for which James was the ideal leader. One reason for his leadership was his relationship to Jesus. He was the brother of Jesus, and there is no doubt that this relationship was a major reason for choosing him as leader. The traditions consistently recognize that this relationship was important in establishing his leadership. The importance of this link is confirmed by the tradition concerning the leadership provided by other members of the family after the death of James.

The martyrdom of James advanced his reputation within Christian Judaism, where his role was understood as one in a succession of righteous sufferers or martyrs. He stands not only in the Jewish succession of righteous sufferers but also in the select company of early Christian martyrs: Jesus, Stephen, and James the Just. A tradition of interpretation of the deaths of the first two has impacted on accounts of the martyrdom of James, providing evidence of the stature and significance of James. Not even Peter and Paul are accorded the dignity of having accounts of their martyrdom set in the same terms as the martyrdoms of Jesus and Stephen. Just James is the righteous sufferer, the righteous martyr whose dignity must be understood in relation to the best and the greatest. Thus there is a tradition, even within the Great Church, in which the significance of the martyrdom of James was recognized and in which he was confessed to be "the most righteous of men." This tradition strains strangely against the suppression of the significance of his leadership role. Even when he is recognized as the first bishop of the Jerusalem church, the recognition appears to be accorded grudgingly.

James is undisputedly recognized as the first bishop of the Jerusalem church. While there are traditions that indicate that his appointment was dependent on the appearance of the risen Jesus directly to him, there is a tendency to make his authority dependent on the apostles. Eusebius reported that Clement of Alexandria wrote that, after the ascension, Peter, James, and John chose James the Just as bishop of Jerusalem, although another quotation in Eusebius implies James's leadership from the time of the resurrection. Eusebius subjects James to the authority of all the apostles in a way that provides evidence of a struggle between the Great Church, represented here by the apostles, and the independent authority of James.

James was the leading authority in Christian Judaism, and there is evidence of conflict with the emerging Great Church. Because Christian Judaism became alienated from the Great Church quite early, the authority of James fell into other hands. Gnostic sources which venerate James were concentrated in Syria in areas where Jewish Christianity was strong after the Jewish war. Gnosticism associated with the name of James (as well as Thomas) derives from Christian Judaism. In this tradition James is not only viewed as an authority figure, the first bishop of Jerusalem, but also as a revealer figure. His role as revealer is (as was the case with his role as bishop) based on his intimate relationship to Jesus. Not only were he and Jesus members of the same family who were nourished by the milk of the same mother; after the resurrection James also was greeted by an intimate kiss initiated by Jesus. The closeness of the two is the essential guarantee of the ultimate mysteries mediated by Jesus through James. As with tradition of the direct appointment of James by Jesus, so here the Great Church sought to embrace James within the authority of the arms of the apostles. Clement wrote that after the resurrection Jesus revealed the higher knowledge to James the Just, John, and Peter.

At that time the authority of James within Christian Judaism and certain Gnostic circles was such that he could not be ignored. It was not an option to condemn James to the company he was then keeping. Marginalized as he was in the documents of the New Testament, even there his role was such that he could not be ignored or denied. The only option was to rehabilitate him. In this case rehabilitation allowed certain of the emphases to stand. The reputation of James for righteousness and as a martyr could be put to the service of the Great Church. His intimate relationship to Jesus and his unique role of leadership within the church of his day were, however, embarrassments that had to be "toned down." His relationship to Christian Judaism was also a problem as the church by now was dominantly Gentile. James's worst fears had come to pass. The mission to the Gentiles, and in particular the circumcision-free mission, had alienated Christian Judaism from the majority of Christians, and the existence of Christians who were not circumcised and did not keep the Mosaic law jeopardized the relationship of Christian Jews to other Jews.

In retrospect, James's struggle with Paul over the terms of a mission to the Gentiles and the consequences this would have for Christian Judaism shows James to have been both clear and farsighted. Paul, as a visionary, saw the implications of the gospel for the world. In this he might have been correct theologically. In retrospect his stated hope that the success of the mission to the nations might stir the Jews to jealousy because the nations were sharing what was the birthright of the Jews, while the Jews "missed out," now reads like a rationalization to justify his action in the face of criticism (Rom 11:13–14). James saw that Paul's style of mission to the Gentiles spelled the end of Christian Judaism—indeed, the end of a viable mission to the Jews—because it was a mission from outside of Judaism rather than an authentic rediscovery of the reality of Judaism from within its own resources. Not only did James stand squarely within the historical reality of Judaism; so also, he believed, did Jesus.

On the other side Paul was driven by a burning question from which he could not hide. "Is God the God of the Jews only? Is he not the God of the Gentiles also?" To this he could only answer—for he was the prisoner of a vision and by it he was driven—"Yes, of the Gentiles also, since God is one, and he will justify the circumcised on the ground of their faith and the uncircumcised through their faith" (Rom 3:29). Paul asserts that affliction and glory come equally to the Jew first and also to the Greek. His basis for making this assertion was, "For there is no respect for persons [προσωπολημψία] with God" (Rom 2:9–11). The Epistle of James, in its own way, was opposed to favoritism, and the reader is exhorted not to hold the faith and at the same time show favoritism to people (ἐν προσωπολημψίαις, James 2:1).

James was bound to the fate of his people and would die a martyr at their hands just a few years before the destruction of Jerusalem, their religious and cultural center. Paul was the prisoner of a vision and he would die in the city which symbolized (in Acts) the goal of the mission to the nations and at the hands of those who were the object of his mission, Romans in the city of Rome. Through his involvement in the collection for the poor saints in Jerusalem Paul hoped to keep the two missions bound together. The delivery of that collection proved, in one sense, to be his undoing. The collection, as a token of goodwill and a sign of indebtedness of the Gentile Christians to the Christian Jews, was unequal to the task of binding the two together. We cannot know if Paul journeyed to Rome with no regrets or whether James experienced forebodings not only concerning his own future and the future of his nation but also (and especially) concerning the future of Christian Judaism. James struggled to maintain the messianic faith in Jesus as a viable faith for Jews. The weight of history crushed him and his tradition so that scarcely an adequate memory remains of his heroic struggle. Perhaps that is because the world has always honored the winners. James struggled valiantly, and in his lifetime it may be that his struggle was the most dazzling adornment of the faith. But James and his cause were lost, so that in the end all we have is just James.

Such is the way of the world with its dismissive attitude and its delight in cutting down the "tall poppies." But justice it certainly is not! By any fair evaluation James must loom large in the history of early Christianity. Although Matthew should ultimately be seen as a Petrine Gospel, it achieved its present form only by assimilating a variety of traditions under the dominant influence of tradition that reflected the perspective of James of Jerusalem (M). It remains an open question how far M actually represents the mind of the historical Jesus as distinct from Mark. It certainly remains close to the mind of James, and this perspective has continued to be a challenge, not only to Paul with his law-free mission to the nations but also to the church down through the ages. Just what is the relationship of Christian faith to Judaism, of the gospel to the law? To Paul the questions came more personally and directly. "Does this mean that we are using faith to undermine the law? By no means: we are upholding the law" (Rom 3:31). "I ask then, 'Has God cast off his people?' Of course not!" (Rom 11:1). James and the circumcision mission ensured that such questions were not easily set aside, and Paul, with his law-free mission, ensured that the universal scope of the gospel continued to challenge the circumcision mission.

The righteousness of James in absolute devotion and loyalty to God became legendary. Apart from God, who is righteous, and Jesus Christ the righteous, righteousness is associated more with James than with any other early Christian figure; in fact "Righteous" became his defining title or characteristic. While attempts to explain the title frequently stress the piety of James, it is likely that the use of this epithet was closely related to the suffering of James as a martyr. His martyrdom was a consequence of his struggle for the poor against the rich and powerful. Here he was as good as the word in the epistle bearing his name, refusing to show favoritism to the rich and powerful. The church down through the ages has needed to hear this challenge to take a stand on the side of the poor, weak, and powerless. The last word then is James the Just, James the faithful, James the righteous.

Robert Eisenman's *James the Brother of Jesus* (New York: Viking, 1997)

Robert Eisenman's magnum opus *James the Brother of Jesus: The Key to Unlocking the Secrets of Early Christianity and the Dead Sea Scrolls* arrived on my desk on the 20th of May. My own manuscript on James was substantially finished in 1994. At long last it is being typeset and I expect page proofs by the beginning of June. With limited time before they arrive there is also much to be done by way of the preparation of indices and last-minute checking of other details, all in the midst of a busy teaching job. Nevertheless, the appearance of 1,100 pages on James cannot be ignored, even if earlier works on this subject by the same author have been dealt with in my final chapter. I must admit that my heart fell when I read in the introduction (p. xxxiii) that this is the first of two projected volumes. Readers may imagine the sense of relief when I discovered, toward the end of the book (p. 959), that the second volume is to be but half the length of the first. Though Eisenman indicates that the second volume has already been prepared, I fear I cannot wait. My own work has already been too long delayed.

Having now read the book, the task remains to deal with it in the time and space available. There is no option but to deal with this volume as if it is the complete work, even though the second volume has been signaled. To cover Eisenman's *James* in just a few pages is an impossible task. Yet something of worth can be done, especially because, while the book is a massive increase in the details of coverage, Eisenman appears not to have changed his views on any major issue. No important ancient source has been overlooked, but there is no significant dialogue with contemporary scholarship on early Christianity or the scrolls.

Eisenman's book on James is both erudite and eccentric. Not only are the conclusions at variance with mainstream scholarship, but his methods of handling evidence and developing arguments are also different from those employed by mainstream scholars. Perhaps this is why there has been little dialogue between Eisenman and other critical treatments of the subject. In the 1,100 pages there is scarcely a reference to any contemporary scholar. In one sense it is refreshing, in the midst of a tradition of recycling the views of other scholars, to find a scholar who pays wholehearted attention to the primary sources. But this treatment leads to problems when that scholarship has identified problems in approaches related to those which Eisenman himself adopts. Leaving aside the long-standing difference between Eisenman and the vast majority of scroll scholars over the date of the scrolls and the identification of the "main players" in those documents, which Eisenman says he has largely deferred to the second volume, there is his use of the Pseudo-Clementines, which is crucial for his hypothesis, and his appeal to connections based on the identification of common root words.

Before proceeding with detailed discussion we may note the way Eisenman describes the structure of his work. Volume one treats "James' relationships to the New Testament, early Church sources, and the problem of the brothers of Jesus generally" (p.xxxiii). It is confined to "delineating the parameters of James' existence, his importance for his time . . . , the Scrolls being used peripherally for purposes of external comparison and verification only" (p. 959). If such is the case, we have a very detailed account of that peripheral use.

Volume two will deal with Paul's final confrontation with James over the charge that Paul was teaching Jews everywhere to "apostatize" from Moses (p. 520). It will also explore "the Pella flight and James' relationship to Eastern conversions and communities generally, . . . providing a more detailed, in-depth, and point-for-point analysis of his link-up with the Dead Sea Scrolls and an identification of the document now popularly known as '*MMT*' as a letter (or letters) to 'the Great King of the Peoples beyond the Euphrates' Agbarus or Abgarus or the character we shall encounter as Queen Helen of Adiabene's favourite son, King Izates" (p. xxxiii). It will explore more fully (they are explored at some length in the first volume, pp. 86–88) the parallels between James and the Qumran Teacher of Righteousness. Volume two will start where the first leaves off, with events connected with the death of James, dealing with the true meaning of James's rain-making and more systematically with his three or four confrontations with Paul and treating meticulously the parallels between James and the Teacher of Righteousness and the relationship of Paul to the Liar in the scrolls (p. 959).

The published book is in six parts, each with multiple chapters, preceded by an introduction and concluded with an epilogue. The six parts, and their chapter divisions, are as follows:

> Part 1: Palestinian Backgrounds—1) James; 2) The Second Temple and the Rise of the Maccabees; 3) Romans, Herodians, and Jewish Sects;

4) First-Century Sources Mentioning James; 5) Early Church Sources and the Dead Sea Scrolls.

Part 2: The Historical James—6) The First Appearance of James in Acts; 7) The Picture of James in Paul's Letters; 8) James' Succession and the Election to Fill Judas *Iscariot's Office;* 9) The Election of James in Early Church Tradition.

Part 3: James' Role in the Jerusalem of His Day—10) James' Rechabitism and Naziritism; 11) James' Vegetarianism, Abstention from Blood, and Consuming No Wine; 12) James' Bathing and Clothing Habits; 13) James as Opposition High Priest and *Oblias.*

Part 4: The Death of James—14) The Stoning of James and the Stoning of Stephen; 15) The Death of James in Its Historical Setting; 16) The Attack by Paul on James and the Attack on Stephen; 17) The Truth about the Death of James; 18) Peter's Visit to Cornelius and Simon's Visit to Agrippa.

Part 5: The Brothers of Jesus as Apostles—19) The Apostleship of James, *Cephas,* and John; 20) James the First to See Jesus; 21) Last Supper Scenarios, the Emmaus Road, and the Cup of the Lord; 22) Jesus' Brothers as Apostles; 23) Simeon bar Cleophas and Simon the Zealot.

Part 6: Jamesian Communities in the East—24) Judas the Brother of James and the Conversion of King Agbar; 25) The Conversion of Queen Helen and the *Ethiopian Queen's* Eunuch; 26) Judas Thomas and Theuda the Brother of the Just One.

There are several reasons why this book is so long with a second volume to follow. Because Eisenman differs from other scholars in his reconstruction of the history of the Qumran Sect and its relation to early Christianity, all of this must be argued before his understanding of James can be set out. Earlier brief treatments failed to convince scholars, so the present approach is aimed to overwhelm opposition with a wealth of detail.

Dating is important. Although most scholars use a combination of external and internal evidence, Eisenman plays down the importance of external evidence (pp. 46–47). While he argues that texts represented by only one copy are likely to be first-century-CE compositions, he majors on the primacy of linguistic connections (pp. 8, 9, 11, 83, 86, 87) by means of which he detects common persons in diverse references (pp. 839–40). Eisenman thinks that the connections show that the Gospels and the scrolls are contemporary documents though the authors of the Gospels knew the scrolls and absorbed allusions from them (p. xx) into their portrayals of the family of Jesus and the apostles. This means that the Dead Sea Scrolls become the key to the interpretation of the Gospels rather than the reverse.

As a basis for his treatment of James, Eisenman sets out the history of the sects in relation to Roman and Herodian power (p. 47). The establishment parties were made up of Pharisees, establishment Sadducees, and Herodians. Then there were the Zealots, purist, anti-accommodation Sadducees, the Jerusalem community led by James (pp. 374–75, 381, 484–85, 831). That these were overlapping groups seems clear in that Eisenman speaks of Zealot Essenes (pp. 833–34) and Qumran Zealots (p. xxxv) and refers to James as a Zealot (pp. 9, 194, 374–75, 381, 389, 490). The anti-establishment movement was both nationalistic and messianic (pp. 45–46, 65). Per this analysis there were two groups of Sadducees, the one adopting an accommodation policy in relation to foreign power and the other being fiercely nationalistic, the one rejecting resurrection and the other affirming it. The Qumran Sect was an expression of the latter in each case, while the Sadducees of Josephus and the New Testament (which Eisenman, p. 58, argues is dependent on Josephus) are an example of the former.

On this reading the Pharisees were not the popular party (pp. 38, 40), but they dominated the Sadducees in the Herodian period (p. 483), which Eisenman thinks was the situation in the time of Jesus and James as "pictured in the New Testament" (p. 43). This is contrary to the picture left by Josephus, who indicates the leading role of the Sadducean high priest Ananus in the execution of James. The same can be said of the New Testament depiction of the role of Caiaphas in the execution of Jesus.

Eisenman tends to use different language to describe the anti-establishment party. Indeed, James is said to be the center of the opposition alliance in Jerusalem (p. xix), and that alliance precipitated the uprising in 66 CE. This picture of James as zealous for the law, which included a willingness to die for the mark of circumcision (p. 48), is said to apply to James and his more famous brother Jesus, of whom James was the true successor (pp. xx, 7, 87–88). But James is opposed to the Jesus of scripture who has been conformed to the image of "overseas Christianity" (pp. xxxii–xxxiii), which Hellenized what had been a messianic and nationalistic movement into an otherworldly mystery cult (p. 6). Establishment Judaism followed a parallel development in Rabbinic Judaism (p. 6). In Christianity this development, which Eisenman lays largely at the feet of Paul, was brought to a definitive expression in the reign of Constantine through the efforts of Eusebius and other like-minded persons (p. 6 and see p. xxxvi). It differed from Rabbinic Judaism in that it was opposed to the law while Rabbinic Judaism was pro-law (pp. 6, 39), but both survived by a policy of accommodation.

Because Eisenman argues that there was but one form of messianism in Palestine (p. 65), the Dead Sea Scrolls become determinative for his interpretation of Judaism and the Jesus movement. He argues that the uprisings against Rome were messianic, as shown by the currency of "the star prophecy" (pp. 39, 45–46, 253–56). In the first uprising both Josephus and Yohanan ben Zachai made use of the star prophecy (p. 69), and it is clearly linked to Bar Kochba in the second uprising (pp. 252–53), which was supported by the eminent Rabbi Akiba. While this is a welcome response to some trends that downplay the importance of messianism in pre-70-CE Palestine, it looks very much like an oversimplification. Rather, the evidence suggests that various kinds of Judaism gave expression to a variety of messianic expectations. But, by asserting a common messianic movement, Eisenman has predisposed his argument to the recognition that messianic expectations, such as with James or Bar Kochba or Qumran, all belong to a common movement which can be described variously as messianic, nationalistic, opposition, Zealot, Sadducean or Zadokite.

The "language circle" involving the consonants Z-D-K is important because in the Hebrew of the time only consonants were written. Thus these three letters might indicate *Zaddik, Zadok*, or even *Zadduk*. James the Just is linguistically connected to this circle, which links him to the righteous and also to the Zadokite Sadducees of Qumran, or so Eisenman argues (pp. 371–75). Likewise he argues that Matthew was responsible for the mistaken identification of the town of Nazareth with the designation of Jesus as a Nazorean (pp. 241–57, 939–43). Eisenman notes that neither the Old Testament nor Josephus mentions any town of Nazareth in Galilee, suggesting that this identification is an overwriting of N-Z-R identifying a Jewish sect of Nazoreans or that it could be a Nazirite reference, linking James (on the basis of the evidence from Hegesippus) to an ascetic purist group. This argument assumes the reliability of Hegesippus on this point. Eisenman asserts that what James was, so also was his more famous brother (pp. xx, 7, 87, 88, 963). Just how one reconciles this argument with the Q passage (Luke 7:33–34 and Matt 11:18–19) where the asceticism of John the Baptist is contrasted with the eating and drinking of Jesus, who is reportedly described as "a glutton and drunkard," is unclear. This is hardly likely to have been concocted by Jesus' supporters, nor was Paul (Eisenman's archvillain) a supporter of drunkenness.

Eisenman argues that the presentation of the apostles as peaceful fishermen reveals an important language circle (p. 504) connecting the early Christian writings and the Dead Sea Scrolls. Reference to "casting down nets" plays on key ideological language from the scrolls (p. xxxvi and 220, 450, 452, 504, 505, 509, 752–54, 773, 774, 841, 957, 961). This language of "throwing down" is also said to be integral to the portrayal of the deaths of James and of Judas. Described as "Galilean" language (p. xxvi), this connects James to the Galilean Zealot movement, associated with Judas the Galilean and with Judas Iscariot.

Rather than being written in a code which the initiated can crack, the Jewish story has been "overwritten" (in the Gospels and Acts) from the perspective of what Eisenman call "overseas Christianity"—Pauline Christianity, which was Hellenized and anti-Jewish (p. 55). This overwriting has obscured the relationship of earliest Christianity to the messianic Zealot movement and the prominence of James as a leader among those who resisted assimilation. He argues that the overwriting regularly obscures the family of Jesus. James is thus revealed as a Zealot leader of the opposition alliance (pp. xi, 9, 12, 194, 211, 374–75, 381, 389, 490).

The language of "casting down" associated with Galilee and the deaths of Judas and of James finds focus in the verb βάλλω which Eisenman reduces to the consonantal stem B-L because, although this is Greek, in the Hebrew of the time only consonants were written. This enables him also to appeal to the association of the devil with Judas (διάβολος) and to a whole circle of language including Bela, Balaam, Belial (p. 504). The association of James with Judas then goes in two directions. The appointment of a twelfth apostle to replace Judas is written over the appointment or election of James as the replacement of Jesus (pp.123–24, 184, 202, 412–13, 955, 958). The association with Judas also symbolizes the Zealotism of James. This ingenious piece of detection fails to carry conviction because of the nature of the linguistic argument upon which it depends.

Another aspect underlying Eisenman's reconstruction is his reevaluation of the early Christian sources. First, he asserts that all documents received by Western Christianity have been Hellenized under the influence of "overseas Christianity." Acts and the letters of Paul remain important for understanding the role of James, while other evidence concerning the brothers remains buried in the Gospels. Both the Gospels and Acts have been overwritten in a way that obscures the role of the family and Acts is dependent on Paul historically and doctrinally (p. 54). Even in Matthew the post-resurrection Jesus validates the Pauline Gentile mission (Matt 28:19–20; p.55). Eisenman thinks that better history lies detectable not far below this overwriting and that by detecting language circles connected with the scrolls and other sources not determined by "overseas Christianity," such as the Clementine *Recognitions,* it is possible to recover better history than Paul and Acts have provided.

Clearly the Pseudo-Clementines fall outside the recognized writings of the Great Church. As we have seen, they present James as the great leader of the mother Church, whose authority is recognized everywhere, even by Peter. The opponent of James is known as the "enemy" and the "liar." In the language circle Eisenman connects him with "the spouter of lies" and "enemy" of the Righteous Teacher of Qumran. He provides linguistic data to support the view that Paul was the liar (pp. 126–27, 145–48) and the "enemy" (pp. 146, 453). In the *Recognitions* the enemy is identified as Saul, and he makes an attack on

James on the Temple steps but does not kill him. Aspects of the martyrdom accounts found in Clement of Alexandria and Hegesippus overlap this account, which differs from the account given by Josephus, in which James was stoned to death at the instigation of Ananus. Reading below the surface of the Christian accounts with insight from Josephus, Eisenman proposes two attacks on James, one by Paul in the 40s, which was not fatal, and a second assault by Ananus in 62, which brought about the death of James (pp. 452, 585). He then finds evidence of the attack by Paul, asserting that the account of the martyrdom of Stephen (p. 7, 12, 121, 124, 186, 258, 452, 529, 839–40) has been overwritten on an account of an attack by Paul on James.

While Eisenman does not specifically so indicate, dating the attack in the 40s places it at a time following Paul's "conversion" to the Jesus movement. Nothing in Paul's letters suggests that he attacked other Christian leaders after his conversion. In both Galatians and 1 Corinthians he acknowledges persecuting the church prior to his conversion. No names are mentioned. Apart from Eisenman's hunch that the attack by Paul on James must be fitted in, there is not much in favor of identifying it with the attack on Stephen. While Stephen was stoned, the supposed first attack on James is said to have been carried out by Paul on the Temple steps. Stephen was killed and James was not. Indeed, according to Acts, Saul did not execute Stephen, but stood by, perhaps as a witness. Further, if the attack was thought to have taken place before his "conversion," James is an unlikely candidate because he strictly kept the law. A Hellenist was much more likely to have been the object of Saul's violence.

Given that the sources of the Pseudo-Clementines are probably not earlier than the second half of the second century, it is unlikely that they are independent of Acts (see the discussion above, pp. 187–98). Scholars generally reject any identification of the *Ascents* (*Anabathmoi*), mentioned by Epiphanius, with one of the sources. While the Pseudo-Clementines have been transmitted in an ideological context distinct from the emerging Great Church, it is a mistake to think that those traditions developed without their own ideological biases. The Christian Judaism of the second century was quite different from the Jerusalem community headed by James. The assumption that this work is independent of Acts is also unjustified. In the account of the attack on James, the "enemy" is not named. A marginal note in one of the manuscripts has introduced the name Saul. But this seems to be a deduction based on 1.71, in which a sympathizer brought news that the "enemy" had been commissioned by Caiaphas to go to Damascus in pursuit of believers. With a knowledge of Acts 9:1–2, the "enemy" can be identified with Saul. Without Acts the identification is not possible. Thus there is no independent account of Saul's attack on James. In all of his letters Paul uses only that name, Paul. Given that use of the name Saul is nowhere except in Acts, we might question whether Paul underwent a change in his use of name. The change of name, from Jewish Saul to Roman Paul,

serves a dramatic and ideological Lukan purpose, signaling the clear development of the Pauline law-free mission to the nations. All of this casts grave doubt
on the historical credibility of the Clementine *Recognitions* account of the attack
on James. Dependence on Acts seems certain. The story of Clement is something of a "romance," which is less directly relevant for the study of James
than Eisenman assumes. He has been drawn to it not only by its pro-Jamesian
orientation but also because of its anti-Pauline bias.

Eisenman locates Pauline Christianity with Rabbinic Judaism, both surviving because of an accommodationist policy toward Rome (p. 39). He sees Pauline Christianity and Rabbinic Judaism as continuous with Christianity and
Judaism today (p. 492). Paul's accommodation is exemplified in 1 Cor 9:19–24.
In contrast to this calculated accommodation, Eisenman says, "The Dead Sea
Scrolls provide the counterpoint, as does James—that is, not 'win at any costs'
but martyrdom. Certainly these movements are 'old fashioned,' with commitment to absolute purity, unbending Righteousness and uncompromising integrity, but this is perhaps their charm. . . . If nothing else, their elegance,
steadfastness and total commitment to absolute Righteousness cannot fail to
impress the modern world as it rediscovers them." Eisenman's admiration for
the Qumran community and those like them is unmistakable. On the other
hand, he is enamored by neither Paul nor surviving Rabbinic Judaism, though
it is Paul who particularly raises his ire. He continues without break: "For his
part, Paul pretends not to understand this ethos, or calls it 'weak' (Rom. 14:1ff.
and I Cor. 14:7ff.). Yet, complaining about attachment to circumcision, when
Maccabaean and Zealot martyrs for over two hundred and fifty years had laid
down their lives rather than abjure it, is totally to close one's eyes to the driving
forces in Palestine throughout this period" (pp. 47–48 and see 128–29).

Paul is called anti-Semitic (p. 58) and Pauline Christianity is described as
anti-nationalist and pro-Roman (p. 46). Paul is said to make "an obscene pun"
(p. 274). "Like Paul, who follows a similar *modus operandi* regarding doctrinal
matters, Josephus is an apologist who is completely unaware of his own disin-
genuousness" (p. 493). Clearly Eisenman is no admirer of Josephus either, and
in discussing whether Josephus was a Christian says, "if one wants him, one is
welcome to him" (p. 69). Evidence of Paul's Roman connections and links
with the house of Herod is frequently referred to in a way that implies a negative evaluation (pp. xxxiii, 150, 388–89, 501–502, 534, 738, 797, 831). The
Roman link is supported by reference to Paul's Roman citizenship. But even
this is doubtful, being referred to only by Luke (Acts 16:37–38; 22:25, 26, 27,
29; 23:27) and never by Paul. Indeed, only Luke uses the term "Roman."
Presenting Paul as a Roman citizen could be part of his strategy in portraying
the peaceful progress of the church in the empire. The argument that the
Epaphroditus of Philippians 2:25 was Domitian's secretary, who also had that
name (p. 791), ignores the popularity of this name derived from "Aphrodite."

Eisenman's treatment of Paul is unsympathetic, accentuating anything that seems to be a negative trait and lacking sensitive awareness of his connection to Palestinian Judaism such as is argued by such scholars as E. P. Sanders, among others. The discussion of circumcision fails to note that Paul's objection was to the imposition of circumcision on Gentile believers. The accusation that Pauline Christianity turned a Jewish messianic movement into a Hellenistic mystery cult echoes nineteenth-century criticisms that have long been rejected by Pauline scholars.

Eisenman's evaluation of early Christianity arises from his conclusion that there was only one messianic movement in first-century Judaism. This inclines him to assimilate all messianic movements to his understanding of the Qumran messianic movement. They are all messianic Zealots, messianic Sadducees of the purist anti-establishment ilk, as was James and, apparently, as was Jesus before him. Against this view the evidence suggests a greater diversity of Judaisms and messianic expectations prior to the Jewish war. The Qumran Texts can distort our views because they are the only surviving body of Judaean Jewish literature coming from the period before the war. The war was a turning point for Judaism. Because of this the Qumran Texts provide a unique insight into pre-70-CE Judaism. But the texts are neither totally peculiar to Qumran, sharing many things with other Jewish groups of the time, nor are they totally representative, because they also embody the peculiar emphases and points of view of the sect. Thus points in common do not prove identity unless they can be shown to exist in a comprehensive fashion. Because of this Eisenman's use of the Dead Sea Scrolls as the key to understanding the conflicts between the New Testament and the other early Christian sources is unlikely to unlock the mysteries surrounding James for many readers. His assertion that "the Scrolls allow us to approach the Messianic Community of James with about as much precision as we are likely to have from any other source" (p. 963) makes no allowance for differences between what we know of James and what we know of Qumran.

While Eisenman argues that the question of "Whether James is to be identified with the Righteous Teacher at Qumran or simply a parallel successor is not the point" (p. 963), the language circles he has used connect people. He discusses the important traditions concerning the Zaddikim but nowhere acknowledges that, because the traditions about the Righteous Teacher and James each conform to the genre of the righteous sufferer, the argument for identifying the two is significantly weakened. Much of his argument would break down if those identifications failed to be sustained. Further, throughout the book the impression of the identifications is built up (pp. 235–37). That Eisenman thinks that James was the Righteous Teacher is implied, and the second volume promises a meticulous and even more detailed account of the parallels between the two (p. 959).

Other identifications are of Paul with the "spouter of lies" (pp. and 126–27) and Ananus as the wicked priest (pp. 170–72). The War Scroll is said to be Jamesian (pp. 212–13), implying that James and his followers were Zealots of a warlike kind (pp. 9, 194, 374–75, 381, 389, 490, 983n. 9). Again, on Eisenman's hypothesis, if James was, so then was Jesus. Nothing in the early Christian traditions supports this view. Zeal for the law cannot be shown to involve Zealotism of the *Sicarii* variety.

Another aspect of the evidence of the language circle is overlapping names. Eisenman asks what we are to make of all the Judases (pp. 44, 112, 115, 955, 958) and Matthiases (p. 208). He concludes that these overlaps are clues to overwriting. Judas's link with the Zealots is said to be one ground for the confused overwriting. But the fact is that the Gospel writers have not concealed the presence of Zealots among Jesus' disciples. Further, it is not surprising that certain names should appear frequently without referring to the same persons because a relatively small number of names was in circulation in first-century Palestine. Of these names, those of the patriarchs and the Maccabaean heroes were common, especially the names Jacob, Judas, Simon, and Mary. Eisenman uses these overlaps to uncover links between leaders of the Jesus movement and the family, particularly the brothers of Jesus. Because the known names of the brothers of Jesus—Simon, Judas and James—also appear amongst the twelve, he argues that Zealot members of the family of Jesus are concealed here (pp. xx, 7, 44, 117–18, 139, 143, 534, 958). These are in turn associated with Zealot figures.

Eisenman recognizes the emergence of the Zealot movement from the time roughly coincident with the birth of Jesus (pp. 112–13) but notes that the movement is specifically identified as Zealot by Josephus only from the time of the slaying of the high priest Ananus in 68 (pp. 113–16). Eisenman recognizes Josephus's pro-Roman, anti-Zealot stance (p. 116), which makes unlikely the identification of James as a Zealot, as Josephus wrote positively of him and critically of Ananus for his role in his execution. Once the likelihood of the frequent use of common names is accepted, this sort of detection, which Jerome practiced, becomes unconvincing. The use of the same name need not indicate the same person

Because James has been depicted as a Zaddik, Eisenman is inclined to defend the tradition that Origen, Eusebius, and Jerome attribute to Josephus, acknowledging that the destruction of Jerusalem occurred because of "what they did to James" (pp. 4, 77, 234–35, 395, 399, 414–15, 553–54, 571–74). In support of this view he argues that these three saw the quotation in Josephus independently. The question would then be whether it was genuine quotation or a Christian insertion. Against the latter view Eisenman argued that Origen was outraged by it and railed against it (pp. 4, 65, 395). In fact, what Origen says is that Josephus almost got it right because the destruction was because of what they did to Jesus. Eusebius argues that the destruction was because of what they did to Jesus but that the presence of James and the apostles in Jerusalem held back the destruction until James was martyred. Nevertheless, there is no need to suggest that Origen willfully interpolated the passage. It is notable that Origen gives no reference for the passage and that Eusebius uses the quotation in the same context as Origen. Jerome appears to have derived his quotation from Eusebius. Consequently, we are left with the single witness of Origen, upon whom the other two depend. Given that Josephus elsewhere says that the destruction was because of what they did to Ananus, the authenticity of the saying about James is questionable.

Eisenman also overrates the role of Eusebius. He refers to him as Constantine's archbishop and attributes great influence to him at the Council of Nicaea in 325 (pp. xxxvi, 3, 6). Yet the views of Eusebius, who was a moderate supporter of Arius, did not prevail at the council. The history of this period of the church is more complex than Eisenman has allowed. Nevertheless, he rightly recognizes that dominant developments in the church, after the death of James and the destruction of Jerusalem, obscured the significance of James and the nature of the Jerusalem church in the early period.

Eisenman's hypothesis that James and his followers fit neatly into the Qumran sect as Zealot defenders of the law (pp. 389, 983n. 9) is simplistic and based on flawed methods of argument. The term used there in his argument (ζηλωτής), based on Acts 21:20 (cf. Gal 1:14 on p. 659), refers to the many converts who "are all zealots of the Law." The genitive case probably has the sense of "for the law." Eisenman translates using a capital "Zealots for the Law," implying that they are identified as belonging to the revolutionary Zealots. But when Luke refers to this group, his description is not qualified by "for the law" or anything else (see Luke 6:15). Acts 1:13 refers to Simon the Zealot, who is named as one of the twelve. Only Luke refers to him as a Zealot. In the New Testament only Luke uses this term of the Zealots. Hence there is no cover up. But the same term is also used of those who are "zealots for the law," "zealots for God," "for spiritual things," "for the traditions of my fathers," "for good works," "for what is good" (Acts 21:20; 22:3; 1 Cor 14:12; Gal 1:14; Titus 2:14; 1 Peter 3:13). In none of these is the translation "Zealots" appropriate. Here we have another instance of Eisenman's rather inflexible reading of words as if they always mean the same thing. This is extended to apparently common roots of different words (see pp.374–75) to make a case linking James to the Zealots.

At the same time Eisenman distances Paul from James, giving weight to the Pseudo-Clementines in conjunction with the Dead Sea Scrolls. Here Paul becomes the enemy of James. That there were serious tensions between Paul and James has been well established. The violent enmity argued for by Eisenman cannot be supported in the light of Paul's letters. Even in Galatians, which acknowledges the conflict, an agreement between the two missions is described. Even when this agreement broke down, the two missions remained in an awkward relationship. In Rom 15:25–29, Paul indicates that he is taking up a collection for the Jerusalem community as an expression of gratitude for the spiritual riches the Jewish believers have shared with Gentiles. This is a side of Paul that is absent from Eisenman's book on James. He rightly sees the conflict between Paul and James but exaggerates it by moving James in the direction of the Qumran Zealots, as he sees them, and by moving Paul in the direction of a Hellenistic mystery cult. The reality seems to have been more complex.

Nevertheless, his work, aimed at bringing James out from obscurity, is to be welcomed. His recognition that James championed the cause of the poorer priests against Ananus, the rich high priest, and his supporters (pp. 316, 318, 388, 488, 500, 960) is helpful, as is his observation that the understanding of James as a "pillar" and "Oblias" is illuminated by the tradition of the righteous sufferers, the Zaddikim (pp. 133–39). But he fails to recognize that this connection significantly weakens his case for identifying James with the Righteous Teacher of Qumran, putting in question his use of the scrolls in reconstructing the history of early Christianity.

Bibliography

PRIMARY SOURCES

Bible

The Greek New Testament. Edited by Kurt Aland, Matthew Black, Carlo M. Martini, Bruce M. Metzger, and Alan Wikgren. 3rd ed. (corrected). Stuttgart: United Bible Society, 1983.

The HarperCollins Study Bible, New Revised Standard Version with Apocryphal/Deuterocanonical Books. Edited by Wayne A. Meeks, Jouette M. Bassler, Werner E. Lemke, Susan Niditch, and Eileen M. Schuller. San Francisco: HarperCollins, 1993.

Novum Testamentum Graece. Edited by Barbara and Kurt Aland, Johannes Karavidopoulos, Carlo M. Martini, and Bruce M. Metzger. 27th edition. Stuttgart: Deutsche Bibelgesellschaft, 1993.

Synopsis Quattor Evangeliorum: Locis parallelis evangeliorum apocryphorum et patrum adhibitis. Edited by Kurt Aland. Stuttgart: Württembergische Bibelanstalt, 1964.

Apocrypha and Pseudepigrapha

The Apocrypha and Pseudepigrapha of the Old Testament in English: With Introductions and Critical and Explanatory Notes to the Several Books, 2 vols. Edited by R. H. Charles. Oxford: Clarendon Press, 1913.

The Apocryphal New Testament: A Collection of Apocryphal Christian Literature in an English Translation based on M. R. James. Edited by J. K. Elliott. Oxford: Clarendon Press, 1993.

New Testament Apocrypha, 2 vols. Edited by Wilhelm Schneemelcher, English translation edited by R. McL. Wilson. Philadelphia: Westminster, 1963, 1965.

The Old Testament Pseudepigrapha, 2 vols. Edited by James H. Charlesworth. New York: Doubleday, 1983, 1985.

Jewish Sources

Dead Sea Scrolls

The Dead Sea Scrolls in English. Translation, notes, and introduction by Geza Vermes. Harmondsworth: Penguin, 1987.

The Dead Sea Scrolls Translated: The Qumran Texts in English. Edited by Florentino García Martínez, translated by Wilfred G. E. Watson. Leiden: Brill, 1994.

Die Texte aus Qumran. Edited by Eduard Lohse. Wissenschaftliche Buchgesellschaft. Darmstadt: United Bible Society, 1964.

Josephus

Jewish Antiquities, 7 vols. Translated by H. St. J. Thackeray, Ralph Marcus, and Louis Feldman; completed and edited by Allen Wikgren. LCL. Cambridge and London: Harvard University Press and William Heinemann, 1930, 1933, 1934, 1937, 1963, 1965.

The Jewish War, 2 vols. Translated by H. St. J. Thackeray. LCL. Cambridge and London: Harvard University Press and William Heinemann, 1927, 1928.

Josephus: The Jewish War. Translated, with an introduction, by G. A. Williamson. Harmondsworth: Penguin, 1970.

Mishnah

The Mishnah. Translated, with introduction and explanatory notes, by Herbert Danby. London: Oxford University Press, 1933.

The Mishnah: A New Translation. Translated by Jacob Neusner. New Haven: Yale University Press, 1987.

Early Fathers

Alexandrian Christianity. Edited by Henry Chadwick. LCC. Philadelphia: Westminster, 1954.

The Ante-Nicene Fathers, 10 vols. Edited by Alexander Roberts and James Donaldson. Grand Rapids: Eerdmans, 1951–1953.

The Apostolic Fathers, 2 vols. Translated by Kirsopp Lake. LCL. Cambridge and London: Harvard University Press and William Heinemann, 1912, 1913.

Documents of the Christian Church. Edited by Henry Bettenson. Oxford: Oxford University Press, 1956.

Early Christian Fathers. Edited by Cyril C. Richardson, LCC 1. Philadelphia: Westminster, 1953.

Early Christian Writings. Translated by Maxwell Staniforth. Harmondsworth: Penguin, 1968.

Early Latin Theology. Edited by S. L. Greenslade. LCC. Philadelphia: Westminster, 1956.

A New Eusebius. Edited by J. Stevenson. London: SPCK, 1968.

The Nicene and Post-Nicene Fathers, 2d series, 14 vols. Edited by Philip Schaff and Henry Wace. Grand Rapids: Eerdmans, 1952–1969.

Patrologiae Cursus Completus, 382 vols. Edited by Jacques-Paul Migne. Paris: Garnier, 1928–1967.

Augustine

The Nicene and Post-Nicene Fathers, 1st series, vols. 1–8. Edited by Philip Schaff. Grand Rapids: Eerdmans, 1956.

The Works of Aurelius Augustine, Bishop of Hippo, 15 vols. Edited by Marcus Dods. Edinburgh: T & T Clark, 1871–1876.

Clement of Alexandria

The Stromata, or Miscellanies, Fragments, Who is the Rich Man That Shall be Saved? Translated by William Wilson. ANF vol. 2. Grand Rapids: Eerdmans, 1989.

Epiphanius

The Panarion of Epiphanius of Salamis: Book 1 (Secs 1–46). Edited and translated by Frank Williams. Nag Hammadi Studies 35. Leiden: Brill, 1987.

The Panarion of St. Epiphanius, Bishop of Salamis. Translated by Philip R. Amidon. New York: Oxford University Press, 1990.

Eusebius

The Ecclesiastical History, 2 vols. Translated by Hugh Jackson Lawlor and J. E. L. Oulton. London: Macmillan, 1927, 1928.

The Ecclesiastical History, 2 vols. Translated by Kirsopp Lake, J. E. L. Oulton, and Hugh Jackson Lawlor. LCL. Cambridge, Mass.: Harvard University Press, 1926, 1932.

Eusebius: Church History, Life of Constantine the Great, and Oration in Praise of Constantine. Edited by Philip Schaff and Henry Wace. NPNF 1, 2d series. Grand Rapids: Eerdmans, 1979.

Eusebius: The History of the Church. Translated and edited by G. A. Williamson. Harmondsworth: Penguin, 1965; revised edition, 1989.

Hippolytus

Hippolytus: Refutatio Omnium Haeresium. Edited by Miroslav Marcovich. Patristische Texte und Studien 25. Berlin and New York: Walter de Gruyter, 1986.

Irenaeus and Justin Martyr

Against Heresies, ANF vol. 1. Grand Rapids: Eerdmans, 1989.

Works. Translated by John Keble. London: James Parker, 1872.

Jerome

Against Helvidius: The Perpetual Virginity of the Blessed Mary. NPNF vol. 7, 2d series, pp. 344–46. Grand Rapids: Eerdmans, 1956.

Commentaire sur S. Matthieu. Translation and notes by Emile Bonnard. Livres 1–2. SC 242. Paris: Cerf, 1977.

De viris illustribus. Edited by E. C. Richardson. TU 14/2. Berlin: Akademie, 1896.

Lives of Illustrious Men. NPNF vol. 3, 2d series, pp. 359–84. Grand Rapids: Eerdmans, 1956.

Origen

The Ante-Nicene Fathers: Original Supplement to the American Edition (Peter, Tatian, Commentaries of Origen). Edited by Allan Menzies. ANF vol. 10. Grand Rapids: Eerdmans, reprinted 1969.

Contra Celsum. Edited by Henry Chadwick, LCC. Philadelphia: Westminster, 1980.

Sozomen

Sozomen, Salaminius Hermias, *Historae Ecclesiasticae.* Edited by P. Schaff. NPNF vol. 2, 2d series. Grand Rapids: Eerdmans, 1957.

Tertullian

The Writings of Quintus Septimus Florens Tertullianus. Translated by S. Therwall and P. Holmes. ANCL 11, 15, 18. Edinburgh: T & T Clark, 1872–1880.

The Writings of Tertullian. Edited by A. Cleveland Coxe. ANF vol. 3. Buffalo: Christian Literature Publishing, 1887.

Clementine Homilies and Recognitions

Ante-Nicene Christian Library, vols. 3 and 17. Edited by A. Roberts and J. Donaldson. Edinburgh: T & T Clark, 1867, 1870.

The Twelve Patriarchs, Excerpts and Epistles, the Clementina, Apocrypha, Decretals, Memoirs of Edessa and Syriac Documents, Remains of the First Ages. Edited by A. Roberts and J. Donaldson. ANF vol. 8. Grand Rapids: Eerdmans, 1989.

Nag Hammadi

The Nag Hammadi Library in English. Edited by J. M. Robinson. New York: Harper & Row, 1977, 1988.

SECONDARY LITERATURE

Adamson, James B. *The Epistle of James,* NICNT. Grand Rapids: Eerdmans, 1976.

———. *James: The Man and His Message.* Grand Rapids: Eerdmans, 1989.

Aland, Kurt. "Der Herrenbruder Jacobus und der Jacobusbrief." *ThLZ* 69 (1944): 97–104.

———. "Jacobus," RGG III, 525–26.

Bachmann, E. T., ed. *Word and Sacrament I*, vol. 35 of *Luther's Works*. Philadelphia: Muhlenberg, 1960.

Bagatti, Bellarmino. *The Church from the Circumcision: History and Archaeology of the Judaeo-Christians*, CmSBF 2. Jerusalem: Franciscan Print Press, 1971.

Baigent, Michael, and Richard Leigh. *The Dead Sea Scrolls Deception*. New York: Summit Books, 1991.

Balch, David L., ed. *Social History of the Matthean Community: Cross-Disciplinary Approaches*. Minneapolis: Fortress, 1991.

Balzer, K., and H. Köster. "Die Bezeichnung des Jacobus als OBLIAS." *ZNW* 46 (1955): 141–42.

Barnard, Leslie W. "The Origins and Emergence of the Christian Church in Edessa in the First Two Centuries AD." *Vigilae Christianae* (1968): 61–75.

Barr, James. *The Semantics of Biblical Language*. London: Oxford University Press, 1961.

———. *Biblical Words for Time*. London: SCM, 1962.

Barrett, C. K. *The Pastoral Epistles*. Oxford: Clarendon Press, 1963.

——— *The First Epistle to the Corinthians*. London: A & C Black, 1968.

———. *New Testament Essays*. London: SPCK, 1972.

———. "Pauline Controversies in the Post-Pauline Period." *NTS* 20/3 (1974): 229–45.

———. *Essays on Paul*. London: SPCK, 1982.

———. *Freedom and Obligation: A Study of the Epistle to the Galatians*. London: SPCK, 1985.

———. *Acts: A Critical and Exegetical Commentary on The Acts of the Apostles*, vol. 1. Edinburgh: T & T Clark, 1994.

———. *Paul: An Introduction to His Thought*. London: Geoffrey Chapman, 1994.

Barton, Stephen C. *Discipleship and Family Ties in Mark and Matthew*, SNTSMS 80. Cambridge: Cambridge University Press, 1994.

Bauckham, Richard. *Jude and the Relatives of Jesus in the Early Church*. Edinburgh: T & T Clark, 1990.

———. "James and the Jerusalem Church." In *The Book of Acts in Its Palestinian Setting*, ed. Bauckham, vol. 4 of *The Book of Acts in Its First Century Setting*. Grand Rapids: Eerdmans, 1995.

———, ed. *The Book of Acts in Its Palestinian Setting*, vol. 4 of *The Book of Acts in Its First Century Setting*. Grand Rapids: Eerdmans, 1995.

Bauer, Walter. "The Abgar Legend." In *New Testament Apocrypha*, vol. 1, edited by Wilhelm Schneemelcher, 437–44. Philadelphia: Westminster, 1963.

———. *Orthodoxy and Heresy in Earliest Christianity*. Translated by R. A. Kraft and G. Krodel. Philadelphia: Fortress, 1971.

———. *A Greek-English Lexicon of the New Testament and Other Early Christian Literature*. Translated and edited by William F. Arndt and F. Wilbur Gingrich. Chicago: University of Chicago Press, 1979.

Baur, Ferdinand Christian. "Die Christuspartei in der korinthischen Gemeinde, der Gegensatz des petrinischen und paulinischen Christentums in der alten Kirsche, der Apostel Petrus in Rom." *TZTh* (1831): 61–206.

————. *Paul, the Apostle of Jesus Christ: His Life and Work, His Epistles and His Doctrine*. London, 1978 (from the German edition of 1876).

Beker, Johan Christiaan. *Paul the Apostle*. Philadelphia: Fortress, 1980.

Betz, Hans Dieter. *Galatians: A Commentary on Paul's Letter to the Churches in Galatia*. Hermeneia. Philadelphia: Fortress, 1979.

————. *Essays on the Sermon on the Mount*. Philadelphia: Fortress, 1985.

Bianchi, Ugo, ed. *Le Origini dello Gnosticismo: Colloquio di Messina*. Leiden: Brill, 1967.

Black, Matthew. *The Dead Sea Scrolls and Christian Origins*. London: Thomas Nelson, 1961.

Blass, Friedrich, and Albert Debrunner. *A Greek Grammar of the New Testament and Other Early Christian Literature*, trans. and ed. Robert W. Funk. Chicago: University of Chicago Press, 1961.

Blinzler, J. *Die Bruder und Schwestern Jesu*, SBS 21. Stuttgart: Katholisches Bibelwerk, 1967.

Böhlig, Alexander. "Zum Martyrium des Jacobus." *NovT* 5 (1962): 207–13.

————. "Der Jüdische und Judenchristlichen Hintergrund in gnostischen Texten von Nag Hammadi." In *Le Origini dello Gnosticismo: Colloquio de Messina,* edited by Ugo Bianchi, 109–40. Leiden: Brill, 1967.

————. "Jacob as an Angel in Gnosticism and Manicheism." In *Nag Hammadi and Gnosis: Papers Read at the First International Congress of Coptology (Cairo).* NHS 14. Leiden: Brill, 1978, 122–30.

Brandon, S. G. F. *The Fall of Jerusalem and the Christian Church*. London: SPCK, 1957.

————. *Jesus and the Zealots*. Manchester: Manchester University Press, 1967.

————. "The Death of James the Just: A New Interpretation." In *Studies in Mysticism and Religion Presented to G. Scholem . . . ,* ed. E. E. Urbach et al., 57–69. Jerusalem: Magnes Press, Hebrew University, 1967.

Brooke, A. E. *The Commentary of Origen on St. John's Gospel*, 2 vols. Cambridge: Cambridge University Press, 1896.

Brown, Raymond E. *The Death of the Messiah*. Garden City, N.Y.: Doubleday, 1994.

————."The Gospel of Peter and Canonical Gospel Authority." *NTS* 33 (1987): 321–43.

————, and J. P. Meier. *Antioch and Rome*. New York: Paulist Press, 1983.

Brown, S. K. *James: A Religio-Historical Study of the Relations between Jewish, Gnostic, and Catholic Christianity in the Early Period through an Investigation of the Traditions about James the Lord's Brother*. Ph.D. dissertation, Brown University. Ann Arbor: University Microfilms, 1972.

Bruce, F. F. "Justification by Faith in the Non-Pauline Writings of the New Testament." *EQ* 2.4 (1952): 66–77.

————. *Peter, Stephen, James and John*. Grand Rapids: Eerdmans, 1980.

Bultmann, Rudolf Karl. *History of the Synoptic Tradition*. Oxford: Oxford University Press, 1968.

Campenhausen, Hans Freiherr von. "Die Nachfolge des Jakobus. Zur Frage eines urchristlichen 'Kalifats.' " *ZKG* 63 (1950–51): 133–44.

Carroll, K. L. "The Place of James in the Early Church." *BJRL* 44 (1961): 49–71.

Catchpole, David R. "Paul, James and the Apostolic Decree." *NTS* 23 (1977): 428–44.

Clark, K. W. "The Gentile Bias in Matthew." *JBL* 66 (1947): 165–72.

Cohn-Sherbok, Dan. "Some Reflections on James Dunn's 'The Incident of Antioch (Gal. 2.11–18).' " *JSNT* 18 (1983): 68–74.

Conzelmann, Hans. "Analyse der Berkenntnisformel I Kor. 15, 3–5." *Evangelische Theologie* 25 (1965): 1–11.

———. *History of Primitive Christianity.* Nashville: Abingdon, 1973.

———. *1 Corinthians: A Commentary on the First Epistle to the Corinthians.* Hermeneia. Philadelphia: Fortress, 1975.

Cranfield, C. E. B. *The Gospel according to St Mark.* Cambridge: Cambridge University Press, 1972.

Cross, Frank Moore. *The Ancient Library of Qumran and Modern Biblical Studies.* Grand Rapids: Eerdmans, 1980.

Crossan, John Dominic. "Mark and the Relatives of Jesus." *NovT* 15 (1973): 81–113.

———. *Four Other Gospels: Shadows on the Contours of Canon.* Minneapolis: Winston, 1985.

———. *The Historical Jesus: The Life of a Mediterranean Jewish Peasant.* San Francisco: HarperSanFrancisco, 1991.

Crouzel, Henry. *Origen.* Translated by A.S. Worrall. Edinburgh: T & T Clark, 1989.

Danielou, Jean. *Origen.* London: Sheed & Ward, 1955.

———. *The Theology of Jewish Christianity.* London: Darton, Longman & Todd, 1964.

Davids, Peter H. *Commentary on James.* NIGNTC. Grand Rapids: Eerdmans, 1982.

Davies, William David, and Dale C. Allison. *Matthew: A Critical and Exegetical Commentary on the Gospel according to Saint Matthew,* vols. 1 and 2. Edinburgh: T & T Clark, 1988, 1991.

Dibelius, Martin. *James: A Commentary on the Epistle of James.* Revised ed., revised by Heinrich Greeven, translated by Michael A. Williams, edited by Helmut Köster. Hermeneia. Philadelphia: Fortress, 1976.

Dodd, C. H. *Historical Tradition and the Fourth Gospel.* Cambridge: Cambridge University Press, 1963.

Drijvers, H. J. W. *Cults and Beliefs at Edessa.* EPRO 82. Leiden: Brill, 1980.

Dunn, James D. G. *Unity and Diversity in the New Testament.* London: SCM, 1977.

———. "The Relationship between Paul and Jerusalem according to Galatians 1 and 2." *NTS* 28 (1982): 461–78.

———. "The Incident at Antioch (Gal. 2.11–18)." *JSNT* 18 (1983): 3–57.

———. "Echoes of the Intra-Jewish Polemics in Paul's Letter to the Galatians." *JBL* 112/113 (1993): 459–77.

———, ed. *Jews and Christians: The Parting of the Ways A.D. 70–135.* Tübingen: J. C. B. Mohr (Paul Siebeck), 1992.

Dupont-Sommer, André. *The Essene Writings from Qumran.* Oxford: Blackwell, 1961.

Easton, Burton Scott. "The Epistle of James," *Interpreters Bible*, vol. 12, pp. 9–11. New York: Abingdon, 1957.

Eisenman, Robert H. *Maccabees, Zadokites, Christians and Qumran.* Leiden: Brill, 1983.

———. *James the Just in the Habakkuk Pesher.* Leiden: Brill, 1986.

———. "Playing on and Transmuting Words: Interpreting Abeit-Galuto in the Habakkuk Pesher." In *Papers on the Dead Sea Scrolls in Memory of Jean Carmignac,* edited by Z. J. Kapera, 177–96. Krakow, 1991.

————, and M. Wise. *The Dead Sea Scrolls Uncovered*. Shaftsbury, Dorset, and Rockport, Mass.: Element Books, 1993.

Eisler, R. *The Messiah Jesus and John the Baptist according to Flavius Josephus' Recently Rediscovered 'Captive of Jerusalem' and Other Jewish and Christian Sources*. London: Methuen, 1931.

Elliott-Binns, Leonard Elliott. *Galilean Christianity*. London: SCM, 1956.

Feldman, Louis H., and G. Hala, eds. *Josephus, Judaism and Christianity*. Leiden: Brill, 1987.

Ferguson, Everett, et al., eds. *The Encyclopedia of Early Christianity*. New York: Garland, 1990.

Fitzmyer, Joseph A. "The Biblical Basis of Justification by Faith: Comments on the Essay by Professor Reumann." In *Righteousness in the New Testament*, by J. Reumann, J. A. Fitzmyer, and J. D. Quinn, 193–227. Philadelphia: Fortress, 1982.

Fredrikson, Paula. "Judaism, the Circumcision of Gentiles, and Apocalyptic Hope: Another Look at Galatians 1 and 2." *JTS* 42 (1991): 532–64.

Freedman, David Noel. *The Anchor Bible Dictionary*. 6 vols. New York: Doubleday, 1992.

Freyne, Sean. *Galilee from Alexander the Great to Hadrian, 325 BCE to 135 CE: A Study of Second Temple Judaism*. Wilmington, Del.: Michael Glazier, 1980.

Funk, Wolf-Peter. *Die Zweite Apocalypse des Jacobus aus Nag-Hammadi-Codex V*. Berlin, 1976.

Furnish, Victor Paul. *Jesus according to Paul*. Cambridge: Cambridge University Press, 1993.

Gardner-Smith, P. *Saint John and the Synoptic Gospels*. Cambridge: Cambridge University Press, 1938.

Gärtner, Bertil. *The Theology of the Gospel of Thomas*. London: Collins, 1961.

————. *The Temple and the Community in Qumram Scrolls and the New Testament: A Comparative Study in the Temple Symbolism of the Qumram Texts and the New Testament*. Cambridge: Cambridge University Press, 1965.

Gertner, M. "Midrashim in the New Testament." *JSS* 7 (1962): 283–91.

Ginzberg, Louis. *The Legends of the Jews*. Philadelphia: Jewish Publication Society of America, 1947.

Goulder, Michael D. *A Tale of Two Missions*. London: SCM, 1994.

Grant, Robert McQueen. *Eusebius as Church Historian*. Oxford: Clarendon Press, 1980.

————, and David Noel Freedman. *The Secret Sayings of Jesus*. London: Collins, 1960.

Green, Joel B., Scot McKnight, and I. H. Marshall. *Dictionary of Jesus and the Gospels*. Downers Grove, Ill.: IVP, 1992.

Griggs, C. Wilfred. *Early Egyptian Christianity: From Its Origins to 451 CE*. Leiden: Brill, 1991.

Grobel, K. *The Gospel of Truth: A Valentinian Meditation on the Gospel: Translation and Commentary*. London: A & C Black, 1960.

Guelich, Robert A. *Mark 1–8.26*. Word Biblical Commentary 34A. Dallas: Word Books, 1989.

Gundry, Robert Horton. *Mark: A Commentary on His Apology for the Cross*. Grand Rapids: Eerdmans, 1993.

————. "A Responsive Evaluation of the Social History of the Matthean Community in Roman Syria." In *Social History of the Matthean Community*, edited by David L. Balch, 62–67. Minneapolis: Fortress, 1991.

Gustafsson, B. "Hegesippus' Sources and his Reliability." In *Studia Patristica III*, edited by F. L. Cross, 227–32. TU 78. Berlin, 1961.

Haenchen, Ernst. *The Acts of the Apostles*. Philadelpha: Fortress, 1971.

Harnack, Adolf von. "Die Verklärungsgeschichte Jesus, der Bericht des Paulus [1 Kor 15.3ff.] und die beiden Christusvisionen des Petrus." *SPAW.PH* (1922): 62–80.

Hartin, P. J. *James and the Q Sayings of Jesus*. JSNTSS 47. Sheffield: JSOT, 1991.

Havener, I. *Q: The Sayings of Jesus: With a Reconstruction of Q by Athanasius Polag*. Wilmington, Del.: Michael Glazier, 1987.

Hawthorne, Gerald F., Ralph P. Martin, and Daniel G. Reid. *Dictionary of Paul and His Letters*. Downers Grove, Ill.: IVP, 1993.

Hedrick, Charles W., and Robert Hodgson Jr., eds. *Nag Hammadi, Gnosticism and Early Christianity*. Peabody, Mass.: Hendrickson, 1986.

Hengel, Martin. *Judaism and Hellenism*. 2 vols. London: SCM, 1974.

———. *Acts and the History of Early Christianity*. London: SCM, 1979.

———. *The Charismatic Leader and His Followers*. Translated by James Greig. New York: Crossroad, 1981.

———. "Jacobus der Herrenbruder—der erste 'Papst?' " In *Glaube und Eschatologie: Festschrift für W.G. Kümmel zum 80. Geburtstag*, edited by E. Grässer and O. Merk. Tübingen: J. C. B. Mohr (Paul Siebeck), 1985.

———. "Die Jacobusbrief als antipaulinische Polemik." In *Tradition and Interpretation of the New Testament: Essays in Honor of E. Earle Ellis*, 148–78. Edited by G. Hawthorne and O. Betz. Grand Rapids: Eerdmans, 1988.

Hill, Craig C. *Hellenists and Hebrews. Reappraising Division within the Earliest Church*. Minneapolis: Fortress, 1992.

Hintlian, Kevork. *History of the Armenians in the Holy Land*. Jerusalem: Armenian Patriarchate Printing Press, 1989.

Hooker, Morna D. *The Gospel according to Saint Mark*. Peabody, Mass.: Hendrickson, 1991.

———, and S. G. Wilson, eds. *Paul and Paulinism: Essays in Honour of C. K. Barrett*. London: SPCK, 1982.

Horsley, G. R. *New Documents Illustrating Early Christianity*. Vol. 2. North Ryde, U.K.: Macuarie University, 1982.

———. *New Documents Illustrating Early Christianity*. Vol. 4. North Ryde, U.K.: Macuarie University, 1982.

Horsley, Richard A., with John S. Hanson. *Bandits, Prophets and Messiahs: Popular Movements in the Time of Jesus*. Minneapolis: Winston, 1985.

Hort, F. J. A. *Judaistic Christianity*. London: Macmillan, 1904.

Houlden, James Leslie. "A Response to James D. G. Dunn." *JSNT* 18 (1983): 58–67.

Howard, George. "Was James an Apostle? A Reflection on a New Proposal for Gal. 1.19." *NovT* 19 (1977): 63–64.

———. *Paul: Crisis in Galatia: A Study in Early Christian Theology*. SNTSMS 35. Cambridge: Cambridge University Press, 1979.

———. *The Teaching of Addai*. SBL Texts and Translations 16; ECL Series 4. Chico, Calif.: Scholars Press, 1981.

Jeremias, Joachim. *Jerusalem in the Time of Jesus*. Translated by F. H. and C. H. Cave. London: SCM, 1967.

Jewett, Robert. *Paul's Anthropological Terms: A Study of Their Use in Conflict Settings*. Leiden: Brill, 1971.

Jones, F. Stanley. "The Martyrdom of James in Hegesippus, Clement of Alexandria, Christian Apocrypha, including Nag Hammadi: A Study of the Textual Relations." In *Seminar Papers Society of Biblical Literature 1990*. Atlanta: Scholars Press, 1990, 322–35.

Jouassard, G. "La personnalité d'Helvidius," *Mélanges J. Saunier*. Lyon, 1944, 139–56.

Kelly, J. N. D. *A Commentary on the Pastoral Epistles*. New York: Harper & Row, 1963.

———. *Jerome: His Life, Writings and Controversies*. New York: Harper & Row, 1975.

———. *A Commentary on the Pastoral Epistles*. New York: Harper, 1963.

Kittel, Gerhard, et al. *Theological Dictionary of the New Testament*. 9 vols. Grand Rapids: Eerdmans, 1964–1974.

Kleinknecht, Karl Theodor. *Der leidende Gerichtfertige*, WUNT 2/12. Tübingen: J.C.B. Mohr (Paul Siebeck), 1984.

Klijn, Albertus Frederik Johannes. "The Study of Jewish Christianity." *NTS* 20 (1973–74): 419–31.

———. *Jewish Christian Gospel Tradition*. Leiden: Brill, 1992.

Knibb, Michael A. *The Qumran Community*. Cambridge: Cambridge University Press, 1987.

Knopf, R., ed. *Das Urchristentum*, by Johannes Weiss. Göttingen: Vandenhoeck & Ruprecht, 1917.

Knox, W. L. "The Epistle of St James." *JTS* 46 (1945): 10–17.

Köster, Helmut. *Introduction to the New Testament*. 2 vols. New York: Walter de Gruyter, 1982.

Kooiman, W. J. *Luther and the Bible*. Philadelphia: Muhlenberg Press, 1961.

Lawlor, Hugh Jackson. *Eusebiana: Essays on the Ecclesiastical History of Eusebius Bishop of Caesarea*. Oxford: Clarendon Press, 1912.

Laws, S. *A Commentary on the Epistle of James*. London: A & C Black, 1980.

Liddel, H. G., and R. Scott. *A Greek-English Lexicon: With Supplement 1968*. Oxford: Clarendon Press, 1985.

Lightfoot, J. B. *Saint Paul's Epistle to the Galatians: A Revised Text with Introduction, Notes, and Dissertations*. London: Macmillan, 1874.

———. *Biblical Essays*. London: Macmillan, 1893.

Lipsius, Richard Adelbert. *Die apokryphen Apostelgeschichten und Apostellegenden*, II.2. Braunschweig: G. Westerman, 1884.

Lohmeyer, E. *Galiläa und Jerusalem*. FRLANT 52. Göttingen: Vandenhoeck & Ruprecht, 1936.

Lohse, Eduard. *Die Texte aus Qumran*. Darmstadt: Wissenschaftliche Buchgesellschaft, 1964.

Longenecker, Richard N. *The Christology of Early Jewish Christianity*. SBT 2nd series 17. London: SCM, 1970.

Lüdemann, Gerd. *Paul, Apostle to the Gentiles*. Philadelphia: Fortress, 1984.

———. *Opposition to Paul in Jewish Christianity*. Minneapolis: Fortress, 1989.

Maier, J., and J. Schreiner, eds. *Literatur und Religion des Frühjudentums*. Würzburg: J. C. B. Mohr, 1973.

Malbon, Elizabeth Struthers. "Fallible Followers: Women and Men in the Gospel of Mark." *Semeia* 28 (1983): 29–48.

———. *Narrative Space and Mythic Meaning in Mark*. San Francisco: Harper & Row, 1986.

Marcus, Joel. "The Evil Inclination in the Epistle of James." *CBQ* 44, no.4 (1982): 606–21.

Martin, R. P. *James*. Word Biblical Commentary 48. Waco, Tex.: Word Books, 1988.

Massebieau, L. "L'Epître de Jacques: est-elle l'oeuvre d'un chrétien?" *RHR* 32 (1895): 249–83.

Mayer, A., and W. Bauer. "The Relatives of Jesus." In *New Testament Apocrypha*. Edited by Wilhelm Schneemelcher, English translation edited by R. McL. Wilson, vol. 1, pp. 418–32. Philadelphia: Westminster, 1963.

Meier, J. P. *A Marginal Jew: Rethinking the Historical Jesus*. 2 vols. New York: Doubleday, 1991, 1994.

———. "Matthew and Ignatius: A Response to William R. Schoedel." In *Social History of the Matthean Community: Cross-Disciplinary Approaches*, edited by David L. Balch, 178–88. Minneapolis: Fortress, 1991.

Mayor, J. B. *The Epistles of St. James: The Greek Text with Introduction, Notes and Comments*. 1897. Reprint, Grand Rapids: Zondervan, 1954.

Meyer, A. *Das Rätsel des Jacobusbriefes*. Giessen: Topelmann, 1930.

Moulton, W. F., and A. S. Geden, eds. *A Concordance of the Greek New Testament according to the Texts of Westcott and Hort, Tischendorf and the English Revisers*. Edinburgh: T & T Clark, 1897.

Mosshammer, Alden A. *The Chronicle of Eusebius and Green Chronographic Tradition*. London: Associated University Presses, 1979.

Munck, Johannes. *Paul and the Salvation of Mankind*. London: SCM, 1959.

———. "Jewish Christianity in Post Apostolic Times." *NTS* 6 (1980): 103–16.

Neirynck, F. "The Sayings of Jesus in I Corinthians." In *The Corinthian Correspondence*, edited by R. Bieringer, 141–76. Louven: Peters, 1996.

Neusner, Jacob. "The Formation of Rabbinic Judaism: Yavneh from AD 70–100," *ANRW* II.19.2, 3–42.

———. *The Mishnah: A New Translation*. New Haven: Yale University Press, 1987.

———. *The Classics of Judaism: A Textbook and Reader*. Louisville: Westminster/John Knox, 1995.

Oberlinner, Lorenz. *Historische Überlieferung und christologische Aussage: Zur Frage der "Bruder Jesu" in der Synopse*. FZB 19. Stuttgart: Katholisches Bibelwerk, 1975.

Overman, J. Andrew. *Matthew's Gospel and Formative Judaism: The Social World of the Matthean Community*. Minneapolis: Fortress, 1990.

Pagels, Elaine. *The Gnostic Gospels*. London: Weidenfeld & Nicolson, 1979.

Painter, John. "The Church and Israel in the Gospel of John." *NTS* 25 (1978): 525–43.

———. *The Quest for the Messiah: The History, Literature and Theology of the Johannine Community*. Nashville: Abingdon, 1993.

———. *Reading Mark: Worlds in Conflict*. London: Routledge, 1997.

Pesch, Rudolf. *Das Markusevangelium*. HTKNT. Freiburg: Herder, 1977.

Phillips, G. *Doctrina Addai*. London, 1876.

Pratscher, Wilhelm. *Der Herrenbruder Jacobus und die Jacobustradition*. Göttingen: Vandenhoeck & Ruprecht, 1987.

Prideaux, Richard. "The Place of the Epistle of James in the Growth of the Primitive Church." Unpublished M.A. thesis, La Trobe University, Melbourne, 1985.

Puech, Henri-Charles, and Gilles Quispel. "Les Ecrits gnostiques du Codex Jung." *Vigilae Christianae* 8 (1954): 1–51.

Rabil, Albert. *Erasmus and the New Testament: The Mind of a Christian Humanist*. San Antonio: Trinity University Press, 1972.

Ramsay, William. *St Paul the Traveller, and Roman Citizen*. London: Hodder & Stoughton, 1895.

Reumann, John, Joseph A. Fitzmyer, and Jerome D. Quinn. *Righteousness in the New Testament*. Philadelphia: Fortress, 1982.

Reynolds, Joyce Marie, and Robert Tannenbaum. *Jews and Godfearers in Aphrodisias: Greek Inscriptions with Commentary. Proceedings of the Cambridge Philological Association*. Suppl. 12. Cambridge: Cambridge University Press, 1987.

Ropes, James Hardy. *The Epistle of St James*, ICC. Edinburgh: T & T Clark, 1916.

Rudolph, Kurt. "Gnosis und Gnostizismus, ein Forschungsbericht." *ThR* ns 34 (1969): 121–75, 181–231, 358–61; 36 (1971): 1–61, 89–124.

———. *Gnosis: The Nature and History of Gnosticism*. Translated by R. McL. Wilson. San Francisco: Harper & Row, 1983.

Saldarini, Anthony J. *Matthew's Christian-Jewish Community*. Chicago: University of Chicago Press, 1994.

Schmithals, Walter. *Paul and James*. SBT 1/46. London: SCM, 1965.

———. *The Office of an Apostle*. Nashville: Abingdon, 1969.

Schnackenburg, Rudolf. "Das Urchristentum." In *Literatur und Religion des Frühjudentums*, edited by J. Maier and J. Schreiner. Würzburg, 1973.

Schoedel, William R. "Ignatius and the Reception of Matthew in Antioch." In *Social History of the Matthean Community*, edited by David L. Balch, 129–77. Minneapolis: Fortress, 1991.

Schoeps, Hans Joachim. *Theologie und Geschichte des Judenchristentums*. Tübingen: J. C. B. Mohr (Paul Siebeck), 1949.

Schofield, G. *In the Year Sixty Two: The Murder of the Brother of the Lord and Its Consequences*. London: Harrap, 1962.

Schürer, Emil. *The Jewish People in the Age of Jesus Christ: A New English Version*, revised and edited by G. Vermes, F. Millar, M. Black. 4 vols. Edinburgh: T & T Clark, 1973, 1979, 1986, 1987.

Schwarz, Eduard, "Zu Eusebius Kirchengeschichte, I. Das Martyrium Jacobus des Gerechten." *ZNW* 4 (1903): 48–66.

Segal, Alan F. "Matthew's Jewish Voice." In *Social History of the Matthean Community*, edited by David L. Balch, 3–37. Minneapolis: Fortress, 1991.

———. *Paul the Convert: The Apostolate and Apostasy of Saul the Pharisee*. New Haven: Yale University Press, 1990.

Segal, J. B. *Edessa: The Blessed City*. Oxford: Clarendon Press, 1970.

Seitz, O. J. F. "Antecedents and Significance of the Term δίψυχος." *JBL* 66 (1947): 211–19.

———. "Afterthoughts on the Term 'Dipsychos.' " *NTS* 4 (1958): 327–34.

Smallwood, E. Mary. "High Priests and Politics in Roman Palestine." *JTS* 13 (1962): 14–34.

———. *The Jews under Roman Rule: From Pompey to Diocletian: A Study of Political Relations.* Leiden: Brill, 1981.

Smith, D. Moody. *John among the Gospels: The Relationship in Twentieth-Century Research.* Minneapolis: Fortress, 1992.

Smith, Morton. *Jesus the Magician.* San Francisco: Harper & Row, 1978.

Smith, Terence V. *Petrine Controversies in Early Christianity: Attitudes towards Peter in Christian Writings of the First Two Centuries.* WUNT 2/15. Tübingen: J. C. B. Mohr (Paul Siebeck), 1985.

Spitta, F. *Der Brief des Jacobus untersucht.* Göttingen, 1896.

———. *Zur Geschichte und Literatur des Urchristentums.* Göttingen: Vandenhoeck & Ruprecht, 1896.

Stanton, G. N. *A Gospel for a New People: Studies in Matthew.* Edinburgh: T & T Clark, 1992.

Stowers, Stanley Kent. *A Rereading of Romans: Justice, Jews, and Gentiles.* New Haven: Yale University Press, 1994.

Strack, Hermann Leberecht, and P. Billerbeck. *Kommentar zum Neuen Testament aus Talmud und Midrasch.* 2 vols. Munich: C. H. Beck, 1926, 1959.

Stevenson, J., ed. *A New Eusebius.* London: SPCK, 1968.

Strecker, Georg. *Der Weg der Gerechtigkeit: Untersuchung zur Theologie des Mattäus.* Göttingen: Vandenhoeck & Ruprecht, 1971.

———. "On the Problem of Jewish Christianity." In W. Bauer, *Orthodoxy and Heresy in Earliest Christianity*, translated by R. A. Kraft and G. Krodel, 241–85. Philadelphia: Fortress, 1971.

———. *Das Judenchristentum in den Pseudoklementinen.* TU 70/2. Berlin: Akademie, 1981.

Streeter, Burnett Hillman. *The Four Gospels: A Study of Origins Treating of the Manuscript Tradition, Sources, Authorship and Dates.* London: Macmillan, 1924.

———. *The Primitive Church: Studies with Special Reference to the Origins of the Christian Ministry.* London: Macmillan, 1929.

Tannehill, Robert C. "The Disciples in Mark: The Function of a Narrative Role." *JR* 57 (1977): 386–407.

———, ed. *Pronouncement Stories. Semeia* 20 (1981).

Taylor, Vincent. *The Gospel according to St Mark.* London: Macmillan, 1966.

Thiering, B. E. *Jesus the Man.* New York: Doubleday, 1992.

Thompson, M. B. *Clothed with Christ: The Example and Teaching of Jesus in Romans 12.1–15.13.* JSNTSS. Sheffield: JSOT, 1991.

Urbach, E. E. et al., eds. *Studies in Mysticism and Religion Presented to G. Scholem.* Jerusalem: Magnes Press, 1967.

van Unnik, W. C. "The Origins of the Recently Discovered 'Apocryphon Jacobi.' " *Vigilae Christianae* 10 (1956): 149–56.

VanderKam, James C. *The Dead Sea Scrolls Today*. Grand Rapids: Eerdmans, 1994.

Vermes, Geza, trans. and ed. *The Dead Sea Scrolls: Qumran in Perspective*. Philadelphia: Fortress, 1982.

Vielleux, Armand, trans. *The Life of Pachomius and His Disciples*. Vol. 1 of *Pachomian Koinonia*. Kalamazoo: Cistercian Publications, 1980.

Van Voorst, Robert E. *The Ascents of James: History and Theology of a Jewish-Christian Community*. SBL Dissertation Series 112. Atlanta: Scholars Press, 1989.

Walter, Nikolas. "Paulus und die urchristliche Jesustradition." *NTS* 31 (1985): 498–522.

Ward, R. B. "James of Jerusalem." *RestQ* 16 (1973): 174–90.

———. "James of Jerusalem in the First Two Centuries." *ANRW* II.26.1, 779–812.

Webber, M. I. "ΙΑΚΟΒΟΣ Ο ΔΙΚΑΙΟΣ: Origins, Literary Expression and Development of Tradition about the Brother of the Lord in Early Christianity." Ph.D. dissertation, Fuller Theological Seminary, 1985.

Wedderburn, A. J. M. *Paul and Jesus: Collected Essays*. JSNTSS 37. Sheffield: JSOT, 1989.

Weiss, Johannes. *Das Urchristentum*, edited by R. Knopf. Göttingen: Vandenhoeck & Ruprecht, 1917.

Wenham, David. "The Meaning of Mark 3:21," *NTS* (1974–1975): 295–300.

———. "Acts and the Pauline Corpus II. Evidence of Parallels." In *The Book of Acts in Its Ancient Literary Setting*, ed. Bruce W. Winter and Andrew D. Clark. Vol. 2 of *The Book of Acts in Its First Century Setting*. Grand Rapids: Eerdmans, 1993.

———. "The Meaning of Mark 3:21." *NTS* 21 (1974–75): 295–300.

Wilkinson, John. *Jerusalem as Jesus Knew It: Archaeology as Evidence*. London: Thames & Hudson, 1978.

———. *Jerusalem Pilgrims before the Crusades*. Jerusalem: Ariel, 1977.

Wilson, R. McL. *Studies in the Gospel of Thomas*. London: Mowbrays, 1960.

Windish, H. *Die Katholischen Briefe*. HNT 16. Tübingen: J. C. B. Mohr (Paul Siebeck), 1951.

Winstedt, Eric Otto, ed. "A Coptic Fragment Attributed to James the Brother of the Lord." *JThS* 8 (1907): 240–48.

Wolverton, Wallace Irving. "The Double-minded Man in the Light of Essene Psychology." *ATR* 38 (1956): 166–75.

Zandee, Jan. "Gnostische trekken een Apocryphe Brief van Jacobus," *Nederlands Tijdschrift* 17 (1963): 401–22.

Zuchschwerdt, E. "Das Nazirät des Herrenbruders Jacobus nach Hegesipp (Euseb, h.e. II.23.5–6)," *ZNW* 68 (1967): 276–87.

INDEX OF BIBLICAL AND
ANCIENT SOURCES

Early Christian Fathers

3.7.7–9	133, 143–44, 171n. 30, 207, 257
3.10.1	146
3.11.1	124, 144, 146, 148, 151, 171n. 30, 207
3.11.12	119
3.12.1	144, 146
3.15	188
3.19.1–3.20.7	43n. 2, 147–49, 150n. 108
3.19.1	148, 150
3.20.1	148, 151
3.21	188
3.31.3	209
3.32.1–6	43n. 2, 149, 151
3.32.5	148
3.32.6	119
3.32.7–8	119
3.32.8	147n. 97
3.32.10	153
3.33.1–3	149n. 106
3.34	188
4.5.1–5	155
4.5.1–4	5n. 6, 114, 147, 153
4.6.4	152
4.8.2	119
4.8.4	119
4.12.1	119
4.22.4	112, 124, 144, 145, 146, 151, 152–54
4.22.8	120
4.32.1	119
5.6	188
7.19.1	113, 114, 147, 154–56, 194
7.32.29	154n. 117

Hippolytus, 106n. 3, 160

REFUTATION OF ALL HERESIES

5.25, 167, 174

Hegesippus, 4, 5, 14n. 6, 106, 115, 116, 117, 118, 119–30, 133, 141, 150–51, 152–58, 167, 175, 177, 179–81, 183, 189, 196, 197, 255, 270, 283

Ignatius, 88, 89, 95, 215

EPHESIANS

12.2	89
19	215

Irenaeus, 183, 215

AGAINST HERESIES

1.3.2	164
1.6.1	168
1.7.2	168
1.21.2	168
1.21.5	168
1.24.2	126
1.28.1	126
1.30.14	164
3.3.2–4	196
4.16.1	235
4.33.9	168n. 21, 169

Jerome, 2, 4, 18, 81, 120, 182–85, 198, 200, 213–20, 235, 242

AGAINST HELVIDIUS

3	214n. 43
9	214n. 44
11	214n. 45
17	214n. 46
18	215n. 49

LIVES OF ILLUSTRIOUS MEN

2	81
33	214

COMMENTARY ON ST. MATTHEW

Preface	215n. 48

DIALOGUE AGAINST THE PELAGIANS

2.4	217n. 55

INDEX OF MODERN AUTHORS

317

INDEX OF SUBJECTS